T0419625

RELIGION AND SPIRITUALITY

THE LIFE AND LEGENDS OF SAINT FRANCIS OF ASSISI

Religion and Spirituality

Additional books and e-books in this series can be found on Nova's website under the Series tab.

Historical Figures

Additional books and e-books in this series can be found on Nova's website under the Series tab.

RELIGION AND SPIRITUALITY

THE LIFE AND LEGENDS OF SAINT FRANCIS OF ASSISI

CANDIDE CHALIPPE

Copyright © 2018 by Nova Science Publishers, Inc.

All rights reserved. No part of this book may be reproduced, stored in a retrieval system or transmitted in any form or by any means: electronic, electrostatic, magnetic, tape, mechanical photocopying, recording or otherwise without the written permission of the Publisher.

We have partnered with Copyright Clearance Center to make it easy for you to obtain permissions to reuse content from this publication. Simply navigate to this publication's page on Nova's website and locate the "Get Permission" button below the title description. This button is linked directly to the title's permission page on copyright.com. Alternatively, you can visit copyright.com and search by title, ISBN, or ISSN.

For further questions about using the service on copyright.com, please contact:
Copyright Clearance Center
Phone: +1-(978) 750-8400　　　Fax: +1-(978) 750-4470　　　E-mail: info@copyright.com

NOTICE TO THE READER

The Publisher has taken reasonable care in the preparation of this book, but makes no expressed or implied warranty of any kind and assumes no responsibility for any errors or omissions. No liability is assumed for incidental or consequential damages in connection with or arising out of information contained in this book. The Publisher shall not be liable for any special, consequential, or exemplary damages resulting, in whole or in part, from the readers' use of, or reliance upon, this material. Any parts of this book based on government reports are so indicated and copyright is claimed for those parts to the extent applicable to compilations of such works.

Independent verification should be sought for any data, advice or recommendations contained in this book. In addition, no responsibility is assumed by the publisher for any injury and/or damage to persons or property arising from any methods, products, instructions, ideas or otherwise contained in this publication.

This publication is designed to provide accurate and authoritative information with regard to the subject matter covered herein. It is sold with the clear understanding that the Publisher is not engaged in rendering legal or any other professional services. If legal or any other expert assistance is required, the services of a competent person should be sought. FROM A DECLARATION OF PARTICIPANTS JOINTLY ADOPTED BY A COMMITTEE OF THE AMERICAN BAR ASSOCIATION AND A COMMITTEE OF PUBLISHERS.

Additional color graphics may be available in the e-book version of this book.

Library of Congress Cataloging-in-Publication Data

ISBN: 978-1-53614-505-2

Published by Nova Science Publishers, Inc. † New York

This Jubilee Edition of the Life and Legends of St. Francis of Assisi is Respectfully Dedicated to all Members of the Third Order in the City of Cleveland and Vicinity, above all, to the Nobel Patrons and Zealous Workers of Our Tertiary Branches.

CONTENTS

Introductory Note		ix
Preface by the Author		xi
Chapter 1	From His Birth to His Time at the Church of St. Mary of the Angels	1
Chapter 2	From His Time at the Church of St. Mary of the Angels to 1218	43
Chapter 3	From His Travel to Perugia to His Appointment of Brother Elias to Vicar General	103
Chapter 4	From His Third Order of Penance to the Time of His Last Illness	159
Chapter 5	From the Time of His Last Illness to the Honors Paid to Him after His Death	229
Conclusion		243
Index		311

INTRODUCTORY NOTE

The Life and Legends of St. Francis of Assisi by Father Candide Chalippe, O.F.M., need no apology. The work was first published at Paris in 1727. It is not only well written and reliable withal, but also instructive, elevating and inspiring. The facts and legends mentioned are drawn from the oldest and most reliable sources. The abundance of incidents and anecdotes not to be found elsewhere make the volume eminently interesting, while the reflexions and applications which the author now and then interweaves with the narrative are so replete with practical hints on spiritual life, that they will undoubtedly produce the best spiritual results in the reader. The style though simple, at times graphic, is very pleasing; the narrative flows on with equal ease and freedom.

In 1852 a priest from the Oratory of St. Philip Neri made a translation into English from what was then the latest French edition. This French edition came from the press in 1850. With the English translation the original work appeared in an abridged form. The original work is divided into six books, the English translation contains but half of these, so rearranged for the sake of clearness that they form five books. Most elucidations of the original work regarding characteristics of St. Francis, events and dates that are doubtful, are omitted, likewise most of the writings of St. Francis. The former were and still are undergoing changes, owing to new historical researches and discoveries made by students of Franciscan sources, while the latter were but lately again newly translated into English and edited as completely as possible with many critical notes and references of great value by the scholarly Father Paschal Robinson, O.F.M.—The Writings of St. Francis of Assisi by Father Paschal Robinson, O.F.M. The Dolphin Press, 1906.

The marvellous progress the Third Order of St. Francis is making in this country causes the story of the life of St. Francis that is herewith presented to the public in a newly revised edition to be especially welcome. For all Tertiaries know that mere devotion to St. Francis is of itself not sufficient to acquire the spirit of their Seraphic Father; all are aware that membership in the Third Order does not necessarily argue the possession of this spirit—and yet, every real Tertiary desires nothing more than to acquire the poor, humble, loving spirit of St. Francis. This spirit can scarcely be acquired, unless the life of St. Francis be well known, meditated upon and imitated as far as practicable. The Life and Legends of St. Francis of Assisi by Father Candide Chalippe, O.F.M., is peculiarly adapted to help Tertiaries to perform this task; the spirit of St. Francis breathes in every page. Not once, but several times may Tertiaries read this book to great advantage. With every reading new items of interest will be discovered, new lessons will present themselves to be learnt, new inspirations will be imparted to the soul from above. The more this book is read, the more it will be loved; the more it is studied, the more it will be admired. For Tertiaries a book of this kind is a necessity; it is as necessary for them as a text-book is for a scholar.

May this wonderful work spread in the future even more rapidly than before, may it receive the hearty welcome it deserves among the innumerable Tertiaries and clients of St. Francis of Assisi and be to them a sure guide to God's abundant graces in this world and to life everlasting in the next.

PREFACE BY THE AUTHOR[*]

Wherein the prejudices of certain persons against miracles which are recorded in the lives of the Saints are shown to be both unreasonable and dangerous, and that the miracles attributed to Saint Francis are very well authenticated.

A very common failing amongst men is to adopt one extreme in the endeavor to avoid another, and sometimes not to perceive that the extreme into which they fall is greater than that which they had sought to flee from. To insure themselves against weak incredulity, some have imbibed such prejudice against the miracles in the Lives of the Saints, that they cannot endure to hear of them; the very ideas of miracles, revelations, ecstasies, visions, apparitions, are hateful and disgusting to them; all that is said on these subjects they look upon as fabulous and incredible; they call in question the most undeniable evidence, or attribute these wonders to natural and unknown causes. The wonders which are recorded in the Life of St, Francis, afford an opportunity of grappling with these prejudices.

In the first place, no man using his right reason will reject the wonders recorded in the Lives of the Saints, because of their impossibility. Miracles are extraordinary events, which break through the laws of nature, and exceed the force of all natural causes; it is only necessary to make use of our reason to be aware that God, whose power is infinite, having freely established these laws, may, whenever He thinks fit, break through them Himself by the ministry of His creatures, whom He makes use of as He pleases; that these suspensions

---

[*] This is an edited, reformatted and augmented version of "The Life and Legends of Saint Francis of Assisi", by Father Candide Chalippe that was previously published in Paris, 1727. The views, opinions and nomenclature expressed in this book are those of the authors, and do not reflect the views of Nova Science Publishers Inc.

may enter into the external designs of His wisdom and providence, and that they occur by successive acts, without there having been any change in Him, because it is an act of His will which causes them, as it does every other thing. Now this proves that miracles are possible, and that there is no impossibility in the wonders recorded in the Lives of the Saints.

In the second place, these wonders ought not to cause an incredulous surprise in any sensible person who pays due attention to the wonders of nature. "Man," says St. Augustine, "sees extraordinary things happen, and he admires them, while he himself, the admirer, is a great wonder, and a much greater miracle than any things which are done by the intervention of man. There is nothing more marvellous done in the world, which is not less wonderful than the world itself. All nature is full of what is miraculous; we seem unconscious of it, because we see those things daily, and because this daily repetition lowers them in our eyes. And this is one reason why God has reserved to Himself other things out of the common course of nature, on which He shows His power from time to time, in order that their novelty may strike us; but when we consider attentively, and with reflection, the miracles we constantly see, we find that they are far greater than others, however surprising and uncommon these may be."

The holy doctor admits that the prodigies which are out of the common course of nature, and which are properly called miracles, are to be viewed with astonishment, since they are works of God, worthy of admiration; he only requires that the surprise they cause shall be qualified by a consideration of the wonders of nature, to which he likewise gives the name of miracles, in a more extended sense: on the same principle, and a fortiori, what there is surprising in them should not make them appear to us incredible. An enlightened mind does not believe in miracles which are communicated to him, unless due proof of them is adduced; but it is not because what is wonderful in them renders him incredulous, because he sees more marvellous things in the universe and in himself. If men who apply themselves to the study of nature, are pertinacious in refusing to believe in the miracles of the saints, it is because they do not make use of the light they have received, and do not reason deductively; they have only sought to gratify their curiosity, or to gain credit for their discoveries; and do not some of them lose themselves in their speculations, and become impious, even so as to recognize no other God than nature itself?

In the third place, faith in the great mysteries of religion must incline us to believe in the wonders we read in the Lives of the Saints. Are we, then, not called upon to say to those whose prejudices we oppose: "As you belong to the society of the faithful, you not only believe that three Persons make only one God; that the Son of God was made man; that the dead shall rise again; but also, that Jesus Christ becomes every day present on our altars, under the species of bread and wine, at the words of consecration; and you believe all the other astonishing wonders that are proposed to you in our holy religion: why, then, do you find such repugnance in believing those of the Lives of the Saints, which are far inferior to the former"?

It is useless to say in answer, that these last are only based on human testimony, which we are not obliged to receive; that the mysteries are propounded to us by Divine authority, to which we are bound to submit; for this is not the question before us. We only compare one wonder with another, and we maintain that the belief in the one should facilitate the belief in the other. In fact, if we believe with a firm and unshaken faith what God, in His goodness, has been pleased to effect for the salvation of all men, and what He continues daily to effect in the Eucharist; may we not easily convince ourselves that He may have given extraordinary marks of His affection for his most faithful servants?

In the fourth place, similar wonders to those which are found in the Lives of the Saints are also found in the Holy Scriptures. Raptures, ecstasies, frequent visions and apparitions, continual revelations, an infinity of miracles, miraculous fasts of forty days, are things recorded in the Old and New Testaments. We believe all these wonderful circumstances, and we are obliged to believe them, although they far surpass our understanding; on what, then, shall we rely for maintaining that the wonders recorded in the Lives of the Saints are improbable, and that we may reasonably call them in question? Reason, on the contrary, marks them as so much the more probable and worthy of credit, as we know and believe similar ones which we may not doubt of. Christians should be accustomed to what is marvellous, and require nothing but proofs for the most unusual prodigies.

In the fifth place, the promise which Jesus made that the power of working miracles should be given to true believers, gives authority to the belief in miracles in the Lives of the Saints. "Amen, amen, I say to you, he that believeth in me, the works that I do he shall do also, and greater than these shall he do; because I go to the Father. And whatsoever you ask the Father in my name, that will I do." "And these signs shall follow them that believe: In my name they shall cast out devils; they shall speak with new tongues; they shall take up serpents; and if they shall drink any deadly thing, it shall not hurt them; they shall lay their hands upon the sick, and they shall recover." Our Saviour, according to the doctrine of the Holy Fathers, has promised the gift of miracles, not to each one of the faithful in particular, but to the Church in general; and His promise is for all times, when the good of religion requires its accomplishment. Heretics pretend that it only related to the days of the apostles, and that miracles were only required for the establishment of the faith. What right have they to limit the words of the Son of God? Do they imagine that they understand the Scriptures better than the holy doctors? How will they prove that since the time of the apostles there have been no combinations of circumstances in which the good of religion shall have required that miracles should be performed? They were required for the infidels, to whom the Gospel has been preached in different centuries, as well as for the Greek and Roman idolaters, to whom it was first announced. The Church has required them to silence the heretics who have successively endeavored to impugn her dogmas, and to strengthen the faith of her own children. They have been always useful for manifesting the eminence of virtue, for the glory of God, for the conversion of sinners, for reanimating piety, for nourishing and strengthening the hopes of the good things of another life. We are, therefore, justified in saying that the promise of Jesus Christ is for all times, in certain occasions, and that the belief in the miracles in the Lives of the Saints is authorized thereby.

In the sixth place, that there have been miracles in the Lives of the Saints are facts, the proofs of which are unquestionable. The Acts of the Martyrs, which have always been read in the Church, and the genuineness of which has been admitted by the most talented critics, contain recitals of the most wonderful events: the confessors of the faith instantaneously cured, after having undergone the most cruel tortures; wild beasts tamed and crouching at their feet; lights and celestial voices, apparitions of Jesus Christ and His angels, and many other wonderful circumstances.

In the first six centuries there are scarcely any ecclesiastical writers and Holy Fathers who do not record miracles worked by the servants of God, and by their relics; and they speak of them as of things which they have either seen with their own eyes, or were of public notoriety.

Saint Justin Martyr, in the second century, speaking of the power of Jesus Christ over the demons, in his Apology, addressed to the Emperors Marcus Aurelius and Lucius Verus, and to the Roman Senate, says: "You have proofs of what passes before your eyes, and in your city, and in all the rest of the world; for you know that many of those possessed, not having been able to be delivered by your exorcists, enchanters, and magicians, have been so by the Christians who have exorcised them in the name of Jesus Christ, who was crucified under Pontius Pilate."

Saint Ireneus assures us that in the same century some true disciples of Jesus Christ had received supernatural gifts, which they made use of advantageously for other men: "Some," says he, "drive away devils; and this is certain, that often those who have been delivered embrace the faith, and join the Church. To others it is given to know the future, and to have prophetic visions. Others cure the sick by the imposition of hands, and restore them to perfect health. Very often, even in every place, and for some requisite cause, the brethren solicit, by fasting and fervent prayers, the resurrection of a dead person, and obtain it; these dead, thus revived, have lived with us for several years afterwards. What shall I say further? It is not possible to enumerate the extraordinary gifts which the Church receives from God, and what she operates in every part of the world, in favor of the nations, in the name of Jesus Christ crucified."

"We can," says Origen, writing against Celsus, "show an immense multitude of Greeks and barbarians who believe in our Lord Jesus Christ; there are some who prove their faith by the power of working miracles. They cure the sick by invoking their God, the Creator and the Sovereign Lord of all things; and the name of Jesus Christ, our Saviour, of whose Gospel they recite a part. We ourselves have seen several sick persons delivered from the most formidable maladies, and the cured are too numerous to be counted."

Tertullian, in his Apology, and in another work, records plainly the miraculous fall of rain which was obtained from heaven by the prayers of the Christian soldiers, which saved the army of the Emperor Marcus Aurelius, which was reduced to the last extremity. He proves the truth of this fact by the very letter of the emperor. We have also authentic proofs of this event in the authors and records of paganism itself. Tertullian, likewise, tells us that the pagans received extraordinary graces by means of the Christians, some of which he quotes, and he adds: "How many persons of distinction, without mentioning other people, have been thus delivered from the devil, and cured of their evils!"

St. Cyprian upbraided an idolater in the following terms, while refuting him: "The gods whom you adore we exorcise in the name of the true God, and they are compelled to leave the bodies which they possessed. Oh, if you chose to see and hear them, when suffering under the power of our words, as if they were spiritual scourges, and feeling the secret operation of the Divine Mastery! They howl terrifically, entreat of us to spare them, declare, in presence of their adorers, whence they came, and confess a future judgment. Come and be convinced of the truth of what we say; to be at least moved. Those whom you adore, fear us; those to whom you pray, entreat of us to spare them; those whom you revere as sovereigns, are as prisoners in our hands, and tremble as so many slaves. We interrogate them, and in your presence they declare what they are; they cannot dissemble the impostures which they make use of to deceive you."

Such are the miracles which many of God's servants operated in the second and third centuries, and which cannot be called in question. How many different kinds are recorded in subsequent times by St. Basil, and by St. Gregory of Nyssa, in the life of St. Gregory Thaumaturgus; by St. Athanasius in the life of St. Anthony; by Sulpicius Severus, in the life of St. Martin; by St. Chrysostom, St. Jerome, St. Ambrose, St. Augustine, St. Paulinus, in many parts of their works; by Theodoret, in his religious history; by Pope St. Gregory, in his dialogues; by St. Hilary of Arles, St. Ouen, and very many others worthy of credit!

These saintly and learned Bishops, Avitus, Metropolitan of Vienne, Stephen of Lyons, Eon of Arles, conferring with the Arians, in presence of Gondebauld, King of the Burgundians, after having proved the consubstantiality of the Word, by the testimony of the Scripture, and by powerful arguments, offered to give additional proof thereof by miracles, if the heretics would promise to acquiesce in consequence; and quoted the example of St. Remigius, Apostle of the French, who was then living, and setting up the faith on the ruins of idolatry by a multitude of prodigies.

The miracles operated by means of relics are neither less well authenticated, nor less celebrated; they were known to the whole world. St. Augustine was an eyewitness of them; being at Milan when St. Ambrose discovered, by means of a revelation, the spot where the bodies of SS. Gervasius and Protasius reposed. He saw a great many miracles performed in Africa by the relics of St. Stephen, of which he makes mention in his book of the City of God, written for the confutation of the most learned of the pagans, wherein he says that, to quote only those operated in the Dioceses of Calame and Hippo, several books would not suffice. Nicetius, Bishop of Treves, writing to Clodosvinda, or Glotinda, Queen of the Lombards, to exhort her to solicit the conversion of King Alboin, her husband, advised her to make use of the visible miracles which were operated at the tomb of St Martin, and by the invocation of St. Germanus, St. Hilary, St. Lupus, St. Remigius, and St. Medardus. They were so evident, that the heretics dared not call them in question, and could not deprive them of their splendor. God made use of these for the conversion of kings, and of the entire nations.

In all ages after the six first centuries, the prodigies of the Lives of the Saints are noticed by numerous authors of all countries, whose talents, learning, probity, holiness, and dignity, render them respectable to the most searching critics. They are supported by incontrovertible evidence, by juridical depositions, by authentic acts, and by splendid monuments which have been erected to their memory by bishops, princes, magistrates, cities and kingdoms to perpetuate the recollections of these splendid achievements. We find that the saints have made numerous predictions, which have been justified by the event; and that, either moved by the Spirit of God, or compelled by obedience, they have admitted the supernatural operations which they felt in their souls. Finally, the prodigies which are found in the Lives of the Saints have always been considered as indubitable facts amongst the faithful; the Church recognizes them, and they form one of the objects of their piety and devotion; no one is placed in the catalogue of saints whose sanctity has not been attested from heaven, by means of miracles; and she takes such rigorous precautions, and carries their strictness so far, that, according to all human prudence, it is impossible she should be deceived.

We now ask whether it can be permitted to think and to say that such facts are absolutely false, and should only be looked upon as fables unworthy of credence? In such case it would be necessary to abrogate the rule judiciously and universally received in the world, that facts which have nothing incredible in themselves are not to be controverted when duly proved; it would be also necessary to refuse credence to all that is related in sacred and profane history; to lay down as a maxim to believe nothing but what we see, and to refuse to receive the testimony of the honorable people with whom we live. Now, this is what is requisite to prove and convince every man of good sense that the prejudice against the miracles of the Lives of the Saints is quite unreasonable; but this does not point out its quality sufficiently; it is senseless and ridiculous, it is rash, and, what is more, it is dangerous.

Whoever denies what the Fathers of the Church attest as having seen, or having been authentically informed of, must conclude that they were either very credulous, or deceived the people. To refuse to believe the marvels which have reached us by an uniform and universal tradition, is to call in question all tradition; to render all its channels suspicious, and to cause it to be looked upon as a questionable proposition. What can be thought of the saints, if the miraculous graces, which they certify that they have received from God, are to be treated as chimeras; if the accomplishment of what they have foretold, is to be attributed to chance? What even can be thought of their most heroic victims? What opinion will be formed of their acts? Will they be deemed more trustworthy in other matters? When it is asserted that there have been no miracles since the days of the apostles, it must be said, by a necessary consequence, that the Church, which grounds canonization on miracles, makes use of falsehood in that most solemn and religious act, and that the public worship which the Church directs is uncertain. Now this very much resembles heresy; for the great principles of religion teach us that on these occasions the Church receives peculiar enlightenment from the Holy Ghost, by which she can neither be deceived herself, nor can she deceive others.

These miracles, it is said, are not articles of faith, and the Church does not oblige us to believe them. As if nothing was believed in the world but such things as are of faith; as if it was not dangerous obstinately to reject those things which are sanctioned by the authority of the Holy Fathers, by reason and by piety, by tradition and by the Church, and which cannot be rejected without fatal consequences!

This incredulity attacks, moreover, one of the proofs of the divinity of Jesus Christ, which the fathers adduced against the pagans. St. Chrysostom having asserted, on the subject of the miracles of the martyr, St. Babylas, that our Saviour, on the night of His Passion, had promised to those who should believe in Him, the power of working these miracles, adds: "It had been antecedently seen that many had taken upon themselves the character of masters, who had disciples, and who boast of performing wonders; nevertheless, we do not hear of any who had ventured to promise their disciples the same power. The insolence of their impostures did not go so far, because they knew that no one would believe them; all the world being convinced that it is only given to God to make a similar promise, and to fulfil it." On this principle the holy doctor proves that Jesus Christ is God, since He has given to those who believe in Him the power of working miracles, which His disciples actually did, and which His servants now do. St. Augustine makes use of the same proofs, in his book of the City of God. Thus the miracles of the saints have in all ages been adduced as proofs of the Divinity of our Saviour; and this is what those endeavor to do away with, who, without reflection, consider them as fables.

Another danger is, that they speak of these marvels according to their own prejudices. They openly say that they do not believe them, and that persons ought not to have the weakness to believe them; they speak contemptuously of the books in which they are recorded; they cannot endure that they should form part of panegyrics of the saints. They make use of impious derisions, and turn into ridicule the faithful who credit them, and they censure the conduct of the Church which consecrates them. Such discourse sanctions heresy and licentiousness; worldlings and the indevout applaud it, the tepid seem to consent to it, and the falsely devout approve it; it is a scandal to the weak, and a dishonor to religion.

It is also to be feared that prejudices against what is wonderful in the Lives of the Saints may spread to other subjects, if we only judge from the principles which are the cause of them. For, in what do these principles consist? They are not grounded on reason or religion; they must, therefore, have a basis of incredulity for everything which they do not understand: the foolish vanity of being thought singular; ignorance, which boldly repudiates what it knows nothing of; keeping company with libertines; a conformity of feeling with heretics, and the spirit of the world, which is the enemy of all piety. Such calamitous causes give room to fear the most fatal effects.

In general, the liberty only to believe those things which we choose, on points in which religion is concerned, is very dangerous; it often makes a destructive progress, for its first attempts embolden it. Persons are easily persuaded that all miraculous narratives are false, though the Church guarantees the truth of many; and when this same Church pronounces on dogmatical facts, declaring: such and such propositions to be heretical which are in such and such a book, and exacts an interior submission of heart and mind, do these doubters show more docility? Do they not cloak their disobedience by a respectful silence, always ill kept and finally broken through by open rebellion? Do we not see persons in the world speaking irreverently of relics, purgatory, indulgences, and even of the holy mysteries, after having treated contemptuously the marvels of the Lives of the Saints?

Certain critics admit these marvels, but have imbibed the idea that falsehood is so mixed up with the truth, that they cannot be separated but by using certain rules, which they take upon themselves to lay down. This prejudice is not less dangerous, nor less unreasonable than the other.

Because some inconsiderate writers, who cannot be too severely censured, have given scope to their imagination in certain legends, and have employed fiction for the embellishment of their narratives, the doubters pretend that the whole history of the saints is full of impostures; nevertheless, pure sources have been the basis of their authentic acts, in the works of the Fathers, and in an infinity of authors well worthy of credit, and in the Bulls of Canonization. An Asiatic priest, as related by St. Jerome, who quotes Tertullian, composed false acts of St. Thecla through an ill-understood sentiment of devotion:—does it follow from that that the truth of many other acts which were there read, and which we still possess, is to be set aside? Moreover, the Church has remedied the evil; she has rejected the false prodigies; she has expunged from the legends the indiscreet additions; a new edition has been long since placed in the hands of the faithful, which only contains the well-authenticated and certain miracles.

A learned man has demonstrated that the rules of these critics for the elucidation of these miracles are not judicious; that they are extravagant, and that it would be risking too much to follow them; that they are contradictory, and not in unison with each other; that it often happens that they reject or admit miracles against their own principles. If they find splendid ones, and many of them in the same legend, they hold them to be suppositions or altered, although, the oldest and most authentic documents contain similar ones; they reject them as false, without assigning any reason in proof of their having been falsified; they pretend that the authors who have recorded them were too credulous, though they received other articles on the testimony of these same authors. In order to believe them, they require perfect certainty, although they give credit to many circumstances in ecclesiastical and profane history on mere probabilities. One of them professes not to omit a single miracle which is vouched for by good authority, nevertheless, he suppresses many of the most considerable; and many of those which he feels compelled to bring forward, he does so in terms which mark doubtfulness, to say nothing more.

Thus, the ultra-critics while admitting the wonders of the Lives of the Saints, reduce them to nothing by rules, which they invent for separating truth from falsehood, as those who profess to believe an infallible authority in the Church make that infallibility to depend on so many conditions, that they may always maintain that the Church, dispersed or assembled, has never come to any decision in opposition to their errors.

It is, they say, the love of truth which induces them to examine most scrupulously the miracles of the saints; nothing should be believed, or be proposed to belief, but what is true. But Bossuet said of bad critics: "They are content, provided they can pass for more subtle observers than others, and they find themselves sharper, in not giving credit to so many wonders." The love of truth does not consist in denying its existence, where so many persons of first-rate genius have found it; it does not depend on rendering obscure the light it sheds, nor in giving to the public Lives of Saints accompanied by a dry, bitter, and licentious criticism, calculated to throw doubt on all that is extraordinary in them, and thereby to give scandal. The learned Jesuits, the continuators of Bollandus, show, by the precision of their researches, that they are sincere lovers of truth, but we do not see that they endeavor to diminish the number of miracles: "They have no idea of taking them for fictions; nothing astonishes them in the lives of the friends of God, provided it be well attested." Father Thomassen, of the Oratory, in his treatise on the Celebration of Festivals, speaks of a miraculous event which occurred in the sixth century, and which is reported by Bollandus, and he adds: "These sorts of miracles are by no means articles of faith, but nevertheless, they are not to be rejected by sage and considerate persons. Upon reading the works of St. Cyprian, St. Augustine, St. Ambrose, and St. Jerome, and those of St. Gregory of Nyssa, of St. Basil, and St. Athanasius, we can have no doubt that these fathers had no difficulty in believing similar occurrences, similarly attested. St. Augustine, indeed, has related several much more incredible; and it is greatly to be feared that to set one's self above the Augustines, the Jeromes, the Gregories, and the most learned Fathers of the Church, must be the effect of a most dangerous pride."

It is objected that the multitude is credulous; that it likes the marvellous, and should not be exposed to believe untruths. But credulity is far less dangerous than incredulity; the one admits of cure much easier than the other; the former, in proper limits, may be very useful, the latter engenders nothing but evil. Some one has said, that the love of the marvellous is the ancient malady of mankind; it would, perhaps, be more accurate to say, that it is a remainder of their original greatness; and that, being created to witness the marvels of the Divinity, they are impelled, by an interior impulse, to believe whatsoever seems to them to approach to them, until such, time as their visions shall be fully gratified. This impulse only becomes a malady when it receives wonderful things which are absurd, or without any foundation. Aversion from the marvellous, which has its origin in the weakness of a mind oppressed by sin, is a much greater malady, and may have most dangerous consequences, in a wholly marvellous religion which we must love. These marvels are displeasing in pious narratives, where they are fully proved, and they are sought for in theatrical compositions, where they are mere fictions: the distinction is dishonorable to Christians. Finally, as to the falsehood: What risk does the pious multitude run, in believing the miracles of the Lives of the Saints? They find nothing in them which is not proved, or worthy of belief; nothing but what may very prudently be believed; nothing but what is edifying; and this, according to St. Augustine, is a sufficient guarantee from falling into any dangerous credulity.

We should be very dangerously credulous, if we put our faith in false and deceitful miracles, which only tend to seduce the mind, and corrupt our belief. We are warned in the Gospel, that "there shall arise false christs and false prophets, and shall show great signs and wonders, insomuch as to deceive (if it be possible) even the elect;" and St. Paul teaches us that Antichrist, "that man of perdition, will come according to the working of Satan in all power, and signs, and lying wonders." The father of lies has often inspired the heretics to produce miracles, which they have asserted to have been performed by persons of their party, living or dead, from whence they inferred that God authorized the doctrines they taught. Ecclesiastical history furnishes many examples of this, and there are some very recent ones.

But Jesus Christ has furnished us with a sure and infallible rule to avoid the contagion: it is to hear the Church; it is to consider those only as true miracles of which she approves, and of which she sanctions the publication; it is to believe firmly that no one who is in revolt against the Church will ever perform a miracle favorable to his sect, whatever appearance of austerity, piety, charity, or sanctity, he may put on; which St. Thomas bases mainly on this principle: that it is impossible that God, who alone can give the power of working a true miracle, shall ever communicate that power to confirm a false doctrine; from whence it follows, that all the miracles produced by sectarians, notwithstanding all their evidence, and all their pretended attestations, must neither be examined nor listened to, and must only be looked upon as purely natural effects, or as impostures, or as delusions and diabolical operations. This is the way in which St. Augustine expresses himself on the subject of the miracles which the Donatists claimed to have performed, and claimed as evidence in favor of their schism. Let Catholics, therefore, reject with horror the false prodigies of sectarians, but let them piously give credit to the miracles of the saints, without paying attention to the ultra-criticism which strives to throw doubts upon them; and let them be intimately persuaded that the Church, which approves of them, has founded that approval on evidence irreproachable.

The marvels which are found in the Life of St. Francis are perfectly well attested. That Life was first written by Thomas de Celano, one of his companions, who was directed by Pope Gregory IX. to compile it, and who afterwards added a second part on additional memoirs. John or Thomas de Ceperano, Apostolic Notary, who was a staunch friend of the Saint, published at the same time what he knew of his actions. Crescentius de Jesi, General of the Order of the Friars Minors, gave directions, by circular letters, to collect and transmit to him whatever had been seen or learnt, relative to the sanctity and miracles of the blessed Father. He addressed himself particularly to three of his twelve first companions: Leo, his secretary and his confessor; Angelus and Rufinus: all three joined in compiling what is called "The Legend of the Three Companions." The others noted separately what they had themselves seen, and the things which they had learnt from others. Saint Bonaventure, being at the head of the Order, was urgently entreated, by the general chapter, to write the life of their holy Patriarch. With the intention of learning, with certainty, the truth of the facts, he went expressly to Assisi, "There," he says, in the preface to his work, "I had frequent and serious conferences with those who had been in the confidence of the great man, and who were still living; and principally with those who were most intimately consociated with him, and who have become the most faithful imitators of his holy life, to whose testimony we must undoubtedly give credit, because their acknowledged sanctity assures us that they have spoken truth." Now, what can the most exact and severe criticism wish more, in order to give warranty to the marvels in the Life of St. Francis, than contemporaries, ocular witnesses, holy persons, his own companions, who lived with him and enjoyed his confidence?

The legend of Saint Bonaventure was spread everywhere, as soon as it appeared, and was everywhere highly approved: there are many manuscripts of it. Lipoman, Bishop of Verona, caused it to be printed in 1556. No one ever attempted to call its accuracy in question. Octavian quoted it, in his petition to Pope Sixtus IV. for the canonization of the holy doctor, in 1482.

The first legends have been preserved in manuscript; the celebrated annalist of the Order of Friars Minors, Luke Wading, saw them and made use of them. He was one of the most learned men of his time, and all other learned men have been loud in his praise, not only on account of his profound erudition, but because he was so ardent a lover of truth, which he sought for with great care, and having developed it, nothing could hinder him from publishing it and committing it to writing.

The uprightness of his heart was conspicuous on a certain occasion, which is too honorable to him for us to pass it over in silence. He had been one of the examiners nominated by Pope Innocent X. to inquire into the writings of Jansenius, Bishop of Ypres, and he had convinced himself that the five propositions which appeared to be censurable in those writings might be tolerably explained in a certain theological sense. Those who are themselves upright are not easily brought to think ill of others, particularly in difficult affairs, and they sometimes endeavor to justify them, through charitable feelings, which are praiseworthy in principle, but which may have evil consequences, when a doctrine is in question which has been widely spread, and which is supported by a cabal. Wading, seeing that the five propositions were censured by various constitutions of the Pope, made a report on the whole affair, with the following beautiful declaration, worthy of a truly Catholic Doctor: "If, before this decision, any one shall have been of a different opinion (as to the five propositions) on whatever reasonings, or whatsoever authority of doctrine, he is now obliged to bend his mind to the yoke of faith, according to the advice of the apostle. I declare it to be what I do with all my heart, condemning and anathematizing all the aforesaid propositions, in all and every sense in which His Holiness has proposed to condemn them, although, before this decision, I thought they might have been maintained in a certain sense, in the manner I have explained in the suffrage which has been just seen."

We may feel assured that a man of this upright character, such a lover of truth, and, moreover, one of such eminent talents, would not have made use of the two Legends of Thomas de Celano and that of the Three Companions, without having ascertained their correctness. Moreover, the critics of his time, who were particular, and in great numbers, had it in their power to examine them as those of our times have, also, since they are still extant in the convent of St. Isidore at Rome.

The first, which was composed under the Pontificate of Gregory IX., was quoted by Luke, Bishop of Tuy, when he wrote against the Albigenses, in 1231. It is to be found in the Abbey of Longpont, of the Order of Citeaux, in the diocese of Soissons, and in the Abbey of Jouy, of the same order, in the Diocese of Sens. The Legend of the Three Companions is in the king's library, at the Recollets of Louvain, and in their convent at Malines.

These are the principal sources which were consulted by Wading for writing the Life of St. Francis, which forms part of the first tome of his Annals. He also consulted the acts and public monuments, the constant tradition, and some manuscripts of the thirteenth century, which contain other testimonials from the companions of St. Francis, and were published by contemporaries who lived with them, who collected their very words, and who are worthy of credence. But the most marvellous thing which he relates, relative to the actions of the Saint, he has taken from the legends, as well as a great number of the splendid miracles which were operated by his intercession after his death, and of which Pope Gregory IX. was fully informed, as he declares in the Bull of Canonization.

All modern authors who have given the Life of St. Francis in various languages, have adhered mostly to Wading; in this work, also, we have made a point of following him; and the learned, who have so much esteem for that great man, will agree that we could not have taken a better guide. Baillet admits that, among the writers of the Life of St. Francis, Luke Wading is one of the most careful and most accurate; and yet he taxes him with not having written methodically, when he adds: "After all the labors of so many persons, who have been zealous for his glory, we are still compelled to wish for a methodical history of his life." Whoever may read the Annals of Wading, and his notes on the works of St. Francis, will find in them as much method as research and accuracy; but according to some ultra-critics, it is not considered writing methodically, when marvels which they dislike are permitted to find their way into history.

Baillet might have said that it has been long a subject of complaint that we have not in our language a complete and methodical Life of St. Francis. This complaint is the more just, as the saint had a particular liking for France; he had learned the language with so much facility, and spoke it so readily, that they gave him the name of Francis, although he was baptized John. Paris was one of the first objects of his zeal; he would even have gone thither, if a cardinal had not detained him in Italy for reasons which related to his Order. Not having it in his power to undertake this mission, which he had much at heart, he destined for it some of his principal followers.

There are some who affect to think that, in the Lives of the Saints, their example should alone be proposed to the public, imagining that the miracles they have performed can nowise contribute to the edification of souls; and two authors of this century have ventured to suppress all miracles in the Lives of Saints which they have published. The Church, nevertheless, causes them to be recited in the Divine Office, and they are carefully related by the holy fathers; neither does any author of repute, of the centuries preceding, fail to bring them forward. In fact, no one can deny that they add great resplendency to the merits of the saints, and, consequently, give great weight to the example they afford us. They uphold and increase the idea we have of the power of God, of His providence, His justice, His bounty, and His mercy, by which they excite us to glorify, love, and serve Him; and, in showing His special good-will to His servants, they induce us to invoke their mediation with confidence. Moreover, miracles strengthen the faithful in their faith, because, being performed in the bosom of the Catholic Church, they confirm the truth she teaches. Now, it is not of less consequence to strengthen faith, than to propose that which tends to the correction of morals, particularly when incredulity makes as much progress as licentiousness. Moreover, the miraculous actions of the saints frequently contain most salutary instructions, and are always accompanied by virtues which may be imitated, which will be very apparent in the Life of St. Francis.

Some may, perhaps, think that his virtues are too transcendent for imitation, and content themselves with admiring them, without gathering any fruit from them. A celebrated heresiarch admired them in this manner, in the last century. Bossuet remarks, in his excellent "History of the Variations," that "Luther reckoned among the saints not only St. Bernard, but also St. Francis, St. Bonaventure, and others of the thirteenth century; and that St. Francis, amongst all the rest, appeared to him to be an admirable character, animated with wonderful fervor of mind." But the faithful in admiring his virtues, must not think them not to be imitated, for they consisted in following the Gospel; and they are all obliged to live according to the precepts of the Gospel.

Rev. Candide Chalippe, O.F.M.

Chapter 1

FROM HIS BIRTH TO HIS TIME AT THE CHURCH OF ST. MARY OF THE ANGELS

We here offer, to the pious reflections of the faithful, the life of a man who proposed to himself to practise literally the precepts of the Gospel, to conform himself entirely to Jesus Christ crucified, and to inspire the whole world with God's love.

Such a purpose must seem great to all those who can appreciate true grandeur by the light of religion. In its contempt of the goods of the world, it manifests an elevation of mind far above the ostentation of the ancient philosophers; in its deep humiliations, an heroical courage; in its extreme simplicity, the most exalted sentiments; in its weakness, and in the apparent foolishness of the cross, the strength and wisdom of God. The infidels themselves admired all this, and it will be not less meet to revive the fervor of Christians, and to increase the veneration they have always entertained for St. Francis.

He was born at Assisi, a town of Umbria, in Italy, in the year 1182, under the Pontificate of Lucius III. Peter Bernardo, his father, was a rich merchant, whose principal commercial transactions were with France. His mother, whose name was Pica, had only two sons, Francis and Angelo. The latter married at Assisi, and some of his descendants were still at Assisi in 1534.

God, who has often condescended to usher in His saints by portents, was pleased, at the birth of Francis, to give signs of what he would be during his life. For some days Pica had suffered great pains, without being able to give birth to her child, when a man, dressed as a pilgrim, came to tell her that she would only be delivered of her infant in a table; he would be born on straw. Although this communication appeared most strange, relatives, nevertheless, acted upon it. The patient was removed to the nearest stable, where she was successfully delivered; an event which may well be looked upon, as in the intention of Providence, thereby to mark the conformity of the holy man to Jesus Christ, poor and humble; as much, at least, as the creature can be in conformity with the Creator, and the servant with the Master of the universe.

This stable has been turned into a chapel, called in Italian, "San Francesco il piccolo"—"St. Francis the Little." Over the door the following words, in very old writing, are inscribed:

> "This chapel was the stable of the Ox and the Ass, Where Francis was born, the mirror of the world."

His mother had the name of John given to him at his baptism, his father being then absent in France. A stranger presented himself as his godfather, and he was accepted as such; whether it was that something extraordinary was perceived in this person, or that they had been struck with astonishment at the first event. The uniform tradition at Assisi is, that this stranger disappeared after the ceremony, and that he left the impression of his knees on a marble step of the altar, which is shown in the cathedral church, with the baptismal font, on which these words in Italian are engraved:—"This is the fountain in which the Seraphic Father, St. Francis, was baptized."

At the return from the baptismal ceremony, a man, who seemed to have been sent by God, as well as the other two, or rather an angel in human form, came to beg that he might be allowed to see the child and hold it. He took it in his arms, caressed it a good deal, and impressed upon its right shoulder a well-formed cross, as a mark of his consecration, recommending the nurse to take particular care of the child, not to expose him to the snares of the devils, who had a foresight that he would one day wage a severe war against them. One of these evil spirits was obliged to confess by the mouth of one possessed, whom they were exorcising, that the princes of darkness, alarmed at the birth of Francis, had tried various ways to take away his life; and it was the Saint himself who expelled this devil afterwards. These portents, marvellous as they are, are less surprising, when we consider the singular and marked favors which heaven destined for him.

His parents brought him up with great care, and he was put to study with the clergy of the Parish of St. George. After he had acquired some knowledge of letters, he was initiated in commercial affairs, the correspondence of which necessitated his learning the French language; he acquired it with so much ease, that his father gave him the name of Francis, a name which he bore ever after.

Bernardo and Francis pursued their avocation in a very different manner. The first, with no other object than his worldly interest, thought of nothing but his profits, and had no other care than that of accumulating. Francis, who had not a particle of avarice, and had less thought of his profit than of dealing with honor, traded with nobler and more elevated feelings. But he loved the world, he frequented society, and spent a good deal in dress, festivities, and parties of pleasure. His father frequently reprimanded him on the subject of his expenses, but his remonstrances had little effect, because he had no consideration of the value of money, and he wished to be distinguished amongst his young companions, who always considered him as their leader. His mother, who was tender and generous, had more patience with him; and she said to those who spoke to her of his profusion, that from what she remarked in his conversation, in his actions, and even in his amusements, she had reasons to hope something great when he should come to maturer years.

Indeed, in all his demeanor, excellent prognostics for the future were observable: his temper was exquisite, mild, and condescending, his manners were agreeable and very polite; he was lively, and had great good sense: he was brave, and had a strong inclination to be generous, even to give beyond his means. Although he plunged into the vain amusements of the world, there was nothing blamable in his moral conduct. By the special protection of heaven, he avoided the rocks on which youth is too often wrecked; he preserved the inestimable treasure of purity; it was also remarked that he was distressed at any licentious expressions, and never made any reply to them.

God had imprinted in his heart great feelings of compassion for the poor, which increased from his infancy, and which induced him to afford them liberal aid, so that, following the Gospel precept, "Give to every one that asketh thee," he made a resolution to give to all who should ask alms of him, and principally if they should solicit it for the love of God. This feeling for the love of God had its effect upon him, even then, notwithstanding his dissipation; he could seldom hear the expression made use of, as he has since admitted, without being sensibly affected. It having once happened to him, in the hurry of business, to turn away a poor person who had asked a charity for the love of God, his conscience smote him immediately, and he ran after the poor man, relieved him amply, and made a promise to God that he would never refuse a single individual as long as it was in his power, when an alms should be asked for His love,—a promise which he faithfully kept to his death, and which, as St. Bonaventure remarks, was of essential service in increasing the grace and love of God in his heart. What is there more likely to bring down the grace of conversion and sanctification, and increase the love of God, than the practice of works of mercy?

The amiable qualities of Francis rendered him a favorite throughout the town, where he was looked up to as the flower of the youth, and great hopes were entertained for the future in his regard. A man of simple manners, but enlightened from above, caused a still greater esteem to be entertained for him. When he met him in the streets, he spread his cloak on the ground before him, and as a reason for showing him so unusual a mark of respect, exclaimed:— "This young man will soon do great things: he will deserve all sorts of honors, and will be revered by the faithful." Francis, who was unconscious of the designs of God, did not understand the meaning of this prediction. He knew not that these honors were to be rendered him only after severe humiliations, according to the words of the Gospel. Engrossed by the affairs of the world, and attached to its vanities, he thought little of this Divine truth, and he had less taste for it; nevertheless he hoped that he should some day receive the honors which others foretold, and which God permitted him likewise to predict of himself in an affliction which came upon him.

The towns of Assisi and Perugia were at war with each other; he was taken prisoner with some of his fellow-citizens: whether it was that he had taken up arms in the service of his country, or that he was beyond the limits of the town of his commercial affairs. His captivity, however, did not affect his spirits, he preserved his cheerfulness and good humor. His companions, who were dejected and cast down, were offended at this, and upbraided him with it, saying that he might, at least out of feeling for them, disguise them, disguise his satisfaction. "I am very sorry for you" he replied, "but as to myself, my mind is at ease and I am thankful that it is so. You see me now a prisoner, but at a future period, you will see me honored by the whole world." There was one among the prisoners whose quarrelsome temper and extreme ill humor caused him to be shunned by the others. Francis entreated them to draw a distinction between his person and his defects, and to bear with him: not being able to induce them to do so, he had the charity to keep him company himself, and by his good advice, he rendered him more gentle. All were so delighted with his goodness of heart, that they sought his friendship.

Liberated from captivity, he returned to Assisi, where God visited him with a long and severe illness, which reduced him to a state of great weakness. This was to prepare his soul for the influence of grace. As soon as he could walk, he wished to enjoy the beauty and air of the country; but he failed to be pleased therewith, and was even disgusted with what he had previously liked the most; he felt contempt for what he had before esteemed, and his own conduct appeared to him to be senseless. This change surprised him much, but it did not as yet make any alteration in his heart. The return of health renewed his attachment to the world, his ambition and vanity revived; he entertained fresh hopes of greatness, and paid once more great attention to his dress. Thus it frequently happens that when God sends illness to worldly persons with a view to their conversion, these have no other effect than momentary reflections and promises, which are soon forgotten on the return of strength.

However, Francis became more and more charitable, and gave to all the poor either money or his clothes. Having met a poor and ill-clad officer who was of a noble family, he saw in him the poverty of Jesus Christ, the King of kings, and being moved to pity, he gave him the new suit of clothes he had on.

The following night God showed him in his sleep a great and magnificent palace, full of warlike arms, all marked with the sign of the cross, to give him an idea of the reward his charity was to receive. He asked whom all that belonged to; and he was answered, that the arms were for his soldiers.

Not as yet understanding the meaning of mysterious dreams, he took this as a token of the success he was to have in warlike achievements, without suspecting that the crosses he had seen had a totally different signification. At that time Walter, Count of Brienne, in Champagne, was waging active war against the emperor, in the kingdom of Naples, on the subject of the claims of his wife Alberia, the eldest daughter of Tancred, King of Cicily, who had been some years dead. Francis resolved to offer him his services, in the hope of gaining military honors. He attached himself to an officer of distinction, who belonged to the count's army, and he set out with a good retinue, after having assured his friends that he was sure of acquiring great renown.

He first went to Spoleto, and there Jesus Christ addressed these benevolent words to him during the night: "Francis, which of the two, think you, can be of the greatest service to you: the master or the servant, the rich or the poor?" "It is the master and the rich," he answered without any hesitation. "Why then," continued our Lord, "do you leave God who is the master and rich, to seek man, who is the servant and poor?" "O Lord!" exclaimed Francis, "what is it your pleasure I should do?" Jesus Christ then said to him: "Return to your town; what you have seen signifies nothing but what is spiritual. It is from God, and not from man, that you will receive their accomplishment." The very next morning he retraced his steps towards Assisi, to await the orders of the Lord, without troubling himself as to what the world should say as to this precipitate return.

His friends came as usual to propose a party of pleasure. He received them, as was his custom, with great politeness, and feasted them magnificently to bid them, thus honorably, an eternal adieu. On parting from them, he found himself suddenly struck with the vanity of all terrestrial things, and with the grandeur of all that is heavenly, by a communication from the Spirit of God, full of mildness, but so internal, and so forcible, that his senses were brought into a state of inaction, and he himself remained motionless. He afterwards told his confessor, that, if he had been torn to pieces in this state of rapture, he would not have felt it; that, in that moment, he could only feel at the bottom of his soul. The company, quite alarmed, drew near him; and when he had recovered his usual serenity, they enquired of him, laughing, what had occasioned his extraordinary reserve; if, perhaps, he was not thinking of taking a wife? "It is so," he replied: "I shall take one, but one so noble and so beautiful, that such another will not be found in the whole world." Evangelical poverty, which he afterwards embraced, was the spouse to which the Holy Ghost inspired him to allude.

After this divine favor he disembarrassed himself as much as possible of his commercial affairs, to beg of God to know what He would have him do; and he usually went to pray in a grotto with a confidential friend, who left him there in entire liberty. The frequent recourse to prayer excited in his heart so ardent a desire for the celestial country, that he already looked upon everything that was earthly as nothing. He felt that this happy disposition contained a treasure, but he did not as yet know how to possess himself of the hidden prize. The Spirit of God merely insinuated to him that the spiritual life, under the idea of traffic, must begin by a contempt of the world,—and under the idea of warfare, by a victory over self.—All spirituality not based upon these two Divine lessons, will never have anything solid in it.

Francis had soon occasion to put these lessons in practice. As he was riding across the plains of Assisi, he perceived a leper coming straight to him. At first he felt horror-stricken, but calling to mind that he had formed a resolution to labor to attain perfection, and that, in order to be a soldier of Jesus Christ, it was necessary to begin by obtaining a victory over self, he dismounted, kissed the leper, and gave him an alms. When he again mounted his horse, he no longer saw any one, though he looked all round the plain. Filled with astonishment, and transported with joy, he fell on his knees to thank God, and formed firm resolution to aim at still greater perfection. This is the effect of generous and courageous efforts, they draw down fresh graces, and reanimate our courage. He acquired also more inclination for retirement, he had no longer any liking but for solitude, for those places which were adapted to the holy sorrow of penance, where he unceasingly addressed himself to God in fervent prayer, accompanied by lamentations, which cannot be described: God at length favorably heard him.

His fervor daily increasing, insomuch that he was wholly absorbed in God, Jesus Christ appeared to him as if attached to the cross. His soul, at this stupendous scene, was wholly penetrated, and, as it were, dissolved, and the image of his crucified Saviour became from that time so strongly and intimately imprinted on his heart, that every time it recurred to his mind, he had a difficulty in restraining his sobs and tears.

In this marvellous apparition he was made aware that these words of the Gospel were personally addressed to him: "If any man will come after Me, let him deny himself, and take up his cross and follow Me." He received from them that foretaste of poverty and humility which became his characteristics, and so ardent a charity inflamed his heart, that he had the courage to devote himself to the service of the lepers. Before this day they were so much his horror, that, far from allowing them to be in his presence, as soon as he saw them, at whatever distance, he turned away from them, and if they were near he passed on quickly, holding his nose. But for the love of Jesus crucified, who was pleased to represent Himself to the Prophet Isaias under the despised figure of a leper, he lowered himself to attending upon them in their hospitals, where, having abundantly supplied them with alms, he made their beds, dressed their sores, and performed for them the most abject services; he often even kissed their hands and their faces with great feelings of commiseration. The words which our Saviour one day addressed to him while at prayer, stimulated him to continue this charitable exercise, notwithstanding his natural repugnance: "Francis, if thou desirest to know My will, thou must despise and hate all that thou hast loved and wished for till now. Let not this new path alarm thee, for, if the things which now please thee must become bitter and distasteful, those which now displease thee, will become sweet and agreeable." Shortly before his death he declared that what had seemed to him most bitter in serving the lepers, had been changed into what was pleasing both for soul and body; and all those who strive to overcome themselves for the love of God feel, as he did, that the severest practices are soon softened down by the unction of grace.

The sight of Jesus Christ fastened to the cross made him feel the misery of the poor so intensely, that he would have wished to employ all he had, and his own person, in their relief. Sometimes he did strip himself to clothe them; and when he had not enough to satisfy them all, he unsewed or tore his clothes to divide among them. In the absence of his father he caused much more bread to be brought to table at their meals than was necessary; and when his mother asked the reason, he said, "that it was in order to give more quickly to those who came to ask for food." This pious mother saw with pleasure the charity of her son; and far from endeavoring to check it, she was not displeased at his leaving her alone at table, while he took to the neighboring sick the viands of which he stinted himself. An equally lively and respectful zeal induced him to come to the aid of such priests as were in want; he took particular care to provide for the decoration of the altars, in order the better to assist at the divine service. He bought the finest linen, and distributed it to the poor country churches to be employed at the sacrifice of the mass; and when this august sacrifice was about to be celebrated, if anything was wanting, or if the altar was not properly found in everything requisite, he would offer himself to the officers of the church, in order to supply what was required either from his purse or by his personal assistance.

But all these good works did not come up to what he had figured to himself as requisite for perfection. He could have wished to withdraw into some distant country, there to practise voluntary poverty, which had already inflamed his heart. At first he resolved to go to Rome, to visit the tomb of St. Peter, moved by that grand devotion which God has often inspired in His saints, and which has been so frequent since the fourth century. He also proposed to himself to solicit from the Almighty, by the intercession of the Prince of the Apostles, the grace to carry out the resolution he had come to of leading an Apostolic life. After having recited his prayer in this holy place, he noticed that in the crowd of people some made but a slender offering, while others made no donation whatever. "What then," said he, "is devotion grown so cold? How is it that men do not offer all they have, and do not even offer themselves on a spot where the ashes of the Prince of the Apostles repose? How does it happen that they do not decorate with all possible magnificence this Peter, on whom Jesus Christ has founded His Church?" He contributed to the best of his power, leaving a considerable sum for that purpose; and what he had wished was subsequently executed. The Sovereign Pontiffs, and in particular Sixtus V, who was a religious of his Order, have rendered the Basilica of St. Peter so sumptuous and magnificent, that it is now the admiration of the universe.

On going out of the church, he saw a multitude of poor, whom he immediately joined, as much for the affection he had for them, as for the love of poverty. He gave his clothes to him who appeared to be the most necessitous. The following day, having dressed himself with propriety, he set out on his return to Assisi, praying God to guide him in the ways of holy poverty.

The devil, who was sensible that the young man would become confirmed in his intention if he persevered in prayer, appeared to him under a most terrific form, and threatened him, if he persisted, to render him a dreadful deformity like unto an old woman of the town, who was so hideous that he could not even look at her. But the newly-enlisted soldier of Jesus Christ, who began to be inured to warfare, laughed at the threats of the tempter, and was more urgent in his prayers, for which purpose he chose underground places, where he could better defend himself against the snares of his enemy. The fruit of these holy exercises was a lively sorrow for the use he had made of the first years of his youth, and a great perseverance in the mortification of his senses, in order to bear the cross of Jesus Christ in his body, as he bore it in his heart.

It was thus that Francis acted before having changed his habit, or quitted the world. St. Bonaventure says that he had then no other master from whom he received instructions than Jesus Christ; nevertheless, an author quoted by Wading, assures us that he sometimes consulted the Bishop of Assisi. We may here say, in order that there may be no seeming contradiction between the two, that he received instructions from Jesus Christ only because he was inspired by Him, but that he communicated with the bishop on the points on which he had been inspired; and we may be the more assured of this, as we shall see hereafter that this prelate had his confidence, and that there is reason to think that he was his spiritual Father.

The servant of God, walking and meditating one day out of Assisi, near the church of St. Damian, which was very old and falling into ruin, was moved by the Holy Spirit to enter it to pray. There, prostrated before the crucifix, he repeated three times the following beautiful words, which gave him great interior consolation, and which he subsequently made frequent use of: "Great God, full of glory, and Thou, my Lord Jesus Christ! I entreat you to enlighten me and to dispel the darkness of my mind, to give me a pure faith, a firm hope, and an ardent charity. Let me have a perfect knowledge of Thee, O God! so that I may in all things by guided by Thy light, and act in conformity to Thy will." He cast his eyes, filled with tears, upon the crucifix, when a voice came forth from it, and he heard distinctly these words repeated three times, not interiorly, but loudly pronounced: "Francis, go and repair my house, which thou seest is falling into ruin." So wonderful a voice, in a place where he was alone, alarmed him greatly, but he felt immediately the salutary effects of it, and he was transported with joy.

The sense of these words chiefly related to the state of the Church which Jesus Christ had purchased at the price of His blood, which the holy man was to repair in all its defects by his ministry and the labors of his disciples, according to the explanation which the Holy Spirit gave to him of them subsequently, which he communicated to his brethren, as St. Bonaventure tells us.

Nevertheless, the powerful protection which he received from heaven for the repair of the church of St. Damian, was an indication that the same words were to be understood to relate to that building also: as the sacred oracles had a twofold literal sense in the mouths of the Prophets, one of which related to events which were at hand, and the other to a distant time, and to mysteries wholly spiritual.

Francis came to himself; he left the church fully resolved to undertake its repair, and left money in the hands of a priest named Peter, who did the parochial duties of it, to keep a lamp burning before the crucifix, promising to give more, and to employ all he had for the use of this holy place.

The voice which had issued from the crucifix renewed in his mind and heart the impression of the mystery of the Passion. He felt himself interiorly wounded through the wounds of Jesus Christ, and he shed such burning tears, that his eyes were quite inflamed, and, as it were, full of blood, when he returned from prayer. To make his body participate in the sufferings which penetrated his very soul, and to punish himself for the levities of his youth, he imposed on himself a very rigorous abstinence, with various other kinds of mortification.

The eagerness he felt to commence the repair of St. Damian's church, suggested to him means by which the work might be begun. After having fortified himself by the sign of the cross, he took from his father's stores several pieces of cloth, which he sold at Foligno, together with his horse. He came back on foot, and offered the money respectfully to the priest of St. Damian for the repair of the church, and in aid of the poor; humbly entreating him to allow him to remain some time with him. The priest consented to receive Francis, but refused the money, fearing the displeasure of his father; and Francis, who had utter contempt for money, not valuing it more than so much dust, when it was of no use for good works, threw it upon one of the windows of the church.

The heretics of the last century, who calumniated the Saint for many things, have deemed it criminal in him to have taken these pieces of cloth from his father's stores. St. Bonaventure is of a different way of thinking; he has not thought that this action required justification; on the contrary, he calls the sale of the cloth and of the horse a fortunate bargain. And, indeed, without going into the right which the son may have had in the commercial affairs of his father, in consequence of their partnership, and of his age of twenty-five, had he not reason to think that, having received orders from heaven to repair a church, God, who is the Master and Dispenser of all goods, permitted him to employ a portion of the goods which were under his paternal roof, since he had no other means of obeying the injunction? But it is an extraordinary case, which must not be drawn into precedent. The general rule of Christian morality is, that children may not dispose of anything without the permission of their parents even under the pretext of piety.

Bernardo on his return from a journey, having heard what his son had done, came in great wrath to St. Damian's with several members of his family; and Francis, who had not yet sufficient strength of mind to encounter the storm, and wished to avoid the first ebullition, went and hid himself in the priest's room. Three contemporary authors assure us that, having placed himself behind the door, and pressing himself against the wall, when the door was opened he was miraculously let into the wall, so that he was not seen by those who were looking for him.

When his father was gone, he retired secretly into a cavern, which was known only to one servant, from whom he received what was necessary for his immediate sustenance, and where he occupied himself in continual prayer, shedding abundance of tears, in order that he might be delivered from those who pursued him, and be able to accomplish the work which God had inspired him to undertake.

After having passed a month in this place, he considered that it was in God alone that he ought to hope, without putting any confidence in his own exertions, and this thought filled him with interior joy, and raised his depressed spirits. Reproaching himself, therefore, with his pusillanimity, he left his cavern and went straight to the town, as a soldier, who, feeling ashamed of having fled, returns intrepidly to the charge. Of what is not he capable, who is fully persuaded that he can do nothing of himself towards his salvation, but that he can do ll through God who imparts strength to him? On these two principles the saints have undertaken, and carried into execution, the greatest things.

The inhabitants of Assisi, who saw his face all pale and wan, and who remarked how changed were his conversation and opinions, thought that his mind was disturbed. He was called a madman, they threw mud and stones at him, and followed him, hooting and calling after him. But, without paying attention to these insults, and being on the contrary well pleased to bear these marks of the holy folly of the cross, the servant of God continued his way as if he had been deaf and insensible.

Bernardo being told that his son had returned, and was made the object of public derision, went immediately in pursuit of him, reproached him bitterly with his conduct, seized him and dragged him to his house, where he beat him severely, and confined him in a hole under the staircase. This severity had no effect in shaking the resolution of the holy prisoner; he even acquired more firmness, and encouraged himself to suffer by the words of the Gospel: "Blessed are they that suffer persecution for justice' sake, for theirs is the kingdom of heaven."

A short time after, when his father was on a journey, his mother, who did not approve of the severity with which he was treated, and who moreover had no hope of overcoming his constancy, set him at liberty. He gave thanks to God for it, and made use of it, to return to the church of St. Damian. Bernardo, not finding him in his confinement at his return, was not content with upbraiding his wife in the severest terms, but went off to St. Damian's to drive him out of the country if he should not succeed in bringing him back. Francis, to whom God had given strength, presented himself boldly to his father, and told him decidedly that he cared not for his blows, nor for his shackles—that he was prepared willingly to suffer all sorts of evils for the name of Jesus Christ. His father, seeing that there was nothing more to hope in his case, thought of nothing further than to get back the money for the cloth and the horse. He found it in the window where Francis had thrown it, when the priest refused its acceptance, and then his wrath was somewhat appeased.

Avarice, which is never satisfied, induced Bernardo to believe that his son had other money, and he had him summoned before the city magistrates, to account for it. Francis appeared before their tribunal and told them that he had changed his state of life, that God had delivered him from the slavery of the world, and that he had nothing more to do with its affairs. The magistrates, who knew his conversion and his perseverance, saw something grand in his demeanor, and told his father, who urged them to put interrogatories to his son, that this affair ought to be carried into the bishop's court. Bernard addressed himself to that authority, not only to compel his son to give up what money he had, but to force him to renounce his claims to any paternal inheritance. Francis, who was a sincere lover of poverty, cheerfully consented to all that was required of him, and said that he would willingly appear before the bishop, who was the pastor and father of his soul. As soon as he was there, without waiting for his father to make his demand, and without saying anything himself, he gave up what money he still had, and then stripped off his clothes, even to his shirt, under which it was seen that he wore a hair-shirt, and gave them up to his father, addressing him in the following beautiful words: "Until this time I have called thee father on earth; but from henceforward I may boldly say, Our Father who art in Heaven, in whom I have placed all my treasure, and all my confidence."

The prelate, who was a man of great worth, admiring this excess of fervor, and moved even to tears, rose up, and embracing the servant of God, covered him with his cloak, and ordered his servants to bring such clothing as was necessary for him. It was no doubt by a dispensation of Divine Providence that a bishop pressed to his bosom him who was to combat so strenuously for the service of the Church. They brought an old cloak belonging to a laborer, who was in the employ of the bishop, which Francis received with great satisfaction, and with which he clothed himself, making on it a cross with some mortar which he met with accidentally; thus manifesting what he wished to he, a half-naked poor one, and a crucified man. This occurred in the year 1206, when he was in his twenty-fifth year. St. Bonaventure, who gives the name of spiritual intoxication to the admirable fervor with which he stripped himself in order to be able to follow Jesus Christ nailed on the cross, says that, moreover, in order to avoid the shipwrecks of the world, he fortified himself with the representation of the wood which was the instrument of our salvation.

Emancipated from the ties of worldly desires, as he had wished to be, he now sought for some sequestered spot, where alone and in silence he might listen to the voice of God. In a wood, through which he was passing, singing the praises of God in the French language, some thieves surrounded him and asked him who he was. "I am the herald of the great King," he replied, in a prophetical sense, with perfect confidence in God. On receiving this answer, they beat him cruelly, threw him into a hole that was full of snow, and ridiculed the title he gave himself. When they had left him, he again began to sing the praises of God in a louder voice than before, delighted to have had an opportunity of suffering. At a neighboring monastery, where he implored alms, which he received as a contemptible beggar, they employed him for some days in the vilest affairs of the scullery. But seeing that this interfered too much with his spiritual exercises, he came to Gubbio, where one of his friends, having recognized him, gave him, in order that he might be more decently clad, a hermit's dress, a short tunic, a leathern girdle, shoes, and a staff.

In this penitential habit, he subjected his body to additional austerities; and in order to fulfil all the functions of humility, to which he was much attached, he devoted himself to the service of the lepers. He was constantly seen in their hospitals, moving about in all directions to aid them, preventing all their wants, showing the greatest compassion for them, washing their feet, cleansing their sores, removing the matter, and, by a wonderful effort of charity, kissing their disgusting ulcers. He received from God in reward the gift of healing; and this was a figure of the Evangelical cures, which he was soon to apply to the diseases of the soul.

Among many proofs which St. Bonaventure adduces of his having the gift of healing miraculously, he mentions that of a man of the Duchy of Spoleto, whose mouth and cheeks were eaten away by a dreadful cancer, and for whom all sorts of remedies had been fruitlessly employed. This man met Francis returning from Rome (whither he had been to implore the assistance of the blessed Apostles), who, out of great respect, wished to kiss his feet; this the humble Francis prevented, but kissed the cancerous face, which was instantaneously cured. The same saint remarks: "I know not which is most to be admired, such a kiss, or such a cure!"

The servant of God, who now acknowledged no other country than heaven, and who was fearful of being the cause of some of his father's violences, proposed to himself to take up his abode in Gubbio and devote himself to the exercises of charity, without returning to Assisi; but calling to mind the order which had been given him by the voice which came from the crucifix, to repair the Church of St. Damian, he thought himself bound to obey it, at least by "questing" for what was requisite for working at it. The profound humility which he had acquired by the degradations he had subjected himself to, gave him the courage he required for begging in his native town, where he had been known to have possessed everything in plenty. Having cast aside all bashfulness for the love of Jesus Christ poor and crucified, he went through the centre of Assisi as one inspired, publishing the glories of God, and soliciting stones for the repair of the church; addressing his fellow-citizens with simplicity, thus: "Whosoever will give me a stone, shall have a reward; whoever will give two shall have a double reward; and he who gives three shall be rewarded threefold."

Many treated him with contempt, and turned him into ridicule. Others could not understand how a young man of a good and opulent family, with excellent prospects, hitherto considered as the model of the young men of the place, could demean himself to such a degree as to beg in his native town. Some thought that such a change could only come from God, and were greatly moved by it. But the new-made pauper, having no respect for the opinions of men, and receiving cheerfully the insults put upon him, after the example of Jesus Christ, thought of nothing but the church of St. Damian, for which he quested so successfully, that many persons, moved by his exhortations, furnished sufficient for its repair. He himself worked at it daily, and carried the materials on his shoulders as a common laborer, without any regard for his body, which was emaciated by the rigors of penance and fasting.

The priest of St. Damian took compassion on the pious workman, and took care to provide him with a substantial meal when he came in from work. Francis having received this charitable succor for some days running, reflected on his situation, and said to himself as he afterwards told his disciples: "Will you find everywhere a priest who has so much consideration for you? This is not the sort of life you have chosen: go, then, henceforward from door to door, as a poor man, and solicit food for the love of God, with an empty plate, on which you will put whatever may be given you. For it is thus you must live for the love of Him who was born poor, who lived poorly, whom they affixed naked to the cross, and who was put after His death into another man's tomb." One must be very dead to self, have great contempt of the world, and a sincere love of God, to entertain such feelings and carry them out.

The following day he took a plate, and went begging from door to door, and sat down in the street to eat. At the first mouthful he took of this disgusting mess, he felt a nausea in his stomach, which made him recoil. Animated at the same instant by the love of poverty, he became ashamed of his weakness, and reproached himself for the feeling; after which, he ate the remainder without reluctance, and with so much relish, that he thought he had never eaten a better meal. He also felt an interior joy and strength in his body, which enabled him to bear with pleasure, for God's sake, whatever might be most severe or bitter. After having returned fervent thanks to the Father of the poor, who had given him so wonderful a taste, he went to the priest and entreated him to take no further trouble with respect to his nourishment, "because," he said, "I have found an excellent purveyor, and a very able cook, who can season his dishes in a superior way." He often used such jocose expressions, which were as much the effect of the spiritual joy he felt, as of his natural lively and joyous turn of mind.

Bernardo, vexed in the greatest degree at seeing his son begging and exposed to the jeers of the public, was inflamed with anger, and either turned from him when he met him, or cursed him. Francis admitted that these curses affected him more than any other suffering he endured, and he hit upon a method of protecting himself. It was to take another poor and miserable man with him, who should be as a father to him. He was engaged to bless Francis, making the sign of the cross on him whenever his father cursed him. Francis then said to Bernardo: "Believe me, my father, that God can give me, and indeed has given me, another father, from whom I receive blessings for your curses."

His brother Angelo, a young man full of the love of the world, also mocked him, and turned him into ridicule. Seeing him one day in church shivering with cold in his poor hermit's dress, and praying devoutly, he said to one of his friends: "Go and ask him to sell you a little of his sweat!" Francis replied, "I do not choose to sell my sweat to men; I can sell it at a better price to God." If all Christians thought thus, they would not suffer much pain for the world, which pays so ill, and they would do much for God, who rewards so magnificently.

The pauper of Jesus Christ gained many other victories over himself in the quest he had taken upon himself for the building of St. Damian. He suffered with admirable patience the persecution of some worldly persons, who treated him as a fool, and insulted him in a thousand ways. Every time that it happened to him to blush when he met any of his acquaintances or friends, he reprimanded himself as if he had committed some great fault; he humbled himself the more, and begged for alms more submissively, to take down all influence of pride. One day when he was begging for oil for two lamps which he wished to keep constantly burning before the crucifix, from which the miraculous voice had been heard, he went into a house where some persons of his acquaintance were collected together for gaming. Their sight struck him, and gave him a feeling of shame which induced him to retire. He had scarcely left the door, when, thinking on what he had done, he considered himself guilty of a great want of firmness, and he immediately returned to the place where they were at play, he acknowledged his fault before all present, and begged boldly for the lamps of the church in the French language, which set the company into an immoderate fit of laughter. Such efforts show the truth of the remark of St. Ambrose: that the saints were no less liable than ourselves to fall into faults; but that they had greater care to practise virtue, and to correct the faults into which they fell.

Pious and well-thinking persons remarked that the conduct of Francis was maintained with an equality of fervor, and they found a high degree of wisdom in what appeared to the generality of the world to be littleness of mind and folly. These opinions gradually spread and brought over many to esteem and venerate him; even those who had despised and insulted him, came forward to solicit his forgiveness.

The prior of the monastery where he had served in the kitchen, who was then at Assisi, and who there became acquainted with his rare virtues, showed him great respect, begged him to pardon the treatment he had received, and excused himself, by saying, that he could not then be known under the miserable disguise under which he had hid himself. The man who had foretold that he would do great things, added to this prediction, while applauding himself: "You know what I before said to you of this young man; you only see the beginning of his holiness, but you will see the continuation: Jesus Christ will do wonders through him, which all the world will admire."

The dispositions which were now entertained in his regard, procured for him the means of completing the repairs of St. Damian towards the close of the year 1206. In the course of this work, it was remarked that he said to those who passed by, "Assist me in finishing this building; there will be a monastery here some day of poor females of holy life, whose reputation will tend to glorify our Heavenly Father throughout His Holy Church." This was a real prophecy, the accomplishment of which was witnessed five years afterwards, when he placed there the holy virgin Clare and her companions, whom he had consecrated to Jesus Christ. This prophecy was so well known, that Saint Clare inserted its very words in the will she made in the year 1253.

At the beginning of the year 1207, Francis, not to remain idle, undertook a new work. He proposed to restore the church of St. Peter, which was at a little distance from the town, in consequence of the devotion with which the purity of his faith inspired him towards the Prince of the Apostles; and this intention was soon put in force, because, it having been seen how carefully he had made use of the donations he had received for his first work, he was now furnished with what he required, more readily and more abundantly. He now was desirous of effecting some essential repairs to a third church or chapel, about a mile from Assisi, which was very ancient, but so deserted and in such a state of ruin, that it only served as a refuge for herdsmen in bad weather: its name was St. Mary of the Angels, and Ottavio, Bishop of Assisi, thus describes its foundation:

> "In the year of 352, a year after the appearance in the heavens of a luminous cross on the 7th of May, in broad daylight, over the City of Jerusalem, which extended from Mount Calvary to the Mountain of Olives, a cross which was more brilliant than the sun, as St. Cyril, then bishop of that city, and one of the eye-witnesses of the phenomenon, relates in his letter to the Emperor Constantius,—four holy hermits came from Palestine into Italy, and obtained from Pope Liberius leave to remain in the Valley of Spoleto, and settled themselves in the vicinity of Assisi, with the permission of the authorities of the town. There they built a chapel which was called St. Mary of Josaphat, because they placed in it

a relic of the sepulchre of the Blessed Virgin, and because the altar was consecrated by the title of her glorious Assumption. In the sixth century it was given to the Religious of the Order of St. Benedict, who enlarged and strengthened it; and it was afterwards called St. Mary of the Angels." We shall soon explain the reason of this. It was also called Portiuncula, because of some portions of ground which the Benedictines of Mount Saubazo possessed in the vicinity.

We can easily understand that a man without any property, who was poor and a beggar, could not have accomplished these works without assistance from above; but St. Bonaventure finds in it a still further mystery. He says that Divine Providence, who guided Francis in all his actions, preordained things in such manner, that he repaired three churches previous to instituting there his orders, in order that the material temples should be the types of the three spiritual edifices which he was to raise up; and that passing from what is perceptible to the senses, to what is only apparent to the mind, and rising gradually to what is still more elevated, he was enabled to give to the Church of Jesus Christ three descriptions of soldiery able to combat for the reformation of morals, and worthy to triumph gloriously in heaven. We may add, that the austerities, labors, and humiliations of the servant of God had been for the two previous years as so many strokes of the hammer, which rendered him a chosen and living foundation-stone on which these sacred edifices might be based. Such is the method which is adopted by our Lord. He prepares all things, and brings them successively to perfection; instead of which, men are always hurried, and often endeavor in the way to perfection to advance faster than the grace which directs them.

Of the three churches which Francis had repaired, he chose that of St. Mary of the Angels for his residence, in order to honor the Mother of God and the Celestial Intelligences. St. Bonaventure says that he was often favored by visits from Angels, on account of the frequent apparitions of these blessed spirits there. The man of God passed days and nights there in fervent prayer, when he entreated the Blessed Virgin, that as she had conceived and brought forth the Word of the Father, full of grace and truth, she would have the goodness to obtain for him a participation therein; it was there also, that, by the merits of this powerful advocate, he had the happiness to conceive and bring forth, if it may be so expressed, his evangelical life; the precious fruit of grace and truth, which the Son of God had come to bring upon earth.

One day when he was assisting in this church at a mass of the Apostles, which he had requested the priest of St. Damian to say, he listened attentively to the Gospel where this form of life is prescribed by our Saviour for the mission of His Apostles: "Do not possess gold, nor silver, nor money in your purses; nor scrip for your journey, nor two coats, nor shoes, nor a staff." After mass, he asked the priest to explain these words to him; he understood the sense of them well, and impressed them well on his heart, finding in them the image of that poverty which he loved: "This is what I seek for," he exclaimed, quite overjoyed, "this is what I desire with my whole heart." At the same instant he threw away his purse with a feeling of horror for money, he took off his shoes, he replaced his leather girdle by a cord, and devoted his thoughts to putting in practice what he had just heard, and to conforming himself in all things to the Evangelical rule. It is a vocation similar to that of St. Anthony, of whom St. Athanasius relates, that having heard in the church these words of Jesus Christ, "If thou wilt be perfect, go sell what thou hast, and give it to the poor," he went immediately to put this counsel in practice, in order to attain perfection.

The hermit's tunic, which Francis still retained, appeared to him too delicate; he therefore got one coarse and rough, of an ash gray, which came down to the feet, and the sleeves of which reached to the fingers; to this he added a hood, which covered sufficiently the head and face. This description of dress he continued to wear during the remainder of his life, except that the tunic and hood had sometimes more or less length or breadth, as is seen in his habits which are preserved with great veneration at Assisi, at Mount Alvernia, and at Florence. Seeking nothing but poverty and humility, he chose the dress that was the plainest, the most despicable, and the most likely to make himself despised by the world, whose vanities he held in utter contempt; it was also the dress most like to that of the shepherds, and other country peasants, who chose it to protect them from the weather; or rather he imitated the prophets, who only covered themselves with a sack, to which he afterwards added a short cloak.

All the events just narrated happened in the year 1208, which is reckoned the first year of the Order of St. Francis, because it is the one in which he took the habit, which he gave in the following year to such as chose to imitate him, and in which the first stone was laid which served as a foundation for this spiritual edifice.

Then God inspired him to preach, to exhort sinners to repentance, and to cause evangelical perfection to be loved in the world. Although he expressed himself in a very plain manner, his discourses had nothing in them that was low; they were solid and animated with the Spirit of God, and so effectually penetrated the hearts of his hearers, that every one was surprised at it. He always began them by the following salutation, which he afterwards declared had been revealed to him by God; "May the Lord grant you His peace." It was noticed that a very pious man, who was in the habit of addressing the two following words to all whom he met, "Peace and weal,—Peace and weal!" was not seen in Assisi after Francis began to preach; as if he wished it to be understood that his mission had ended by the presence of him whose precursor he was. In fact, this new preacher was in truth an angel of peace sent from heaven to reconcile a great number of sinners with Jesus Christ, and to draw down on them all sorts of benefits.

He joined to the ministry of the word the exercise of every sort of virtue, and applied himself particularly to prayer, where the sufferings of our Blessed Saviour made such impression on his soul that he groaned and sobbed aloud, when he found himself at liberty. One of his friends, passing by the church of St. Mary of the Angels, having heard him, went in, and seeing him bathed in tears, reproached him with it as of a weakness unbecoming in a man. "I weep for the Passion of my Lord Jesus Christ," answered Francis, "and I ought not to be ashamed of weeping openly before the whole world." This enviable emotion was in the heart of St. Augustin, when he said to his people: "The Passion of Jesus Christ, which the Church puts every year before us, moves and affects us as if we saw Him personally stretched on the cross; there are none but the impious who can be insensible to it.—As for me, I wish to lament with you in considering this affecting spectacle. This is the time in which to weep, to acknowledge ourselves criminals, and to pray for mercy. Which of us would have it in his power to shed a sufficiency of tears to equal the merit of so great and so worthy a subject of grief?" Every Christian ought to blush, if he is wanting in these sentiments of gratitude and love.

The words and actions of Francis soon became noised abroad. Some became converted, and embraced the penitential course he preached. Others formed the resolution of leaving all and joining him. The first was Bernard de Quintavalle, a rich and discreet man, of one of the best families of Assisi, who had great influence in the town, and guided it by his advice. This respectable man, as St. Bonaventure called him, considering the contempt with which Francis viewed all the things of this world, was desirous of ascertaining whether it was in truth an effect of sanctity, or of littleness of mind. He invited him, therefore, to supper and to sleep at his house, and had a bed prepared for him in his room. While he feigned to sleep soundly, he saw by the light of a lamp Francis get up, fall on his knees, melt into tears, his eyes raised to heaven, his arms crossed, pronounce slowly these words: "Deus meus et omnia," —"My God, and my all," which he repeated during the whole night.

So ardent and so tender an expression is quite convincing that he was then in an exalted state of contemplation, where interior communications made him sensible that the Lord was especially his God, and filled the whole soul. Happy he who can with truth say, Deus meus et omnia. For this it is requisite that he should belong wholly to God, and that the world should be nothing to him.

Bernard did not interrupt Francis in his holy exercise, but, filled with devotional feelings, he said to himself, "Truly this is a man of God." After having put him to other proofs, he resolved to give all his goods to the poor and follow him, and he put this question to him: "If a man had received from his master a certain portion for several years, and then wished no longer to make use of it, what do you think it would be best for him to do?" Francis said in answer, that he ought to return it to the master from whom he had received it. "It is I," replied Bernard, "who have received a great deal from God, and much more than I have deserved; I return it willingly into His hands, and place it at your disposal; for I mean to attach myself to you." At these words, Francis, delighted to find that God began the accomplishment of his works by so worthy a personage: "Your intention," he said, "is one of great importance; you must consult God upon it, to learn from Him how you are to put it in execution. Early to-morrow morning we will ask the Curate of St. Nicholas, who is known to be a most worthy man, to say a mass for us, and after having heard it, we will continue in prayer till the hour of Tierce." We see in this the mode of acting of one who has the spirit of God; he hurries nothing, he has recourse to prayer, and he makes use of the ordinary practices of the Church.

The following day they did what they had proposed; after which, Francis, who had great devotion to the three Persons of the Blessed Trinity, opened three times in their honor the book of the Gospels, entreating the Almighty to confirm, by the testimony of their texts, Bernard's holy resolution. At the first opening they found the following: "If thou wilt be perfect, go sell all thou hast, and give it to the poor." At the second: "Take nothing for the journey." At the third: "If any man will come after Me, let him deny himself, and take up the cross, and follow Me." Then Francis, addressing himself to Bernard, said: "There is the life we must lead, the rule we must follow, you and I, and all those who shall desire to join us. Go thou and put in execution what thou hast just heard."

The new disciple, intimately convinced that his design came from God, sold, as fast as he could, all his effects, from which he got a considerable sum, which he had carried to the Square of St. George, and distributed it entirely among the poor whom he could collect. Francis then gave him a habit similar to his own; he called him his eldest son, and was always tenderly attached to him: he was indeed a most holy man.

Peter of Catania, Canon of the Church of St. Ruffinus, the Cathedral of Assisi, edified by the self-denial and charity of Bernard, was disposed to become a disciple of the same master, and received the penitential habit on the same day, which was the 16th of April. All three retired to a hut which had been deserted, near to a rivulet called Rivo Torto, on account of its winding so very much.

Seven days after that, a very pious man called Giles, who was greatly looked up to in Assisi, on his return from the country learnt what his two fellow-citizens had done, which had excited the admiration of the whole town, and felt an ardent wish to imitate them, and thus carry out an intention he had entertained of devoting himself to the service of God. He passed the following night in prayer, when he was inspired to offer himself to Francis, for whom he had already great esteem, on account of the extreme contempt of the world and of himself, which was remarked in the whole of his conduct. In the morning he went to the Church of St. George, whose festival it was, there to implore the saint's intercession, that he might find him whom he was seeking, of whose abode he was ignorant. Seeing out of the town three roads, without knowing which to take, he addressed the following prayer to God: "O Lord, most holy Father, I entreat Thee by Thy mercy, if I am to persevere in this holy vocation, so to guide my steps that I may arrive at the place where Thy servant lives whom I am seeking." He took one of the three roads as God inspired him; and as he walked full of his holy project, Francis, who was at prayer in a neighboring wood, came out to meet him.

As soon as Giles saw him, he went to him, and threw himself at his feet, and begged the favor of being received into his society. The holy man, who was at once satisfied of the faith and piety of the postulant, replied: "My brother, your request is that God would receive you as His servant and soldier. This is no small favor. It is as if the emperor were to come to Assisi, and wish to make choice of a favorite; each one would say, 'I wish to God it may be myself.' It is thus God has made choice of you." He assured him that his vocation came from heaven and exhorted him to persevere. Then presenting him to Bertrand and Peter, he said: "Here is a good brother, whom God has sent us." And when he was alone with them, he told them that Giles would one day excel in sublime virtue.

After a slender meal, and a spiritual conference, Francis set out with his new postulant for Assisi, to procure what was requisite for clothing. On the way, a woman having asked charity of them, the Saint turned to Giles, and with an angelic countenance, said: "My dear brother, let us give this poor woman the cloak you have on for the love of God." Giles gave it immediately, and it seemed to him that this alms ascended to heaven, which filled him with great joy. They begged at Assisi for some very coarse cloth, with which Francis clothed his third disciple, in the small hut where he instructed him in the religious exercises of a religious life.

Francis did not permit his disciples long to enjoy the sweetness of a life of retirement. Having informed them that they were bound to go forth to instruct their neighbors by unstudied words and an edifying life, he sent Bernard and Peter into Emilia, and set out himself with Giles for the March of Ancona.

These apostolic men preached everywhere the grandeur and goodness of God, the obligation of each one to love Him, to obey His love, and to do penance. When they wanted the necessaries of life, they rejoiced, as if it were a treasure that they had purchased at the price of all they had possessed. Some persons received them obligingly, and did them good offices; but the singularity of their dress, and the rigor of their mode of life, shocked most of those who saw them. They were even frequently insulted, covered with mud, dragged by their hood, and severely beaten: this they joyfully bore, judging from the interior profit which they derived from it, that it was greatly to their advantage.

Their virtue, nevertheless, caused them to be treated at times with respect, and honors were even rendered to them. This mortified them, Giles in particular, who only gloried in the mortifications which he suffered for Jesus Christ's sake, and could not bear to be so honored. He said to his father: "When men honor us, we lose our glory." He also expressed to him his dissatisfaction that the mode of greeting which he had taught them, "May the Lord grant you His peace," was ill received by the men of the world. "Pardon them," replied Francis, "for they know not what they do. I verily assure you that hereafter there will be many nobles and princes who will respect you and your brethren, when you shall address those words to them." He foretold to him likewise that his Institute would spread, and that it might aptly be compared to a net which a fisherman casts into the river, with which he catches a multitude of fish.

The pious missionaries having gone through several towns, and given great satisfaction, returned to the hut at Rivo Torto, when a fourth disciple offered himself: his name was Sabbatin.

Morique, a religious of the Order of Crosiers, or cross-bearers, was the fifth. Being sick, and in extremity, given over and abandoned by the medical men of the hospital of St. Saviour of Assisi, where all strangers were received, he got himself recommended to the prayers of Francis, who willingly prayed for him, and mixed a little crumb of bread with the oil of the lamp which burnt before the altar of St. Mary of the Angels. This he sent him by two of his brethren, saying to them: "Take this to our dear Brother Morique. The power of Jesus Christ will not only restore him to perfect health, but will cause him to become a generous soldier, who will enter into our militia, and will persevere in it." The sick man had hardly swallowed the remedy when he was quite cured, and he soon after entered the Institute of his charitable physician, in which he lived in prodigious austerity during a long life, and enjoyed perfect health.

A sixth disciple, called John, and surnamed De Capella, began well, but finished ill. He was employed to distribute to his brethren what was given to them in alms, and he took willingly the trouble of procuring for them what was wanted. But by little and little he got attached to temporal things, went too much abroad, and was very much relaxed from the regular discipline. The holy founder having frequently reprimanded him severely, and without effect, he threatened him for his contumacy with a severe illness and a miserable death. In fact, this unworthy religious was stricken with a horrible leprosy, which he had not patience to endure. He forsook the poor of Jesus Christ, his companions, and, letting himself fall into despair, he hanged himself, as Judas had done.

St. Antonius remarks that the life of St. Francis was in conformity with that of Jesus Christ, even in the circumstance of having had an unworthy disciple. He only became such by his depraved will; but God in His wisdom made him serve as an example to show that we may be lost even in the most holy states of life if we cease to labor with fear and trembling for our salvation. Peter Rodulphus, Bishop of Sinigaglia, in the Duchy of Urbino, adds, that the loss of one of the first children of St. Francis, and still more that of Judas in the Apostolic College, should induce those who are inclined to think ill and contemptibly of a whole order, on account of the ill-behavior of some individual, to reform their method of forming their opinions.

Among the instructions which Francis gave to his disciples, he laid great stress on poverty, the practice of which might appear to them to be very severe. In order to render them wise herein by experience, and to make them feel that their subsistence depended on the charity of the faithful, he took them all into Assisi, and made them beg from door to door. This voluntary mendicity, which seemed new, and which had hardly been seen till then, drew down upon them derision, contempt, rebuffs, and angry words. In one place they were treated as sluggards and idlers, and turned away with curses; in another they were told they were fools to have given up their own property to go begging from other people. The parents and relatives of those who were thus begging, asserted that their families were dishonored by these practices, and made loud complaints. There were, however, some who respected their poverty, and aided them with good will. Such was the feeling of the public of those times in regard to evangelical poverty, which differs but little from what it is in our own days.

After this quest, Francis went to report to the Bishop of Assisi the proceedings of his new soldiers. This worthy prelate, who greatly valued him, and gave him his support on all occasions, could not help telling him then, that he thought the sort of life he had chosen, in which they gave up all possessions whatsoever, hard and grievous. "As to me," replied the holy man, "I find it still harder and more grievous to possess anything; for one cannot take care of what one possesses without much solicitude and embarrassment. It gives rise to lawsuits, which must be undertaken; sometimes people are obliged to take up arms to protect it; and all this extinguishes the love of God and of our neighbor." The bishop approved of his remarks, and once more promised him his protection. It is true that the state of voluntary poverty in which a person possesses nothing whatever, has its inconveniences; and where does human corruption fail to find such? But it cannot be denied that the state in question is very favorable to salvation, since it is based upon the counsel of Jesus Christ; and that, on the contrary, the possession of property is dangerous for salvation, since He Himself has said emphatically: "How hardly shall they that have riches enter into the kingdom of God."

While the Evangelical poor continued at Rivo Torto, the Emperor Otho IV, who was on his way to Rome with a great train, in order to be consecrated and crowned by Innocent III, passed by their hut. They were too mortified to pay any attention to the pomp of his retinue; but Francis ordered one of them to go to the emperor and tell him that all the glory which surrounded him would be but of short duration. The religious obeyed, and boldly told the emperor what had been commanded. The prediction displeased the prince, who, nevertheless, admitted from the event that it was well founded. For, having violated his coronation oath, and committed various injustices towards the Church, he was excommunicated the following year by the same Pope; and afterwards deprived of his empire, and abandoned by the whole world. It is thus that the greatness of the world, so fickle in itself, and always put an end to by death, falls sometimes even before that, by misconduct, and by the just judgments of God.

Zeal for the salvation of souls induced Francis to move his small troop into the Valley of Rieti. He halted at an abandoned hermitage on a large rock, which he thought to be a convenient place for entering into conversation with God.

Being at prayer one day on this rock, and ruminating in the bitterness of his soul on his past years, he was assured, by a fresh inspiration of the Holy Ghost, that his sins were forgiven him, which filled him with joy. We cannot doubt but that his sins had been remitted him at the period of his conversion, by sincere contrition and the sacrament of penance. But in this happy moment he received the assurance thereof by revelation, and he learnt at the same time that the remission was entire, that is to say, that all the temporal punishment due to his sins had been remitted.

St. Bridget, whose revelations are sanctioned and respected by the Church, relates that she learnt from our Saviour that, when Francis retired from the world to enter on the way of perfection, he obtained from God a lively sorrow for his sins, which enabled him to say: "There is nothing on earth which I am not heartily willing to give up; nothing so laborious and so toilsome that I would not joyfully endure, nothing that I would not undertake, according to the strength of my body and soul, for the glory of my Lord Jesus Christ; and I will, as far as is possible, excite and induce all others to love God with their whole hearts, and above all other things." Such beautiful sentiments, well lived up to and exemplified by actions and conduct, would give us, not an entire assurance as to the remission of our sins, but a firm and well-founded confidence thereof.

The holy penitent received with this plenary indulgence the grace of an ecstasy, wherein, by a bright illumination from on high, God communicated to him what was to occur to his order. When he returned to join his disciples he said:—"Take courage, my dear children, rejoice in the Lord. Be not cast down at the smallness of your numbers. Let not my simplicity nor yours alarm you, for God has shown me clearly that, by His blessing, He will spread this family of which He is the Father, into all parts of the world. I should wish to be silent on all that I have seen, but charity compels me to communicate it to you. I saw a great multitude coming to us to take a similar habit, and to lead the same life. I saw all the roads filled with men who walked hither, and hastened themselves very much. They came in great numbers, French, Spaniards, Germans, English, and from almost all nations. The noise of such as come and go, to execute the orders of holy obedience, till sounds in my ears."

So magnificent a prediction reminds us of the prophet Isaias on the establishment of the Church: "Jerusalem, thou who sayest, I am barren! lift up thine eyes and look all around thee. All this vast multitude surrenders itself up to thee. I see them coming from afar—some from the North, others from the West, others from the land of the South; a thousand will come forth from the smallest among them, and from the very least a great people."

The event has verified, in the eyes of the universe, the prophecy of the holy Patriarch. There was in a very short time a great number of religious; his order extended itself to all parts with astonishing rapidity, and it has multiplied itself so wonderfully for seven centuries, that it may be looked upon as a representation of the birth and progress of the Church.

The disciples, greatly comforted by what they had just heard and persuaded that their master had the spirit of prophecy, entreated him to inform them what would in future be the situation of his Order. He explained to them in parables the good which would be effected by it, and at the same time the relaxations which would be introduced into its discipline, in order that the graces of God, which were to be bestowed on it, might excite their utmost gratitude, and that the fear of their weakness and want of fervor might render them vigilant and humble.

The odor of sanctity which issued through the environs of the hermitage, and the holiness of their lives, brought many persons to them for instruction, and to profit from the edification they would receive. A very worthy person, whose name was Philip the Long, was desirous of entering the state of Evangelical poverty. Francis made him his seventh disciple, and he brought them all back to the hut at Rivo Torto. In this holy retreat he spoke to them frequently of the Kingdom of God, of the contempt of the world, of renouncing of their own will, of the mortification of the senses, and other maxims of a spiritual life. He opened to them also his intention of sending them into the four parts of the world; for, with the seven children which evangelical poverty and simplicity had given him, it was his wish to bring all the faithful to penance, and to generate them in some measure anew by the word of truth, to give them, or rather to restore them, to Jesus Christ. In fine, he told all his disciples openly, but with great humility, that he Divine Majesty had, in His wisdom, decided to employ them, and the companions they should aggregate to their community, to renew the face of the earth, by their preaching and their example, in order that the losses the Church had sustained by the corruption of morals, might be made good; and that it was for this purpose that grace had put it in their power so promptly to exercise the holy ministry. In order to prepare them for this mission, he made them the following discourse, which is worthy of being recorded at full length, in the words in which it has been preserved by his companions, to whom it was addressed:—

"Let us consider, my dear brethren, what our vocation is. It is not only for our own salvation that God has called us by His mercy, but it is for the salvation of many others. It is in order that we should exhort all the world, more by example than by words, to do penance and to keep the Divine precepts. We are looked upon as senseless and contemptible, but let not this depress you; take courage, and be confident that our Lord, who conquered the world, will speak efficaciously through you. Let us be cautious, after having given up all, not to lose the kingdom of heaven for a trifling gain. If we find money anywhere, let us consider it as valueless as the dust which we tread under our feet. Let us not judge and despise the rich who live in luxury and wear the ornaments of vanity. God is their Lord, as He is ours; He may call them and justify them; we must honor them as our brethren, and as our masters. They are our brethren, because we have all the same Maker; and they are our masters, because they befriend the good by the assistance they afford them. Go then, and exhort men to do penance for the remission of their sins, and for peace. You will find some among the faithful mild and good, who will receive you with pleasure and willingly listen to you. Others, on the contrary, people without religion, proud and violent, will censure you, and be very hostile to you. But make up your minds to bear all this with humble patience, and let nothing alarm you. In a very short time many learned and noble persons will join themselves to you, to preach to kings, to princes, and to nations. Be therefore patient in tribulations, fervent in prayer, and fearless in labor. Be unassuming in speech, be grave in your manner, and grateful for the favors and benefits you may receive. The kingdom of God, which is eternal, will be your reward. I entreat the one and only God, who lives and reigns in three Persons, to grant it to us, as He doubtless will grant it to us, if we are faithful to fulfil all that we have voluntarily promised."

This discourse filled them with fresh ardor. They threw themselves at the feet of the holy man, and joyfully received the orders he gave them, in addressing to each one of them these words of the psalmist, which he was accustomed to repeat when he gave those instructions which required obedience: "Cast thy care upon the Lord, and He shall sustain thee." Having divided the routes they were to take, by forming a cross which pointed to the four quarters of the globe, and knowing that he was to be the model for his brethren, he took one side for himself with a companion, and sent the other six, two and two, to the other sides. Wherever they found a church, they prostrated and made use of this formula, which they had learnt from their Father: "We adore Thee, O most holy Lord Jesus Christ! here and in all Thy churches which are in the whole world, and we bless Thee for having redeemed the world by Thy holy cross." They had a great veneration for all chapels, for all crosses, and for all that had any relation to the worship of God. As soon as any one addressed them, they wished him peace, and instructed him in the way to gain it. If any one appeared to them to have strayed from the way of salvation, they endeavored to bring him back in a mild and humble manner. In their sermons they spoke ingenuously whatever was inspired them by the Holy Ghost, pointed out the true way to heaven, showed what were the duties of charity, and endeavored to bring all to love and fear the Creator and keep His holy commandments.

When they were asked from what country they came, and to what profession they belonged, they replied: "We are penitents come from Assisi;" for they would not as yet give the name of religion to their society. There were worthy people who received them with pleasure; but there were many others who disapproved of their habit, their institute, their discourses, imagining also that it was dangerous to give them house-room, and that alms ought not even to be given to them; so that these poor of Jesus Christ, cast off on all sides, had often to pass he nights under porticos.

Bernard and Giles went as far as Florence. A pious individual named Guy offered them some money, which they refused, and when it was wished to know from them, why, being so poor, they would not take it, they made this answer: "We have left all that we possessed, according to the Evangelical counsel. We have voluntarily embraced poverty, and we have renounced the use of money." So perfect a detachment, joined to an ardent zeal for the salvation of souls, and to sublime virtues, and particularly a patience full of meekness and charity in the midst of insults and injurious treatment, caused them to be looked upon in the town as holy personages; they were consulted in cases of conscience, and dwellings were offered them.

While these Apostolic men continued their mission, Francis, guided by the Spirit of God, returned to the hut at Rivo Torto, where he received four additional disciples: Constantius, or John of St. Constantius; Barbarus; Bernard of Viridant, or Vigilantius; and Sylvester, who was a priest He was the first in the order, and his vocation was marvellous, of which the following are the circumstances.

He had sold some stones to St. Francis for the Church of St. Damian, and had received the payment of their value. When he saw him preside over the distribution of the property of Bernard de Quintavalle, he complained of having been injured in the sale of the stones, and demanded a compensation. The servant of God, who did not choose to have any dispute with him on the subject, taking a bag full of money, gave him handfuls, saying: "Take this for the payment you demand from me, but which I do not owe you." He offered him some a second time, but Sylvester would not take it, but left him well satisfied with what he had got. At night the injustice of what he had done occurred to him; he conceived a sincere sorrow for it, asked pardon of God, and promised to restore what he had extorted to the prejudice of the poor.

Nevertheless, he formed his opinion of Francis according to the ideas of the world, and he looked with disgust on his mode of life. God was pleased to will that he should be cured of this prejudice, which was dangerous for his salvation, and that he should surrender himself to the saint as one of his disciples, which was effected by means of a mysterious dream. During the night he saw a horrible dragon, which surrounded the town of Assisi, as if about to destroy it, together with the entire country. Francis immediately came forth, and from his mouth there came forth a golden cross, which reached up to heaven, and the arms of it extended to the extremities of the earth, and its splendor put the dragon to flight. Having had this dream three successive nights, he perceived in it something divine, and he went and related it to Francis, with the minutest exactness. This humble servant of Jesus Christ, far from having the least complacency at it, only made use of it to admire the goodness of God who grants such favors, and to animate himself to combat the infernal dragon with renovated energy, and publish the glory of the cross of our Saviour. But Sylvester, profiting by the grace attached to the vision, was not satisfied with restoring what he had unjustly extorted; he resolved, moreover, to leave all that he possessed, to embrace poverty under the guidance of Francis, which his affairs did not permit him to carry into execution till the end of the year 1209. St. Bonaventure says, that on authentic proof of the truth of the vision was the holiness of the life he led when in the order. In fact, he undertook so sincerely to walk in the footsteps of Jesus Christ, and made such vast progress in prayer, that, according to the account of this blessed Father, he conversed with God in a manner nearly similar to what is written of Moses: "That the Lord spoke to him as a man is accustomed to speak to his friend."

Francis, full of the tenderest feelings for his children, was desirous of having them all assembled together. He entreated the Lord, who had in former times congregated the people of Israel dispersed among the nations, to do him a similar favor in regard to his small family, and his prayer was heard. The six who were out on missions returned to Assisi from various places, as if they had acted in concert, without having any notice given them. The pleasure which their return gave him was greatly increased by the sincere and modest recital which they made him of all that had passed in their travels for the glory of God and the benefit of their neighbor. They gave an account, with evident joy, of the outrages and blows they had endured and suffered, pleased to have been found worthy to undergo those trials in the service of Jesus Christ. The last comers envied them, and were only consoled by the thought and hope that a time would come when they would be employed in this holy warfare, and, should an opportunity be given them, of displaying equal courage; the seniors embraced the latter, and congratulated them on having chosen this holy estate of life: they all exhorted each other to perseverance.

Their common Father brought them up in the practice of the most rigorous penances, but with the utmost mildness and kindness. He did not impose upon them any considerable number of prayers because he was not desirous of compelling devotion, and rather wished that these exercises of piety should be spontaneous. He only then prescribed to them to say daily, for each part of the Divine Office, the Lord's Prayer three times, and to hear Mass, at which he desired they should employ themselves in meditating on the mystery. It is, in fact, the very best way of assisting at the Holy Sacrifice, and the faithful should be advised to practise it. But those are not to be censured who make use of vocal prayer during Mass, provided they do so with attention and piety in the very spirit of the mystery;—since there is nothing in prayer but what is good, and because, moreover, every one has not the talent of meditation.

The servant of God, considering that the number of his brethren increased, thought seriously of forming a Rule for them, and having assembled the eleven, the number they then were, he said to them: "I see, my dear brethren, that God, in His infinite goodness, proposes to extend our society; it is therefore necessary that we should prescribe for ourselves a rule of life, and go and give an account thereof to the most holy Roman Pontiff; for I am persuaded that in matters of faith, and in such as concern religious orders, nothing can be done which is pure and stable without his consent and approbation. Let us then go and find our Mother, the Holy Roman Church. Let us make known to our Holy Father the Pope, what God has deigned to begin through our ministry, in order that we may pursue our course according to his will, and under his orders."

A celebrated Bishop of France said, in an assembly of his clergy: "Paul, having returned from the third heaven, came to see Peter, in order to give a form to all future ages, and that it be established forever, that, however learned or holy we may be, were any of us another St. Paul, we must see Peter." These sentiments are in entire accordance with those of St. Francis, and contain an important principle, from which it is easy to deduce the consequence.

All the disciples applauded the proposal of their master, declaring that they were ready to receive the rule that he would give them, and to go to Rome to solicit its confirmation. Francis betook himself to prayer, and composed, in a plain, unadorned style, in twenty-three chapters, a rule of life, the immovable basis of which was the observance of the Gospel; to which he added some exercises, which he considered necessary for the sake of uniformity. Besides the three vows of Poverty, Chastity, and Obedience, they renounced all possessions whatsoever, and they bound themselves to live on charity without ever receiving money. Clerics and laymen were alike admitted to embrace this Institute, under the name of Friars Minor. There were also some regulations relative to the Divine Office, prayer, the practice of virtue, fasts, the bareness of the feet, preaching, and the missions, which will be noticed when we come to speak of the second rule which the Patriarch gave in the year 1223, which they keep in his Order, and which is nothing more than an abridgment of the first. This first having been read and accepted, Francis with his brethren set out for Rome, to which, through humility, he chose that Bernard de Quintavalle should lead them.

They pursued their journey with great simplicity, only speaking of God and of things calculated for edification; they often retired to some by-place for the purpose of praying, without troubling themselves where they should pass the night; and God raised up persons who received them hospitably. By an effect of His Providence, they went out of their way to go to Rieti, where they remained two days. Francis met in one of the streets an officer of the army, whose name was Angelo Tancred. He was quite unknown to him, but, nevertheless, he accosted him by his name, and said: "Angelo, you have worn long enough your spurs, your sword, and your belt; it is time that you should have a thick cord instead of a belt; the Cross of Jesus Christ instead of a sword; and mud and dust instead of spurs. Follow me, therefore, and I will make you a soldier of Jesus Christ." At the very moment the officer quitted all things, followed Francis, took his poor habit, and became his twelfth disciple, who now by their number resembled the twelve Apostles, whose lives they revered. This wonderful conversion shows that God sometimes moves sinners by his active and powerful grace; as when He said to Matthew, "Follow me," and Matthew followed Him. But it must also make us reflect that, in the ordinary course of things, He invites to repentance by graces, the impressions of which upon the mind are not so active.

The holy Patriarch continued his route, placing his entire confidence in God; but the others became alarmed at their own simplicity, they were fearful that it would impede their design; but God removed their fears by a vision which their holy Father had. It seemed to him that he was walking along a way where there was a very high tree. Coming near it, he went under it to admire it, when all on a sudden he felt himself raised up in the air by divine power, so that he had reached the top of the tree, and that from thence he easily made the tallest branches bend quite to the ground. The Holy Spirit pointed out to him that this was a presage of the favorable issue of his application to the Apostolic throne. This filled him with joy, and his recital of it to his brethren renovated their courage.

The Bishop of Assisi, whom they found at Rome, received them with great kindness. The sight of them at first gave him some uneasiness, being apprehensive that it was their intention to leave his diocese, and that his people would be deprived of the examples of these holy men. But having learnt from them the motive of their journey, he promised them to use his influence in their favor, and gave them hopes of succeeding through the intervention of Cardinal John of St. Paul, Bishop of Sabina, who was his intimate friend.

This prelate was of the Colonna family; he was the friend of the poor, and of all worthy persons; he was respected for his many eminent qualities, and had great authority at the Roman court. What the Bishop of Assisi had already told him of Francis and his companions, of their holy life, and of the singularity of their Institute, had excited in him a great wish to see them. As soon as he had heard of their arrival, he had them brought to his palace, received them with great honor, and was so pleased with their conversation, that, after having assured them of his favor, he begged them to consider him from thenceforward as one of themselves. He also declared himself their protector, and by his interference he soon procured for them the friendship of the principal persons in the Sacred College, particularly that of Cardinal Ugolini, nephew to the Pope, and subsequently Pope by the name of Gregory IX.

Francis, who was anxious to get his affairs expeditiously brought to a termination, got himself introduced to the Pope by an officer of his acquaintance. The Pope, who was walking at that moment in a place called the Mirror, and being deeply engaged respecting some difficult affairs of the Church, would not so much as listen to him, but repulsed him rudely as a stranger of no very respectable appearance. The servant of God humbly withdrew; and it is recorded that he then restored to sight a blind man who had had his eyes torn out. The Holy Father saw in his sleep a palm-tree grow slowly at his feet and become a fine large tree. Pleased with what he saw, but not understanding its meaning, he learnt by a Divine inspiration that the palm-tree represented the poor man whom he had ungraciously repulsed the day before. As soon as it was day, he gave directions that the poor man should be sought for. He was found in the hospital of St. Anthony, and came to the feet of the Pope, and laid before him the rule of life he followed, with energetic though humble solicitations for His Holiness's approval thereof.

Innocent III, a Pontiff of great wisdom, acknowledged the candor and the admirable courage and zeal of the servant of God. He received him into his favor as one truly poor in Jesus Christ, and he was inclined to comply with his request; however, he postponed doing so, because his mode of life appeared novel to some of the cardinals, and so much, beyond what human strength could endure; the evil times, and the coldness of charity, making them think it very difficult and almost impossible for an order to subsist without possessing any effects whatever.

Cardinal John of St. Paul was indignant at these obstacles, and he expressed himself with great warmth to the other cardinals in presence of the Pope. "If you reject the prayers of this poor man, on the pretence that his rule is novel, and too austere, let us take care that we do not reject the Gospel itself; since the rule of which he solicits the approval, is in conformity with what the Gospel teaches; for, to say that Evangelical perfection, or the vow to practise it, contains anything unreasonable and impossible, is to blaspheme against Jesus Christ, the author of the Gospel." The Pope, struck with this reasoning, said to Francis: "My son, pray to Jesus Christ that He may make known His will to us, that so we may favor your wishes." The servant of God retired to pray, and soon after returned and set forth this parable.

"Most Holy Father, there was a beautiful young girl, who was very poor, and who lived in a wilderness. The king of the country, who saw her, was so charmed with her beauty that he took her for his wife. He lived some years with her, and had children, who all resembled their father, and had, nevertheless, the beauty of their mother; he then came back to his court. The mother brought up her children with great care, and after some time said to them: 'My children, you are born of a great king, go and find him, tell him who you are, and he will give you all that is befitting your birth. As to myself, I will not leave this desert, and I even cannot.' The children went to the king's court, who, seeing their resemblance to himself, and that they had the beauty of their mother, received them with pleasure, and said to them: 'Yes, you are my true children, and I will support you as the children of a king; for, if I have strangers in my pay, if I maintain my officers with what is served at my table, how much more care should I not have for my own children, the offspring of so beautiful a mother! As I love the mother extremely, I will keep the children she has had by me at my court, and I will feed them at my table.'

"This king, most Holy Father," continued Francis, "is our Lord Jesus Christ. This beautiful girl is poverty, which, being everywhere despised and cast off, was found in this world as in a desert. The King of kings coming down from Heaven, and coming upon earth, was so enamored of her, that He married her in the manger. He has had several children by her in the desert of this world, Apostles, Anchorites, Cenobites, and many others, who have voluntarily embraced poverty. This good mother sent them to their Father with the marks of royal poverty, as well as of her humility and obedience. This great King received them kindly, promising to maintain them, and said to them: 'I who cause my sun to shine on the just and on sinners, who give my table and my treasures to pagans and to heretics, food, clothing, and many other things, how much more willingly shall I give to you what is necessary for you,—for you and all those who are born in the poverty of my much-cherished Spouse.'"

"It is to this celestial King, most Holy Father, that this Lady, His spouse, sends her children whom you see here, who are not of a lower condition than those who came long before them. They do not degenerate; they have the comeliness both of their Father and their mother, since they make profession of the most perfect poverty. There is, therefore, no fear of their dying of poverty, being the children and heirs of the Immortal King, born of a poor mother, of the image of Jesus Christ, by the virtue of the Holy Ghost; and being to be brought up in the spirit of poverty in a very poor order. If the King of heaven promises that such as imitate Him shall reign with Him eternally, with how much more confidence ought we believe that He will give them what He usually gives, with so much liberality, to the good and to the bad."

The Pope listened very attentively to the parable and to its application. He was greatly pleased with it, and had no doubt but that Jesus Christ spoke by the mouth of Francis. He was also convinced by an interior light of the Holy Spirit, that in him a celestial vision which he had but some days before would be accomplished, and which, as St. Bonaventure informs us, he himself related. While he slept, he saw that the Lateran Church was on the point of falling, when a poor and miserable man supported it on his shoulders. On which he exclaimed: "Yes truly, it is that man who will support the Church of Jesus Christ by his works and by his doctrine." He thus foretold the great service Francis and his children would render to the universal Church, which indeed they have rendered, and, for the last six centuries, have not ceased to render: this was what was prefigured by the vision; although it has been remarked as something very singular, that the Lateran Church has been repaired, improved and ornamented by three Popes, the children of the blessed Patriarch, to wit, Nicholas IV, Sixtus IV, and Sixtus V.

Innocent III, moved and greatly affected by these celestial portents, conceived for Francis a most tender friendship, which he preserved ever after. He approved his rule verbally, granted him several other favors, and promised many more. After having received in his own hands the profession of the founder, and of those who accompanied him, he directed him to preach penance in all parts, and to labor for the extension of the Catholic faith. In order to enable them to employ themselves more freely in preaching, and to assist the priest with greater dignity in the performance of the holy mysteries, he directed that the lay brethren who were then with them, should receive the Tonsure, and wear small crowns; he even conferred minor orders on them, and deacon's orders on Francis, whom he constituted Superior General of all the Religious of the Order of Friars Minor, present and to come. Those who were present promised obedience to Francis, and Francis promised to obey the Pope. The pious Pontiff gave this new Patriarch, with paternal kindness, instructions in various matters which related to the well-being and strengthening of the Institution, and he assured him of his peculiar favor; and finally, having embraced each one of them, he gave them his blessing, and dismissed them filled with joy and consolation.

We have witnessed these favors renewed in 1723 by Innocent XIII, of happy memory, the fifth Pope of the ancient and illustrious house of the Counts of Segni, to which Innocent III belonged. The Holy Father, assisted by four cardinals, had the goodness to preside at the general chapter of the Order of St. Francis, held at Rome in the convent of Ara Coeli, making known to all Christendom on that splendid occasion, that he looked upon the Friars Minor as his children, as much from family affection, as from his dignity of Supreme Pontiff.

The illustrious author of the "Variations," who quotes the Abbot of Ursperg, says that it was to give the Church true poor, more denuded and more humble than the false poor of Lyons, that Pope Innocent III approved the institution of the Friars Minor assembled under Francis, who was a model of humility, and the wonder of the age. The false poor, who are also known by the name of Vaudois, and are placed in the number of heretics by Pope Lucius III, assumed the exterior of poverty and humility, although they had none of the spirit of poverty and humility. They were filled with hatred of the Church and its ministers, whom they reviled in their secret assemblies. In 1212 they feigned submission, and had the daring to go to Rome, to solicit the approbation of the Holy See for their sect, but they were rejected by the Pope, and from that time were obstinate and incorrigible heretics.

Conrad, Abbot of Ursperg, who was at Rome when they came there in 1212 with Bernard their master, remarks that the Friars Minor were very different from the false poor, practised poverty with sincerity, and were free from all errors; that they went barefooted in winter, as well as in summer; that they received no money, and lived wholly on alms, and were in everything obedient to the Holy Apostolic See; an obedience which will ever be a mark by which true virtue may be distinguished from false.

Francis, finding himself protected by the Almighty, and authorized by the Pope, acquired great confidence. He placed his most apostolical Order under the immediate protection of the holy Apostle, whose tomb he visited. He took leave of the Cardinals, John of St. Paul, and Ugolini, whom he made acquainted with his intentions, and to whom he expressed his great gratitude; then he took his departure from Rome with his twelve companions, and bent his steps to the Valley of Spoleto, there to practise and preach the Gospel.

On the way he conversed with them on the means of adhering faithfully to the rule, and relative to the manner in which they should strive to attain perfection, so that they might be examples to others. One day the conference lasted so long, that the hour for their meal passed by without their having stopped; finding himself tired, they went a little out of the way to rest. They were very hungry, but they had no means of satisfying their craving. There then came to them a man who brought them a loaf, and immediately disappeared, without their having had it in their power to notice from what side he had come, or which way he had gone from them. Then, says St. Bonaventure, Divine Providence came to the aid of the poor of Jesus Christ, when all human assistance failed them. They were well aware that the company of their holy founder procured them this favor from Heaven; and the miraculous nourishment they had just received, which renovated the strength of their minds as well as that of their bodies, by the interior consolation they received from it, inspired them with a firm resolution never to swerve from the poverty to which they had devoted themselves.

Pursuing their route towards Orta, they came in the plain near that town to a church which had been deserted, and where, having offered up their prayers, they agreed to stop, until such time as they should learn where it was God's intention they should settle themselves. From thence they went, daily, to the town to preach penance in the public places; and it was with much fruit for the salvation of souls. The people began to feel attached to them; and as they saw that on their quest they refused everything but what was strictly necessary, they took very many things to the church in which they had retired, and those considered themselves fortunate who could make themselves useful to them. They even came in crowds to see them, and to listen to the discourses of these new men, whose actions and whose speech made them appear as persons descended from heaven.

But Francis, who found that this concourse of people interrupted and disturbed their spiritual exercises, determined to leave this place. The very beauty of it decided him to do so. It was a most agreeable spot; on one side there were meadows covered with beautiful flowers; on the other, a thick wood, where birds carolled the livelong day; near the church there was a fine spring, and a rivulet, whose waters murmured pleasantly around them; the view of the whole plain, with that of the town beyond it on the heights, was all that could be wished. The holy man was fearful lest so delicious an abode should enervate the minds of his disciples, that the vigor of their intellect, so requisite for penitential reflections, should become relaxed when surrounded by objects so pleasant to the senses; and lest that which inspired gladsomeness should make them lose the seriousness necessary in prayer, and deprive them of the spiritual delight which is felt therein. Thus, as a skilful general who was the leader of the soldiers of Jesus Christ, and only followed His intentions, he made his little band raise their camp at the end of a fortnight, and resume their march towards the Valley of Spoleto.

In the way they counselled together whether they should communicate with the world, or whether they should retire into some solitary retreat. Francis, not choosing to trust either to his own lights or to those of his companions, had recourse with them to prayer, to ascertain what the will of God was on this head; and he learnt by a revelation, St. Bonaventure says, that God had sent him expressly to gain souls which the devil was endeavoring to draw away from Jesus Christ. He therefore resolved to dedicate himself to this holy employment, and to live a life which should be useful to his neighbor rather than to himself; being likewise animated thereto by the example of Him of whom St. Paul said: "One died for all." With this view he continued his route to the Valley of Spoleto, and brought his brethren to the hut at Rivo Torto, near Assisi, where he had been before.

One must feel surprised that St. Francis, with all the assurances he had of his vocation, could have doubted for a single instant that he had been sent by God for the spiritual service of his neighbors. But his doubts only had their rise in the powerful attractions he had for contemplation, which the tenderness of his conscience made him fearful of resisting, by employing himself in the exercises of an active life; and it was this that lessened his inclination for the functions of Apostolicity; for, according to the doctrine of the Fathers, and of Saint Bernard in particular, there are no more worthy ministers of the Gospel than such as devote themselves to conversation with God in retreat, and who leave that retreat to preach the doctrines of salvation only when they have reason to think that God calls upon them to do so. Our Lord, who thus in his wisdom permitted that His servant should labor under this uncertainty, revealed to him already that he was destined to labor for the salvation of souls, and we shall see, further on, that He assured him again by other revelations.

The hut in which these men devoted to evangelical poverty had retired, was so small and so confined, that, far from being able to lie at full length in it, there was barely room for them to sit, insomuch that their Father was obliged to assign to each his place by writing his name on the joists, in order that they might pray and take their rest without being incommoded. They remained some time in this miserable habitation, which might be looked upon more as a tomb for the living, or rather for such as were dead to the world; and they bore it for the love of God, with more fraternal charity and gaiety than can be described. The life they led there was so laborious, and so poor, that frequently, not having a morsel of bread, necessity compelled them to search the country for herbs and roots, which they ate with satisfaction; preferring to be nourished with tears rather than with any other food.

Their most frequent exercise was prayer, and that more mental than vocal, because they had not as yet books for saying the Divine Office. A wooden cross, of moderate size, which Francis had fixed in the middle of the hut, round which they prayed, served them instead of a book. They meditated on it unceasingly, and read in it with the eyes of faith, instructed by the example of their saintly chief, who often discoursed to them on the Passion and Cross of Jesus Christ.

However, they wished to learn from him what vocal prayers they ought to recite; and he told them, as our blessed Saviour had told the Apostles: This is the prayer that you will say: "Our Father, who are in heaven, hallowed be Thy name," etc. To which he added the Act of Adoration which he had before taught them: "Lord Jesus Christ, we adore Thee in all the churches in the whole world, and we bless Thee for having redeemed the world by Thy holy Cross." He likewise taught them to praise God in all things, to make use of all creatures, to raise up their minds to Him, to have great respect for priests, to be inviolably attached to the true faith, which is believed and taught by the Holy Roman Church, and to confess it plainly. His faithful disciples put in practice all that he taught them, and conformed to all his maxims, which they did in still greater perfection after the marvel which we are about to relate.

Francis being one Saturday in Assisi, in order to preach on the Sunday morning in the cathedral, as it was his custom to do, retired to a small shed in a garden belonging to the canons of the church, to pass the night in contemplation, which he usually did. About midnight, a fiery car of great brilliancy, on which there was a globe as bright as the sun, and which gave a light equal to that of noon, entered into the hut in which the brethren were collected, and moved round it three times. Some of them were watching and praying; the others, who were taking a little rest, awoke. It is not to be said how great their astonishment was when they found themselves enlightened, as well interiorly as exteriorly, by this penetrating light, which manifested to them the state of their consciences.

St. Bonaventure remarks on the subject of this marvellous light, on the testimony of those who had been witnesses of it, that they understood well, by this luminous and burning figure, God represented to them the lively and holy flames which illuminated their Father, who, though absent in the body, was present with them in spirit, in order that, as true Israelites, like unto Eliseus, they might look up to and imitate this new Elias, whom He had appointed the light and guide for spiritual men. Doubtless, he continues, the Lord, who opened the eyes of the servant of Eliseus, that he might see around that Prophet, that "the mountain was full of horses and chariots of fire," would also, at the prayer of Francis, open those of his disciples to shew them the marvel which was operating in their favor.

At his return from Assisi, the Father conversed with his children on the prodigy which they had witnessed, and took occasion from it to confirm them in their vocation. He entered in detail as to the secret dispositions of their consciences; he foretold them many circumstances relative to the increase of his Order; he made known to them, in fine, so many sublime things beyond human ken, that they became perfectly aware that the Spirit of God rested fully on him, and that their greatest security would be in a conformity of themselves to his life and doctrine.

People were so greatly moved and affected by his virtues and his discourses, that many presented themselves to join his Order, but he declined as yet to receive them, because the hut was too small for the twelve he had; but he availed himself of the opportunity to say to these: "My dear brethren, God, in His goodness, has made known to me that He proposes to increase our poor family. I cannot receive those who wish to join us, until I have a place large enough to admit all. We require a larger habitation, as well as a church, where we may hear mass, say the Divine Office, and deposit in peace those of our society who may die. Let us therefore go to our lord Bishop and the canons. Let us earnestly entreat of them, for the love of God, to cede to us some church near the town, and to put our rising Order under cover in some part of their domain. If they cannot assist us, we will go and ask the same favor of the Religious of Mount Soubazo."

The Bishop of Assisi and the Canons had it not in their power to promote such views, having no church at their disposal; but the Abbot of Mount Soubazo, with the consent of the community, granted him for himself and his brethren the chapel of St. Mary of the Angels, or of Portiuncula, which he had put into repair, but he added this condition, that, if the Institution became more extended, this church should be always considered the place of its origin, and the chief monastery.

Francis received the present, and accepted the condition with great thankfulness. He came and told his brethren of it, expressing the pleasure he felt, in having, for the first church of his Order, a church of the Blessed Virgin, very small and very poor, obtained by begging, and in which he had first taken upon himself the Apostolic life.

On the same day he went to St. Mary of the Angels, where a pious ecclesiastic of Assisi was living, whose name was Peter Mazancoli, to whom the care of that church had been intrusted after it had been repaired. He communicated to him the cession which the Religious of Mount Soubazo had made to his Order, and begged him to come and live with his brethren.

As true piety, which is charity itself, is never jealous, and is delighted in what is of advantage to its neighbors, the ecclesiastic embraced Francis, and assured him how desirous he was to see the Blessed Virgin honored and praised in this place, which she loved, where concerts by the angelic host were constantly heard. As a proof of this, he called a laborer of the vicinity, who certified to have several times heard in the night melodious canticles, and to have seen a great light come forth from the windows.

The experience of Francis himself was an additional proof. For, being in prayer during the following night in order to recommend his family to the protection of the Blessed Virgin, he saw on the altar, by means of a splendid light, our Saviour Jesus Christ, His holy Mother, and a multitude of angels, who cast upon him looks of great benignity. He adored, and recited these words: "O most holy Lord, King of Heaven, Redeemer of the world, sweet Love! and thou, O Queen of Angels! by what excess of goodness do you come down from heaven into this small and poor chapel?" He immediately heard this reply: "I am come with my Mother to settle you and yours in this place, which is very dear to us." All then disappeared, and Francis exclaimed: "Truly this place is holy, which ought to be inhabited by angels, rather than by men. As long as I possibly can, I will not leave it; it shall be, for me and mine, an eternal monument of the goodness of God!" It became, in fact, a great object of devotion and veneration for himself and his brethren, particularly after it had been revealed to him that, among all the temples consecrated under the name of the Blessed Virgin, this was the one for which she had the greatest attachment.

At break of day he sent for the other religious by his companions, with directions to bring with them the few pieces of furniture which they had in the hut at Rivo Torto, in order to place them in the house adjoining the church of St. Mary of the Angels, which the pious ecclesiastic willingly gave up to them.

He communicated to the new guests the sanctity of the place they were about to inhabit, and recommended them to live therein holily, never ceasing to praise the Lord. Then he said to them: "You must be very grateful to the Benedictine Fathers for the benefit they have conferred upon us. They have consecrated all the habitations we shall hereafter have, by this house of God, which is the model of the poverty which must be observed in all the houses of our Order, and the precious germ of the holiness which we must seek for in it."

But, in order to show that he did not live there as on a property wholly his, as well as for a mark of his gratitude to his benefactors, he took care to have taken yearly to the Abbey of Mount Soubazo, as a ground-rent, a basket of fish, a species of mullet, which is taken in quantities in the River Asi, or Chiascio, near the Church of St. Mary of the Angels. The Friars Minor have always cherished the feelings of the blessed Patriarch for the Order of St. Benedict. They will ever manifest, with sincerest gratitude, that it is to this great order, so ancient and so celebrated in the Church, that they are indebted for their first establishment, and for many other benefits.

Chapter 2

FROM HIS TIME AT THE CHURCH OF ST. MARY OF THE ANGELS TO 1218

It was therefore in the small Church of St. Mary of the Angels, or of Portiuncula, that Francis laid the foundations of the Order of Friars Minor, which spread over the whole earth with wonderful rapidity. This holy place was, as it were, the cradle of the Institute, and the nursery of the houses of the religious; the source which supplied a great river, which was divided into various channels; the citadel from whence numerous brave warriors went forth to encounter the enemies of the Church; the school which has produced a very great number of saints, and a multitude of learned men, whose doctrine and piety have been equally celebrated.

The new habitation, less confined than the hut of Rivo Torto, enabled the Patriarch to receive the postulants who had before presented themselves; among whom may be noticed, Leo, Rufino, Masseo of Marigan, and Juniper:—Leo, whom Francis chose for his confessor and secretary, and whom he generally called Pecorella Di Dio (the sheep of God), on account of his admirable candor. Rufino, of whom he said: "I learnt, by a revelation, that he is one of the most faithful and of the most pure souls that there is in this world, and I should have no fear of giving him, though in a mortal body, the title of Saint, since he is already canonized in heaven." Masseo, whom he often sent, instead of going himself, to converse with persons of piety, in order not to be interrupted in his own meditations, because this religious added great mildness and suavity of manner to a rare talent of speaking about heavenly things. Juniper, whom he found so valuable for his evangelical simplicity, for his contempt of himself, and for his great desire to attract upon himself the contempt of the world, that, alluding to his name, he used to say good-humoredly: "I wish to God we had a wood full of such Junipers."

The charitable father had all his children in his heart, and he brought them up with a tenderness truly maternal. He was the first to go from door to door, to ask charity to provide for their wants; sometimes he even went alone, to spare them the mortification of begging, under the impression that they might still retain the prejudices of the world on this head. But the weakness of his frame not admitting of his providing for all, and his religious being bound to subsist on charity alone, he resolved to teach them to solicit it for the love of God, and he made them the following exhortation, which they have recorded:—

"My very dear brethren and well-beloved children, be not ashamed of soliciting alms, since our Lord became poor in this world for the love of us, and that, following His example, we have chosen this state of the most perfect poverty. For, if we have made this choice for the love of Jesus Christ, we must not blush at begging in our quality of poor. Heirs of the kingdom of God should not blush at what is a pledge of their heirship. Yes, we are heirs of heaven; this is a benefit which our Lord has obtained for us, to which He has given us a right, as He has to all those who choose to live in a state of holy poverty. I make known to you as a truth, that a great number of the most noble of the age will become members of the Order, who will consider it an honor to solicit alms, and who will look upon it as a favor to be permitted to do so. You, therefore, who are the very first of the Order, do this cheerfully; do not refuse to practise what you will have to teach these saintly personages. Go, then, and with the blessing of God solicit alms, full of confidence and joy, more than would be felt by him who should offer a hundred for one. For it is the love of God you offer in asking, when you say, 'For the love of God, bestow your charity on me;' and in comparison with this divine love, heaven and earth are as nothing."

To mitigate the reluctance still felt by some of them, he brought forward the two following motives: "The bread which holy poverty causes to be collected from door to door, is the bread of angels, because it is the good angels who inspire the faithful to bestow it for the love of God. It is thus that the words of the prophet, 'Man ate the bread of angels,' are fulfilled in these holy poor ones. God has given the Friars Minor to the world in these latter times, that the elect may have it in their power to practise what will cause them to be glorified by the Supreme Judge, when He will address them in these mellifluous words: 'What you did to one of these, the least of My brethren, you did it to Me.' It is pleasing to solicit charity in the capacity of a Friar Minor, whom our Master seemed to designate expressly by the appellation, 'the least of My brethren.'"

The disciples, persuaded and moved by this appeal, went of their own accord to quest in the neighboring places, to get the better of the natural repugnance they felt to it. At their return they presented themselves to their Father with satisfied countenances, which delighted him, and by a holy emulation they were proud of the things they had collected for the love of God. One of them returning one day with much cheerfulness, singing loudly the praises of the great Benefactor of men, Francis took from him the weighty wallet, which was full of bits of bread, placed it on his own shoulders, kissed the shoulders of him who had carried it, and came and said publicly: "So it is that I wish my brethren to go always on the quest, and return from it: ever gay, and glorifying God for all the good which He does in our favor."

The blessed founder employed himself day and night unceasingly in inspiring them with the love and practice of the most sublime virtues; he warned and exhorted each one of them in particular, and he made discourses to them when collected, on the most essential heads; and this again he enforced by his own good example; knowing that they were called by God to train up those who would embrace his rule in the different parts of the earth, and that on the instruction of the one depended that of the others.

Under such a master, with the powerful assistance which they received from Heaven, they made in a short time such considerable progress, that the latest comers were not less competent for the exercise of the Evangelical ministry than the first. Altogether animated with the same spirit, watching, fasting, praying, penetrated with the fear of God, full of holy desires, they resembled in a great degree the primitive Church confined in the supper-room. Francis, who was perfectly acquainted with their most inward feelings, and with the intentions of Divine Providence, thought that he ought not to delay sending them forth on missions according to the idea of St. Chrysostom, who says that the Apostles, who were commissioned to labor in the conversion of the world, were necessarily separated, and that it would have been very prejudicial to the interests of the universe had they kept together longer.

But, as he had not yet heard them preach, he desired prudently to judge by his own experience of their respective talents. Having assembled them together, he desired Bernard de Quintavalle to speak on the mysteries of religion. He immediately obeyed, and spoke beautifully on the several points. Peter of Catania was directed to set forth the greatness of God, which he did with as much facility and learning as if he had been long perfect in the art of preaching. A third was called upon to give an exhortation on avoiding sin, and practising virtue, which he complied with in powerful language. In short, they all handled the subjects which were allotted to them, so as plainly to show that wisdom was given to them from on high.

After they had made this essay in preaching, or rather this masterpiece of eloquence, Jesus Christ, who had inspired their thoughts and words, appeared in the midst of them in the form of a very beautiful young man, and gave His blessing to each of them successively, with wonderful benignity. This astonishing vision threw them into a rapturous transport; after which, Francis addressed them as follows:

"My brethren, and dear children, give abundant thanks to God most powerful, and to His Son, our Lord Jesus Christ, for having deigned to have communicated celestial treasures through the speeches of the most simple of men; for it is God who causes infants to speak, who opens the mouths of little children, and makes the tongues of the most ignorant eloquent: His goodness renders Him compassionate to the world, which is loaded with crime. He has resolved to warn men of the woes into which they are plunging themselves; and in order to root out from amongst them the works of the devil, which are sins, He has chosen vile and despicable preachers, so that no one shall have reason to glorify himself before Him, and that every one shall acknowledge that all the good which is done comes from Him. Although there are few among you of whom it can be said that they have worldly wisdom, or are powerful or noble, yet it is you whom the Lord hath chosen for this important work. It is His will that you should go into all parts to honor Him by your actions and by your words, bringing to His fear and to His love such as have strayed into evil ways."

"Prepare yourselves therefore to set forth; gird your loins according to the commands of Jesus Christ; be courageous; put on the armor of faith; be devoted to the service of the Gospel; always prepared to let yourselves be carried away as clouds, whithersoever the Spirit of God may direct you, by the guidance of obedience, to shed the dew of the divine word on the dry and arid soil of hardened hearts. For our Lord has not called you into this Institute to think of nothing but saving your own souls quietly, without any fatigue, in the hearts of your country, and in the bosom of your families; His intention is, that you carry His name and His faith into the nations, and before the kings of the earth. Now, lest we should appear to be slow in carrying His will into execution, we will immediately, giving him the name of Brother Humble, on account of the humility he found in his heart.

At Crotona, to which place he next took the word of God, there was another young man named Guy, who, moved by his preaching, had invited him to dinner: "This young man," said Francis, "will enter our militia to-day, and will sanctify himself in this town." He was the oldest of his family, brought up in study and in virtue, and the excellence of his conduct exceeded even that of his education. He frequented the churches and the sacraments, he gave great alms, and visited the sick to assist them; he wore a hair-shirt, and chastised his body severely, to enable him to preserve his virginal purity. He had made a vow to do this. After the dinner, he knelt down and petitioned for the habit of a Friar Minor, which he received in the principal church of the town, in the presence of a numerous concourse of people, after having first fulfilled two conditions which the father had prescribed for him: The first was, to give to the poor all that he had inherited by his right of primogeniture; the second was, to renounce all the rest of his fortune. It was in the same town that he lived a most holy life, as had been foretold, honored by many miracles; now by permission of the Holy See, he is publicly invoked.

The love of prayer and retirement made Francis wish to find in the neighborhood of Crotona a fit place for building a house suitable for the education of his novices. Guy pointed one out to him in the valley, near a place called Celles. This location greatly pleased him, because it was solitary; and by the aid of some pious persons, he built a very poor dwelling, which he soon filled with novices, and where he received the celebrated Brother Elias, of whom we shall have much to say hereafter.

Having spent nearly two months in preaching at Crotona, and in forming his novices at the Convent of Celles, he was inspired to pass over to a desert island in the middle of the Lake of Perugia. Lent was drawing near. He recommended the care of the house to Sylvester, without letting him know what his own intention was; and on Ash-Wednesday he caused himself to be taken to the island by a boatman, having with him only two loaves of bread. The boatman was a worthy man and his friend. He begged him not to tell any one where he was, and only to come to him on the Wednesday of Holy-Week, to take him back to the shore.

Having made himself there a sort of hut in one of the thickets, to preserve himself from the cold, he had his intercourse with God alone during two and forty days; and his fast was so rigorous, that of the two loaves he brought with him he only ate half a one.—In ecclesiastical history we meet with examples of these miraculous fasts, of which the Holy Fathers have had an assured knowledge, and which the weakness of human nature was enabled to sustain by virtue of the Spirit of God, which supported them. The fruit which they were to derive from it, was to animate the faithful to keep, with as much exactness as was in their power, the fasts prescribed by the Church, and particularly the fast of Lent, which many principal motives of religion render so venerable.

On Wednesday in Holy-Week, the boatman went to fetch Francis and bring him back to Crotona. On the passage the Saint stilled a storm, by making the sign of the cross on the waves; and as soon as he had landed he went to the Convent at Celles, where he passed the remainder of the Holy-Week with his brethren. His confidant did not think it necessary to keep the secret of the marvellous fast. The rumor spread, and many persons went to the island to see and venerate the hut in which he had lived. The miracles which were wrought there by the merits of the Saint, induced some persons to build there; and gradually a small town arose, where later a church was built, with a convent of his Order, near a spring at which he had drunk; sick were afterwards cured there.

After the Easter solemnities, he placed a superior in the convent; then having tenderly embraced the religious, he made the sign of the cross on them, and separated himself from them to go to Arezzo.

This town was at that time greatly agitated by internal dissensions, which were likely to bring on its entire ruin. Francis being lodged in the suburbs, where he had been hospitably received, saw over the town, with the penetrating sight which the Almighty had given him, devils who excited the citizens to massacre each other, and who appeared to be transported with joy. To put these evil spirits to flight, he sent Sylvester, as his herald, and gave him this command: "Go to the gate of the town, and standing before it, order the devils, in the name of the Almighty God, and in virtue of obedience, instantly to retire." Sylvester, who was a man of extraordinary simplicity, praising God beforehand for what was about to happen, went as fast as possible, and cried out with all his might: "All you devils who are here, begone, go far from hence. It is in the name of God and of His servant, Francis, that I call upon you to go." At this very moment the citizens, who were on the point of flying to arms, came to an understanding on the points which were in dispute, and peace was restored to the town. On which St. Bonaventure remarks, that the obedience and humility of Francis had obtained for him that absolute power over the proud spirits who fear and fly from the sublime virtue of the humble.

It became known in Arezzo who the author was of so sudden a reconciliation, because the words which had been spoken by Sylvester had been heard. Francis was sought for and brought into the town in a sort of triumph, notwithstanding the efforts he made to escape from this honor. He preached in the great square on the love of peace, and on the means of preserving it; pointing out to them that dissensions and quarrels came from, and are promoted by, the evil spirit. The magistrates entertained him at the town-house, and had a convent built for his Order according to his wishes, that is to say, according to holy poverty; in which he placed some worthy subjects who had presented themselves to him. A child was brought to him who was quite distorted; he took it into his arms, and it forthwith became straight. This miracle, and several others which he performed during his stay, proved that God had given him as much power over bodily complaints as over the evil spirits.

From Arezzo he bent his steps to Florence, preaching with great success throughout the route. The lords of Ganghereto received him with great respect, and were so pleased with the holiness of his life, that they begged his acceptance of a field and a small wood for the service of his religious. He set up a hut there, where his infirmities compelled him to remain some time. After preaching and prayer, to which he daily gave some time, one after the other, he employed himself in building a small wall round a spring of water which he got miraculously, and which still flows, the water of which God was pleased to render salutary.

As soon as his health was in some degree restored, he continued his way towards Florence, where he went to lodge in the hospital. The following day he preached in the town, and was listened to as a saint. They gave him a small dwelling near the church of St. Gall, about five hundred paces from the city, in which he received several novices, who rendered themselves illustrious by their exalted virtues; among whom John Parent is particularly noticed, who was a native of Carmignano, near Pistoria.

His conversion was attributable to a very peculiar circumstance. As he was walking one evening in the environs of the town, he saw a swineherd who was endeavoring to drive his pigs into a stable, and who, being in a great passion because, instead of going in, they dispersed themselves in all directions, called out to them in his anger: "Swine, get into this stable as judges get into hell." He had scarcely said the words, when these animals went quietly in. That which might have appeared to this magistrate nothing but an impertinence, struck him, and made so strong an impression upon him, that, having seriously reflected on the dangers incurred by a judge (which are indeed very great) as to salvation, he threw up his magistracy, and retired to Florence. There he saw Francis, examined his conduct, admired his virtues, and felt himself called by God to imitate him. An only son of his had a similar vocation. The father and the son divided their all among the poor, and became disciples of the Saint, whose prophecy began thus to be fulfilled: that the wise and learned of the world would enter into his Order.

Such a conversion sets before us this important truth: that the Spirit breatheth where He will; that the Lord gives His grace sometimes to what is most common, most simple, and even most base, according to the notions of the world; that it is necessary to be attentive, that we may not receive the grace of God in vain; and that, little as it may seem at first, by being carefully attended to, it may have the most beneficial results. Not to be thankful for it, to neglect it, to resist it, is a heavy loss.

While Francis was at St. Gall, he foretold a thing which the event justified a few years afterwards. Three men at Florence brought each a child to receive his blessing. As soon as he was apprised of it, he went into the garden and gathered five figs, then he came in, and gave one to the first of the children, one to the second, and three to the third, to whom he addressed the following words: "You will be my dear child." That one, when he had attained the proper age, took the habit of the Friars Minor, and was called Brother Angel, which he deserved by his angelic life, which was the fruit of his great devotion to the Blessed Virgin, from whom he received very marked favors.

From the month of October, 1211, to the beginning of 1212, the man of God visited the Towns of Pescia, Pisa, San Miniato, Sarthiano, Cetona, and other places in Tuscany, where he made many wonderful conversions, and left some of his brethren to continue the work of God. We shall relate, at the end of his life, the great honors which were publicly shown him,—honors which he received with the greatest humility, and yet with the most generous sentiments.

The brethren whom he had dispersed in the other provinces of Italy, and who partook of his apostolic spirit, labored on their part with great zeal and success. They founded many establishments, and formed many disciples, whom they sent to the holy Founder in order to receive the habit of the Order from him.

They mention particularly what happened at Bologna to Bernard de Quintavalle. As soon as he made his appearance, his extraordinary and very poor habit made him looked upon as a person not worthy of notice. He went to the great square in order to preach the truth of salvation, and he went there several times without having collected an audience. Children and idle people surrounded him; some pulled him by the hood, others threw mud and stones at him; and he was daily assailed with fresh outrages, which he bore with exemplary patience.

A lawyer, having noticed this, made his reflections on it, and it occurred to him that his conduct might be attributed to virtue rather than insensibility. One day, then, he came up to Bernard and asked him who he was, and what he had come to do at Bologna. "You will know who I am," replied Bernard, "if you will take the trouble to read what I now offer you." It was the Rule of Francis, of which he had a copy, and which he placed in his hand. The lawyer having read it with astonishment, said to those who accompanied him: "I own I have never seen anything so perfect or so heroic as this mode of life. Those who ill-use this man are very criminal; he ought, on the contrary, to be loaded with honors, as a special friend of God." Then, addressing himself to Bernard, he said: "If you will follow me, I will give you a place in which you may serve the Lord." Bernard, having accepted the offer, was taken to the house of his benefactor, who received him with affection, and gave him a house, which he furnished with everything necessary, and promised to protect him and his companions. After this, Bernard was so highly respected in Bologna, that people considered themselves fortunate if they could get near him, touch him, or even see him. This truly humble man, mortified at the honor which was shown him, went to Francis, and said, "My Father, all is in good order at Bologna. But send any other religious thither rather than me, for I have no longer any hopes of being useful there: it is even to be feared that I may lose many graces on account of the great honors I receive." This prudent mistrust of himself was as pleasing to the holy Father as the affection of the Bolognese, to which he responded by sending them several of his disciples, who subsequently spread the Order throughout all Romagna.

The holy Patriarch returned some time before Lent to St. Mary of the Angels, where his first care was to examine rigidly whether in his Evangelical progress some worldly dust might not have adhered to him in consequence of his communications with seculars; and in those instances in which the extreme delicacy of his conscience gave him room for self-reproach, he purified himself by very severe penitential observances. He then applied himself carefully to the formation of the novices, whom he had collected from various places, and he preached during the Lent at Assisi.

His discourses, backed by his example, and his prayers and exhortations, animated by an ardent zeal, were so efficacious, that in the town and county of Assisi a very great number of persons was converted, and the fire of divine love was kindled in every heart. "Then," says St. Bonaventure, using the words of the Holy Scriptures, "the vine of the Lord spread its branches and bore flowers of a most agreeable odor, and produced fruits of glory in abundance." There were many young girls who made vows of perpetual virginity; amongst whom, says the same holy doctor, the Blessed Clare appeared as the most beautiful plant in the garden of the Celestial Spouse, and as a star more brilliant than all the others.

This illustrious maiden was the daughter of a rich and noble family of Assisi. The Cavaliere Favorine, or Favarone, her father, was descended from the ancient and powerful houses of Scifi and Fiumi. Her mother, of equal high birth and exalted piety, was called Hortulana. She had the talent of joining the care of her household to the practice of good works, and to regulate her time so well, that she found enough in which to visit, with the consent of her husband, many holy places: she even made a pilgrimage to the Holy Land. If this practice is no longer usual in these days, particularly as regards distant countries, it arises from the circumstances of the times being very different, and from there having been a great change in manners. But Christian piety does not permit us altogether to condemn (independently of abuses) voyages or journeys of devotion, since they are sanctioned by the examples of the saints, have been approved by the Fathers of the Church, and since at one time they were directed as sacramental penances for certain sinners.

Hortulana had three daughters, Clare, Agnes, Beatrix. Being about to be confined of the first, and praying to God before a crucifix in a church for a safe delivery, she heard a voice, which said to her: "Woman, fear not, thou wilt bring forth, without danger, a light which will illuminate a vast space." This was the reason she gave the name of Clare to the daughter to whom she gave birth, in the hopes of seeing the accomplishment of what it might signify.

Indeed, from her earliest years, her virtue shone as an aurora, the prognostication of a fine day. She received with docility the instructions of her mother, and her whole conduct was the fruit thereof; the exercise of prayer became familiar to her; she every day recited the Lord's Prayer a number of times, which she marked with small stones, in order to be exact in the daily number she had assigned for herself. In that she resembled the solitary of the Desert of Seethe, who kept an account of the number of his prayers, offering them to God three hundred times each day. Naturally tender and compassionate to the poor, she aided them voluntarily, and the opulence of her family enabled her to assist them abundantly. But, in order to render her charities more agreeable to God, she sent to the poor, by confidential persons, the nicest eatables which were served to herself. The love of God, with which these holy practices inflamed her heart, inspired her with a hatred of her own body, and showed her the vanity of all the things of this world. Under her own costly dresses, which her situation in society obliged her to wear, she constantly had a hair-shirt; and she cleverly refused a proposal of marriage which her parents wished her to accept, recommending to God her virginity, which she intended to preserve in entire purity. Although she was at that time confined in the bosom of her family, and solely intent on sanctifying herself in secret before the eyes of God, her virtue became the subject of admiration, without her being conscious of it, and drew down upon her the esteem and praise of the whole town.

The great celebrity which the sanctity of Francis gained in the world, could not be unknown to young Clare.—Aware that this wonderful man renewed a perfection on the earth which was almost forgotten, she wished much to see him and to have conversations with him. Francis also, having heard the reputation of Clare's virtues, had an equal desire to communicate with her, that he might tear her from the world and present her to Jesus Christ. They saw and visited each other several times. Clare went to St. Mary of the Angels with a virtuous lady, a relation of hers, whose name was Bona Guelfucci; Francis also came to see her, but always taking the necessary precautions to have the pious secret kept. She placed herself entirely under his guidance, and he soon persuaded her to consecrate herself to God. An interior view of eternal happiness inspired her with such contempt for the vanities of the world, and filled her heart with such divine love, that she had a complete loathing for finery, which it was not as yet permitted her to throw aside; and from that time she entered into engagements to live in a state of perpetual virginity.

The holy director did not choose that so pure a soul should continue longer exposed to the contagion of the world. She had herself come to him some days before Palm-Sunday to hasten the execution of her intention; he told her to assist at the ceremony of the delivery of palms dressed in her usual ornaments, to leave Assisi the following night, as our Blessed Saviour had left Jerusalem to suffer on Mount Calvary, and to come to the church of St. Mary of the Angels, where she would exchange her worldly ornaments for a penitential habit, and the vain joys of the world for holy lamentations over the Passion of Jesus Christ.

On the 18th of March, being Palm-Sunday, Clare, magnificently dressed, went with other ladies to the Cathedral Church, and as she remained in her place out of bashfulness while the others crowded forward to receive the palms, the bishop came down from the altar, and carried a palm branch to her, as a symbol of the victory she was about to gain over the world.

The following night, accompanied as propriety required, she arranged her flight as her spiritual Father had directed, and according to the earnest wish of her soul. Not being able to get out by the front door, of which she had not the key, she had the courage and strength to break open a small door which had been blocked up with stones and wood, and she repaired to the church, where Francis and his brethren, who were saying their matins, received her with great solemnity, bearing lighted tapers in their hands. They cut off her hair before the altar, and after she had taken off her ornaments with the help of the females who accompanied her, she received the penitential habit, consecrating her virginity to Jesus Christ, under the protection of the Queen of Virgins, while the religious chanted hymns and canticles.

It was a touching scene to see a young noble lady, only eighteen years of age, in solitude, in the middle of the night, renounce all the advantages and allurements of the world, put on sackcloth and a cord, and devote herself to a rigorous system of penitential exercises, solely for the love of God. Similar sacrifices can only be made by a supernatural virtue; they prove that the religion which inspires them is divine; and justly does St. Ambrose consider them to be far above the most heroical pagan virtues.

It must be remarked, moreover, that the Church of St. Mary of the Angels, which was the cradle of the Order of the Poor Evangelical Brethren which Francis had just established, was also the place where Clare made profession of the same poverty, that she subsequently prescribed to the Order of Women, which she instituted together with the holy Patriarch. This gives to the two orders the pleasing consolation of knowing that they belong to the Mother of God from their origin, and that she is specially their mother.

As soon as the ceremony was over, Francis, who was always guided by the spirit of wisdom, took the new bride of Jesus Christ, followed by her companions, to the monastery of Benedictines of St. Paul, there to remain until Divine Providence should provide a dwelling for her.

When morning dawned, and her parents learnt what had occurred during the night, they were overwhelmed with grief. They equally disapproved of what Clare had done, and of the manner in which she had carried her intention into execution; and they went in great numbers to the monastery of St. Paul, to compel her to leave it. At first they spoke to her in mild and friendly terms; they represented to her that she was choosing a vile and contemptible state of life, which was disgraceful to her family, and that there was no precedent in the whole country of such an occurrence. After which they attempted by violence to force her from the monastery; which they might easily have done, because in those times the religious females did not keep strict enclosure, beside which her relations were all military men, accustomed to acts of violence.

Clare uncovered her head to show them that she was shorn; and she protested, clinging to the altar, that nothing in the world should tear her from Jesus Christ. Either because they had too much respect for religion to venture to violate so holy an asylum, or that God restrained them by His power, they molested her no farther. She had only to resist the fresh efforts they made to induce her to return to her father. But the love of God gave her courage to resist with such determined firmness, that, giving up all hopes of conquering her, they left her in peace.

A short time after, Francis removed her from the Monastery of St. Paul to that of St. Angelo de Panso, of the same Order of St. Benedict, near Assisi, to which she drew her sister Agnes. The conformity of their inclinations and manners, which rendered them tenderly united, had made them sensibly feel their separation. Clare was greatly grieved that Agnes, at so tender an age, should be exposed to the dangers of the world. She prayed fervently to the Almighty to cause her sister to feel the sweets of His grace, so that she might grow disgusted with the world, and become her companion in the service of Jesus Christ. Her prayer was soon favorably heard, for, a fortnight after her consecration, Agnes came to her, and declared that she was decided to give herself wholly to God. "I return Him thanks," replied Clare, "for that He has thus relieved me from the uneasiness I was in on your account."

The indignation of the family was extreme, when it became known that one sister had followed the other. On the morrow, twelve of its principal members hastened to the Monastery of St. Angelo. At first they feigned to have come in a peaceful mood; but, having been admitted, they turned to Agnes, for they had no longer any hopes of Clare, and said: "What business have you here? Come immediately home with us." She replied that she did not choose to leave her sister, when one of the knights, forgetting himself altogether, attacked her furiously, struck her with his fist, kicked her, pulled her down by the hair, and the others carried her off in their arms. All that this innocent lamb could do, thus torn by the wolves, was to cry out: "My dear sister, come to my aid; do not let them separate me from Jesus Christ." Clare could give her no assistance, but by praying to God to render her steadfast, and to check the violence of her ravishers. This prayer was followed by a miraculous effect, similar to what the Church records in the life of the illustrious virgin and martyr, St. Lucia.

As the relations of Agnes dragged her down the mountain, tearing her clothes, and scattering her hair along the road, because she continued violently to resist, she became suddenly so heavy, that they were unable to raise her from the ground, even with the help of persons who flocked from the fields and the vineyards. They were blind to the finger of God in so extraordinary an event, and they even made a jest of it; for ill-disposed persons, like the Pharisees of the Gospel, do not submit to the evidence of miracles, but carry their impiety to the length of turning all miracles into ridicule. The one which God was pleased to perform in the person of Agnes, threw her uncle, whose name was Monaldi, into such a rage, that he raised his arm to strike her in such a manner as would have killed her, if the Divine power had not arrested the blow by bringing such an excessive pain into the limb as to disable it; this pain lasted a considerable time. This is a grand lesson for those parents who prevent their children from consecrating themselves to God in a religious state. If they do not experience in this world the effects of His anger, they ought to fear the consequences of the anathema in the next with which the Council of Trent menaces, not only them, but those also who compel their children to embrace a religious state.

Clare came to the field of battle, where she found her sister half dead. She entreated the relations to retire and to leave her in her care, which they regrettingly did. Agnes then rose with great ease, glad to have had a share in the cross of Jesus Christ. She returned to the monastery with her sister, to consecrate herself to God under the direction of Francis, who cut off her hair with his own hands, and instructed her in the duties of the state she was about to enter. Clare, not having her mind quite at ease in the Monastery of St. Angelo, removed to the house which adjoined the Church of St. Damian, the first of the three which he had repaired, and where he had foretold that there would be one day a monastery of poor females, who should lead a sanctified life, and whose reputation would cause our Heavenly Father to be glorified.

Clare had scarcely fixed herself there, when the fame of her sanctity spread all around, and produced wonderful effects. The influence of grace was so great, that there were many persons of all sexes and all ages, of all states of life, nobles and rich, who took to a religious life. They mutually incited each other in families, as St. Jerome tells us that it occurred in all Africa, when the illustrious virgin, Demetrias, moved by the exhortation of St. Augustine, took the holy veil. It was even seen that married persons separated by mutual consent, and entered separate convents: and those who could not do this, strove to sanctify themselves in the world. The virtues of the holy spouse of Jesus Christ, as a precious perfume, attracted pure and innocent souls, who made the house of St. Damian a numerous community, and the cradle of the Order of the Poor Clares, or Poor Ladies, the second of the three orders which were established by St. Francis. He appointed Clare Abbess of St. Damian, although her humility made her wish to be the servant of the others, and he only overcame her repugnance by enforcing that obedience which she had promised him.

It was there that this holy abbess was enclosed during a period of forty-two years in the practice of the most eminent perfection, and which we shall have an opportunity of referring to, when we come to speak of her rule.

After Francis had regulated the spiritual exercises of these nuns, provided for the enclosure, and placed the house in good order, he turned in his mind things personal to himself, as to what should be his future way of life. In order to come to a decision, he consulted those of his brethren with whom he was in the habit of having familiar intercourse, and proposed to them his difficulties as follows:

> "My brethren, what do you advise me? Which of the two do you think best: that I shall give myself to prayer, or that I shall go forth to preach? To me it seems that prayer is what is most advantageous to me, for I am a simple person, who am not a good speaker, and I have received the gift of prayer, rather than that of speech: moreover, we gain much by prayer; it is the source of graces; but, in preaching, we only distribute to others what God has communicated. Prayer purifies the heart and the affections; it unites us to the sole true and sovereign good, and strengthens us in virtue. Preaching renders the feet of the spiritual man dusty; it is an employment which dissipates and distracts, and which causes regular discipline to be relaxed. In fine, in prayer we speak to God, and we listen to Him; we converse with the angels, as if we lived an Evangelic life. In preaching we must have much condescension towards men, and, living with them, we must hear and see, speak and think, in some measure as they do, in a human way. But there is one thing which seems to prevail over all this before God, which is, that the Only Son, who is in the bosom of His Father, and is the Sovereign Wisdom, came down from heaven to save souls, to instruct mankind by His example and by His word, to redeem them by His blood, and to make of this precious blood a bath and a celestial beverage: all that He had He gave up liberally and without reserve for our salvation. Now, having bound ourselves to do all things according to the model given us in His person, it seems more in conformity to the will of God, that I should give up my own repose in order to labor for the benefit of others."

After all these reflections, he continued in an anxious state of uncertainty as to the course he ought to take; and this man, who had wonderful knowledge through the spirit of prophecy, had no light thrown on his doubts by prayer: God permitting at that time that he should not be sensible to the evident proofs he had, that he was called to the apostolic life.

We have already seen that powerful attractions to a contemplative life had given rise to similar difficulties arising in his mind. As he wished in all things to act faithfully and perfectly, his principal care was to apply himself to the virtues which he knew, by the inspiration of the Holy Spirit, to be most agreeable to God.

St. Bonaventure says that this was the ground of his doubt, and he gives two reasons why God permitted that the Saint should not have been able to solve the difficulty, the solution of which appeared so easy. The first is, in order that the heavenly oracles which had announced that Francis was destined to preach the Gospel, should give a more exalted idea of the merits of that ministry; to this may be added, that it was of consequence that it should be known with certainty that the holy Founder and his disciples were destined by Heaven to labor for the salvation of souls, since in after times it has been found that some of their adversaries have contested it. Secondly, the doubt of the servant of God was useful in preserving his humility and rendering it still greater. In the capacity of a Friar Minor, he was not ashamed of seeking the advice of the least of his brethren, he who had been taught such elevated things from the Sovereign Master. It was likewise one of his maxims throughout his whole life, and of the principles of the sacred philosophy, of which he made profession, to address himself to the simple as well as to the learned, to the imperfect as well as to the perfect, to the young as to the old, with the ardent desire to find from intercourse with them in what way and by what means he could best serve God according to His good pleasure, and raise himself to the greatest perfection.

Finally, we must not be surprised that he entreated God to grant him additional proofs of his vocation, after having received such convincing ones by revelations, by miracles, and from the mouth of the Vicar of Jesus Christ; when we see in the Sacred Scriptures, that Gideon, having been chosen by God to fight the enemies of His people, and this choice having been manifested by the apparition of an angel, by a miracle and by a revelation, he nevertheless begged the Lord to give other miraculous signs, in order to be still further assured of it, and his prayer was granted. Would to God, that, without asking for miracles and without expecting them, all vocations, particularly those for the holy ministries, and other affairs of conscience, were examined on such sound principles, and weighed by means as likely to deserve the light of Heaven.

In order to know how finally to decide, Francis sent two of his religious, Philip and Masse, to Brother Sylvester the priest, who was then on the mountain near Assisi, continually intent on prayer, begging him to consult the Lord on the subject of his doubt, and to let him know the result. He made a similar application to Clare, recommending her to put the same question to her sisters, and particularly to the one who should appear to her to be the most pure and most single-minded. The venerable priest and the consecrated virgin gave similar answers, and pronounced that it was the will of God that Francis should go forth to preach.

When the two religious returned, Francis received them with great respect and affection; he washed their feet, embraced them, and gave them their meal. He then took them into the wood, where he knelt barcheaded and inclined, with his hands crossed upon his breast, and said to them: "Now tell me what my Lord Jesus Christ commands me to do?" "My very dear brother, and my Father," replied Masse, "Sylvester and Clare received precisely the same answer from our Lord Jesus Christ, which is, that you set out to preach; because it is not for your salvation alone that He called you, but for the salvation of others also; and for them He will put His words into your mouth."

Then Francis, moved by the Spirit of God, as the prophets had been, and inflamed by the fire of charity, rose up, saying: "Let us then go in the name of the Lord;" and he set out with two of his companions, Masse of Marignan, and Angelo of Rieti. He walked so fast to obey the words of Heaven, that it was easy to see that the Lord acted upon him, and that he had received fresh strength from above for the ministry of preaching. His companions were the more convinced of this by the very extraordinary wonders which were worked by him on the route.

The apostolical preacher went first to Bevagna, where he pronounced an excellent discourse on the love of God; after which, in presence of the whole audience, he restored the sight of a blind girl by putting spittle three times on her eyes in the name of the Blessed Trinity. This miracle had a salutary effect on a number of sinners, who were converted; and many of them joined him who was the instrument of the Divine Power.

So many souls gained to Jesus Christ in one place, stimulated him to carry the faith into the Levant. The triumph of martyrs, whose charity could not be extinguished by the violence of persecutions, excited in him a holy jealousy. Burning with similar fire, he wished to offer himself, as they had done, a sacrifice, in order to mark his gratitude in some measure, by the effusion of his blood, for the goodness of Jesus Christ, who vouchsafed to die for our salvation, thus the better to excite others to love Him. But he desired to have the sanction of the Sovereign Pontiff for this undertaking, and therefore bent his steps to Rome, preaching as he went the truths of salvation, which God confirmed by miracles.

Arrived at Rome, he sought an audience with the Pope. Innocent III still filled the Papal throne; he first communicated to him the wonderful extension of his Order, the holy lives of his brethren, and the design which God had to bring about a reformation of morals in the world, which was growing old, and was visibly in a state of decay. Then he disclosed the project he had of transporting himself to the lands of the Mahometans and Tartars, to endeavor to give them some knowledge of the Gospel. It must be remarked, that the Saint attributed to the world that decay which is the effect of old age, but he did not extend this to the Church, because he well knew that, although old, she was not infirm. St. Augustine says, that her old age is always young, fresh, vigorous, and that she bears fruit in abundance. The Pope, who was very religious, was highly gratified at the fortunate success which he now learnt had attended the Saint's labors; he willingly granted the servant of God leave to preach to the infidels, and he affectionately gave him his blessing.

Two sermons which Francis preached at Rome procured him two disciples, Zachary and William; the one was a Roman, the other was an Englishman. John de Capella, of whom we have before spoken, having left the Order about this time, and having had a similar end to that of Judas, William was substituted for him, as St. Mathias had filled the place of the traitor in the Apostolate, and William was afterwards always considered as the twelfth of the first companions of the Patriarch.

A Roman widow, very noble and very rich, called Jacqueline de Settesoli, having heard the Saint preach, was very anxious to have an interview with him. He agreed to it, although reluctantly, and he gave her such salutary instructions, that she committed the care of all her affairs to her two sons, who were afterwards senators, in order that she might apply herself to the sanctification of her soul, employing the gift of tears which God had given her, to weep incessantly the neglects of her past life. This lady and St. Clare were the only two persons of the female sex with whom the servant of Jesus Christ had any intimate relations on the subject of their salvation; which ought to serve as a caution for this sort of direction lest it be too greatly multiplied,— and be unholy.

As there is no affection more solid or more effective than that which is grounded on charity, the pious widow rendered to Francis and his brethren all the good offices in her power. When they came to Rome she provided them with lodgings, she fed them, clothed them, and assisted them in their sicknesses with the tenderness of a mother. It was she who procured for them from the Benedictines of the Abbey of St. Cosmas beyond the Tiber, a refuge in the Hospital of St. Blaise; and this hospital with its church was entirely ceded to them by the same religious order in the year 1229, at the request of Pope Gregory IX; it is to this day the Convent of St. Francis of Ripa. Thus the Friars Minor are indebted to the children of St. Benedict for the first establishment they had in Rome, as well as for that of St. Mary of the Angels, or Portiuncula, the first of the whole Order.

Francis, having terminated his business at Rome, returned to St. Mary of the Angels, where he communicated to his brethren his intention of proceeding to the Levant. He exhorted them in the strongest terms to perfect themselves in the exercises of a religious life; he left them Peter of Catania as superior during his absence, and set out with one companion for Ascoli. At that place they were extremely anxious to see and hear this admirable man, who was everywhere looked upon as a saint: he had scarcely arrived in the town when all flocked to him; whichever way he went, a crowd followed him; every one was anxious to get near him, and they pressed upon each other in order only to be able to touch his miserable habit. His presence and preaching in this town procured him thirty disciples, some priests, and some laymen, whom he placed in different houses of the Order.

The desire of martyrdom which he aspired to from the infidels, did not admit of a longer stay at Ascoli; he therefore made for the sea-side, and embarked on board a vessel which was bound for Syria. But on the passage the winds became adverse, and they were obliged to come to anchor off Sclavonia, where he remained some days in hopes of finding some other vessel bound to the Levant. Not finding any, and perceiving that his intention had been foiled, he applied to some seamen who were about to sail to Ancona, to take him on board their vessel for the love of God. They refused obstinately to do so, because he had no money wherewith to pay his passage; notwithstanding this, the holy man contrived to slip secretly on board with his companion.

An unknown person came on board the vessel and brought provisions with him, saying to one of the passengers: "Worthy man, I confide these provisions to you, for the use of two poor religious who are secreted in the vessel; take care of them, and give food to them when required." Who could this charitable purveyor be? There is reason to think, with St. Bonaventure, that he was sent by God to the assistance of these two poor religious, who were only poor for love of Him. Stormy weather rendered the passage disastrous; they could neither carry sail, nor return to land. All the sailors' provisions were expended: there was nothing left but the provisions put on board for the two religious. Divine Providence was pleased to multiply these, inasmuch that they sufficed for all who were in the vessel for several days, during which they were still at sea, before they reached Ancona. The sailors, astonished at this miracle, were convinced that the poor man whom they had refused to receive on board, had, by his merits, saved their lives, and they returned thanks to God for His mercy.

After having landed, Francis went to several places, spreading the word of God as a precious seed, which produced an ample harvest. Many came to see him from afar, so greatly had his reputation been disseminated. A celebrated poet came amongst others, having heard his entire contempt for the things of this world spoken of. He was of the class of persons who were called in Provence Troubadours, who invented fables, and composed different pieces of poetry, which were sung in the houses of the nobles. The art of versifying in the vulgar tongue was uncommon in those times, and was only practised by the nobility. The Italians imitated the people of Provence, and translated into their language the best compositions of the Troubadours. The poet of whom we are speaking excelled in this art, and the Emperor Frederic II had crowned him as the Prince of Poets, which caused him to be usually called "The King of Verse."

Coming then to see Francis, he passed through the Borough Town of San Severino, and entered the church of a monastery, where the Servant of God was preaching on the mystery of the Cross. He listened to him at first without knowing him; but God disclosed Francis to him in the course of the sermon, by two shining swords pierced through the Saint cross-wise, one from the head to the feet, and the other from one hand to the other through the breast; from this he became aware that the preacher was the holy man of whom so much was spoken. The first impression which the vision made upon him was, that he ought to lead a better life; but the words of the preacher filled him with such compunction, that he felt as if he had been pierced by the sword of the spirit which came out of his mouth. He went after the sermon to renounce in Francis' hands all the vanities of the world, and to embrace his Institute. Francis, seeing him pass so perfectly from the agitations of the world to the peace of Jesus Christ, gave him the name of Brother Pacificus.

St. Bonaventure adds, that he was a man of so much holiness that he received the additional favor from God of seeing on the forehead of his Blessed Father a great T, painted in a variety of colors, which threw a remarkable softness on his countenance. This letter, which represents the cross, showed the interior comeliness which the love of the cross gave to his soul.

Watchfulness and affection inspired the Father with the wish to return to Tuscany, to visit the establishments he had founded there the preceding year, and to learn from his own inspection how they progressed in the ways of God. The family of the Ubaldini, which is among the most illustrious of Florence, gave him a convent which had been built and founded by their ancestors for the religious of the Order of St. Basil, in the sixth or seventh century, some leagues from the city, in the middle of a wood, and which had been since occupied by hermits. He put some of his companions into it, and returned towards the end of October to St. Mary of the Angels, preaching, as was his custom, in all the places he passed through. The repose he allowed himself after so much fatigue, was that of applying himself to the instruction of his disciples, and addressing discourses to them full of wisdom.

At the end of this year he had an attack of ague, which became quartan, and reduced him to a great state of languor. The bishop of Assisi, who was a most charitable prelate, and his particular friend, having heard of his illness, came to see him, and, notwithstanding his resistance, had him removed to his palace, where he attended to his recovery with the charity of a pastor and the affection of a parent. His religious came to him there to seek the light they required. They also brought to him such postulants as presented themselves, and those who were recommended to him (at times there were thirty or forty) by the missionaries he had in various parts of Italy; for none were then received who had not been examined by the founder himself. A young gentleman from Lucca came with tears in his eyes, to entreat him to give him the habit. "Unfortunate young man," said the Saint, "why do you attempt to show by your eyes what is not in your heart? You have, without due consideration, formed a plan which you will soon as lightly give up." In fact, a few days after he went home with two of his relations who had come in search of him, and he thought no more of becoming a religious.

The servant of God, having regained some portion of strength during his residence with the bishop, by relaxing in the severity of his abstinences, which were extreme, became irritated with his own body, and was inflamed with the desire of humbling himself: "It is not right," he said, "that people should think me austere, while I am pampered in secret." Upon which the spirit of humility suggested to him an act, which St. Bonaventure records, not as an example, but as a prodigy, to be compared only with those extraordinary things which God commanded the Prophets to perform. He rose, and accompanied by a great number of his brethren, he went to the great Square of Assisi, assembled the people, and led them to the cathedral. Then he caused himself to be dragged by the vicar of his convent from the church to the place of execution, stripped, and with a cord round his neck, as the Prophet Isaias. There, weak as he still was, and shivering with cold, he addressed the assembly with surprising energy, and said in a loud voice: "I assure that I ought not to receive honor as if I were a spiritual man. I am a carnal, sensual, and greedy man, whom you ought thoroughly to despise." The hearers, who knew the austerity of his life, struck with such a scene, admitted that this extraordinary humility was more to be admired than imitated.

Nevertheless, the holy doctor, whom we have just named, finds in this some wholesome instruction. It teaches us, he says, that, in the practice of virtue, we must avoid with great care everything having any tendency to hypocrisy, repress the slightest approaches of vanity, and have a sovereign contempt for praise. The humble Francis, who strenuously labored for his interior sanctification, did many things with a view of rendering himself contemptible, endeavoring, above all, to prevent men from being deceived in the idea they might have formed of his sanctity. This is the characteristic of true devotion; it has no borrowed exterior; it is, or it endeavors to be, all that it seems.

The religious whom Francis had sent into Lombardy, fulfilled the mission in an admirable manner. They acquired so much esteem at Milan by their preaching and by their good example, that the archbishop of that city, Henry Satalas, gave them an establishment there, which became considerable later, by the liberality of the Milanese.

One of the fruits of their apostolic labors was the vocation of a young man of rank, who was rich and talented, and who solicited the habit of the Order. Upon their acquainting him that, to become a Friar Minor, it was requisite to renounce all temporal goods, he immediately disposed of all of which he was then master, and distributed the greater part to the poor, reserving the remainder to pay the expenses of his journey to Assisi, where he was told that it was necessary to present himself to the founder, who alone had the power of receiving novices.

He induced some of his relations and friends to accompany him, and took with him a considerable number of servants; one of the religious was also requested to go with them, in order to introduce the postulant, and favor his reception. When they arrived at St. Mary of the Angels, Francis, seeing such a number of persons, and such an appearance of vanity, asked the religious who was with them, who these lords were, and what they wanted? He answered: "My Father, this is a young man, learned and rich, of one of the first families of Milan, who wishes to become your disciple." Francis replied, before them all, smiling: "This young man does not seem to me to be fit for our Order, for, when people come with so much pomp, which is the mark of a proud spirit, to embrace a state of poverty, we are led to believe that they have not yet sufficient contempt and aversion for the world, and that they are not prepared wholly to relinquish it. But I will consult our brethren on the subject."

He assembled them all, and asked their opinion, which was not to receive him, because he had still a fund of pride, and because the love for the splendor of the world was not yet eradicated from his heart.

The young man who was present burst into tears; and Francis, who was moved with compassion, said: "My brethren, will you receive him if he consents to serve in the kitchen? it will be the means of inducing him to renounce the vanities of the world." They assented on this condition, which the postulant willingly agreed to, protesting that he was prepared to do anything that was required of him. The Father embraced him, after having returned to those who accompanied him his money and his equipage. He sent him to the hospital of St. Blasius of Rome, there to act as cook; and the young novice attained to such perfection in that humble employment, that Francis judged him worthy to be placed over others, and made him superior of the same place.

The line adopted in respect to this young man shows evidently, that for the religious profession neither birth, nor riches, nor talents, are to be heeded, but that the essential qualifications principally to be considered for this holy state, are, to be sincerely prepared to die to the world and to self.

At the beginning of the year 1213, the fever of which Francis had been cured at the bishop's palace of Assisi recurred; sometimes it was tertian, sometimes quartan, but always with great severity. He bore the suffering with great equanimity, because of the hatred he felt for his body, and from the patience taught by Jesus Christ. The violence of the fever which burned his body, was, in his opinion, a lesser evil than the fire of temptations which inflame the soul; his sufferings appeared to him again. All the saints have had a like way of thinking, and the principles of Christianity admit of no other. The only uneasiness the sickness gave to the holy man, was its having prevented him putting in force the intentions he had in view for the salvation of souls. But charity, which is ever active, suggested to him to exhort the faithful in writing, as he could not do so in person; he therefore addressed them a short letter, couched in the following terms:—

"O how happy are all those who love God, and who worthily practise all that Jesus Christ has taught in His holy gospel. Thou shalt love the

Lord thy God with thy whole heart, and with thy whole soul, and thy neighbor as thyself. Let us love and adore God with great purity of mind and heart; for that is what He seeks for above all things. He has said that the true adorers shall adore the Father in spirit and in truth, and that they who adore Him, must adore Him in spirit and truth. I salute you in our Lord."

This short letter was still fresh from his hand, when an infinity of copies were made of it, so anxious were all people to see anything that came from the hand of so holy a person. In this simple and brief exhortation they admired the candor of his soul and the extent of his charity, and, in reading it, they were moved by a power which penetrated the soul; for the words of the saints have a secret unction which is not found elsewhere.

These spiritual services, and others which Francis rendered to his neighbor, with the continual instruction he gave to his brethren, were his occupations during his sickness, and until such time as returning health permitted him to do more. He was somewhat better in the spring, as is usually the case with those who have the quartan ague; but his extraordinary austerities had so weakened his constitution, that he never wholly recovered his health, and the remainder of his life was little else than a state of languor.

As soon as he could commence travelling, he committed the care of his Order to Peter of Cantania, and set out with Bernard of Quintavalle and some others, in order to go to Morocco, through Spain, to preach the Gospel to the Miramolin and to his subjects, in the hopes of attaining by this means the crown of martyrdom, which was the great object of his wishes.

The servant of God did not reach Spain till near the end of the year, because he had stopped in various places to preach, to visit the houses of his Order, and to receive accounts of others. His whole route was a succession of miracles, and other remarkable things, which contain admirable instructions.

At Foligno, the sign of the cross which he made on the house of his host, protected it from various accidents, and particularly from fire, which did no damage to that dwelling, although the adjoining houses were three or four times on fire: the flames were even seen to take a contrary direction. At Spoleto, knowing that a rich man thought ill of his Institute, and refused his brethren alms, he asked him only to give him a loaf; and, having received it, he divided it among his religious, and directed them to say the Lord's Prayer and the Evangelical Salutation three times, for the person who had given it. Their scanty meal was scarcely finished, when this man came to ask forgiveness for the harshness he had shown them, and he was, after that, the best friend of their convent, so good an idea of their Institution had the saint impressed upon him.

At Terni, the bishop who had listened to one of Francis' sermons, ascended the pulpit when he had done, and said to the people:—"My brethren, the Lord, who has often enlightened His Church by men illustrious for their science, has now sent you this Francis whom you have just heard, a poor illiterate man, and contemptible in appearance, in order that he may edify you by his word and his example. The less learned he is, the more does the power of God shine in his person, who chooses those who are foolish according to the views of the world, to confound all worldly wisdom. The care which God takes of our salvation obliges us to honor and glorify Him; for He has not done the like to other nations."

Francis followed the prelate, fell on his knees, kissed his hand, and said:— "My lord, in very truth, no one has ever done me so much honor as I have this day received from you. Some attribute to me a sort of sanctity, which noway belongs to me, and which ought to be referred to God alone, the author of every perfect gift. But you, my lord, have wisely separated what is valuable from what is vile, the worthy from the unworthy, the saint from the sinner; giving the glory to God, and not to me, who am but a miserable mortal. It is, indeed, only to God, the King of Ages, immortal and invisible, that men should give honor and glory for ever and ever." The bishop, even more pleased with this specimen of his humility than with his preaching, embraced him affectionately.

In the same city, by the sign of the cross he rendered some sour wine perfectly good, and that before persons who had tasted it in its acid state. But he performed a much greater miracle, which was universally admired, on a young lad who had been just crushed by the fall of a wall; having had him brought to him, he applied himself to prayer, and, extending himself on the corpse, as the Prophet Eliseus had done on the child of the Sunamite, he restored him to life.

In the County of Narni, he was lodged in the house of a worthy man who was in great affliction for the death of his brother, who had been drowned, and whose body could not be found, so that it might be buried. After having privately prayed for some time, he showed a spot in the river where he said that the body certainly was at the bottom; it had been stopped there by the entanglement of the clothes. They dived at that place and found the body, which he restored to life in the presence of the whole family.

The fever, and a severe stomach complaint, caused him to faint in a hermitage which had been given him near the Borough of St. Urban, and he asked for some wine to recover from the weakness which had ensued. As there was none to be had there, he had some water brought to him, which he blessed, by making the sign of the cross over it, and it was instantly changed thereby into excellent wine. The little that he took of it renovated him so promptly, that it was a double miracle. Upon which St. Bonaventure remarks, that this wonderful change is a type of the change he had effected in his heart, in casting off the old man to put on the new.

In the City of Narni, he cured a man who had lost the use of his limbs for five months from palsy, employing no other remedy than a sign of the cross, which he made over his whole body; this he did at the request of the bishop of the place, and by virtue of the same sign he restored the sight of a blind girl. Being at Orti, he straightened a child, who was so deformed that its head touched its feet. At San Gemini, he prayed, with three of his companions, for the wife of his host, whom the devil had possessed for a long while, and the evil spirit left her. Such evident miracles, publicly performed, and in great numbers, gave a wonderful splendor to his sanctity. In the archives of the Town of Poggibonsi, in Tuscany, the act of donation of a house given to him is preserved, which commences thus:—"We cede to a man named Francis, whom all the world considers as a saint," etc.

The discourses of so holy a man, of one so gifted with the power of miracles, had the greatest effect upon the hearts of his hearers, and made the people very anxious to have houses of his Order established among them. He settled some of his religious at Foligno, at Trevi, at San Gemini, at Sienna, and in several other places.

Fresh disciples joined him from all quarters, but he did not receive any until he had strictly examined their vocation. A young gentleman, having heard him preach at Monte Casale, a town in the Appennines, came to acquaint him with the design he had long formed of entering his Order. "You must think seriously of it," replied Francis; "for the kind of life we lead must appear very hard to those who have been tenderly brought up." The young man answered courageously: "My Father, are not you and yours of the same nature as I am, and formed of the same earth? I hope, with God's help, to bear without much inconvenience what my fellow-men can bear so willingly." These ideas were very pleasing to the Patriarch, and the postulant was received. It must be admitted that man has resources of strength which he might make use of to imitate the saints in many things, if he were not wanting in exertion and confidence in God.

From Monte Casale Francis passed over the Appennines, and went through the Valley of Marecchia to reach Monte Feltro, or St. Leo. He learnt on the road that the lord of that town was about to be knighted at his castle, where he was giving a grand feast, accompanied by games and theatricals, to a numerous assembly of the nobility, among whom was Count Orlando Catanio, lord of Chiusi Nuovo, and of all the Casentino. Being near the castle, and hearing the sound of the trumpets, which denoted that the revelry was about to begin, he said to his companions:—"Let us go hither also, and let us combat the devil with all our might, who never fails in these rejoicings to lay his snares into which many fall; for it is our duty to labor everywhere and in all places for the salvation of souls." He went up to the castle, and heard the solemn mass with all those who accompanied the new knight. As soon as it was over, he took a position on a height near the church, in order to preach from thence, and the crowd gathered round him to listen.

He took the following Italian words for his text:—"Tanto e il ben che aspetto, che d'ogni pena mi diletto:" which means—"the good which I hope for is so great, that to obtain it all suffering is pleasurable." He proved his text by this passage from St. Paul:—"The sufferings of this life are not worthy to be compared with the glory to come;" by the example of the apostles, who were filled with joy for having been found worthy to suffer for the name of Jesus; by the example of the martyrs, who willingly exposed themselves to torments and death, that they might obtain heaven; and, finally by such cogent reasons, so pathetically set forth, that all the auditors admired the doctrine, and felt what he wished to inspire them with. They found in the preacher something divine, which commanded respect, and they fixed their looks upon his countenance as if it had been that of an angel.

Count Orlando, more impressed with what he had heard than the rest, went after the sermon to embrace the preacher, and he entreated him particularly to instruct him in the affairs of his salvation. Francis, who, in addition to his ardent zeal, had much discretion and suavity of manner, said:—"Count, go now and do honor to your friends whom you have invited, and we will talk of this affair at a more convenient time." The count, complying with this advice, joined the nobility who waited for him, and did not forget to take care of the servants of God. The feast having ended, he returned to the prudent director, with whom he had a lengthened conversation, with which he was so much struck, that in order to have the comfort of seeing familiarly the religious of the Institute, he offered Francis the Mountain of Alvernia, with a promise, if he agreed to it, of building there a convent.

As this was a lonely place, very fit for contemplation, Francis gladly accepted the offer, and promised to send two of his brethren to Chiusi, before he should leave Italy. He did in fact send them, and the count having received them as angels sent from heaven, he took them to Mount Alvernia, where they fixed upon a spot which appeared to them an apt location for a church. Fifty soldiers who had been brought thither began immediately to fell timber, and a place was cleared, where hutting was set up to lodge the religious, in which they dwelt until the church and convent were built. These are the circumstances under which the Friars Minor were settled on this mountain, which subsequently became so celebrated in the Christian world by the stigmata of St. Francis. The place was ceded to them by an authentic document which the count gave them, and which is preserved in the original in the archives of the convent. We shall speak further of this holy place when we come to relate the first visit the Saint paid it on his return from Spain.

He continued his journey through Bologna, from whence, after having visited his brethren, he came to Imola. He first went to offer his respects to the bishop, and asked permission to preach to his people. "I preach," replied the bishop coldly, "and that is quite enough." Francis bowed humbly, and retired; but an hour afterwards he returned, and the bishop, surprised and angered at seeing him again, asked him what he could possibly want? to which he replied, in a tone of sincere humility: "My lord, if a father drives his son out of the house by one door, it is right that the son should return through another." The bishop mollified by this mild address, embraced him with affection, and said: "From henceforth you and your brethren may preach in my diocese. I give you a general leave, it is what your humility has merited." Is there anything which can soften minds and obtain favors sooner than this virtue?

The humility of Francis was accompanied with great courage, which rendered him firm and confident in the most imminent dangers, this was owing to the great confidence he had in God. Night overtook him once when he was in company with Leo, between Lombardy and the Trevisan Marshes, on a road having on one side the Po, one of the most considerable rivers in Italy, and on the other a deep morass. Leo, much alarmed, exclaimed: "Father, pray to God to deliver us from the danger we are in." Francis, full of faith, replied: "God can, if it is His good pleasure, give us light to dissipate the darkness of the night." These words were hardly spoken, when they found themselves surrounded by a brilliant light, which not only made the way clear to them, but enabled them to see many things on either side of the way, although the darkness was very dense everywhere else. They pursued their route, singing the glories of God; the celestial torch served them as a guide till they reached the place where they were to be lodged, which was then very far off. This miraculous light was a notification to the Saint that it was God's pleasure that he should have a dwelling in the place to which His goodness had led him, and he told this to his companion. The inhabitants made no difficulty in assigning him one, after having heard him preach, and he gave the convent the name of The Holy Fire, as it is still called.

In Piedmont, where he was well received, his preaching, with the reputation of his sanctity, confirmed by many miracles, converted a considerable number of persons, and procured him several houses. From thence he went into Spain, but the writers of his life have not recorded by what route. Now, it is scarcely to be doubted that he went by land, and through France; ancient documents show that he entered Spain through Navarre, and that he arrived in the year 1213 at Logrono, a Town of Old Castile, which had formerly belonged to Biscay.

On the road he came up with a poor and abandoned invalid, for whom he felt so much pity that he directed Bernard de Quintavalle, one of his companions, to stay with him and take care of him, which Bernard willingly undertook to do. At Logrono he miraculously cured a young gentleman who was on the point of death; then he went on to Burgos, where Alphonso IX., (or VIII., according to some,) father of Blanche Queen of France and mother of St. Louis, then was. Francis presented himself before the king, he showed him the rules of his Institute, and entreated him to receive the Friars Minor into his states. This monarch, who, in addition to his political and military talents, had a great fund of goodness and piety, received the holy man very favorably; he condescended to read the rules, and after having conversed with him for some time, gave him leave to build houses in Spain.

Francis now fixed his thoughts only on advancing towards the sea-side in order to embark for Morocco, there to suffer martyrdom, for this was the great object of his wishes. If we only formed our opinion of things by the ordinary rules of prudence, we should be surprised, that a man, visibly sent by God for the institution of a new order of religious, should leave it so short a time after its birth, to seek for death among the infidels. But the saints only thought of following the impulses which the Spirit of God suggested to them, with reference to the works which they had commenced by God's order. St. Anthony, father of a great number of Cenobites, left his monastery, and followed at Alexandria certain confessors of the faith; he attended upon them in prison, and exhorted them under torment to procure for himself the palm of martyrdom. St. Dominic, animated by a similar spirit, had formed the intention of going among the Saracens, only two years after the institution of his order. Francis, thus inspired from above, desired to meet death for Jesus Christ, and left to God the care of his rising family.

This disposition, which was the fruit of ardent charity, was very pleasing to God; it entered into the economy of His providence for the salvation of souls and for the aggrandizement of the new Order, for the Saint did not cease his labors when he took the route which was to lead to martyrdom. Nevertheless, God did not choose that his design should be carried into execution; and His will was made known to His Servant by a violent illness, which put it out of his power to embark for Morocco. Francis gave up his wishes, obeying what was thus signified to him, and came to the resolution to return to Italy for the guidance of his flock, however, he did not set out till the close of the year.

The authors of the Order are agreed in saying that he went to visit the tomb of the Apostle St. James, at Compostella, the capital of Galicia, to which place devotion has attracted, for many centuries past, crowds of pilgrims, and that an angel appeared to him there, and assured him that it was God's will that he should return to Italy, after having founded some establishments in Spain. They also say that he went into Portugal, where he raised to life the daughter of his host at Guimaraens, a town of the diocese of Braganza, which caused him to be spoken of as a saint throughout the whole country; and that he went through nearly the whole of the Kingdom of Arragon and the adjacent provinces; and, finally, they relate the following most extraordinary circumstance:

> Francis being one evening on the banks of the River Orbego, with his companions, where there was no food, a young man of the Town of Novia overtook them, and carried them over on some horses he had with him, and received them hospitably. The gratitude the Saint had was shown by saying: "May the Lord reward you for the kindness you have shown us, when He rewards the just." Some short time after this, the young man, having gone to Rome out of devotion, and having endeavored to put his conscience in a good state, prayed fervently to God, to take him out of this world before he should commit a mortal sin. His prayer was heard; he died. His father desired to have a funeral service said for him, and thirty Friars Minor attended to it without having been asked; none knew from whence they came, nor whither they afterwards went, which made it thought that the assistance was miraculous; and as it as known what the holy man Francis had said to the deceased, it was understood that he had, by this means, procured the reward of the just for him whose hospitality he had received.

Gonzagues, Bishop of Mantua, who had been General of the Order of St. Francis, says, that it is held as certain that St. Francis commenced the establishments of Gasta, Arevalo, Avila, Madrid, Tudela, and caused several other convents to be built. It is easily understood that in the eight or nine months in which he remained in Spain after his illness, he arranged much by himself and by his companions; the old inscriptions which are still seen on the tombs of many Minors are an additional proof. Moreover, it is certain that his holy life and his preaching were of the greatest benefit to souls, and that his Order was received in Spain with an affection which has passed from age to age, from fathers to sons; so that Spain is one of the countries of the world in which we find the greatest veneration for St. Francis, and the greatest consideration for the Order of Friars Minor.

The same bishop tells us, on the testimony of universal and unvaried tradition, of many miracles performed by the Almighty, through the ministry of the holy man. We shall satisfy ourselves by relating one of them, which is warranted by manuscripts and documents.

Francis was lodged at Compostella, at the house of a poor dealer in charcoal, whose name was Cotolai, and he often went to pass the night in contemplation on a neighboring mountain. God made known to him, that it was His will that he should build a convent between two valleys, the one of which was commonly called the Valley of God, and the other the Valley of Hell. He knew that this ground belonged to the Benedictines of Compostella, of the Abbey of St. Pay, or Pelagius, since transferred to that of St. Martin; and, bearing in mind the favors which the religious of this holy order had done him in the gifts of St. Mary of the Angels, and at Rome, he called upon the Abbot and asked unhesitatingly for permission to build a convent between the two valleys. "What will you give me in payment?" said the abbot. Francis replied: "As I am very poor, I have neither money, nor anything else to give you, if you grant me what I ask. Yet what will be most precious to me, I will give you in quit rent yearly—a small basket of fish if they can be caught in the river." The abbot who was a very pious man, admiring his simplicity and his confidence, granted him his request on the condition proposed, and an act to that effect was prepared and signed by both.

The holy man came to Cotolai and told him what had passed between the Abbot of St. Pay and himself, and added: "My dear host, it is God's will that you should build this convent; therefore prepare yourself for the work." "Oh, how shall I be able to do that," answered Cotolai, "I who am so poor, and who live by my daily labor?" "Take courage," said Francis, "take a pickaxe, and go to the spring which is close by; make a hole a little in front of it, and you will find a treasure which will enable you to execute the order of Heaven." Cotolai, relying on the Saint's word, searched as he was bidden, found the treasure, and built the convent, which is known by the name of St. Francis to this day. This fact is narrated in an authentic manuscript in the archives of the Abbey of St. Martin, from whence this is copied; and in two very old inscriptions, one of which is on the tomb of Cotolai and his wife, whose name was Mary de Bicos, and the other over the gate of the church of the convent in which their tomb is. The deed which was executed by Francis and the Abbot of St. Pay, is preserved in the original in the archives of the Abbey of St. Martin of Compostella. The Prince of Spain, Philip the Second, saw it in the year 1554, when he was about to embark at Corunna, to espouse the Queen of England. However, the marvel has nothing in it which should be the cause of much surprise: our Saviour, who made St. Peter find in the mouth of a fish wherewithal to pay the tribute for his Master and himself, could easily cause a treasure of money to be found sufficient to build a house for his faithful Servant Francis.

When the Apostolical man had terminated his mission in Spain, he went to rejoin Bernard de Quintavalle, whom he had left on entering it, in charge of the poor sick man, who was perfectly cured. Francis came through Aragon into Catalonia. The magistrates of Barcelona, where he stopped for a short time, were so pleased with his poverty, his humility, and his other virtues, that, for the sake of having some religious of his Order, they converted the hospital where he was lodged into a convent, the church and cloister of which are still extant, and are venerable from the remembrance of the Saint.

At San Saloni, a small town between Barcelona and Gerona, an adventure occurred to him which seemed purely accidental, but which God turned to good. As he walked by the side of a vineyard, his companion gathered a bunch or two of grapes to refresh himself. He who had charge of the vineyard, perceiving it, came violently upon the religious, beat him and abused him in no measured terms, and took from him his poor cloak. Francis asked to have the cloak back, alleging mildly, that what had been taken had done no injury to the vineyard; and that good feeling required that this assistance should be given to a passer-by who needed it. But, not having succeeded in procuring its restoration, he went to the proprietor of the vineyard, from whom he had no difficulty in getting it back, after having told him what had happened. He then conversed with him on heavenly things with such effect, that the man, devoting himself from that moment to his service, promised to receive hospitably all the Friars Minor who should pass through San Saloni, and furnish them with whatsoever they might require, as far as his means would allow; which he never failed to do as long as he lived. Francis, in return, granted him participation in all the spiritual merits of his Order, and gave him the name of Father of the Friars Minor.

It is from this precedent that the superiors of the Order give letters of filiation, as they are called, in virtue of which the holders participate in the merits of all the practices of the community. This is grounded on the communion of saints, one of the articles of the apostolic symbol by which each member of the faithful who is not excommunicated, and principally if he be in a state of grace, participates in the good works of others. Besides this general communication, the faithful may assist each other by their prayers, and their own merits, as is done in confraternities and all pious associations. This is the way in which the Order of St. Francis, and all other religious orders, manifest their gratitude to their benefactors; in this they do that which St. Augustine says of the ministers of Jesus Christ in regard to the faithful who support them; "They give spiritual things, and only receive temporal ones; they give gold, and only receive brass." Those who know what the communion of saints is, and who neglect nothing which can contribute to their salvation, have great esteem (as, indeed, they ought) for letters of filiation, and strive to live in a Christian-like manner in order to profit by them.

From Catalonia, Francis continued his route through Roussillon, and it is believed that he placed some of his religious at Perpignan, the capital. He then entered Languedoc, which the errors and arms of the Albigenses had alike tended to desolate. The Catholics at that time enjoyed some calm by the valor of the illustrious Simon, Count of Montfort, who had just overthrown the heretics, principally by the celebrated victory obtained, at Muret, over Peter, King of Aragon, whom ill-understood interests had made protector of the Albigenses, to the detriment of religion, and who was killed in that battle. The saintly traveller did not make any stay in Languedoc; perhaps because it was the field destined by Providence to be cultivated by St. Dominic, whose preaching and miracles had made an infinity of conversions, and who was then at Carcassonne, where he gave the nuptial benediction to the marriage of Amaury de Montfort, the son of Simon, with the Princess Beatrice, the daughter of the Dauphin, Count of Viennois. Francis arrived at Montpellier at the time when they were about to open the council, at which Simon of Montfort was loaded with praises, and chosen to be possessor of the City of Toulouse, and the other conquests of the Crusaders; he preached there, and foretold that a convent would be built soon for his brethren at the hospital where he lodged; a prophecy which was fulfilled in the year 1220.

His bad health, the fatigues of his journey, and the rigor of the season, had brought him into a state of great languor, and compelled him to stop one day. His malady gave him a disgust for all sorts of food, and he thought that he could only relish some wild fowl. As he was speaking of it to his companion Bernard, a well-appointed cavalier brought him one ready dressed, saying, "Servant of God, take what the Lord sends thee," after which he disappeared. Francis, admiring the goodness of God, who fulfils the desires of those who fear Him, ate willingly of this celestial food, and was so strengthened by it, that he rose up immediately and continued his journey through Dauphiny and Piedmont; from whence he went to St. Mary of the Angels, continuing to perform the functions of an Apostle and Patriarch of the Order on his way, but not without having to endure the honors which his miracles and the reputation of his sanctity procured him from all parts.

His return was the subject of great rejoicing to his children, to Clare in particular, and to a number of young men, among whom were many nobles and many learned persons who were waiting to be received into the Order.

He was surprised to find a building which Peter of Catania, his own vicar had constructed during his absence; he inquired the reason of it, and Peter having replied, "that it was for the accommodation of their guests, where they might say the divine office more commodiously," He said:—"Brother Peter, this place is the rule and the model of the Order; I choose that those who come to it shall suffer the inconveniences of poverty as well as those who live in it, in order that they may tell others how poorly we live at St. Mary's of the Portiuncula; for if the guests see that they are provided with everything they can wish for, they will expect the same thing in their provinces, and will say, that they only do as they do at Portiuncula, which is the original place of the Institution." He was desirous that the building should be pulled down, and he even directed it to be done; but, upon the representations of the need they had of it, he consented to let it stand. They could not do without room to lodge the number of people who were drawn thither by the rumor of his great virtues, and the multitudes of his religious who came from various parts to consult him.

Those whom he had destined for Mount Alvernia, having come with several others to congratulate him on his return, informed him that Count Orlando had loaded them with favors; that they were settled on the mountain, and that it was the place, of all others, proper for contemplation. This gave him a wish to go thither, and he set out with three companions, Leo, Masse, and Angelo of Rieti. It was his custom in travelling to name one of those who accompanied him as guardian and leader, and he obeyed him humbly in all things. On this occasion, he gave this commission to Masse, desiring him not to disquiet himself about their food, and giving no other instructions, except that the divine office should be punctually and piously recited, that silence should be rigidly observed, and that their deportment should be reserved. He preached, as usual, wherever he went, and performed many miracles.

One night he went into a church which was deserted, in order to pass the night in prayer, knowing from experience that the Spirit of God was communicated more freely to the soul in quiet solitary places. At the beginning of the night, the devils used every sort of artifice to interrupt his prayers and to disturb him. Then they attacked him in person, as St. Athanasius relates that they did St. Anthony, so that they seemed to come to blows with him. The more they annoyed him, the more fervently he prayed, and the more strenuously he invoked Jesus Christ with confidence, in the words of the prophet:—"Protect me under the shadow of thy wings from these wicked ones who pursue me;" and he said to the devils:—"Spiteful and deceitful spirits, do all you can against me, for you can do nothing but what God permits, and here I am, ready to suffer with pleasure all the afflictions it is His pleasure to send me." Then the devils cast themselves upon him with still greater violence; they pushed him about on all sides, they dragged him along the ground and beat him severely. In the midst of his sufferings, he exclaimed:—"My Lord Jesus Christ, I give Thee thanks for all Thy benefits; this is not one of the least; it is an assured mark of the goodness Thou hast for me. Thou punishest my sins in this world to spare me in the next. My heart is ready, O my God, my heart is ready to suffer still more if such be Thy holy will." St. Bonaventure says, that he was often tormented in this manner by demons; but that these proud spirits, not being able either to overcome him, or to bear his constancy, retired in confusion. Such a resistance would repress all the efforts of the tempter when he attacks us invisibly.

In the morning, he could not disguise from his companions what had happened to him, and the extreme weakness which it had brought on obliged him to desire his companions to go to the neighboring village, to procure for him, in God's name, some means of riding on with them. The farmer to whom they applied, having learnt that it was for Francis of Assisi, of whom he had heard so much good spoken, went to fetch his own ass to carry him on, during the journey.

On the way, Francis bethought himself of stopping for a short time at this farmer's to recruit his strength by some poultry and other delicacies of the country; but, wishing to punish himself for having merely listened to such a suggestion, he took up a half-rotten fowl from a dunghill, and smelt at it, saying to himself:—"Here, glutton! here is the flesh of the poultry that you so anxiously wished for; satisfy your longing, and eat as much as you like." To support himself, he ate nothing but bread, on which he sprinkled ashes, and he drank nothing but water. He blessed the house of his host, and promised him very long lineage, who should be neither poor nor very rich. The remembrance of this prediction has been carefully preserved in this place, and the house still exists, bearing the name of St. Francis, where the religious of his Order are always charitably received. This lesson is taught by the apostle:—"That God, by His blessing, gives to charitable persons the means of continuing and multiplying their good works."

The invalid was replaced on the ass, and they took the road to Chiusi which they reached by noon. Count Orlando was greatly pleased to see them, and would have been but too glad to detain them, if only for that day; but Francis would go as soon as dinner was done to Mount Alvernia, whither the count accompanied him.

> "The Mountain Alvernia is on the confines of Tuscany, not far from Camaldoli and Val Ombrosa; it is part of the Apennines, and it rises higher than the adjacent mountains from which it is separated: two rivers flow at its foot, the Tiber and the Arno. On their sides it has rocks so perpendicular and so smooth that they might be mistaken for walls; and on the side on which the top may be reached, no one would dare to attempt the ascent but for the number of beech trees and underwood which hide the precipices. These trees, which are very lofty, hide some extensive and beautiful pasturages. There also an abundance of plants is found called carline or Caroline which is a cure for the plague."

The farmer, who was their guide, made bold to address Francis thus: "Brother, I hear much good spoken of you, and I understand that God has shown you great favors, for which you are greatly indebted to Him; strive, then, to be what it is said you are, and never to change in order that those who have confidence in you may not be deceived; this is a piece of advice I give you." Francis, delighted at what he had heard, dismounted, kissed the man's feet, thanked him, acknowledging the great mercy of God, who had been pleased to cast His eyes on the lowliness of His servant. Although this advice came from a poor countryman, it was nevertheless the very best that could be given to a saint. So true it is that no one should be despised, and that the most simple-minded persons often say more sensible and more spiritual things than men of the greatest genius.

The same man being very thirsty at the steepest part of the mountain, exclaimed loudly: "I shall die, if I cannot get something to drink." Francis immediately alighted, threw himself on his knees, raised his hands to heaven, and prayed until he knew that he had been heard. Then, pointing out a large stone to the man, he said, "Go there quickly, and you will find some living water: it is Jesus Christ who, out of His great mercy, makes it spring from this rock that you may drink." The man ran directly, found water, and drank as much as he required.

No spring had ever been known to be in that place, and no water was ever found there afterwards. Wonderful goodness of the Almighty, exclaims St. Bonaventure, who thus with so much benevolence grants the prayers of His servants. The birds seeing St. Francis and his companions approaching came in great numbers to welcome him to their home.

At length they reached the top of Mount Alvernia, where the religious resided. The father was well pleased with their dwelling, because everything was on a small scale and poor.

Count Orlando returned in the evening and came back next day, bringing something for their dinner. After they had finished their meal, he gave orders for the construction of a small chapel under a very tall beech tree, and a cell, which Francis had asked him for, and, calling the others aside, he said: "Since your founder has given his consent to the donation I made you two years ago of this mountain, you may consider it as yours, and hence both myself and mine will be always devoted to your service whenever you shall need it. You will not be able to please me more than by addressing yourselves to me, looking upon me as your servant; and even, if you will do me that favor, considering me as one of your brethren." After the departure of the count, the holy Patriarch made them the following discourse, relative to the count's kindness, which they took care to commit to writing:

> "My dear children, it is God who thus turns the hearts of the faithful towards His little and useless servants, in which He does us a very great favor. On what we have hitherto received let us place our hopes for what is to come; if that seems but little, the Lord, who is infinitely liberal, will add to it by His goodness still greater benefits, provided we are faithful to Him. Let us, then, leave to Him the care of all that relates to you, and He Himself will feed you, as He fed Elias, Paul, and Anthony in the desert. The birds of the air neither sow, nor reap, nor gather into barns, yet your Heavenly Father nourishes them; how much more will He do this for His servants? If He tries you, it will be only for a time, for it is written, that

He will not suffer the just to waver forever; the eyes of the Lord are on them that fear Him, and on them that hope in His mercy to deliver their souls from death and feed them in famine. Trust not to the princes of the earth, nor to the charitable offers made you by our benefactor, Count Orlando, for cursed is the man that trusteth in man, and maketh flesh his arm. This lord has acted nobly by us, and according to his piety; let us do on our parts what depends on us, and fail not therein; that is to say, let us not have recourse to his generosity, as to a treasure of which we are the masters, and in that regard let us have the greatest reserve that we may not in any respect trench upon holy poverty. Be sure, my dear children, that our best resource for providing for our wants, is to have none to provide for. If we are truly evangelical poor, the world will have compassion upon us, and will generously give us all that is necessary for our subsistence; but if we swerve from holy poverty, the world will shun us; the illicit means which we might take for avoiding indigence, would only make us feel it the more." Is not such a discourse sufficient to show us, that St. Francis had great talents and judgment, joined to great knowledge of the practice of virtue?

Count Orlando had a church built on Mount Alvernia, according to the plan which the Saint had given him, which, it was confidently said, had been given to Francis by the Blessed Virgin, who appeared accompanied by St. John the Baptist, and St. John the Evangelist.

While they were at work at this building and at the cells for the brethren, Francis explored the mountain on all its sides, to discover the sites best adapted for contemplation. He found one, where there were some large openings in the rock, great masses overhanging them, deep caverns, and frightful pits; and what seemed to him to be most curious, there was a rock so split that the interior formed a room with a smooth flooring, and a sort of ceiling which had a small opening which admitted the light. He was anxious to know whether this was the natural formation of the rock, or whether it was not the effect of an earthquake; and, after having recited the seven penitential psalms, he begged God to grant him information on this head. An angel acquainted him, in an apparition, that this had happened at the death of Jesus Christ, when the earth shook and the rocks were rent asunder. This circumstance gave Mount Alvernia additional value in the eyes of the servant of Jesus Christ crucified. He never afterwards saw these openings without thinking of the sufferings his Divine Master endured on the cross, and without wishing that his feelings of compassion might break his heart. In the opinion of the holy Fathers, the rocks which were rent when Jesus Christ expired were reproaches to the Jews for the hardness of their hearts, and this reproach falls equally on Christians who are insensible to His sufferings.

We can have no difficulty in thinking, with Cardinal Baronius, that the rocks on Mount Alvernia were split at the death of our Saviour, since the earthquake was universal, according to the opinions of Eusebius, St. Jerome, and many others, and even according to the testimony of pagan authors.

It is also very credible that the Son of God has manifested to His special servants, some of the effects of this motion of the earth, in order to impress more vividly on their minds the remembrance of His Passion; and may we not think that the Lord, who is the beholder of all ages, as the wise man says, and who had selected Mount Alvernia as the place in which He would do His Servant Francis the favor of imprinting the stigmata on him, as we shall see further on, was pleased to give this mountain some resemblance to that of Calvary, where St. Cyril of Jerusalem assures us, that in his time the rents caused by the earthquake were seen?

Among the masses of rock on Mount Alvernia, there is one much more elevated and much larger than the rest, and which is separated from them by precipices, to which there is no access but by throwing a bridge across. There, as in an insulated citadel, a celebrated brigand had his stronghold, who was called the Wolf, on account of the plunder and murders he committed in the surrounding country, either by himself, or by the gang of which he was the chief. He often, also, by means of a flying bridge, confined travellers in this place, whom he had surprised on the high-roads, and whom he detained till their ransom was paid. The establishment of Francis and his brethren displeased him greatly: people of that sort do not like having neighbors. He gave them several times notice to begone, and he threatened them should they not obey. Their great poverty gave them nothing to fear from thieves, but there was just cause for apprehending that the murderer might massacre them all. Divine Providence, however, saved them by a change which might well be called the work of the Most High. The villain came one day determined upon expelling them, and used the most atrocious language to them. Francis received him with so much mildness, listened to him with so much patience, and induced him by degrees to hear reason, so that his anger entirely fell, and he not only consented to their remaining, but he begged that they would admit him into their poor dwelling. He witnessed during several days their angelic mode of life, and he became so changed, that he determined upon adopting a similar plan. The Saint perceiving that from a ravenous wolf he was become a gentle lamb, gave him the habit of the Order, and the name of Brother Agnello, under which he expiated his crimes by religious penance, of which he rigidly fulfilled all the duties. This fact was of such notoriety, that the rock to which he used to retire has always been called since, and is still known, by the name of Brother Wolf's prison.

All things being put in order at Mount Alvernia, he left it to go to Rome. He passed through Monte Casale, Fabriano, Osimo, Ancona, Macerata, Ascoli, Camerino, and many other places, preaching in all the truths of salvation, gaining disciples, founding houses for his Order, prophesying and working miracles; we shall only put on record here the most remarkable, and those that are most edifying.

God favored him, as He had done St. Ambrose, with power of discovering relics which were hidden. He knew by revelation that there were some in a certain church in which he had prayed, and some business calling him away from thence, he communicated the circumstance to his brethren, desiring them to take them from thence and place them in a more suitable situation; but they either through forgetfulness or neglect did not do so. One day as they were preparing the altar for Mass, they found under the altar-cloth some beautiful bones, from which a sweet perfumed smell issued, and they immediately recollected that these were the relics of which their Father had spoken. At his return he inquired whether they had been disinterred, and the religious, having told him exactly what had occurred, he said: "Blessed be the Lord, my God, who, of His goodness, has done what you ought to have done out of obedience;" but he imposed a penance upon them in expiation of their fault. At the Monastery of Monte Maggiore, a joy and interior consolation which he felt on entering the church, made him sensible that the high altar contained something which had been used by the Blessed Virgin. He spoke of it to the religious, who searched closely, and found that it was true. In ecclesiastical history we find that God had often caused the relics of His saints to be discovered, in order to do them honor, and the Holy Fathers have taught the faithful to venerate them and to preserve them with great care.

While he was preaching at Fabriano in the middle of the market-place, some workmen who were employed at a palace made so much noise, that it prevented his being heard. Having entreated them to be quiet for a short time, to which they paid no attention, he said that the work of those who were building the house would be of no use, because the Lord did not build it, but that it would soon fall; however, that neither man nor beast would be injured by it; and this happened but a few days after it had been finished, as he had foretold. He assured the people at the same town, that at a place called the Poor Valley, his brethren, who were poor, would some day have a habitation. And, in fact, in the year 1292, the town of Fabriano placed Friars Minor there.

When he had reached his convent, Clare, who, being very humble, had accepted only through obedience the quality of Abbess of St. Damian, wished to lay it down into his hands, to which he would by no means assent, because he knew that by the disposition of Divine Providence, she was to form the disciples who were to establish his Order in various places, from whence it was to spread throughout the Church.

Clare had admitted many virgins during the three years she had presided over St. Damian, among whom were some of her own relatives. Beatrice, the youngest of her sisters, came a short time afterwards; and Hortolona, her mother, as soon as she became a widow, decided upon consecrating herself to God, with her three daughters, in the same monastery, where miracles testified to the holiness of her life. Finally, the virtues of Clare were so resplendent, and the miracles which it pleased the Almighty to work by her means, threw so much splendor around her, that, according to the remark of Pope Alexander IV, in the bull of her canonization, the truth of the prediction which was made to her mother, was clearly seen:—"That she would give to the world a light which would even enlighten the world." The sequel of the life of the Father will afford further opportunity for speaking of the daughter.

The Benedictines of Mount Soubazo, in this year, gave the holy Patriarch a convent on this very mountain, two miles from Assisi. It has been called the prison of St. Francis, because he often shut himself up there in contemplation after his Apostolical labors. His oratory is still there, also: his cell, the stone and the wood which served him for bed and pillow, and a copious spring which, by his intercession, he obtained from God.

From the beginning of the following year, 1216, to the 30th of May, the Festival of Whitsuntide, the day on which the general chapter was held, which was the first of the Order, he had as much leisure as he could desire for conversing with God, for giving instruction to his brethren at St. Mary of the Angels, and to the Town of Assisi and its environs. In the assembly, provincial ministers were appointed, to whom power was given for admitting postulants into the Order; which the Founder had previously reserved to himself. One whose name does not appear, was sent into Apulia, and John de Strachia was sent into Lombardy; Benedict of Arezzo, into the Marches of Ancona; Daniel the Tuscan, into Calabria; Augustin of Assisi, into the Terra di Lavoro; Elias of Cortona, into Tuscany. Evangelical laborers were chosen for different nations. Bernard de Quintavalle, for Spain; John Bonella, a Florentine, with thirty companions, for Provence; John de Penna, and sixty of his brethren, for Upper and Lower Germany; Francis took for his share Paris and what is properly called France and the Low Countries.

Among the most considerable establishments which he placed on his route, was that of St. Mary of the Stony Valley, so called from its being situated in a very rocky valley, between two mountains, four miles distant from Fabriano. It was a church dedicated to the Blessed Virgin, with a monastery, which the Religious of St. Benedict had abandoned in order to take refuge in the town, on account of the wars, and it is one of the most beautiful solitudes of all Italy. Devotion to the Mother of God, and the love of retreat, had induced Francis to ask for this place; and it was given him by those who were its proprietors. The first time he went there, he lost his way, with his companion, and asked a ploughman to take him to the valley. "What," says the man, "shall I leave my plough and lose my time, to serve you?" However, he took him to the place, mollified by Francis' mildness, and by his promising him that he should be no loser by so doing: on returning, after receiving the Father's blessing, he found his field quite ploughed.

Some workmen who were employed repairing a house which had been given him, at a place called Trabe Bonata, being very tired, asked him to give them some wine. He sent two of his brethren to procure some in a neighboring village, from some charitable benefactor; but the workmen being very urgent, out of compassion for them he went to a spring, made the sign of the cross over it, and in an instant, instead of water, wine issued from it, which flowed for a whole hour. Those who drank of it published in all places the miraculous effect of the Saint's charity.

In a parish called La Citta, he was very well received by the curate, whose name was Raniero, with whom he became very intimate, so that he was in the habit of visiting him, and going to confession to him. One day after confession he gave him, in a very humble manner, notice, that he, the curate, would become one of his brethren, because they had become too closely united to live different kinds of lives: "But," he said, "this will not happen till after my death." The event verified the prediction: as soon as the curate learnt that his friend Francis shone by an infinity of miracles, and was just canonized, he entered the Order of Friars Minor, and adhered to the rules with great regularity.

The holy man coming to Osimo, was greeted, notwithstanding his great humility, and brought into the town, with great honors. The next day he preached on the vanity of the world, in so persuasive a strain, that all his hearers, penetrated with compunction, turned their thoughts seriously to their reformation, and thirty young men entered his Institute.

On the same journey, he and his companions lodged at the house of a gentleman, the greatness of whose soul equalled the antiquity of his nobility, and whose politeness was joined to piety. The welcome he received there was followed by this open-hearted proffer: "Man of God," he said, "I place my person at your disposal, and all that I possess, all is yours, do as you please with it; if you want clothing, or a cloak, or books, or whatever it may be, take it, and I will pay for it. Be assured that I am wholly at your service. God has given me wealth; I have wherewithal to assist the poor, and it is but just that I do not fail in so doing."

Francis merely at the time contented himself with making those grateful acknowledgments which so handsome and obliging an offer required; but when he left him, he could not refrain from admiring the generosity of this gentleman, and he said to his companion: "Indeed, brother, he would be an excellent subject for our Order; he is humbly thankful for what he has received from God; he loves his neighbor very sincerely; he gives willingly to the poor; and he exercises hospitality from his heart; he is extremely affable and polite; and politeness is sister to charity; it puts down contention and promotes concord; he is naturally benevolent; and this feeling is highly pleasing to our Father who is in Heaven, who causes the sun to rise on the good and on the wicked. So many excellent qualities which I see in this young man, make me wish to have him to be one of us, and I should admit him with pleasure. We must pay him another visit, and exhort him to devote himself to the service of God; perhaps the Holy Ghost may incline him to do so; meanwhile let us implore the Lord to grant our wish, if He judges it right." In fact, they did pray for this purpose.

Some days afterwards they returned to this person's house, who had the curiosity to watch what Francis did in the night; he saw him in prayer, and in an ecstasy raised from the ground, and surrounded by a splendid light, and he felt interiorly a certain celestial fire, which inspired him with an ardent desire to imitate his mode of life. In the morning, he communicated his feelings to the Saint, who was already made aware of them by revelation, and who thanked the Giver of all good gifts for them. The postulant gave all he had to the poor, took the habit of a Friar Minor, and lived holily; preserving always the same affable and polite manners, with which he received the guests of the convents in which he resided. This endeared him still more to the Patriarch, who was very zealous in the exercise of hospitality. The duties of hospitality, lauded by the pagans, taught by the Gospel, enforced by the Apostles, and all the Holy Fathers, are exercised in the Order of St. Francis with so much the more care as, being totally dependent on charity, they consider themselves bound to give all in the same manner, and they apply to themselves these words of the Son of God to the Apostles, on the gift of miracles: "Freely you have received, freely give." This is what draws down the blessing of G which makes so many houses subsist, without any revenue, by the ch the faithful.

The holy Patriarch of the Friars Minor arrived at Rome when ev was preparing for the opening of the Twelfth Ecumenical Council, th Lateran, one of the most numerous ever held in the Church. Innocent convoked it for the extinction of heresies, for the reformation of mo regulating the discipline of the Church, and for the recovery of the Ho by the union of the Christian princes.

Francis came to Rome to induce the Sovereign Pontiff to give approval to the Rule of his Order, which was of the highest impor order that the prelates might have it in their power to distinguish the Jesus Christ, true children of the Church, from certain sectaries of tho who affected, as has been already said, to bear the marks of Apostolic

What the Servant of God required was put in force; the Pope before all the Fathers of the Council, that he approved the Order and of St. Francis, although he had hitherto issued no bull. This is a fact related by the companions of the Saint who wrote his life, and by two of the Order of St. Dominic, Jordan of Saxony, a disciple of that Patriarch, and St. Antoninus. Moreover, in order to avoid too great a v religious orders, the council prohibited the formation of any new o directed that the existing ones should be considered sufficient. Yet it that the Pope could not, in this instance, avoid making known the app he had given to an Order so new and peculiar as was that of the Friars which in the last five years, had spread over Italy, and was establ Rome.

The holy friendship which was subsequently formed between St. and St. Francis, renders it proper that we should here record that St. came also to this Lateran Council, together with Fulke, Bishop of Tou order to propose to the pope an intention he had of instituting an preachers, and that the Pope had seen in a dream St. Dominic suppo Lateran Church, which was falling, in the same way as he had seen supporting it five years before. He praised his undertaking, but tc according to the decree of the council, to return with his brethren, and a rule for the guidance of the order, and then come back to have th confirmed, which the holy patriarch complied with.

The Council of Lateran having terminated its labors, Francis left the beginning of December to return to St. Mary of the Angels.

The Apostolic laborers being all assembled at the feet of their Father, to receive his orders, he addressed them with paternal tenderness, in the following discourse:—

"In the name of the Lord, go forth modestly, two and two, observing strict silence from the morning till after the hour of Tierce, praying to God from your hearts. Let no idle or useless words be heard among you; although you are travelling, your deportment should be as humble and as decorous as if you were in a hermitage, or in your cells. For wherever we are, and, whithersoever we may be going, we have always our vocation with us; our brother, the body, is our cell, and the soul is the hermit, who dwells in it to think of God and to pray to Him. If a religious soul does not dwell quietly in the cell of the body, the external cells will be of little use to him. Behave, then, in such manner in the world, that whosoever may see or hear you, may be moved to devotion, and praise our Heavenly Father to whom alone all glory belongs. Proclaim peace to all men, but have it in your hearts, as well as in your mouths. Give to no one cause for anger, nor for scandal; on the contrary, by your own mildness, induce every one to feel benignly, and draw them to union and to concord. We are called to heal the wounded, console the afflicted, and to bring back those who err; many may seem to you to be members of the devil, who will one day be disciples of Jesus Christ." What Francis said of the inutility of exterior cells, where the soul is not at ease in the cell of the body, is in conformity to these words of St. Bernard:—"You may be alone when you are in the midst of the world, as it may so happen that you may be in the midst of the world when you are alone."

The children of the holy Patriarch received his blessing; and having recommended themselves to the prayers of their companions, they set out for those places to which obedience sent them. The success of the several labors will be adverted to further on. The missionaries for Provence remained some days after the breaking up of the chapter, to receive further instructions relative to their mission. The day of their departure, there were only three loaves of bread in the convent, two of which had been sent there by Clare; these were found sufficient for more than thirty who were present, and there was a great deal to spare, a circumstance which was considered to be a good omen.

Francis, having animated all the others by his zeal, prepared himself for setting out for Paris. Besides the natural affection he had for France, of which he liked the language, as it was familiar to him, he chose this city preferably to many others, because he knew that their devotion was great towards the blessed sacrament, and this was a great attraction for his piety.

May the Parisians ever entertain and transmit to their posterity this fervent devotion of their ancestors, which Pope Urban IV., who was a native of France, stirred up in the hearts of the faithful forty-six years afterwards, by the institution of the Feast of the Most Holy Sacrament, which is celebrated throughout the Church, with so much solemnity. The bull which he issued on this occasion, enters into the strongest and most moving arguments calculated to inspire veneration, love, and the zeal which the precious memorial of the goodness of the Son of God calls for, and to invite to a frequent and worthy participation in the divine mystery, which the Council of Trent has since expressed its anxiety to see reestablished.

Before his departure, Francis undertook to reconcile the members of the illustrious family of the Baselennesi, a long time disunited by unhappy family dissensions, and he succeeded to the satisfaction of all parties. Out of gratitude they had built for him, on one of their estates on a spot near the Tiber, surrounded with very beautiful trees, a convent called St. Angel of Pantanellis.

He chose to go once more to Rome to recommend to the holy Apostles his journey to France. On the road, having seated himself close to a spring to take his meal, he put some pieces of bread, which had been given to him on his quest, and which were very hard and mouldy, on a stone near him; he expressed much satisfaction, and he pressed his companion Masse to give thanks to God for so great a treasure; and he repeated several times the same thing, elevating his voice more and more. "But of what treasure are you talking" said Masse, "at a time when we are in want of many things?" "The great treasure is," replied Francis, "that, being in want of so much, God has had the goodness to furnish us by His providence with that bread and this spring, and to find us this stone to serve as a table."

He went shortly after into a church, where he prayed to God to give him and his children the love of holy poverty; and his prayer was so fervent that fire seemed to issue from his countenance. Full of this celestial ardor, he went towards Masse with open arms, calling him by name with a loud voice; Masse, in great astonishment, going to throw himself into the arms of his Father, was raised into the air several cubits high, and felt such sweetness in his soul, that he frequently afterwards declared that he had never experienced anything like it. After this ecstasy, Francis spoke to him on the subject of poverty in an admirable strain.

When at Rome, in a chapel of the Church of St. Peter, while he was praying with tears that the holy Apostles would give him instructions on the subject of holy poverty and of an Apostolic life, they appeared to him surrounded by lights, and, after tenderly embracing him, said: "Brother Francis, our Lord Jesus Christ has sent us to tell you that He has favorably heard your prayers and tears on the subject of holy poverty, which He Himself had followed, as well as His Blessed Mother, and we, who are His Apostles, after his example. This treasure is granted to you for yourself and for your children; those who shall carefully adhere to it, will have the kingdom of heaven for their reward." The Servant of God, filled with consolation, went to his companion Masse, to whom he communicated what had passed, and they went together to give thanks at the place which is called the Confession of St. Peter, which is his tomb.

While Francis was at Rome, Pope Innocent III died at Perugia. He was of the illustrious house of the Counts of Segni, which has given five popes to the Church, the last of whom was Innocent XIII, of blessed memory. It was at the University of Paris that his merit was first noticed; he shone there above the many who were its honor and its ornament. It was his rare and transcendent qualities which induced the cardinals unanimously to elect him to the pontificate; and these qualities shone with additional splendor when his humility urged his resistance to the election, from which he prayed with unaffected tears to be released. His government and the works he has left to posterity, show, that he had great genius, great science, prudence, and probity, with solid piety, and ardent zeal. "He was," says a French contemporary writer "a man of great courage and great wisdom, who had no equal in his day, and who did marvellous things." He was indeed one of the most eminent men who have filled the chair of St. Peter. The affection he bore to Francis, and the favors he conferred on his Order, have compelled us to do this justice here to his memory.

On the 18th of July, they elected for his successor Cardinal Savelli, who took the name of Honorius III. He was a learned and worthy man. He generally followed the designs of his predecessor, and had a similar affection for the religious orders, of which he gave substantial proofs in the favors he bestowed on that of St. Francis.

Some months after his election, he gave his approval of the Order of St. Dominic. This holy patriarch having returned to his companions to fix upon a rule, as had been recommended to him by Pope Innocent at the Lateran Council, and having adopted the rule of St. Augustine, to which he had added some more austere regulations, came back to Rome to procure the approval of the Holy See. While he solicited it from Honorius, who had arrived from Perugia, he made acquaintance and contracted an intimacy with Francis, in consequence of a miraculous vision which he had in the Church of St. Peter, where he prayed unceasingly with great fervor for the success of his enterprise.

He saw the Son of God seated on the right hand of His Father, who rose up greatly irritated against sinners, holding three darts in His hand, for the extirpation of the proud, the avaricious, and the voluptuous. His holy Mother threw herself at His feet, and prayed for mercy, saying that she had persons who would remedy the evil; and she at the same time introduced to Him Dominic and Francis, as being proper persons for reforming the world, and reestablishing piety; this pacified Jesus Christ.

Dominic, who had never seen Francis, met him next day, recognized him, ran to him and embraced him, saying: "You are my companion; we will work in concert with each other; let us be strictly united, and no one will be able to master us." Francis himself communicated this favor of Heaven to the children of Dominic: and St. Vincent Ferrer, and some other authors quoted by Wading, say that Francis had received a similar favor from Heaven. The event proved the truth of the Vision. Dominic alone, without any human aid, having nothing to command success but poverty, humility, and prayer, obtained the approbation of his order, which was an affair of great difficulty, particularly at the commencement of a Pontificate, when the Pope is occupied by most important affairs.

We may here notice the groundwork of the ardent zeal of the Friars Preachers and the Friars Minor for the glory of the Mother of God. Persuaded that their orders were established under her protection, and that she is especially the mother of their holy patriarchs, they strive by every means in their power to restore the devout veneration due to her. It is the common interest of all the faithful who see that she is, according to the expression of the Holy Fathers, their advocate and their mediatrix; that she prays and solicits for them; that she interposes between them and the wrath of her Son, and appeases Him: this affords great room for confidence in her, and should induce them to invoke her for their conversion and sanctification.

Dominic and Francis, confident of the protection of the Blessed Virgin, entered into a strict friendship and resolved to spare no pains in their exertions for the glory of God, and concerted together as to the best means for attaining their object. Upon which an author quoted by Wading, makes a most appropriate reflection: "It was," he says, "something admirable to see two men, who were poor, badly clad, without power or interest despicable in the eyes of the world, divide between them the world itself, and undertake to conquer it. Who would not have turned their plans into ridicule hearing them seriously consult together on such an undertaking, since they seemed to have so little means of carrying them into execution? Nevertheless, they succeeded; because God selected by their means to confound what is strong." They resembled St. Peter and St. Paul, proposing to themselves, in the same City of Rome, to convert the universe by the preaching of the Gospel; this shows that God made use of means for reanimating the faith, similar to those which He had employed to establish it.

It is reported, that while Dominic and Francis were still at Rome, Angelus, of the Order of the Carmelites, who was afterwards martyred in Sicily, was also there; that, preaching in the Church of St. John Lateran, where the two others were among the hearers, he foretold that they would become two great pillars of the Church; that when the sermon was finished, they foretold to one another what would happen to each of them, and even that Francis would receive the stigmata; then the three together cured a man afflicted with leprosy, and passed a day and a night together in prayer and conversing on holy subjects.

Francis left Rome at the end of the year, intending to continue his journey into France. He passed through Sienna and by Mount Alvernia and arrived at Florence in the month of January, 1217, to pay his dutiful respects to Cardinal Ugolino, who was Papal Legate there. This cardinal, who had declared himself his protector and his friend, when he went to request the approbation of his rule from Pope Innocent III., in 1210, received him with great kindness, detained him some days, inquired into the affairs of his Order, and said to him on the subject of his journey: "Francis, your Order is still in its infancy. You know the opposition it met with in Rome, and you have still there some secret enemies; if there is not some one there to watch over your interests, it will be an easy matter to cause all you have obtained to be revoked. Your presence will go a great way in upholding your work, and those who are attached to you will have a greater stimulus for giving you their support. As to myself, I am from this moment wholly yours."

The holy man, after having thanked the cardinal, replied: "I have sent many of my brethren into far distant countries. If I remain quietly in our convent, without taking any share in their labors, it will be a great shame for me; and these poor religious, who are suffering hunger and thirst, will have great reason to murmur and complain; but instead of that, if they find that I work as much as they do, they will bear their fatigues more willingly, and I shall more easily persuade them to undertake similar missions."

The cardinal, feeling for the sufferings of these missionaries, said: "But why, brother, have you the harshness to expose your disciples to such arduous journeying and to so much suffering?" "My Lord," replied Francis, who was urged by a prophetic spirit, "you think that God has sanctioned the Institute for this country only; but I tell you that He has formed it for the good of the universe, and for the salvation of all men, without excluding the infidels: for religious of this Order will go into their territories; and provided they live in conformity to the Gospel, God will provide amply for all their wants, even among the enemies of His name."

These words made a great impression on the cardinal, who was a very holy man, and increased his affection for Francis, whom he again exhorted in stronger language than before, to remain in Italy to consolidate an Institute which was to have such beneficial results. The Saint having yielded to the reasoning of the cardinal, entreated him to be the protector of the Friars Minor, according to his promise, and to be so good as to be present at the next general chapter; after which he took the road to the Valley of Spoleto.

There he learnt that some of his brethren had been seriously ill-treated by several prelates, and that at the court of Rome there were persons who spoke against his Order. This news confirmed him in the resolution he had taken to remain in Italy; and he named three of his disciples for the French mission, to wit: Pacificus of the Marches of Ancona, the celebrated poet, whose conversion we have related; Angelus, and Albert, both of Pisa.

He likewise intended to request the Pope to nominate a cardinal of the Holy Roman Church, to protect his Order against all who should attack it. Three of his companions, the writers of his life, say, that he was induced to this by a celestial vision in his sleep. He saw a hen endeavoring to gather all her chickens under her wings, to protect them from a hawk; she could not cover them all, and many were about to become its prey; but another large bird appeared, spread its wings over them, and preserved them from the danger. On awaking, Francis prayed our Lord to explain to him the meaning of this, and he learnt that the hen represented himself, and the chickens were his disciples, that the bird with the large wings represented the cardinal, whom they were to solicit for their protector. He told all this to his brethren, and addressed them as follows:—

"The Roman Church is the mother of all the churches, and the sovereign of all religious orders. It is to her that I shall address myself to recommend to her my brethren, in order that her authority may silence those who are hostile to them, and that she may procure for the children of God full and perfect liberty to advance quietly in the way of eternal salvation; for when they shall be under her protection, there will be no more enemies to oppose them, nor disturb them; there will not be seen among them any son of Belial to ravage with impunity the vineyard of the Lord. The holy Church will be zealous for the glory of our poverty; she will not suffer that the humility which is so honorable to her, shall be obscured by the clouds of pride. It is she who will render indissoluble among us, the bonds of charity and peace, rigorously punishing the authors of dissensions. Under her eyes, the holy evangelical observance will ever flourish in its pristine purity; she will never permit these holy practices to flag even momentarily, those practices which shed around them a vivifying light. May the children, then, of that holy Church be very grateful for the great favors which they receive from their mother; let them kiss her feet with profound veneration, and remain forever inviolably attached to her."

The first words of this discourse show that St. Francis was perfectly cognizant of the prerogatives of the Church of Rome, and of the extent of the authority of the Holy See. It was not in vain that he sought her protection, since his Order was established, extended, supported, and sometimes even renovated under this powerful authority; and the attachment to the Holy See, which he so strongly recommended to his brethren, has been so visibly manifested during five centuries, that it has procured for them the esteem and love of all Catholics, as well as the hatred of the heretics, so that they have the honor of having some share in the eulogiums which St. Jerome passed on St. Augustine: "The Catholics esteem and respect you, and, what enhances your glory, all the heretics detest you. They hold me in equal hatred; and if they durst not put both the one and the other of us to death, they have at least the wish to do so." This wish of the heretics has not been without effect as regards the children of St. Francis, for of a thousand martyrs which they reckon in his Order, a very great number of them were put to death with greater cruelty in this and latter times by the sectarians than by idolatrous tyrants. Heresy will be ever so, the daughter of a parent, who, according to the words of Jesus Christ, was a murderer from the beginning.

The holy Patriarch went then to Rome, where he found Cardinal Ugolino, who was returned from Tuscany, to whom he communicated the intention he had of soliciting the pope for a protector. The cardinal at the same time expressed his wish to hear him preach before the pope and the sacred college. Francis excused himself from this as much as he could, assigning for reasons, his ignorance, his simplicity, and his uncultivated mind, which unfitted him for speaking in the most august assembly in the world. But he was obliged to yield to the pressing instances of the cardinal, who entreated him as a friend to comply, and even ordered him to prepare himself for the task, recommending him to compose carefully a sermon wherein there should be as much erudition and reasoning as such an audience required.

Up to that time, the Servant of God had never prepared himself for preaching; he only spoke from the pulpit what the Holy Ghost inspired. Nevertheless, he, in this instance, obeyed the cardinal; he prepared a sermon as carefully as he could, and learned it by heart. When he came into the presence of the Pope, he forgot every part of the discourse, and could not utter a syllable of it. But after having humbly explained the circumstance, and implored the aid of the Holy Ghost, words flowed copiously from his mouth, and he spoke with so much eloquence and animation, that the Pope and cardinal were deeply affected.

Having been admitted to an audience of the Pope in presence of Cardinal Ugolino, he said: "Most Holy Father, I am not in fear of becoming importunate for the interests of your lowly servants, the Friars Minor, while you are occupied with so many important affairs which regard the whole Church. I entreat you to give us this cardinal, to whom we may have recourse in our wants, always under your sanction, since it is from you, the Head of the mystical Body, that all power emanates." The Pope granted his request with alacrity, and recommended the cardinal to take great care of the Order. From that time, the Orders of Friars Minor have always had a cardinal protector, whose powers are extended as the Pope shall see fit; the terms of the Rule, which oblige the Order by obedience to apply for one, show, that it was the intention of Francis, that his powers should be most ample.

Cardinal Ugolino was one of the most accomplished men of the City of Rome; his person well made, his countenance mild and majestic, his genius quick, with great memory and eloquence, possessing in perfection all human sciences, civil and canon-law, and particularly the Holy Scriptures; he was very expert in all public business; a lover of virtue and order, and of a pure and exemplary life.

His first care in undertaking the office of protector, which he did willingly, was, to defend the Friars against all those who attacked them, to conciliate the prelates in their favor and to spread them into all parts for the salvation of souls; his great authority silenced their enemies. As often as his affairs admitted of it, he assisted at their general chapters; then he officiated pontifically. Francis acted as his deacon, and preached. He conformed to the rule of the Institute as much as was in his power, and was, when with them, as one of themselves, and even endeavored to appear as the lowest among them.

A contemporary author, who was an ocular witness, expresses himself thus: "O how often has he been seen humbly to divest himself of the marks of his high dignity; put on the poor habit, and, with bare feet, join the religious in the regular exercises, in order to imitate their evangelical life!" A lively and enlightened faith, a solid and fervent piety, and a superior mind, convinced him that since the time of the abasement of the Son of God, humiliation is honorable, and adds to the splendor of the highest dignities; a truth which is not understood by persons of little faith, by the proud, the indevout, and those of little mind.

This great cardinal respected Francis as much as he loved him; looking upon him as a man sent down from heaven. His presence was a source of pleasure to him, and he often admitted, as the above-quoted author states, that from the time he had made acquaintance with this holy man, as soon as he saw him and heard him speak, all that caused in him uneasiness of mind, or grief at heart was dispelled; his countenance became serene, and his soul was filled with fervor.

Francis, on his side, had great veneration for the cardinal. He insisted on his brethren considering him as the Pastor of the Flock, and, with an attachment as tender as that of an infant for its mother's breast, he gave him in all things marks of the profoundest deference. One day, hearing that he was about to receive a visit from him he ran away and hid himself in the thickest part of the wood. The cardinal had him sought for, and went himself in search for him. Having found him he asked Francis as his friend to tell why he avoided him. "My Lord and my Father," answered the humble Francis, "as soon as I knew that your Grandeur intended to honor me with your presence, me who am the poorest and the most despicable of men, I was covered with confusion, and I blushed at the thought of my baseness, finding myself wholly unworthy to receive so distinguished an honor, for I truly revere you as my Lord and my Father." These feelings were partly owing to a vision he had, which revealed to him that this cardinal would be Pope; he foretold it to him,—this is recorded by St. Bonaventure; and in the private letters which he wrote to him, he put on the heading: To my Reverend Father and Lord Ugolino, who is one day to be the Bishop of the whole world, and the Father of all nations.

The respectful gratitude of the Friars Minor required that we should insert all these anecdotes in memory of Cardinal Ugolino, who honored the holy Patriarch of his Order, as well as that of St. Clare, with his affection, his protection, and his liberality, and who surpassed all his former favors ten years afterwards, when he was Pope under the name of Gregory IX.

When Francis had obtained from the Pope so powerful a protector, and had put his various affairs in order, he set out on his return to St. Mary of the Angels, but he spent the remainder of the year in the Valley of Rieti, where he performed many wonderful things, of which one of his companions has given a very ample account.

At Grecio, or Grecchia, a very dissolute town in which he first preached, no one frequented the Sacraments; no one listened to the Word of God, and marriages within the prohibited degrees were of ordinary occurrence.—By word and example he urged them to repentance and made such an impression that they entreated him to make some brothers stay among them. He willingly agreed to do so, in the hope of their conversion, which took place in a short time; meanwhile he retired to a mountain, from whence he came to Grecio and other places to preach.

On returning one day from Cotanello, a neighboring town, and not being able to find the way to the mountain, he asked a farmer to be his guide. This man excusing himself, saying that there were wolves in that direction that committed great havoc, Francis promised him, and pledged himself as his surety, that he should not be attacked by any wolf either in going or coming back; he found that the Saint was correct, for, in returning, two wolves which were in the way, played with him as dogs do, and followed him to his house without doing him any harm. The farmer reported this over all his neighborhood, and said that, assuredly, the man to whom he had served as guide, must be a great favorite with God, who gave him such absolute command over the wolves. Upon this they assembled in great numbers, and came to the Man of God, entreating him to deliver them from their calamities.

"Two sorts of calamities bore hard upon them," says St. Bonaventure, "wolves and hail." The wolves were so ravenous in the environs of Grecio, that they devoured both cattle and men; and the hail fell every year in such quantity and of such large size, that their crops of corn were destroyed, and their vineyards sorely damaged. Francis preached on this subject, and pointed out to them that scourges of this nature were the punishment of sin; and he ended by saying: "For the honor and for the glory of God, I pledge my word to you, that if you choose to give credit to what I say, and have pity on your own souls, by making a good confession, and showing worthy fruits of repentance, God will look upon you with a favorable eye; will deliver you from your calamities, and render your country abundant in all sorts of good things. But I also declare to you that if you are ungrateful for these benefits, if, like the dog, you return to the vomit, God will be still more irritated against you, and you will feel the effects thereof twofold by the fresh afflictions He will then send." They believed the preacher, and did penance; from that moment the scourges ceased; nothing more was heard of wolves, and there was no more hail; and, what seemed most remarkable, continues St. Bonaventure, was, that when it hailed in the vicinity, the cloud, on nearing their lands, either stopped or went off in another direction. This lasted as long as those people remained faithful to God.

Four authors, in different centuries, who have written the history of the Valley of Rieti, assure us, that when dissoluteness recommenced in that country, the wolves returned and made great havoc. Wading, who wrote in Italy in the 17th century, says, that the inhabitants of the valley admitted this to be the case. It is certain by the testimony of the Holy Scriptures, that the sins of the people call down not unfrequently the scourges of the wrath of God, which may be averted by repentance, or be rendered useful to salvation. But how many afflicted sinners are there, of whom it may be said with the prophet: "O Lord, Thou hast struck them, and they have not grieved; Thou hast bruised them, and they have refused to receive correction; they have made their faces harder than the rock, and they have refused to return."

A knight, whose name was John Velita, who was converted by the preaching of Francis, became his intimate friend, and used often to go to see him and consult him in his hut, which was made of the branches of two large hornbeams intertwined. As he was an elderly man, and very corpulent, whom the steepness of the road greatly fatigued, he begged Francis to come nearer to the town: this would be agreeable to all, and he offered to build him a convent on any spot he should select. The Servant of God assented to the proposal, and, smiling, promised the knight not to settle farther from the town than the distance to which a child could throw a lighted brand. Upon this they went together down the mountain, and when they reached the gates of Grecio, the knight sent the first child he met to fetch a lighted brand, and desired him to throw it as far as he could, not thinking he could throw it very far. But the child, with a strength surpassing that of men, threw the brand to a distance of more than a mile, and it fell on a hill belonging to the knight, and set fire to the wood which covered it, and lit at length on a very stony spot. This prodigy made it clear that God desired that a convent should be built there, and it was cut out of the rock. The oratory, the dormitory, and the refectory, which are still extant, on the ground floor, are only thirty feet long by six broad; precious remains, which show us the love of poverty which planned them.

The Saint founded three other establishments in the Valley of Rieti, at St. Mary of the Woods, at Monte Raniero, or Monte Columba, and at Pui Buscone. These four houses, which are situated on eminences on the four sides of the valley, formed together a cross. In each of them, as in the Town of Rieti, and all around the lake which surrounds it, traces are shown of several miracles which were performed by the man of God.

He returned to St. Mary of the Angels in the Month of January, 1218, and he determined upon convoking a general chapter, which he proclaimed by circular letters, to be held on Whitsuntide of the year 1219, in order that he might be made acquainted with the state of the missions intrusted to his disciples, and that he might send missionaries into parts where there had hitherto been none.

While he was thus occupied by his important projects for the salvation of souls, God, in order to prevent any emotions of pride stealing into his heart, and to maintain in him a profound humility, was pleased to permit that he should be attacked by a violent temptation; it was an extraordinary depression of spirits, which lasted several days. He made every effort to surmount it by his prayers and his tears; and one day when he was praying with more than ordinary fervor, a celestial voice said to him: "Francis, if thou hadst the faith of a grain of mustard-seed, and thou wert to say to this mountain, go thither from hence, it would go." Not understanding the meaning of these words, he asked "what is the mountain"; and he was answered: "The mountain is the temptation." He immediately replied, weeping and humbling himself: "Lord, Thy will be done." And from that moment the temptation ceased, and his mind became perfectly at ease.

The year 1218 was divided between the stay he made at St. Mary of the Angels, for the instruction of his brethren, and some excursions he made to Mount Alvernia and to some other places, where new dwellings were made over to him. His route was always marked by the fruits of his preaching, and by the splendor of his miracles. Passing by Montaigu, above the Valley of Caprese, before a Church of St. Paul, which was being repaired, and seeing that two of the masons could not succeed in lifting a stone, which was to be placed as a jamb for the door, his compassion and zeal induced him to lift it and place it as required, which he did alone, and with a strength which was not that of a mortal. The Abbot of the Monastery of St. Justin, in the Diocese of Perugia, met him, and alighted from his horse to compliment him, and to speak to him on some matters of conscience. After a conversation replete with unction, the abbot, recommended himself humbly to his prayers. Francis replied: "I will pray with all my heart;" and they parted. At a little distance from thence, the Saint said to his companion: "Wait a little, brother, I will here perform my promise." He knelt to pray; and while he was so doing, the abbot, who was riding on, felt his mind inflamed with a suavity of devotion, such as he had never before experienced. He stopped, and the vivid impressions with which God favored him, threw him into an ecstasy. But when he came to himself again, he became aware that it was entirely owing to the prayers of Francis.

On his return from his last journey in 1218, which was much longer than any of the others had been, Francis found that another building, large and commodious, had been erected in his absence, close to the Portiuncula convent. Displeased at seeing this infringement of the rules of holy poverty, he took some of his brethren with him, and went on the roof, to begin to break it down, which he certainly would have carried through, had not some of the people from Assisi, who were there, informed him that the building belonged to the town; that it

had been built by them for the foreign religious, who daily arrived there, it being dishonorable to the town to see them compelled, in consequence of the want of room in the convent, to sleep outside, and even in the fields; that the town had destined this building for their accommodation, and that they would be received there in its name. On hearing this he came down, and said:—"If that, then, is your house, I leave it, and shall not meddle with it; we shall have nothing to do with it, neither myself nor my brethren; take care of it yourselves." It was decided in consequence by a deliberation of the municipality, that the magistrates should provide for the repairs.

Chapter 3

FROM HISTRAVEL TO PERUGIA TO HIS APPOINTMENT OF BROTHER ELIAS TO VICAR GENERAL

The time of the general chapter drew near, of that chapter which became so celebrated by the number of religious which attended it, and by many other marvellous circumstances. Before its assembling, the holy Patriarch proposed to go to Perugia, to confer with the cardinal protector, who was living there, on the affairs of the Order. Wading states, on good authority, that St. Dominic was there at the same time, and that they had several deliberations together with the cardinal, who had a like esteem for both.

One day when they were in serious conversation on the affairs of the Church, the cardinal asked them whether they should consider it advisable for some of their members to be raised to ecclesiastical dignities; "for," said he, "I am persuaded that they would have no less zeal for the glory of God and the salvation of souls, than those bishops of the early ages of the Church, who, although in great poverty, animated by ardent charity, fed their flocks with salutary instructions and the example of a good life."

After a contest of humility between the two patriarchs, as to who should speak first, Dominic, urged by Francis to take the lead, said to him:—"You excel me in humility, and I will excel you in obedience." He then gave the cardinal this answer:—"My lord, my brethren may well consider themselves as holding a very elevated rank. What is there more honorable than teaching others from the Evangelical pulpit? What should well-thinking minds desire more than to be employed in defence of the faith, and to combat the enemies of the Church? For this reason I strenuously desire that my brethren may remain as they are, and I will keep them so as long as I can." Francis made the following reply:—"My lord, my brethren have received the appellation of Minors, in order that they might never have the presumption to become great. If it be your intention that they shall bear fruit in the Church, leave them in their vocation, and never permit them to be raised to prelatures."

The cardinal was greatly edified by their answers, and highly commended the humility of their opinions, but he did not therefore change his views. He thought, on the contrary, that such ministers would be most useful in the Church, considering the corruption of the times.

The Church has since followed the opinion of this eminent dignitary, having made many bishops and cardinals from the two orders, and several have been even elevated to the sovereign pontificate.

But the Friars Preachers and the Friars Minor, who have preserved the spirit of their vocation, have never had any other feelings than those of their holy patriarchs on the subject of ecclesiastical dignities. They have refused them as long as they could, and those who have accepted them, have been compelled to do so by superior authority, which they could not be dispensed from obeying.

Brother Leo, the companion and confessor of St. Francis, who was at Perugia, and who assisted at all the conferences, says, that they spoke much on the propagation of the faith and the salvation of souls; that, having made reciprocal inquiries into the peculiarities of their respective orders, Dominic proposed to Francis to unite them, and make but one order, in order that the difference of the Institute should not divide those whom the intimate friendship of their fathers had closely united. To this proposition Francis replied:—"My dear brother, it has been God's will that our orders should be different, the one more austere than the other, in order to their being by this variety better adapted to human infirmity, and to give an opportunity to such as could not bear a life of very great austerity to embrace one which was somewhat milder." Leo adds, that they took steps for maintaining permanent agreement between the two orders; and, after having mutually praised their congregations, they recommended to their companions who were present, reciprocal respect and friendship for each other; that Dominic requested Francis to give him his girdle, which was a cord with large knots; and, having obtained it after many entreaties, he wore it during the remainder of his life under his habit, as a bond and perpetual symbol of the charity which so intimately united them.

Francis having discussed with the cardinal protector all the affairs of his Order, left Perugia to return to St. Mary of the Angels. As he discoursed on the road with his companion Leo, on the virtue of humility and entire abnegation of self, he said in a moment of fervor:

> "My dear brother, I do not believe myself to be a Friar Minor, and, in truth, I am not one, unless I can bear humbly and with entire tranquillity of mind, all that could happen to me under circumstances which I can figure to myself. I suppose, then, that my brethren came to seek me, with great respect and confidence, to assist at the general chapter which is about to be holden, and solicit me to preach at it. If, after having exhorted them in such terms as God shall have inspired me, they were to rise up against me, and manifest openly that they hold me in aversion, saying:— 'We will no longer have you to govern us; we are ashamed of having such a man as you at our head, who has neither learning nor eloquence, who is simple and ignorant, with very little prudence and experience; therefore, in future, do not have the arrogance to call yourself our superior.' If they were to put other affronts upon me, and to drive me ignominiously from the assembly, I should not consider myself to be a true religious, unless I were to receive all this as patiently and with equal serenity of countenance as I should receive those who would load me with praise and honor."

To this he added: "Assuredly, places of honor are very dangerous to salvation, not only from the vainglory which is to be feared, but likewise from the government, which is very difficult; whereas, in opprobrium, there is nothing but merit to be acquired. If I am removed from the headship, I shall be exempt from being accountable to God for a great number of souls. Prelature is a station of danger, and praise brings one to the very edge of the precipice. In an humble, lowly station, there is much to be gained. Why, then, do we look to and prefer what is dangerous to what has so much more spiritual advantage, since it is for this that time is given to us?" These are sentiments which should be well considered by persons in every station of life, whether they aspire to honors, or fear the losing of them. The profound humility of St. Francis does not admit of a doubt of his having gone through the trial which he here supposes; and even in putting it thus hypothetically, he strengthened in his mind the virtue requisite for supporting it in reality. These sorts of suppositions, which might be stumbling-blocks to the weak, are very useful to those who aspire to perfect humility.

The Friars Minor assembled for the general chapter of their Order at the Convent of St. Mary of the Angels, or Portiuncula, near Assisi, at the Feast of Pentecost, and their number exceeded five thousand. This circumstance is truly amazing, particularly when it is recollected that some remained in their respective convents; that the Order had only existed ten years since its institution; and that the novices had always been admitted by the Founder himself, except since the chapter of the year 1216, when he had given the provincial ministers power to receive them. It is nevertheless certain, that more than five thousand Friars Minor assisted at this celebrated chapter: the fact is attested by four of St. Francis' companions, who were present at it; by St. Bonaventure, who lived with them and by many others.

What can be said on this subject, except that it pleased God to recall in some measure, by the rapid establishment of this Order, the wonderful spread of the Gospel by the preaching of the Apostles? St. Augustine says that the Apostles were as dark clouds from whence lightning and thunder emanated; that, by their poverty and their simplicity, they shone in the eyes of the universe; that, by the powerful virtue and splendor of their admirable actions, they overthrew everything which was opposed to the empire of Jesus Christ, and, in a short time, christianized the world. May we not also say, that Francis and his companions, men poor and simple, were a representation of the Apostles; that Jesus Christ rendered them powerful and eminent in words and works, to bring back sinners to His empire, and that by them, in an inconceivably short period of time, an immense number of Apostolic men was collected and formed who embraced the same Institute, in order to exercise the same ministry? What assists us in comprehending that in ten years it had been possible to build a sufficient number of houses, to contain so many thousand men is, that they were poor and without any income.

The religious of this chapter were lodged in huts made of matting, erected all round the Portiuncula convent, from which this chapter has been called the Chapter of Mats. They were there separated from the world, but perfectly united among themselves, all lovers of watching and fasting after the example of their Father; zealous in prayer and in the recital of Psalms, in spiritual reading, and in readiness to execute all works of mercy, and having no other hope than that of the happiness of a future life.

Cardinal Ugolino, as Protector of the Order, came to preside over the chapter, and all the religious went in procession before him. He opened the assembly on Whitsunday the 26th of May: he officiated pontifically, and preached; and he deemed it his right to inspect the ranks of this holy army of the Lord, in which he found everything in good order. These soldiers of Jesus Christ were not seen wandering about; but all were collected in groups, a hundred in one spot, sixty in another, more or less, and conversing on holy subjects, on their own salvation, or on that of their neighbours, and on the means of reforming the morals of a corrupt world. The cardinal, delighted with so interesting and unusual a scene, said to those who followed him, as Jacob had when he met the angels on his way: "Truly, this is the Camp of God." We might also apply to it what Balaam could not prevent himself from saying, when he saw the Israelites encamped: "How beautiful are thy tabernacles, O Jacob, and thy tents, O Israel!"

Francis, as a general in his camp, went through all the tents; he encouraged his troops to fight valiantly the battles of the Lord, assuring them of receiving assistance from on high, animating some, and fulfilling in every place the duties of a vigilant chief.

He assembled all his brethren, and addressed them in an excellent discourse, of which the following embraces the subject: "We have promised great things; and we have been promised greater. Let us keep the first, and let us sigh after the others: Pleasure is of short duration; the penalty is eternal. Sufferings are light; glory is infinite. Many are called; but few are chosen. Each one will receive according to his deserts."

On this beautiful text he exhorted them, in the most forcible and moving terms, to the practice of virtue and to the duties of a religious life; urging them, above all things, to implicit obedience to our Holy Mother the Church, to a contempt of the world, to purity of mind and body, to a love of holy poverty and humility, to charity, to concord and mildness, to continued watchfulness, and to an ardent zeal for the salvation of souls. He recommended to them to pray for all the faithful, and particularly for the exaltation of the Holy Roman Church, and for the benefactors of the Order. After which he positively forbade them to have any anxiety whatever for anything concerning the body, and he quoted to them these words of the psalmist: "Cast thy care upon the Lord and He shall sustain thee." He had conformed strictly to the rule he laid down, for he had made no provision for the chapter.

St. Dominic, who, out of friendship for St. Francis, had come with six of his companions to this assembly and who heard this discourse, was fearful lest what he said and did was perhaps an exaggeration, and that it might seem to be tempting the Lord, if some steps were not taken for procuring food for so great a multitude. But he was of a very different way of thinking shortly after when he saw arrive from Assisi, Perugia, Spello, Foligno, Spoleto, and many more distant towns, ecclesiastics, laics, nobles, burgesses, and persons of every state of life who brought with them not only what was necessary for the subsistence of such vast numbers, but pressed forward to serve the religious themselves with an emulation of humility and charity.

So marked an interposition of Providence in behalf of these Evangelical poor struck the Patriarch of the Friars Preachers with astonishment; and it is believed that it suggested to him the intention which he carried into execution the year after, when he assembled the first general chapter of his order at Bologna, in which it was resolved that the Friars Preachers should adopt the system of entire poverty, and consider it as the fundamental rule of their order, renouncing forever all property in land, or revenue arising therefrom, even what they had at Toulouse, which the Pope had confirmed to them by his first bull. In dying, he recommended to them this Evangelical poverty as the foundation of their institute; and lest this foundation should be undermined by the prudence of the flesh, he forbade in the strongest terms, on pain of the curse of the Almighty, and of his also, the introduction into the order of any temporal possessions.

May Evangelical poverty that made so strong an impression on the mind of St. Dominic teach the faithful never to be mistrustful of the care of Divine Providence!

However, we are not to look for, or expect miraculous assistance; this is not in the ordinary course of God's dispensations; but after doing all that depends on ourselves, provided there be no irregularity on our part, and that our desires are within the bounds of moderation, without any impatience as to the event, we may assure ourselves that, according to the words of the wise man: "No one hath hoped in the Lord and hath been confounded."

Several prelates, and other persons of quality, who had been invited by Cardinal Ugolino to the Chapter, as to a grand and admirable sight, had the curiosity to examine everything minutely. They saw the religious in their miserable huts, coarsely dressed, taking but a very small portion of nourishment, sleeping on mats spread on the earth with a log of wood for a pillow. They noticed at the same time that they were quite calm, that joy and concord were universal amongst them, and that they were entirely submissive to their saintly founder. Admiring all these things, they said to each other: "This shows that the way to heaven is narrow, and that it is very difficult for the rich to enter into the Kingdom of God. We flatter ourselves that we shall eke out our salvation in the enjoyment of all the comforts of life, having our ease in all things, while these people, to save their souls, deprive themselves of everything, mortify their bodies, and are notwithstanding not without great apprehension. We should like to die as they will, but we do not choose to live as they live." Similar reflections converted a great number of persons, and more than five hundred took the habit of the Friars Minor during the chapter.

The holy Patriarch found that many of his religious submitted themselves to extraordinary mortifications, which either shortened their days or rendered them useless to the Order by the illnesses which were the consequence. He therefor publicly forbade them, by the virtue of holy obedience, to make use of such means, and ordered all who had coats of mail, iron girdles, or other instruments of mortification, to leave them off and deliver them up to him. This was done, and some most extraordinary modes of inflicting self-punishment were discovered. The number of coats of mail and iron girdles which were delivered up were more than five hundred; they were put into a heap, and the Patriarch thought proper to show them to the cardinal and his company, for their edification. They were astonished on witnessing so great a love of such penitential austerities, in men of such pure and holy lives. In their presence he again forbade his dear brethren indiscreet mortifications, which are injurious to the body; representing to them that they either hasten death, or throw the body into such a state of languor and weakness, as makes it unfit for spiritual exercises, or an impediment to the practice of good works. Oh, fortunate and happy times, when it was necessary to check such failings!

God made known to Francis, in a revelation he had during the sitting of the chapter, that the Prince of Darkness, alarmed at the fervor of the new Order, had collected thousands of demons, to concert together on the means of bringing it to ruin; and that one of them, more astute than the rest, had put forth an opinion which it had been decided should be acted upon. It was, not to attack the Friars Minor openly, but to have recourse to artifice; to induce them to receive into their society nobles, learned men, and youths. Nobles, in order by their means to introduce effeminacy in which they had been brought up; learned men, who, proud of their learning, should have a contempt for humility; and youths, who, being weak and delicate, would greatly relax in the regular discipline.

Religion teaches us that there are demons, and that they are subordinate one to the other; that God, when it pleases Him, permits them to tempt mankind, and even torment them corporally; and St. Paul speaks of "the Prince of the powers of this air." We know what Satan did to holy Job; and what our Lord said to St. Peter: "Satan hath desired to have you, that he might sift you as wheat;" and what He stated elsewhere: "When an unclean spirit is gone out of a man, he taketh with him seven spirits more wicked than himself, and they enter in and dwell there." Thus we need have no difficulty in believing that the prince of darkness had collected such a number of demons against St. Francis and his Institute. St. Gregory says, that they attack with greater violence those in whom they find a greater disposition to holiness, and that the principal demons are employed in the attacks on the bravest soldiers of Jesus Christ. What must be the wrath of these malignant spirits against the apostolical men, whose lives are wholly employed in effecting the salvation of souls!

Francis had already been made aware by the words of a young female who was possessed, as St. Bonaventure relates, that the devils, irritated by the injury he did them, had assembled against him, and then he merely said, as Paul did: "I am the stronger." But he was alarmed when he learnt from God Himself the increase of their rage. He retired for two days to an oratory to pray for grace to be able to escape from their snares, and that he might be protected by good angels. His prayer gave him fresh courage; he returned to the chapter, and addressed his brethren with energy on the watchfulness with which it was incumbent on them to work out their salvation, without placing too much reliance on the holiness of their state of life, from which they must be apprehensive lest they should fall off by the machinations of their enemy. "You know," he said, "the examples we have; Satan fell from Heaven, and drew with him a number of the angels; he caused Adam and Eve to be driven from Paradise; he prayed to be allowed to sift the Apostles as wheat is sifted; and he did so with such effect, that one of them betrayed his Master, another denied Him, and all fled when He was captured."

The Saint then explained to them what God had made known to him of the designs of the devil; and in order that the enemy's malignity might fall on himself, he warned them to pay more attention in the reception of advices to the sentiments of the mind than to the advantages of birth; to be very careful that the learned whom they should admit, should be devoid of pride, and were fit to edify others by their humility, and to be careful that such as joined them in the flower of youth, should be informed of all that they would have to practice in future.

For the holy man did not think it requisite, in consequence of Satan's malice, to prohibit noblemen from joining his Order, since their example has great influence, and the elevated sentiments which are found in that class, render them more fit to do great things for the service of God. He did not wish to drive away the learned, since learning is necessary for the exercise of the functions of religion, and since those men who join the knowledge of sound doctrine to an Evangelical life, are most instructive teachers in the Church, for the dissipation of error and the establishment of virtue. He also desired that they should receive such young men as should present themselves in the tenderest age, "because it is good for man to bear the yoke from his youth:" to leave the world, before having any knowledge of it, except through the lights of the Church, and to offer themselves as pure victims, rather than to bring to

Him the remains of a heart stained by the passions; and, moreover, our Saviour said to His disciples, who turned away the children who came to Him: "Suffer them, and forbid them not to come to me." We know that there are in the world censorious people who condemn the custom of permitting young persons to enter into a religious state; it would be easy to show, if it were not for fear of rendering this work too voluminous, that their arguments are based on a superficial foundation, and are contrary to the maxims of Christianity; we therefore content ourselves with saying that at the Council of Trent, which was guided by the Spirit of truth in its discipline, as well as in its dogmas and morality, permission was given to persons of either sex, to make profession as a religious at the full age of sixteen; that rule is authorized by the ordinances of all Christian princes, and it therefore seems very extraordinary that any individuals should be rash enough to oppose their private opinions to so respectable an authority.

Francis, who was desirous of encouraging the fervor of his disciples, apprised them of what they had to fear, and anticipated the smallest inclinations to pride in them, by salutary humiliations. The cardinal protector having one day preached before all the religious of the chapter, and having concluded his sermon by bestowing on them considerable praise, the holy Patriarch asked his permission to address the audience. He foretold to them, and represented in lively colors, all that was to happen to the Order; the temptations to which they were to be exposed; the tribulations they were to suffer; the changes that would be brought in, and their decline. He reproached them with their laxity, and with their want of fervor in cooperating with the peculiar graces they had received from God; he spoke so energetically, that, in censuring their foolish obsequiousness, if such a fault they had, he covered them with confusion. The cardinal was somewhat mortified, and said:—"Pray, why, brother, did you gainsay me, setting the imperfections of your brethren in opposition to the praises I had given them?" "My lord and my father," answered Francis, "I did so, in order to preserve the substance of your praise. I was apprehensive that such praise being given by a person of your exalted rank, might inspire vanity into the minds of those in whom humility has not as yet thrown out deep roots." This affords great matter for reflection for those virtuous persons who voluntarily receive praise, at least when it is artfully administered; and for indiscreet flatterers, who expose virtue to a dangerous trial.

What occurred on the following day, showed that the holy man had received from God the perfect means of appreciating men's minds. Brother Elias, who was the provincial for Tuscany; Brother John of Strachia, who was provincial for Bologna, and several others came to the cardinal protector and entreated him to tell Francis, as from himself, that he ought to listen to the advice of his brethren, among whom there were many learned men, fully capable of governing; particularly as he himself was a simple and unread man, whose ill health did not permit him to bring their affairs into good order. They added, that respect ought to be paid to the ancient rules of St. Basil, of St. Augustine, and of St. Benedict, and that Minors should not differ so widely by a new rule and excessive severity, as if they wished to be better than their fathers.

The cardinal took his time, and then proposed all these things to Francis, as maxims which he deemed good for the government of the Order. The Saint being immediately made aware by the Spirit of God, that these things were suggested by others, rose up from the place in which he had been seated with the cardinal, took him respectfully by the hand, and led him to the brethren who were assembled in chapter, and said:

"My brethren, my brethren, God has called me by the way of simplicity and humility, in order that I might follow the folly of the cross: it is for His glory and my confusion, and for the security of your consciences I am about to tell you what He said to me:—'Francis,' He said, 'I desire that you may be in the world a new little idiot, who shall preach by thy actions and by thy discourses the folly of the cross. Do thou and thine follow me only, and not any other manner of life.' Speak not to me therefore of any other rule, he added, for I shall not follow, nor prescribe any other than that which God has in His mercy given me; those who swerve from it, I fear, will feel the Divine vengeance, and will be covered with confusion, when at length they shall be obliged once more to enter into this path, which God has shown me."

Then addressing himself to the cardinal, he said:—"My lord, these wise people, whom your lordship praises so much, would wish by their worldly prudence to deceive both God and you; but they deceive themselves, endeavoring to destroy what God has ordained for their salvation, through me, his unworthy servant. I attribute nothing to myself of what I do, or of what I say; I rely not on my own lights in the government of the Order; I arrange everything by long prayers with our Divine Father, who governs it sovereignly, and who has made His will known to us by so many manifest signs, in order to bring to perfection the work He has commenced by so miserable a man as I am, for the salvation of souls, and the edification of our holy mother the Church. Those who prefer the wisdom of the world to the will of the Lord, expose themselves manifestly to be lost." Having spoken thus, Francis retired.

The cardinal, who admired the energy of his words, and the light which disclosed to him at once the most secret thoughts, said to the superiors who were abashed:—"My dear brethren, you have seen how the Holy Ghost has himself spoken by the mouth of this apostolical man; his words came forth as a two-edged sword, which has penetrated to the bottom of the heart. Take care that you do not grieve the Spirit of God; be not ungrateful for the favors He has done you. He is truly in this poor man, and manifests to you, through him, the marvels of His power; in listening to him, it is Jesus Christ that you hear; in despising him, it is Jesus Christ whom you despise. Humble yourselves, therefore, and obey him, if it is your desire to please God, and not lose the fruit of your vocation; for I know by experience, that everything which either the devils or men are about to attempt against his Order, is revealed to him. Whatsoever may be said to him with good or bad intention, it is difficult to find him off his guard; neither my advice, nor that of any other person, will turn him from his purpose." The provincials who had given rise to this scene were moved, and submitted themselves to the will of the Patriarch.

Among the religious who had congregated at the chapter, there were many who came to seek a remedy for the ill-treatment they had received in many places out of Italy, which had its rise in two causes; the first was, that they had no authenticated letters to show that their Institute had been approved by the Church; the second was, that the pastors would not allow them to preach. They begged therefore that the Pope might be solicited to give them written testimonials to certify that they had his approbation of their Institution; and, moreover, that they should obtain from the Holy Father a privilege, in virtue of which they might preach wherever they thought proper, even without leave from the bishops.

The holy founder could not hear this second article without indignation. "What my brethren" said he, "are you still devoid of understanding; and do you not know the will of God? It is His pleasure that we should gain the good will of our superiors by our respect for them, and by humility; and then by word and good example, those who are under them. When the bishops see that you live holily, and that you do not encroach on their authority, they themselves will apply to you to work for the salvation of the souls which are committed to their care; they themselves will collect their flocks to listen to you, and to imitate you. Let it be our sole privilege to have no privilege calculated to swell our pride; to give ourselves a confidence which shall be to the prejudice of others, and be the cause of contentions. Let us ask nothing of the Holy See but what is calculated to aid us in serving God, in extending the faith, and in gaining souls under the good pleasure of the prelates, without causing any disturbance among the people."

Some represented that they had found many of the heads of the parochial clergy so harsh, that they had been unable to mollify them, either by entreaties, or by labor, by submissiveness or good example, so as to obtain leave to preach to their parishioners, or to receive from them any corporal assistance; to this Francis replied:

> "My brethren, we are sent to the aid of priests, to make good that in which they may be deficient. Each one will receive his reward, not according to the degree of his authority, but in proportion to his labors. Know, then, that what is most agreeable to God is, to work for the salvation of souls, and that we shall best succeed in this by living in concord with the priests than by living separately from them; if they throw obstacles in the way, God, to whom all vengeance belongs, will give them in His good time what is their due. Be therefore submissive to ecclesiastical superiors, in order to avert, as much as may be in your power, any jealousies. If you are children of peace, you will soon ingratiate yourselves with the clergy and the people, and this will be more acceptable to God than if you gained over the people, and thereby gave scandal to the clergy. Hide the faults of the priests, make good what they are deficient in, and be only in consequence the more humble."

The Religious of St. Francis must not be surprised if they, even in these days, meet with opposition in the exercise of their holy ministries. It is an occurrence which the similarity of men may at all times bring about; and which St. Paul experienced more than any other in the course of his ministry. But let them be careful to put in practice the advice of their Father, in order that they may be able to say in truth with the apostle:—"We have injured no man" And, finally, the advice which he gave them must induce us to notice his moderation and his discretion, in an age when the Church had reason to renew the laments of one of the Prophets against the pastors of Israel.

He judged it proper, by the advice of the cardinal protector, to procure Apostolic letters to make known the approbation his Institute had received; and he obtained them from the Pope, who was then at Viterbo. These were the first which were given to the Order of Friars Minor: their contents are as follows:

Honorius, Bishop, servant of the servants of God, to the Archbishops,
Bishops, Abbots, Deacons, Archdeacons, and other Superior Ecclesiastics—

"As our dear son, brother Francis and his companions, have renounced the vanities of the world, and embraced a state of life which the Roman Church has justly approved; and, following the example of the Apostles, are about to go into different parts to announce the word of God; we beg and exhort you in our Lord, and we command you by these Apostolical letters, to receive as Catholic and faithful, the brothers of this Order, the bearers of these letters who may apply to you, to be favorable to them, and to treat them with kindness, for the honor of God, and out of consideration for us. Given this 3d of the Ides of June, the third year of our pontificate."

Many cardinals and other illustrious persons added their letters of recommendation to those of the Pope, particularly Cardinal Ugolino, the protector of the Order, who testified by a document addressed to all prelates, which certified the intimate knowledge he had of the virtues of the Founder and of his religious, and the great fruit that was to be expected from them for the propagation of the faith, and the benefit of the whole Church. They made a great number of authenticated copies of these letters, to give them to those friars whom Francis had resolved to send in all directions, even into the most distant lands.

Three things were decreed at this general chapter. The first was, that on every Saturday a solemn mass should be celebrated in honor of the immaculate Blessed Virgin Mary. This glorious title of Immaculate, which the general councils of the seventh and eighth centuries, and the ancient fathers of the Church, have given to Mary, has been used by the Council of Trent, which has declared in its decree on the subject of original sin, "that it is not its intention to include therein the blessed and immaculate Virgin Mary, Mother of God." The use which the Friars Minor made of it in 1219, shows clearly that they adopted, as did their sainted Patriarch, the common opinion of the Greek Church, which was already spread in various parts of the Latin Church, in honor of the Conception of the Blessed Virgin, because they thought it wholly pure and exempt from the stain of original sin. Their successors have always, with admirable zeal, maintained this opinion, which God in so far blessed, that they have now the advantage and consolation of seeing the institution of the

Feast of the Immaculate Conception in the whole Church, and of knowing that what was at one time only a pious opinion is now a dogma.

It is proper to notice here, that at the head of the Friars Minor, who supported the proposition of the Immaculate Conception, was the celebrated John Duns Scotus, so respected in the Church for his penetrating genius, for the solidity of his doctrine, and for his singular piety. He silenced his opponents, and his success was so manifested that all considered him to have had the special aid of the Blessed Virgin, and his reasonings were so convincing that the University of Paris admitted them, and declared in favor of the doctrine of the Immaculate Conception, which it has maintained ever since. In the fifteenth century, the faculty of Theology passed a solemn decree on this point, in which it declared that in consonance with the opinions of its predecessors, and in order to oppose the enemies of the Blessed Virgin, it bound itself by oath to maintain the proposition that the Mother of God was preserved from original sin, framing a law, not to receive any doctor who should not take this oath; which practice was continued till the dogma was declared in 1854, when it was no longer necessary.

This is the pious triumph of all the Sons of St. Francis who, in gratitude for so singular a privilege, honor the Blessed Virgin as the Patroness and Protectress of their Order, under the title of her Immaculate Conception, and by celebrating the festival thereof with every possible solemnity.

The second statute directed, that express mention should be made of the names of St. Peter and St. Paul, in the prayer, "Protege nos Domine, etc.," and in another which begins with these words—"Exaudi nos Deus," etc., in memory of what had been revealed to St. Francis, that these apostles interceded powerfully with God for his Institute. This is practised by the whole Church since Innocent IV revised and reformed the Roman Breviary, through Aymon, an Englishman, who was the fifth general of the Order of Friars Minor.

In the third statute it was said that poverty should be apparent in everything, in the convents which they should build; that the churches should be small and low, and that the walls of the rest of the buildings should be of wood or mud. Some difficulties were started to this; many represented that in their provinces wood was dearer than stone, and that walls of masonry, if they were not too high, would better denote poverty, because they would be solid and not compel frequent repair. The holy Founder would not argue this matter with them; for it is remarked that not to give rise to any dispute, and not to give scandal to the weak, he often condescended to the opinions of others in similar matters. Nevertheless he recommended to them all, not to receive either churches or houses which were not in conformity to holy poverty which was their rule.

It was not possible always to follow out his intentions. The prelates and princes who were greatly attached to his Order had beautiful convents built, which his religious could not avoid receiving; and St. Bonaventure even says that a numerous community which has different exercises to perform, requires large houses, although care should be taken that holy poverty should be apparent throughout, and that superfluity should not preponderate over what is reasonably necessary.

The chapter being ended, Francis, following the example of the Apostles, divided the world among his brethren, in order to bring it all in subjection to the Empire of Jesus Christ.

The first mission to Germany had not been successful. Those who had been sent thither by the preceding chapter, not knowing the language, and answering badly the questions put to them, were suspected from their poor and unusual habit to belong to those heretics who were prosecuted in Italy, in consequence of which they were cruelly ill-treated and driven away. The recital which they gave on their return made Germany so unpopular among the brethren that they said that none ought to go there but such as aspired to martyrdom, and that many prayed to Heaven to be preserved from the ferocity of the Germans. Francis did not think proper to send any more there till such time as he should have received some novices from thence who might go there with others; but he sent some into Hungary.

As soon as the several missions had been fixed upon, the missionaries prepared to set out. Before we give an account of St. Francis' voyage to the Levant, we think it desirable to give an abridgment of what his children did in various parts of the world, because the principal glory is due to him, and these proceedings naturally belong to the history of his life.

Benedict of Arezzo embarked with his companions for Greece, where their preaching, backed by the holiness of their lives, and confirmed by miracles, produced abundance of fruit for the salvation of souls, and procured so many houses for the Order that in a very short time it was formed into an entire province, and was called Romania.

Giles and Electe, who anxiously aspired to martyrdom, and who were only lay-brothers, had appeared to St. Francis to be more fit to be sent to the Saracens than even those of the clergy, and they hastened to go into Africa with several others. What chiefly animated the zeal of brother Giles, as the author of his life remarks, was his having heard that the Saracens treated with great cruelty those Christians who spoke ill of the law of Mahomet. When he reached Tunis with a party of missionaries, he generously preached the faith in public, and this continued for some time. A person who was looked up to among the Saracens for his great wisdom, having come forth from his retreat, told the people that they ought to put to the sword all those infidels who spoke against the law of their prophet. Giles and his companions were delighted at the prospect of an early martyrdom; but the Christians with whom they had their domicile, fearing lest they might be included in the massacre, took away these preachers and compelled them to go on board a vessel in the harbor, and did not permit them again to land. As they did not cease addressing the Mahometans who crowded to the sea-shore, with a view to induce them to embrace the faith of Jesus Christ,—their desire to sacrifice their lives for His glory being so ardent,—the Christian residents hastened to have them removed to Europe. Thus seeing that even their fellow-believers were opposed to their views, they returned to Italy.

Electe was more fortunate; during some years he performed the functions of an apostle in another town in Africa, where he received the crown of martyrdom. A body of Saracens rushed upon him while he was preaching, upon which he fell on his knees, grasped the Rule with both hands, asked pardon for his faults from God and from his companions, and then presented his neck to the infidels who took away his life. This did not happen till after the death of St. Francis. He had entered the Order when very young, and had lived in it with great austerity, always wearing a coat of mail on his bare body, so that he prepared himself for the martyrdom of blood by the martyrdom of penance, as was recommended to the Christians in time of persecution.

Those who went into Spain with John Parent proceeded with so much speed that ten of them arrived at Saragossa by the Feast of the Assumption; a very short time after their departure, Bernard de Quintavalle, who was sent into this kingdom after the chapter of 1216 had established two convents, the one at Toledo, the other at Carrion de los Condes, a town in the Kingdom of Leon. Some of his companions had been admitted at Lerida, and at Balaguer, in Catalonia, under very extraordinary circumstances, which are omitted not to be too prolix. Zachary and Gautier, who had been sent into Portugal, had had much to suffer in the beginning; but Queen Urraqua, the wife of Alphonso II, who then reigned, was a most pious princess. She, having caused their Institute to be examined by very learned men, and having had full assurance of the holiness of their lives, now obtained leave from the king for their being received into his states, and permission for their building convents. A house was given them, with a chapel attached to it, of St. Anthony, near Coimbra, where the court then was, and subsequently one on a larger scale at Lisbon.

Princess Sancia, the daughter of Sancho I, and sister of Alphonso II, highly praised by historians for her piety and chastity, protected Zachary, and gave him a third house, called of St. Catharine, at some distance from the Town of Alenquer, which was her own; but in consequence of the distance and the insalubrity of the air, she some years after converted her own palace into a convent, which she gave to the Friars Minor. Gautier, one of Bernard's companions, who had made many great conversions by his virtues and his miracles, near Guimaraens, had built a convent not very far from that town.

While at the convent of St. Catharine, a very queer thing occurred, which we have not thought right to omit here on account of the instruction it contains. One of the ladies, in waiting on the princess whose name was Maria Garcia, often came to have some pious conversation with one of the holy religious, who was very averse to receiving her, because he feared the company of females. One day when he was at prayer, she came to the church, and expressed a wish to see him, but he refused to go to her. The historian says that in order to obtain what she wished for, she did what women generally do under such circumstances, she became more importunate, and cried bitterly, and protested that it would give her great pain if she might not speak to the holy man. He therefore came, to get rid of her importunities; but he brought some straw in one hand, and some fire in the other; he set the straw on fire in her presence, and then said to her: "Although, madam, all your conversations are pious, I refuse to hold them with you in private, because what you see has happened to the straw, is what religious persons have to fear may occur to them if they have private and familiar intercourse with women; and at least they lose the fruits of their holy communications with God in prayer." The lady blushed, retired, and troubled him no more. St. Jerome, who so strongly recommended to ecclesiastics and religious to avoid conversations with the female sex would certainly have approved of this action.

John Parent arrived at Saragossa in the month of August, 1219, with nine of his brethren who were followed by many others soon after; he addressed himself to the Bishop and to the magistrates who assembled to hear him. He explained to them who Francis of Assisi was, his vocation, his mission, his mode of life, his Institute, the approbation given to his Rule by Pope Innocent III and Honorius III, and the testimonials given to him by several cardinals. He remarked to them that the new Order had been exceedingly multiplied in a very few years, and that they had seen more than five thousand religious at the general chapter which had been lately assembled in the neighborhood of Assisi, which was considered to be miraculous; that their Father had sent a great number of his children into all parts of the world to combat vice and encourage virtue, which circumstance should be considered as a bountiful effect of Divine Providence towards His Church, in such calamitous times. He concluded by saying: "If our Institute is agreeable to you, we earnestly entreat you to give us some small place in which we may recite the Divine Office, and fulfil the other ministries which our Founder has recommended to us. Have no anxiety as to our subsistence, for we solicit no part of your goods; we content ourselves with very little; we are poorly clad; work and questing furnish us with all that we require."

All the assembly admired the spirit of humility which prevailed through this discourse, and the reading of the Papal Bull, with the testimonials of the cardinals, were proofs that nothing had been set forth but what was true. They conceived such a liking to the Order, that they took immediate measures for giving to John Parent and his companions a dwelling of which they took possession on the 28th of August.

The Order of St. Francis, as well as that of St. Dominic, began from that time to spread through all Spain. On all sides preachers of the two orders were found, and new convents were erected, as Luke, Bishop of Tuy, a contemporary author, mentions in his chronicle when he speaks of the marvels of the reign of St. Ferdinand, King of Castile and Leon. It would clearly appear that both the one and the other were in the City of Leon about that time, since the same author, in his excellent work against the Albigenses, says that they exerted themselves with great zeal and energy against the heretics, who, to seduce the faithful, published pretended miracles which they asserted to have been performed by the bones of one Arnold a man of their sect who had been dead sixteen years, and they also accused the good religious who exposed their impostures of heresy. Such is the mode adopted by certain sectarians; they endeavored to establish their false doctrine by fictitious miracles; while they insolently refused credence to those which the Catholic Church admitted as certain; and all have sufficient audacity to treat as heretics the orthodox who prove them to be heretics themselves.

The mission to France was equally successful with that of Spain. Pacifico and his companions who began it in 1216, were exposed to hunger, cold, and all other kinds of inconveniences, which men are exposed to suffer when out of their own country, unknown, and destitute of everything, and moreover living an unusual and extraordinary sort of life. They went to that office of the night which is called matins in those churches in which it is said at midnight, as is still the custom at Notre Dame, in Paris. If there was no service in the places where they were, they then prayed by themselves at that hour, and they passed the whole night at the foot of the altar; after which, if no one offered them a meal, they went questing from door to door. The remainder of the day was spent in the hospitals, making the beds of the lepers and other sick, dressing their wounds, and rendering them such other services of humility and charity as they had learned from the example and instruction of their Father Francis. So saintly a life attracted the attention of all, gained their esteem, caused many to embrace the Institution, and procured for them many establishments, notably the one at Paris.

Angelo of Pisa, one of the missioners sent by St. Francis, was the first warden of the Parisian convent. This convent soon became a college, where young men, from all parts of the world came to study, and, subsequently, to take out degrees in the university. Several great men have, in the last five hundred years, rendered this college illustrious.

Pacifico, whom St. Francis had appointed provincial of the French missions, sent some of the religious into different parts of the kingdom, where they were well received. He went with some companions into Hainault, and other provinces of the Low Countries, where, by the liberality and under the protection of the Countess of Flanders, Joanna of Constantinople, he caused many houses to be built.

Thomas de Chantpre, a Canon Regular of St. Austin, and subsequently a religious of the Order of St. Dominic, states, as an eye-witness, a very marvellous thing which deserves to be recorded in the life of St. Francis, since it occurred during his lifetime, relative to his Order. At Thorouth, a town in Flanders, a child of five years of age, whose name was Achaz, of a good family, having seen, in 1219, the habit of the Friars Minor, begged his parents to give him a similar one. His entreaties and tears induced them to gratify him. He was therefore habited as a Friar Minor, with a coarse cord and bare feet, not choosing to have any money, not even to touch it, and he practised as much as was in his power the exercises of the religious. Among his companions he was seen to act as preacher, cautioning them against evil, exciting them to virtue by the fear of the pains of Hell, and by the hopes of the glories of Heaven; teaching them to say the Lord's Prayer, and the Angelic Salutation, and to honor God by genuflections. He reproved such as did anything wrong in his presence, even his own father, if he heard him swear, or saw him in a state of inebriety. "My Father," he would say, with tears in his eyes, "does not our cure tell us that those who do such things will not possess the Kingdom of God?" Being one day at church with his mother, who was dressed in a handsome gown of a flame color, he pointed out to her a crucifix, as a censure on her vanity, and warned her to be careful that the color she wore did not cause her to fall into the flames of Hell, which warning had so great an effect that his mother never after wore anything but the plainest dress. Such a precocious mind, with so much matured wisdom and piety, was universally admired, and every one took pleasure in seeing and listening to this amiable child.

God took him from this world before he had attained his seventh year. In his last illness, he confessed, and solicited most earnestly to be allowed to receive the Body of Christ. The cure not venturing to comply with his request, on account of his tended age, although his reason was so mature and his holiness so manifest, he raised his hands to Heaven, and said, in tender accents:—"My Lord Jesus Christ, Thou knowest that all that I wish for in this world is to receive Thee. I begged for Thee, and have done what I could; I hope with entire confidence that Thou will not deprive me of the happiness of possessing Thee." He then consoled and exhorted his parents and others who surrounded him, after which he gave up his pure soul to God, praising Him, and ejaculating prayers to Him.

The ocular witness adds two circumstances which are very remarkable; the first is, that the religious habit which this holy child wore disappeared, and could never afterwards be found. The second, that the Friars Minor who, as well as himself, went to pray at his grave, could not go through the De profundis which they had commenced, notwithstanding all the efforts that they made to do so; by which they understood, that so pure a soul stood in no need of prayer; and, no doubt, they only endeavored to offer up some under the impression that a mind so early in other respects matured, might have been capable of contracting some stain.

Francis, having despatched his disciples to the several missions allotted to them, as has been said, prepared to go himself to the Levant, with a zeal equal to that with which he had inspired his brethren, when Cardinal Ugolino, the protector of the Order, entered into discussion with him on the subject of the government of the establishment of St. Damian's, in which Clare presided, and of the other monasteries of females which had been commenced on that model.

Cardinal Ugolino, by the advice and authority of the Pope leaving to Francis the guidance of the Monastery of St. Damian of Assisi, took upon himself the direction of all the others who had adopted that rule, and nominated as visitor-general under his orders, a prudent religious of the order of Citeaux, called Ambrose. He gave them the rule of St. Benedict, with constitutions which Wading gives at length. We do not transcribe them here, because, in the year 1224, St. Francis gave them another rule, which will be spoken of later, and which is the only one which ought to be called the rule of St. Clare or of the Second Order.

The holy Patriarch being now about to set out in order to preach the Gospel to the Mahometans of the Levant, resolved to send to those who were in the west, some of his brethren. He chose six for Morocco: Vidal, a very prudent and pious religious, whom he nominated superior; Berard de Carbio, from the vicinity of Narni, who was well versed in the Arabian language; Peter, of St. Geminien, and Otho, who were in priests' orders; and Ajut, and Accurse, who were lay-brethren.—Having sent for them he spoke as follows:—

> "My dear children, it is God who has commanded me to send you amongst the Saracens, to make known His faith, and refute the law of Mahomet. I shall go in a different direction to work for the conversion of the same infidels, and thus I shall send preachers over the whole earth. Prepare yourselves, therefore, to fulfil the will of the Lord. To render yourselves worthy of it, take great care to preserve peace and concord among yourselves, as the ever-subsisting ties of charity. Avoid envy which was the first cause of the loss of mankind. Be patient in tribulations, and humble in success; which is the means of coming off victorious in all encounters. Imitate our Lord Jesus Christ in his poverty, chastity, and obedience; He was born poor, He lived poor, and it was in the bosom of poverty that He died. To manifest how highly He loved chastity, He chose to be born of a virgin, He took virgins for His first soldiers, He kept, and counselled virginity, and He died in presence of two virgins. As to obedience, He never ceased from practising it from His birth to His death on the cross. Place your hopes in the Lord, He will guide and assist you. Take our rule with you, and a breviary, in order that you may be punctual in saying the Divine Office, and be always submissive to Brother Vidal, your superior. My children, although I am greatly pleased to see the good-will with which you embrace this undertaking, yet our separation is painful to my heart from the sincere affection I bear you; but the commands of our Lord are to be preferred to my own feelings; I entreat you to have the Passion of our Lord Jesus Christ always present to your mind; it will strengthen you and powerfully animate you to suffer for His glory."

These apostolic men, encouraged by this address of their Father, replied that they were ready to go into any country and expose themselves to the severest labors for the interests of the faith; that he need not hold out an example for them, by going himself among the infidels, as if his word was not sufficient; that they did not think his orders too strict, and that they expected assistance from above for carrying them into execution; but that they required his prayers and blessing in order to gather some fruit in unknown lands, among barbarous people, enemies of the Christian name. "He," rejoined the Saint, with great animation, "who sends you, it is He who will take care of you; you are under His protection, under the protection of God; you belong no more to me from this moment; I tear you from my bosom to send you as His laborers." They threw themselves on their knees, kissed his hands and prayed for his last blessing which he gave them weeping, in the following terms:—"May the blessing of God the Father be upon you, as it descended on the apostles; may it strengthen you, guide you, and console you in your sufferings. Fear not; the Lord is with you, as an invincible warrior; go, in the name of God who sends you."

We shall speak of their voyage when we come to relate the martyrdom they suffered in Morocco, on the 16th of January, 1220.

At length, Francis, anxious for the crown of martyrdom in which he had been twice disappointed, confided the government of his Order during his absence to Brother Elias, the Provincial of Tuscany, and set out on his voyage to Syria with twelve companions, the principal of whom were Peter of Catania, Barbaro Sabbatino, Leonard of Assisi, and Illuminus of Rieti.

In the Marches of Ancona through which they passed, in order to embark at the last-named place, a young man came to solicit to be received into the society of Friars Minor, and the Saint said to him: "If you have the intention of joining the Poor of Jesus Christ, go and bestow upon the poor all that thou hast." The postulant went away and gave all he had to his parents whom he loved very much, without giving any to the poor. He then returned and said how he had disposed of his property. Francis censured his conduct in the strongest terms, considering him as a man who would be totally useless, and nowise fit for evangelical perfection. "Tender brother," he said to him (for so he called all those whom he considered of no real value), "Tender brother, go thy ways, you have neither left your country nor your kindred; you have given what you had to your parents, and disappointed the poor; you do not deserve to be received into the company of those who make profession of holy poverty. You commenced by the flesh, which is an unstable foundation for a spiritual edifice." This carnal and animal man returned to his parents, resumed his property, and rather than give it to the poor, he gave up the good purpose he had entertained.

The love of his relations did as much disservice to this young man as the love of riches did to him whom our Saviour desired to sell all he had and give unto the poor. Perhaps also he had an intention of finding a resource in what he gave to his relations, which is contrary to the entire renouncing of everything which Jesus Christ requires. For which reason, when St. Bonaventure relates this circumstance, he says, that St. Francis only admitted those into his Order who gave up all they had, and did not in any manner keep anything back.

The man of God received many novices on his way. Many of his brethren in the vicinity accompanied him as far as Ancona, to witness his departure, as sorrowful, as had been the faithful of Miletus and Ephesus, who accompanied St. Paul embarking for Jerusalem, although he had not told them, as the Apostle did, that they would see him no more. The arrival of this holy band was so agreeable to the magistrates at Ancona, that they immediately allotted a spot for the erection of a convent, and had it commenced at their own expense. It was so large that when Francis returned from Palestine he caused it to be reduced out of love for holy poverty, and then he gave the model of a church which is still extant.

The captain of a vessel who was about to take succor to the Christian forces before Damietta, was so good as to receive him, one of twelve, on board his ship. All the religious who were there were desirous of going to sea with him, and each one vied for the preference, not only that they might accompany the Patriarch, but that they might obtain the crown of martyrdom, which they ardently wished for; but not to mortify any of them, and to show no preferences, he prudently and with the mildness of a common father, addressed them as follows:—

> "My very dear children, there is not one of you, from whom I should wish to be separated; I wish you would all accompany me on the voyage I am about to make; but it would have been unreasonable of me to ask the captain of the vessel to take you all. On which account, and that none should have reason to complain, nor to be jealous of the others, I will not make the selection; it must be Made by God." And thereupon calling a child who happened to be on board, he said: "The Lord has often made His will known by the mouth of children, and I have no doubt He will do the same now; let us ask this child, and let us credit what he shall say; God will speak through him." Then asking the child, whether it was God's will that all the religious who were with him should put to sea and make the voyage with him? the child replied with a firm voice: "No, it is not

God's will." He then again asked which of them among those who were there present he should take? The child, inspired by the Almighty, selected eleven, pointing them out with his finger, and going up to them as he named them.

The religious, full of astonishment, were all satisfied: those who were destined to remain behind as well as those who were selected to accompany him. They fell on their knees, received the blessing of their common Father, and separated after having given to each other the kiss of peace.

Francis embarked with his eleven companions; they weighed anchor, and shortly after they reached the Island of Cyprus, where they remained a couple of days. In this interval, one of the religious committed a fault which was soon atoned for. In a gust of passion he made use of some harsh expression to one of his brethren before the others, and before another person who might have been scandalized at the event. Reflecting on what he had done, and being immediately sorry for it, he took up some dung, and, returning to the spot, he put it into his mouth, and began chewing it, saying: "It is but just that he who has offended his brother by his speech, should have his mouth filled with filth." This act of penance was fully satisfactory to him who had been offended, and made such impression on a gentleman who had witnessed the scene, that he offered himself and all he possessed to the service of the Order.

From Cyprus, Francis proceeded to Acre, from whence he sent his companions, two and two, into such parts of Syria in which missionaries were most wanted. He himself preached for some days in the vicinity of the town, where he did some good, and then embarked again with Illuminatus to join the army of the Crusaders who were besieging Damietta. We shall now speak of the Crusade, and of this siege.

At the council of Lateran, which was held in 1215, Pope Innocent III represented so energetically the miserable state to which the Christians in the Holy Land were reduced under the domination of the Saracens, that in order to deliver them from so cruel a slavery, the council ordered the assembly of a similar crusade to that which had been ordered two centuries before, for the same object. The bishops proclaimed it everywhere with great ardor, and the Pope, to give it greater weight, went himself into Tuscany to preach it after having published it at Rome. This great Pope, dying on the 16th of July, 1216, Honorius III, who succeeded him, imitated his zeal, and wrote to the princes and prelates of all Europe, and sent legates everywhere, to urge the execution of what had been decreed in the Council of Lateran. The success was as prompt as it was fortunate, so that at the time fixed, that is, on the 1st of June,

1217, an infinity of crusaders, principally from the North of Europe, were in readiness to set out for Palestine, by land and by sea.

After some expeditions, the crusaders thought that, instead of operations in Palestine, to which they had hitherto confined themselves, it would be advisable to carry the war into Egypt, because it was thence that the sultans sent large armies into the Holy Land against the Christians; and this had been the opinion of Pope Innocent at the Lateran Council. It was therefore decided to lay siege to Damietta, the strongest town in Egypt, and from its situation the key of that kingdom. The first of those who sailed arrived before the place on the 30th of May; they disembarked, and intrenched themselves without meeting with any resistance, and when the remainder of the army arrived, the attack commenced.

The siege lasted nearly eighteen months, with enormous losses, yet some astonishing acts of bravery were witnessed. Coradin, (or Moaddam) the Sultan of Damascus, came with an army much more numerous than that of the Crusaders, and besieged them in their intrenchments; and Meledin, (or Melic Camel) his brother, Sultan of Egypt or of Babylon, having brought an equally numerous army, they drew up their troops in order of battle, on the last day of July, 1219, in the early morning, and appeared before the Crusaders' lines, which they attacked on several points. The battle was obstinately contested; it lasted till night, and the Saracens seemed to have the victory, but it was torn from them, chiefly by the indomitable bravery of the French, supported by the Grand Master of the Temple, and the Teutonic knights, who drove the infidels far from their lines with great slaughter. Dissensions then arose between the cavalry and infantry of the Crusaders. They accused each other of cowardice, a reproach very grating to military men; the consequence was, that a turbulent rivalry ensued, in order to prove which had the greatest courage, and they compelled John de Brienne, King of Jerusalem, who commanded the army, to lead them to the enemy and offer him battle.

It was at this moment that Francis arrived at the camp, having no other arms than those of faith. He said to his companion, with deep sighs:— "The Lord has revealed to me, that if they come to blows, the Christians will be worsted. If I tell them this, I shall be considered an idiot;— and if I do not tell it, my conscience will reproach me; what do you think of it?" His companion, whose name was Illuminatus, and who indeed was filled with light, replied:— "My brother, do not let the opinions of men guide you; it is not the first time that you have been looked upon as one bereaved of sense. Clear your conscience, and fear God more than the world." Francis immediately went and warned the Christians not to fight, and foretold them that if they did, they would be beaten.

Minds were, however, too much excited to listen to sound reason; the words of the Saint were taken for ravings. On the 29th of August, when the heat was overpowering, the whole of the Christian army left their lines and offered battle. The enemy at first retired, in order to draw the Crusaders to an extensive plain, where there was no water, and when he saw that thirst and fatigue had caused their ranks to be broken, he turned suddenly and fell upon the cavalry of the right wing which he took by surprise; it was broken and dispersed; its rout caused the infantry which was supported by it, to flee, and the whole army would have been cut to pieces had not the king, followed by the knights of the three orders of French, Flemish and English, and other troops, placed themselves in front and stopped the Saracens who were pursuing the fugitives and effecting an awful retreat. The Christians lost on this occasion near six thousand men, besides prisoners, among whom were many of considerable note. This loss was the accomplishment of what Francis had foretold; and it showed, adds St. Bonaventure, "that his valuable advice ought not to have been disregarded, since, according to the words of the Holy Scriptures, 'the soul of a holy man discovereth sometimes true things, more than seven watchmen that sit on a high place to watch.'"

The faults of the Crusaders, and the ill-successes which often attended their measures, have given room to minds disposed to censure, to condemn all wars undertaken against infidels, or heretics. Nevertheless, the Crusades, during two centuries, were suggested by the Sovereign Pontiffs, and by the councils of the Church, proclaimed by most holy personages, and authorized by their miracles; led by Christian princes of all Europe, by many of our kings, by a Saint Louis, by men full of religious zeal, such as Godfrey of Bouillon, and Simon, Count of Montfort. Is there not the greatest rashness in including such men as these in one sweeping condemnation? If all the Crusaders had not equally pure intentions; if debauchery insinuated itself into their armies, if prudence did not always regulate their proceedings; if sometimes even success did not crown their best-concerted measures, are these sufficient grounds for blaming the enterprise, or, are we only to judge of measures by the event?

Saint Bernard preached the crusade which was decided on in the year 1144, of which Louis VII, King of France, had first formed the plan, and of which Pope Eugenius III, and the bishops of France approved. The preaching of the holy abbot was publicly supported by a prodigious number of miracles, which even his humility could not dissemble. Two powerful armies, the one commanded by the Emperor Conrad III, the other by the King of France, with the princes and nobility of the states, were calculated to inspire the infidels with terror. Nevertheless, from various causes, nothing could have been more unfortunate than the issue of this war; and, as the loss of these two armies was felt through the whole of France and through the whole of Germany, where St. Bernard had preached, and promised glorious success, public indignation fell upon him, and he was treated as a false prophet. What he wrote to Pope Eugenius in his justification, must be considered as an answer to all those who, even in these days, condemn the Crusades, the result of which was disastrous. He says, that Moses, in God's name, had solemnly promised the people of Israel to lead them into a very fertile land, and that God had even confirmed that promise by splendid miracles; that, nevertheless, all those who went out of Egypt perished in the desert without entering into the land of promise, in punishment of the sins of the people during the journey; that it cannot be said that this punishment was a contradiction of the promise, because the promises which God, in His goodness, makes to man, never prejudice the rights of His justice; and this reasoning the Saint applies to the crimes committed in the armies of the Crusades.

This digression may, perhaps, appear long, but we could not dispense with it for the honor of the religious and of the preceding ages; and, besides, it is connected with the life of St. Francis, who certainly approved of the Crusades, although, by a supernatural inspiration, he blamed a particular enterprise of the Crusaders which had the unfortunate issue which he had foretold.

The ardor of his charity which urged him to labor for the conversion of the Saracens, and to expose himself to martyrdom, induced him to take the resolution to present himself to the Sultan of Egypt. "We saw," says James de Vitry, "Brother Francis, the founder of the Order of the Friars Minor, a simple and unlearned man, though very amiable and beloved by God and man, who was respected universally. He came to the Christian army, which was lying before Damietta, and an excess of fervor had such an effect upon him, that, protected solely by the shield of faith, he had the daring to go to the sultan's camp to preach to him and to his subjects the faith of Jesus Christ."

The two armies were in sight of each other, and there was great danger in going from one to the other, particularly as the sultan had promised a handsome reward in gold to any one who should bring him a Christian's head. But this would not deter such a soldier of Jesus Christ as was Francis, who, far from fearing death, eagerly sought it. He betook himself to prayer, from which he arose full of strength and confidence, saying with the prophet: "Since Thou art with me, O Lord, I will fear no evil, though I should walk in the midst of the shadow of death;" and he set out for the infidel camp.

Two sheep which he met on setting out, gave him much joy. He said to his companion: "My brother, have confidence in the Lord, the word of the Gospel is being fulfilled in us, which says: 'Behold I send you forth as sheep in the midst of wolves.'" In fact, only a very little farther on, some Saracens rushed upon them, as wolves upon sheep, insulted and beat them, and bound them. Francis said: "I am a Christian, lead me to your master;" and God permitted that he should be so led to comply with the desire of His servant. The Sultan Meledin asked him who sent them, and for what purpose they came? Francis answered with courageous firmness: "We are not sent by men, but it is the Most High who sends us, in order that I may teach you and your people the way of salvation, by pointing out to you the truths of the Gospel." He immediately preached to him, with great fervor, the dogma of one God in three Persons, and the Lord Jesus Christ, the Saviour of mankind.

Then was seen verified what our Saviour said to His apostles. "For I will give you a mouth and wisdom which all your adversaries shall not be able to resist or gainsay." Meledin became so mild and tractable, that, admiring the courage of Francis, he listened quietly to him for some days, and invited him to stay with him. The man of God said: "If you and your people will be converted, I will remain for the love of Jesus Christ. And if you hesitate between His law and that of Mahomet, let a great fire be lit up, and I will go into it with your priests, in order that you may see thereby which is the faith to follow." "I do not believe," replied the sultan, "that any of our priests would go into the fire, or suffer any torments for his religion." He answered thus because he perceived that as soon as the fire was proposed, one of the eldest of the priests, one who was of the most considerable of them, got quickly away. "If you will promise me," added Francis, "that yourself and your people will embrace the Christian faith, in case I come forth from the fire safe and sound, I will enter it alone; if I am burnt let it be imputed to my sins; but if God preserve me, you will then acknowledge that Jesus Christ is the true God and Saviour of mankind."

Meledin acknowledged that he dared not accept this challenge, lest it should be the cause of a sedition; but he offered him rich presents which the servant of God despised from his heart as so much dirt. Such entire disengagement from the good things of this world inspired the prince with such veneration and confidence that he entreated the Saint to receive his presents, and to distribute them among the poor Christians or to the churches for the salvation of his soul. Francis who had a loathing of money, and who did not find in the sultan any groundwork of religion, persisted in his refusal of these offers. He, moreover, thought it was time to leave the infidels when he saw no prospect of effecting any good, and where he had no further chance of gaining the crown of martyrdom; and he learnt by a revelation that what he intended was conformable to the will of God. The sultan, on his part, fearing that some of his people might be moved by the discourse of Francis, and, being converted, might join the Christian army, caused him to be escorted with marks of consideration to the Christian camp before Damietta, after having said to him in private: "Pray for me, that God may make known what religion is most agreeable to Him, in order that I may embrace it."

Was it not a sight worthy of God, worthy of angels, and of men, to see on one side Francis, clothed in sackcloth, pale, emaciated, disfigured by his penitential austerities, pass through an army of infidels, and present himself boldly before their sovereign, speak to him against the law of their prophet, and exhort him to acknowledge the divinity of Jesus Christ? and, on the other side, the Sultan of Egypt, the mortal enemy of the Christians, elated by the victory he had just gained over them, and anxious to shed more of their blood, suddenly lose all his ferocity, become mild and tractable, listen attentively to the poor one of Jesus Christ, endeavor to retain him, offer him large presents, admire his poverty, his disinterestedness, his courage, ask the aid of his prayers, that he might know and embrace the true religion, and send him back to the Christian camp with honor? How certain it is that the religion of Jesus Christ will never be made more respectable and amiable to the infidels than by the practice of the exalted virtues which it teaches, and by which it became established in the world.

Another scene which is not less striking in the eyes of piety, is the heart of Francis, burning with anxiety to shed his blood for the glory of his Master, and not being able to satisfy that ardor. Already, in the hope of attaining it, he had embarked for Syria, and contrary winds had driven him back to the Christian shores. He had gone into Spain in order to pass into Africa, when a violent illness compelled him to desist from the undertaking. He thinks he already grasps the palm, when he finds himself in Egypt; in order to hasten the accomplishment of his desires, he places himself in the hands of the infidels, and attacks the tyrant on his throne; when, instead of the opprobrium and tortures which he sought, he finds nothing but mildness and curiosity, attentions and honor. He seeks for martyrdom, and martyrdom flies from him. "It was," St. Bonaventure remarks, "by an admirable disposition of Divine Providence, who chose that the ardent desire of his faithful servant should give him the merit of martyrdom, and that his life should be preserved to receive the glorious stigmata which were to be impressed on his body by a singular prerogative, in reward of his great love for Jesus crucified, who inflamed his heart."

Wading relates, upon the authority of a religious of the Order, who was a contemporary of St. Francis, whose name was Ugolino of St. Mary of the Mount, corroborated by some other writers of the Order, that the sultan was converted and baptized. Some later authors deny this, and remark that they have mistaken the Sultan of Egypt for the Sultan of Ieonium, who never saw St. Francis, and of whom James of Vitry says, that he was believed to have received baptism at his death which happened in the year when Damietta was besieged. It is admitted that Wading was mistaken in quoting this passage to prove the conversion of the Sultan of Egypt, but that does not weaken the evidence of Ugolino. He says that Francis went a second time to the sultan before his return to Italy. He urged him to be converted. The Saint, not being able to induce him to overcome the human obstacles which stood in the way, prayed fervently for him for several successive days, and then felt that his prayers were heard. This he communicated to Meledin, who imbibed still greater affection for him, and wished to detain him, but he departed according to the command that he had received from heaven. Some years after, this prince being dangerously ill, the Saint appeared to two of his religious who were in Syria and ordered them to go to him, instruct him, baptize him, and remain with him till he should expire; all this was complied with. There is nothing in this legend which is not very probable, and which is not consistent with circumstances that cannot be called into question:

1) We have seen, in the narratives of James of Vitry, and of St. Bonaventure, that Meledin said to Francis: "Pray for me, that God may make known to me which religion is most agreeable to Him;" and that he wished to induce him to receive his presents, in order to distribute them to the poor Christians, or to the churches, for the salvation of his soul.

2) After he had seen the holy man, he treated the Christians with great humanity, and shortly after their discomfiture, he sent some of his prisoners to their camp, to offer terms of peace. In the year 1221, their army, which was coming to offer him battle, entangled itself between two branches of the Nile, where it must have inevitably perished. "He behaved to his enemies," says one of our authors, "in such a manner as could not reasonably have been expected from a Saracen, and which in these days would do honor to a Christian prince were he to do it."

3) An author, whose testimony on such a point is beyond suspicion, says, "that this sultan, being on his deathbed, caused a large sum of money to be distributed among the poor Christians who were sick in the hospitals, and that he left a considerable revenue for the same purpose; that he enfranchised many slaves, that he had performed various other acts of mercy, and that his death was greatly lamented by the Christians, whom he spared to the utmost of his power. The Emperor Frederic was inconsolable after Meledin's death, having had strong hopes that he would receive baptism according to a promise he had given him, and that he would strenuously contribute to the propagation of Christianity in the Levant."

4) It may have happened that St. Francis who was then in heaven, appeared to two of the religious of his Order, and that he sent them to Meledin; that these religious instructed and baptized him; and that the thing was done secretly from the circumstances of the times; that the authors of those times were not informed of it, and that Ugolino learned it from the religious themselves. In short, it is not improbable that the conversion of this soul should have been granted to the zeal, labors, prayers and tears of such a friend of God as St. Francis. Thus, the baptism of the sultan is not so very uncertain, and those who have recorded it have not given the Saint praise which may be called false, as Wading has been acrimoniously taxed with. After all, if Meledin was not converted, it is a judgment of God, which those must be fearful of who recommend themselves to the prayers of the pious, forming projects of conversion, and even doing some good works, who yet positively resist the grace vouchsafed them, which requires an effectual change of heart. If he was converted, which is probable, it was a great effect of divine mercy, which sinners must not abuse by deferring their repentance; these graces are very rarely given, and those who wait for them run great risk of their salvation.

There is reason for thinking that Meledin gave Francis and his companions leave to preach in his dominions, since it is well known that the Friars Minor began from that time to spread themselves amongst the Saracens, as James de Vitry says:—"Even the Saracens, blinded as they are, admire the humility and perfection of the Friars Minor, receive them well, and provide them cheerfully with all the necessaries of life, when they go boldly amongst them to preach the gospel; they listen to them willingly, speaking of Jesus

Christ and His doctrine; but they beat them and drive them away if they attack Mahomet, and hold him as a liar and infidel."

An anecdote, related by St. Bonaventure, may have easily happened in those times. A Saracen seeing some Friars Minor, was moved by their poverty and offered them some money, which they refused to accept, and this astonished him. Having understood that it was for the love of God that they refused money, he conceived such a liking for them, that he undertook to provide them with everything necessary as long as he was able to do so. The holy doctor exclaims on this:—"O inestimable excellence of poverty, which is so powerful to inspire a barbarian with such tender and generous compassion!" It would be a shameful and very criminal thing, were Christians to despise and trample under foot this precious evangelical pearl, for which a Mahometan showed such esteem and respect.

While Francis remained in Egypt, he did not gather much fruit from among the infidels; but his words were a fertile seed which his disciples reaped the abundant harvest of, when afterwards sent thither by Gregory IX and Innocent III.

The Saracens were not the only objects of the zeal of Francis. He labored also for the salvation of the Christians in the army of the Crusaders, and some of them became his disciples. James de Vitry, Bishop of Acre, writing to his friends in Lorraine informed them that Renier, the Prior of St. Michael, had joined the Order of the Friars Minor; and that three of the most eminent of his clergy had followed his example, and that it was with difficulty he prevented the chorister and several others from taking the same course, to which he adds that this religious Order spreads fast in the world because it is an exact imitation of the form of the primitive Church, and of the life of the Apostles.

The most ancient records of the Order assure us that after some months' residence in Egypt, the holy Patriarch went to Palestine, and visited the holy places, but they enter into no particulars. What we may safely conjecture is, that God, who led him into the Holy Land, seemed to say to him, as He had said to Abraham: "Arise and walk through the land in the length and in the breadth thereof, for I will give it to thee."

Rather more than a hundred years after his death, the Sultan of Egypt permitted the Friars Minor to take charge of the Holy Sepulchre of our Lord, and they still have the care of it in the midst of the infidels, under the protection of the Eldest Son of the Church. This privilege, which is so honorable for the Order of St. Francis, is justly considered by them as the fruit of the fervent devotion of the blessed Patriarch to Jesus Christ crucified.

From Palestine Francis went to Antioch, the capital of Syria, and passed by the black mountain, where there was a celebrated monastery of the order of St. Benedict. The abbot who had died only a short time before, had foretold that a saintly man would soon come to their house, who was much beloved by God, the Patriarch, of a great Order, who would be poorly attired and of mean appearance, but very much to be revered; in consequence of which the religious, hearing of his coming, went in procession to meet him, and received him with all the honors due to a man of God. He remained some days with them, and the holin ess which they observed in him made such an impression upon them, that they embraced his Institute, placing all their effects at the disposition of the patriarch of Antioch. Some other monasteries followed their example; and, in a few years, there was a flourishing province in that country, which continued until such time as the Saracens ravaged the whole of Syria.

While Francis was thus employed in extending his Order in the East, Brother Elias, who was his vicar-general in the West, was destroying it there. He said to the religious, in their conferences, that the life of their Founder was worthy of the highest praise, but that it was not given to all to imitate it; that among the things which he had prescribed for them, some appeared in the eyes of prudence very difficult of observance, others absolutely impracticable and beyond the strength of man; that, in the opinion of the most prudent, some modification was requisite and some change required, some practices necessary, which were not so strictly regular—by specious insinuations of this nature, he brought over many to his opinions, and even some of the provincials who ventured to represent the simplicity of their Father as imprudent. The vicar-general, nevertheless, in conjunction with the ministers, made some regulations for the government of the provinces which were very useful; but, by a strange inconsistency, at the time when they were talking of modifications, they prescribed total abstinence from meat, and forbade its use either in or out of the cloisters, which was a direct contradiction of the rule, which permits the Friars Minor, except in times of fasting, to eat, according to the terms of the Gospel, whatsoever is put before them.

All those who had the true spirit of God were greatly grieved to see that human prudence was preferred to the divine will, and that the vineyard of the Lord was rendered desolate by Brother Elias. They put up fervent prayers to God for the speedy return of their pastor, so necessary for the flock; and, after having secretly concerted together, they sent Brother Stephen into Syria, to communicate to their Founder what was going on. Stephen went and gave him a full detail of all things. Francis was not cast down by this deplorable intelligence, but he had recourse to God, and recommended to His protection the family he had received from him. As to the regulation which prescribed entire abstinence from meat, he, with great humility, asked the advice of Peter of Catana, who replied: "It is not for me to judge; it is for the legislator to decide thereon, as on all the rest." Francis deferred the decision till his return, and embarked immediately for Italy.

His voyage was not a long one; they soon anchored at the Isle of Candia, from whence they came to Venice where they landed. He sent circular letters to convene the chapter which he proposed holding at the ensuing Michaelmas, to remedy the evil which had been brought about by Brother Elias. He built a small chapel near the Venetian lakes, (Lagunes,) in which two of his religious were to say the Divine Office, in memory of an extraordinary thing which happened to him at this place.

The Saint then went to Padua, Bergamo, Brescia, the island of the lake of Garda, to Cremona and Mantua; at all these places there were convents of his Order. We are assured that St. Dominic joined him on his way; that they conferred together and with John of Navarra de Torniella, Bishop of Bergamo, on the salvation of souls; that they made some pious visits to the solitaries of the valley of Astino, and that the patriarch of the Friars Preachers celebrated Mass there, that of the Minors being the deacon at the service. When they were in spiritual conference at Cremona, the religious came to request them to bless the well, and to solicit the Almighty to purify the water which was thick and muddy. Dominic, at the entreaty of Francis, blessed a vessel full of the water, and caused it to be thrown back into the well, and all water that subsequently was drawn from it was clear and wholesome to drink.

The two saints separated, but, shortly after, met again at Bologna. Francis going to Bologna, met a woman whose son was epileptic, and who came to beg the aid of his prayers. He wrote on a slip of paper some short but very devout ejaculatory prayers which he thought might be taken to the sick youth; they had no sooner been given to him, than he was entirely cured; in gratitude whereof, he placed himself at the service of the Friars Minor in the convent of Parma.

The reputation of the holy man was so great that, according to Sigonius, the streets were choked with the number of students who wished to see and hear him. It was with difficulty that way was made for him to reach the principal square, where he preached in so sublime a manner that they thought they heard an angel and not a man. The greater part of the audience was converted; and many solicited the habit of the Order, among whom were Nicholas of Pepulis, Bonizio, Pelerino, Falleroni, and Riger or Ricer of Modena. Nicholas was that learned jurisconsult who had been so kind to

Bernard de Quintavalle in 1211, when every one had treated him with contempt at Bologna. Bonizio excelled in the love of holy poverty, and was very useful to the Saint in affairs of importance, by the talent he had of managing with prudence. Pelerino and Riger were young gentlemen from the Marches of Ancona, who were students at Bologna—to them Francis foretold all they would do in the course of their lives. The first would only be a lay-brother, although he was well versed in canon-law; it was said of him that when he was in company with men of the world, either from necessity or from charitable motives, he left them as soon as he could; and when he was censured for so doing as being guilty of rudeness, he replied: "When we have sought Jesus Christ our Master, we have never found Him either amongst relatives or amongst our acquaintances." The second attached himself to his holy Patriarch, and strove to imitate him in all things. Although he was eminently favored with the gift of chastity, he nevertheless avoided with great care the conversation of females, and he said to those with whom he was intimate, who were surprised at it: "I should perhaps lose the gift with which I have been favored, by a just judgment of God, if I took fewer precautions: he who loves danger will perish in it."

Here is an authentic testimonial as to one of the sermons which Francis preached at Bologna in the year 1220; it is taken from the Archives of the church of Spalatro, and it is found in the history of the bishops of Bologna, written by Sigonius:

> "I, Thomas, citizen of Spalatro, and archdeacon of the cathedral of the same town, saw, in the year 1220, on the day of the Assumption of the Mother of God, St. Francis preach in the square in front of the little palace where almost the whole city was collected. He began his sermon thus: 'The angels, the men, and the demons.' He spoke of these intelligent beings so well and with such precision, that many learned men who heard him, were astonished to hear such a discourse from the mouth of so simple a man. He did not diverge to draw a moral from different subjects, as preachers usually do, but as those who dilate upon one point, he brought everything to bear upon the sole object of restoring peace, concord, and union which had been totally destroyed by cruel dissensions. He was very poorly clad, his countenance was pale and wan, and his whole appearance was uninviting; but God gave such force and efficiency to his words, that they led to the reconciliation of a great number of gentlemen who were greatly exasperated against each other, and whose irritation had caused the shedding of no small quantity of blood. The love and veneration for the Saint were so universal, and went

so far, that men and women ran to him in crowds, and those esteemed themselves fortunate who could only touch the hem of his garments."

The author who records this testimonial adds that he performed miracles also in Bologna. A child of quality was taken to him, who had what is called a pearl on his eye, which rendered his eye quite blind, and no remedy could be found for it. Francis made the sign of the cross over him from the head to the feet, and he was perfectly cured. Having subsequently entered the Institute of his miraculous physician, he saw much better with the eye on which the pearl had been than with the other. This miracle, which was known throughout the city, increased the zeal and respect which the Bolognese had for the servant of God so much, that they could not tear themselves from him, and they gave him a second house for his Institute, situated in a wood about a mile from the town.

After these apostolical functions, he went to see Cardinal Ugolino, who was then legate in Lombardy, by whom he was received with marks of the most sincere affection. He proposed next to visit the convent of his Order which was close to one of the gates of Bologna, but as soon as he saw it, finding it much more spacious and handsome than was requisite for strict poverty, he turned away his eyes from it, and said indignantly: "Is this the dwelling of the poor Evangelical laborers? Such grand and superb palaces, are they for Friars Minor? I do not acknowledge this house as one of ours, and I do not look upon those who dwell in it as my brethren. I, therefore, order and enjoin all those who wish to continue to bear the name of Friars Minor, to leave this house forthwith, and to give up to the rich of the world buildings which are only fit for them."

He was so implicitly obeyed, that even the sick, among whom was Brother Leo, one of his first companions, who is the relator of this circumstance, were carried out on the shoulders of their brethren and exposed to the air. There they all remained till the arrival of the legate, who, having been informed of what was going on, had come and appeased the holy man. He represented to him that it was necessary to allow the convents to be more spacious, in order that the infirm might have more air for restoring their health; and that such as were well should have more room for relaxing their minds. "But as to the property," he added, "I can assure you that your brethren have no part in it, as it remains entirely to the founders. Moreover, if you have any further scruples on the subject, I declare to you that I take the whole upon myself in the name of the Holy Roman Church."

Francis could not resist the powerful reason of the prudent and pious legate, the protector of his Order. He, therefore, consented that his brethren should remain in the convent; he even ordered them to return to it, but he would not go into it himself, and he chose to take the repose which nature required, in the house of the Friars Preachers, where he passed some days with his friend Saint Dominic.

It would appear that St. Bonaventure had this circumstance in view, when he said: "that if it happened that St. Francis found in the houses which his brethren occupied, anything which looked like property, or that was too elegant, he wished the houses to be pulled down, or that the religious should quit them, because he maintained that the Order was grounded on Evangelical poverty as its principal foundation, so that if this poverty was adhered to in it, it would flourish, but that it would perish if it was set aside."

While the Saint was with the Friars Preachers, one of them, from feelings of compassion, begged him to return to his children, and to pardon the fault they had committed, but he replied: "Indulgence which gives rise to an easy relapse into sin, is not be commended. I will not sanction by my presence what has been committed against holy poverty." This charitable religious endeavored to induce him at least to see them, in order that they might be made aware of their fault, and be corrected. "We will come back here together," he said, "if you do not choose to remain there, after having performed this duty of superior." Francis yielded to this prudent advice; he went to his children, and seeing them grieved and repentant, and ready to receive the penance he might inflict, he pardoned them.

His indulgence did not extend to the provincial, whose name was John de Strachia, one of those who wished to have the rule mitigated in 1219. He censured him severely for having had so beautiful a house built, or, at least, for having permitted it to be built. He upbraided him in strong terms for having, without consulting him, opened a school for the studies of the Friars Minor, and for having made regulations for its conduct more favorable to science than to piety. He did away with this school, because he chose that his religious should pray rather than study, and that the other provincials might learn to be more humble and more religious in all that had relation to studies.

And here we must advert to what happened at a later period; the provincial had the rashness to reestablish the school after the departure of the Founder, who, having been informed of it, and knowing from interior revelation the obduracy of this man, cursed him publicly, and deposed him at the ensuing chapter. The Saint was entreated to withdraw this curse, and to give his blessing to Brother John, who was a noble and learned man, but he answered:

"I cannot bless him whom the Lord has cursed." A dreadful reply which was soon after verified. This unfortunate man died, exclaiming: "I am damned and cursed for all eternity." Some frightful circumstances which followed after his death confirmed his awful prognostic. Such a malediction which pride and disobedience brought upon this learned man, ought to strike terror into those vain men who forsake piety for science, and in whom great talents have no other effect than to produce in them great attachment to their own conceits, and proud indocility, which induces, at length, even a revolt against the Church.

St. Francis was not averse to studies, as will be seen, when, two years after, he caused theology to be taught. But he chose that they should so study as not to extinguish the spirit of prayer. He approved of science, but of that only, which the Holy Spirit calls religious, which is sanctified by the fear of the Lord, of which St. Augustine says: "that it is the companion of charity, and teaches humility."

Cardinal Ugolino proposed to the Servant of God that they should make a retreat of some days together, at Camaldoli, in order to give his body some rest, which was borne down by fatigue, and relax his mind from the various cares which oppressed it. He willingly assented to this, because he liked the life of a recluse. They, therefore, went to this holy solitude, and they remained there nearly a month, solely employed in meditation on heavenly things. The cardinal took a cell at the entry of the desert where it is still to be seen; and Francis took one near it, which had been inhabited by St. Romnald. It has since taken the name of St. Francis' cell, and is only occupied by the prior, or major of Camaldoli. The writers of the country add, that the festival of St. Francis is celebrated solemnly there, and that it is decreed by the statutes that the anthem which the Friars Minor chant shall be sung on that day: Salve, Sancte Pater, &c.

> The two pious solitaries went from thence to Mount Alvernia,
> where they only stayed a few days. The cardinal returned to Bologna,

and

> Francis took the route for Assisi, in order to open the chapter at
> St. Mary of the Angels, as he had given notice.

On the way, St. Bonaventure acquaints us what occurred to him. His infirmities and fatigue having compelled him to mount on an ass, his companion, Leonard of Assisi, who followed him on foot, and was also very much fatigued, gave way to human feelings, and said to himself: "His parents were not the equals of mine; yet, there he rides, and I am forced to trudge on foot and lead him." As he was thus giving way to these thoughts, Francis, to whom God had made known what was passing in Leonard's mind, dismounted, and said: "No, brother, it is not fitting that I should ride while you walk on foot, because you are better born than I am, and are of greater consideration in the world." Leonard, greatly surprised, and blushing for shame, threw himself at his Father's feet, acknowledged his fault, and with tears solicited his pardon.

As soon as the holy Patriarch entered the Valley of Spoleto, his children came in crowds from various parts to meet him, and to congratulate him on his return. He was greatly gratified on seeing them, and communicated freely with them, encouraging the weak, consoling those who were in affliction, censuring such as were in fault, and exhorting them all to adhere strictly to the rules. It was there that he received a confirmation of the complaints which had been made to him in the Levant, against the government of Elias, his vicar general, and he had himself the proof of it.

Elias ventured to present himself to him, in a newer habit and one made of finer cloth than those of the other brethren, the cowl of which was longer and the sleeves wider, and he assumed an air little suitable to his profession. Francis, dissembling what was passing in his mind, said to him before the assistants:—"I beg you to lend me that habit." Elias did not dare refuse: he went aside and took it off and brought it to him. Francis put it on over his own, smoothed it down, plaited it nicely under the girdle, threw the cowl over his head, and then, strutting fiercely with his head erect, he paced three or four times round the company, saying, in a loud voice:—"God preserve you, good people." Then taking the habit off indignantly, he threw it from him with contempt, and, turning to Elias, "That is the way," he said, "that the bastard brethren of our Order will strut." After this he resumed his usual demeanor and walked humbly with his old and tattered habit, saying:—"Such is the deportment of the true Friars Minor." Then, seating himself amongst them, he addressed them in the mildest manner, and spoke on poverty and humility, of which he so forcibly pointed out the perfection, that it seemed to them that those whom they had previously considered the poorest and most humble, had made but small advance in the practice of those two virtues. In fine, he annulled all the novelties which the vicar-general had introduced into the Order during his absence, except the prohibition of eating meat, which he thought it necessary to retain some time longer, lest he might be thought to encourage gluttony.

The means he had taken to curb the foolish vanity of Brother Elias, showed both his prudence and his authority, and made such an impression on his disciples, that there was not one of them who ventured to say a word in favor of the vicar-general, although he had his partisans amongst them. Some time afterwards, the Patriarch had an opportunity of taking off the prohibition of eating meat, in consequence of a wonderful event which is worthy of being recorded.

A young man in the dress of a traveller, came in haste to the door of the Convent of St. Mary of the Angels, and said to Brother Masse, who was the porter:—"I wish to speak to Brother Francis, but I know he is meditating in the woods; call Brother Elias to me, who is said to be learned and prudent, in order that he may satisfy a doubt which presses upon me." The porter was turned away by Brother Elias, and was puzzled what reply to give the stranger, not to scandalize him, and not to say what was untrue. The young man anticipated him, saying: "Brother Elias does not choose to come, I must therefore beg you to go to Brother Francis, in order that he may order him to come to speak to me." Masse went, and did as he was requested, and Francis, having his eyes fixed on heaven, said, without changing his position:—"Go and tell Brother Elias that I order him to speak to the young man."

This order vexed Elias, and he came to the door in great irritation, asking what he was wanted for? "Do not be angry," said the young man, "I ask you, if those who profess to follow the Gospel may not eat whatever is given to them, as Jesus Christ has observed; and if any one may rightfully direct the contrary?" Elias, seizing hastily the door to shut it, said:—"I know all that, and have no answer to give you but: go your ways." The young man replied:—"I cannot tell what you would answer, but I know very well that you ought to give an answer."

When Elias got calm in his cell, he reflected on what had passed, and on what would be proper to say in answer to the question which had been put to him; and, finding it difficult, and being sorry that he had given the young man so ungracious a reception, in whom he thought he had remarked something extraordinary, he returned to speak to him, but he was gone and could not be found. Francis learned from God that it was an angel, and, on his return to the convent, he said to Brother Elias:—"You do what is not right; you turn contemptuously away angels who come from God to visit and instruct us; I greatly fear that your pride will render you unworthy of the humble institution of Friars Minor, and that you will die out of that state." It was then that he revoked the statute which forbade eating meat.

Bernard of Quintavalle returning from Spain and being on the border of a river which he could not cross, the same angel appeared to him in the same form, and greeted him in the Italian language. Bernard, surprised at hearing the language of his country, and taken with the good looks of the young man who addressed him, asked him from whence he came. The angel then told him what had just occurred between him and Brother Elias. He took him by the hand, carried him across the river, and disappeared, leaving him so full of consolation, that he had no fatigue during the remainder of his journey. When he arrived in Italy, and had related the circumstance, with the day and hour, he found that it was in fact the same angel.

Before the opening of the chapter, Francis, reflecting mournfully on the relaxation which had been introduced into his Order by those who ought to have been most zealous in promoting the purity of its observance, had a vision which was very extraordinary. A great statue appeared before him, and he saw it with his bodily eyes; it greatly resembled that which Nabuchodonosor had seen in a dream, the interpretation of which had been given him by the Prophet Daniel. God chose to employ this mode to acquaint the holy Patriarch with the various revolutions which would take place in his Order, and he signified them to him by the statue itself, by the different metals of which it was composed, either thus to modify by these humiliating foreshowings the honor which he derived from being the Founder of so wonderful a work as that of the establishment of his Order; or to inspire him with the intention of sending up fervent prayers to heaven, which should draw down graces on his flock at all times, which, in fact, he did with a profusion of tears; or, in fine, it was a foresight given him of the relaxations which would be introduced, to enable him to advise his religious to be more vigilant, as St. Paul had predicted the errors and irregularities which were to occur in the Church, in order to excite the vigilance of the bishops.

In Nabuchodonosor's vision, a stone was separated from the mountain, which, striking the feet of the statue, shivered it to pieces; the statue was wholly broken, and disappeared. This did not occur in the vision which Francis had; for the great body of religion which it represented, which has had its vicissitudes, as all others (and with more lustre than any, because of its more extensive and greater exposure to the eyes of the public) has nevertheless continued to have existence, to maintain itself, to serve the Church at all times, and to furnish it with saints. It has even often renewed itself with features which bring to mind its primitive beauty; by which it may be said to be a type of the mystical body of Jesus Christ, which notwithstanding the decay of ages, does not cease to have vigorous and healthy members who are as fervent as those of the earliest periods.

The holy Founder having listened to all that was said against the government of Brother Elias, and to what he had alleged in his justification, held his chapter on the Festival of St. Michael, in the Convent of Portiuncula. He substituted Brother Gratian, in the place of Brother John of Strachia, as Provincial of Bologna, of which we have spoken before; and Brother Peter of Catania, in place of Brother Elias. Peter had been the second of his disciples, and into his hands he committed the whole guidance of his Order, not only because he did not think himself able to look to it in person, on account of the multitude of religious now belonging to it, and on account of his infirmity, but in order to improve himself in the virtue of humility, to which he was so much attached.

He then assembled them and said:—"I am now dead to you all; there is Peter of Catania, who is your superior, whom henceforward we must all obey, you and I," and prostrating himself at the feet of Peter, he promised to obey him in all things as minister general of the Order. This title of minister general was displeasing to the religious, who did not wish it should be given to any one during the lifetime of their Father, and they agreed that he who took his place should only have the title of vicar general.

Francis being on his knees, with his hands clasped, and his eyes lifted up to heaven, said, with affecting emotion: "My Lord Jesus Christ, I recommend to Thee this family, which is Thine own, and which up to this moment Thou hast confided to me. Thou knowest that my infirmities incapacitate me from having any longer the care of it; I leave it in the hands of the ministers; if it should so happen that on their part, negligence, scandal, or too great severity, should be the cause of any one of the brethren perishing, they will render to Thee, O Lord, an account of it at the day of judgement."

From that time till his death he continued as much as it was in his power in the humble state of an inferior, although he did not fail to communicate to the superiors the lights which God gave him for the good government of the Order, and on several occasions he could not avoid acting as its Founder and General.

St. Dominic, his friend, had similar feelings as to the employments of office. In this year he held the first chapter of his Order at Bologna, and wished to resign the station of superior, of which his humility made him consider himself incapable and unworthy; but his religious would not permit it. These have been the feelings of all the saints, because they knew that, for the purpose of salvation, it is safer to obey than to command. Eight days before the chapter, Pope Honorious issued a bull addressed to Francis, and to the superiors of the Friars Minor, by which he forbade them to receive any one to profession, unless after a twelvemonth's probation, and directing that, after profession, no one whosoever should leave the order; forbidding, also, any persons from receiving such as should quit it. What gave rise to this measure was that, at the commencement of the Order of Friars Minor, and of that of the Preachers, there were some who made their profession without a novitiate, according as the superiors thought proper under different circumstances, and this sort of precipitate engagement was found to have its inconveniences.

Peter of Catania, acting as vicar general, and finding that he could not provide for the multitude of religious who came to the Convent of St. Mary of the Angels, as to the chief monastery of the Order, thought that, in order to provide for this, some portion of the property of the novices might be retained; on which he consulted Francis to know whether he thought the suggestion proper, and if he would permit it. Francis said: "My dear brother, God preserve us from this sort of charity, which would render us impious in respect to our rule, in order to acquire consideration in the sight of men." The vicar then asking what he should do for the relief of the guests; "Strip the altar of the Blessed Virgin," replied Francis, "take away all the ornaments which are there; the Lord will send you what is requisite to restore to his Mother what we shall employ in charity. Believe firmly that the Virgin will be pleased to see her altar stripped, rather than that there should be any contravention of the Gospel of her Son;" and he took occasion again strenuously to recommend holy poverty.

He also said many things relative to books, to science, and to preaching, which will be recorded in another part of his life. Brother Casar of Spires, who had been professor of theology before becoming a Friar Minor, and who was a man of great piety, having heard all that the Father said on the subject of science, and the learned, had a long conversation with him on the state of his soul, and on the observance of the rule, which he concluded thus: "My Father, I have made a firm resolution, with God's grace, to observe the Gospel and the rule, according to the instruction of Jesus Christ, until my death; and now, I have a favor to ask you, which is that, if it may happen in my lifetime that some should swerve from it, as you have foretold, you give me your blessing from this moment, and your leave to separate myself from such transgressors, in order that I may adhere to the rule alone with those who have a like zeal with myself." Rejoicing at this proposition, Francis embraced him and blessed him, saying: "Know, my son, that what you solicit is granted to you by Jesus Christ, and by me;" and placing his hands on his head, he added: "Thou art a priest forever according to the order of Melchisedech"—the holy man desiring to have it understood thereby that all the promises he had received from Jesus Christ, would have their accomplishment to the end, in those who adhered to the rule.

It was at this time that he addressed a letter to the religious of his Order, and particularly to the priests, upon the profound veneration which we ought to have for that august mystery of the Eucharist.

In the course of the year 1220, Francis received the news of the martyrdom of the five religious whom he had sent to Morocco. We must relate the circumstances, more at length, since they belong to the life of the holy Patriach, who gave this mission to these valorous soldiers of Jesus Christ, and since they are the first martyrs of the Order.

Berardus, Peter, Otho, Ajut, Accursus, and Vital, their superior, having left Italy for Morocco, after having received their Father's blessing, as has already been noticed, arrived shortly after in the kingdom of Arragon. There Vital was detained some time by a lingering illness, which induced him to think that it was not God's will that he should continue his journey. He therefore let the other five proceed, who soon reached Coimbra, and were favorably received by Urraca, queen of Portugal, the wife of King Alphonso II. This princess conceived so high an opinion of their virtue and placed such confidence in them, that she entreated them to pray to God to inform them of the time at which she should die. They promised to do so, although they considered themselves unworthy of making such a request; but they were so favorably heard, that they foretold to the queen that they were to suffer martyrdom with all the circumstances thereof; that their relics would be brought to Coimbra, and that she would receive them honorably, after which she would be called from this world. Predictions which were fully verified. They went from thence to Alanquer, where the Princess Sancia, sister to the king of Portugal, approving their plans, induced them to put secular clothing over their religious habits, without which precaution they would not have been able to pass into the territories of Morocco.

Having reached Seville, which was then occupied by the Moors, they remained a week concealed in the house of a Christian, where they threw off their secular clothing. Their zeal induced them to go forth, and they got as far as the principal mosque, which they attempted to enter in order to preach to the infidels, but they were driven back with loud cries and severely beaten. From thence they went to the gate of the palace, saying that they were ambassadors sent to the king from Jesus Christ, the King of kings. They were introduced, and said many things relative to the Christian religion, to induce the king to be converted and receive baptism; but they afterwards added much against Mahomet and against his law, which irritated him to such a degree, that he ordered them to be beheaded; but being mollified by the entreaties of his son, he was satisfied with having them confined at the top of a tower, from whence he had them removed to the ground-floor, because, from above, they continued to speak of Jesus Christ, and against the prophet, to those who entered the palace. Having caused them to be again brought before him, he engaged to pardon them, if they would change their religion: "Prince," they replied, "would to God that you would have mercy on yourself! Treat us as you think proper. It is in your power to take away our lives, but we are sure that death will lead us to a glorious immortality." The king, seeing their unshakeable firmness, sent them, by the advice of his council, to Morocco, with Don Pedro Fernandas de Castro, a gentlemen of Castile, and some other Christians.

They found there the Infant Don Pedro of Portugal, who had retired to that country in consequence of some misunderstanding which he had with his brother, King Alphonso, and who now commanded the troops of the king of Morocco. This prince received them with great respect and charity as apostolical men, and had them provided with everything necessary for their subsistence. Knowing what had occurred to them at Seville, in consequence of their preaching, and seeing that, consequently, they were still in a state of great weakness, he endeavored to dissuade them from doing the same thing in Morocco; but the generous missionaries, solely intent upon their pious object, ceased not to preach without any fear, wherever they met with any Saracens.

One day, when Berardus was giving instruction to the people and was declaiming against Mahomet from a wagon, the king passed by, going to visit the tombs of his predecessors, and seeing that he continued his talking notwithstanding his presence, he thought the declaimer must be out of his mind, and instantly directed that all the five should be driven out of the town, and sent back to the country of the Christians. The Infant Don Juan gave them an escort to convey them to Ceuta, whence they were to embark. On the road, they got stealthily away from their escort, and returned to Morocco, where they recommenced preaching in the great square. The king, being informed of this, became greatly irritated, and had them imprisoned, in order to starve them to death. They were there twenty days without food or drink.

During this time the heat became so excessive and caused so much sickness, that it was thought that the hand of God fell heavily upon them to avenge his servants. The king became alarmed, and by the advice of a Saracen named Abaturino, who loved the Christians, he liberated the prisoners. They were extremely surprised to find that, after twenty days' confinement, without any nourishment whatsoever, they came out in full health and strength.

As soon as they had left the prison, they were anxious to recommence their preaching; but the other Christians, who were apprehensive of the wrath of the king, opposed themselves to it, and had them taken to the place of embarkation; but they again made their escape, and returned to Morocco. Then the Infant Don Pedro was induced to keep them in his palace, and to place guards over them to prevent their appearing in public.

This prince being obliged to set out, some short time after, to take the command of the army which the king sent against some rebels, he took the Friars Minor with him, as well as several other Christians, fearing lest, during his absence, they should escape from those who had charge of them. As he returned victorious, his army was three days without water, and was reduced to the greatest distress. Brother Bernardus resorted to prayer, and having made a hole in the ground with a pickaxe, he caused a spring to flow from it, which sufficed for the whole army, and enabled them to fill their goat-skins, after which it dried up. So palpable a miracle procured for them from all parts the greatest veneration. Many even went so far as to kiss their feet.

When they returned to Morocco, the Infant continued to take the same precautions as before, to prevent their appearing in public; nevertheless, they found means to get out secretly one Friday, and to present themselves before the king, as he was passing, according to his custom, to visit the tombs of his predecessors. Berardus again got upon a wagon, and spoke in his presence with astonishing intrepidity. The king, irritated beyond control, gave orders to one of the princes of his court to have them put to death. This prince only had them put in prison, because he had witnessed the miracle which we have recorded above.

They were very ill-treated in this confinement, but continued to preach even there, when there were either Christians or Saracens to listen to them. All this occurred towards the end of the year 1219.

At the beginning of the year 1220, the Saracen prince who had received the order to put them to death, having sent for them from the prison, found them very firm in their faith, and that they spoke with the same boldness against their prophet Mahomet. He was so enraged at this, that, forgetful of the miracle he had witnessed on the return of the army, he directed them to be kept separated and tortured in various ways. They tied their hands and feet, and dragged them along the ground by a cord fastened round their necks, and they were so cruelly scourged that their bowels nearly protruded. Thirty men who were employed for this cruel service did not leave them till they had poured boiling vinegar and oil into their wounds, and rolled them upon broken pieces of earthenware covered with straw.

Some of those who guarded them, saw a great light which came from Heaven, and which seemed to raise these religious up, with an innumerable number of other persons; they thought that they had left the prison and entered it in great haste, where they found them in fervent prayer.

The king of Morocco, informed of what had been done, desired that they might be brought into his presence. They brought them to him, their hands tied, and they were driven in with blows and cuffs. A Saracen prince who met them endeavored to induce them to embrace the law of Mahomet. Brother Otho rejected the proposition with horror and spat on the ground, to mark his contempt of such a religion; this brought upon him a severe box on the ear, upon which he turned the other side, according to the direction of the Gospel, and said to the prince:—"May God forgive thee, for thou knowest not what thou doest."

When they had reached the palace, the king said to them: "Are you then those impious persons who despise the true faith, those foolish persons who blaspheme the prophet sent from God?" "O king," they answered, "we have no contempt for the true faith; on the contrary, we are ready to suffer and die in its defence; but we detest your faith, and the wicked man who was its author." The king, imagining that he might perhaps gain them over by the love of pleasure, of riches or of honors, said to them, in pointing out to them some Saracen women whom he had brought there on purpose: "I will give you those women for wives, together with large sums of money, and you shall be highly esteemed in my kingdom, if you will embrace the law of Mahomet; if not, you shall die by the sword." The confessors of the faith answered without hesitating: "We want neither your women nor your money: keep those for yourself, and let Jesus Christ be for us. Subject us to what tortures you please, and take away our lives. All suffering is light to us, when we think of the glories of heaven." Then the king, having lost all hopes of overcoming them, took his scimitar, and with his own hand split their skulls in two; and thus was completed the martyrdom of the five Friars Minor, on the 16th of January, 1220.

Their bodies, having been dragged out of the town and cut to pieces by the infidels, were collected by the Christians; and the Infant Don Pedro took them into Spain, from whence he sent them into Portugal to King Alphonso, not daring as yet to revisit his own country. This king, accompanied by Queen Urraca and some of the grandees of the kingdom, came with the clergy to meet them, and had them placed with great pomp in the monastery of Regular

Canons of the Holy Cross, at Coimbra, where they still are. The celebrated miracles which were achieved there in great numbers as well as those which were performed in Morocco, and on the way to Europe, are recorded by contemporary authors, who have written their acts. Pope Sixtus IV recognized them solemnly as martyrs, in the year 1461, and gave permission to the religious to say their office.

At the time of their death, the Princess Sancia of Portugal, was in the act of prayer; they appeared to her with a bloody scimitar in their hands and told her that by their martyrdom they were on their way to heaven, where they would pray to God continually for her and would thus reward the good she had done them.

What they had foretold Queen Urraca, as to the time of her death, came to pass, and her confessor, a canon regular of Santa Cruz, a most exemplary man, of great piety, was made acquainted with it by a very marvellous vision. A short time after the bodies of these glorious martyrs had been placed in the church of this monastery, he saw in the middle of the night the choir filled with religious, who were singing very melodiously, which surprised him exceedingly, neither knowing what brought them there, nor how they got in. He asked one of them, who replied: "We are all Friars Minor. He whom you see at the head, is Brother Francis, whom you have longed so much to see; and the five who are more resplendent than the rest, are the martyrs of Morocco, who are honored in this church. Our Lord has sent us hither in order to pray for Queen Urraca, who is dead, and who had great affection for our Order; and he has willed that you should see all this, because you were her confessor." The vision disappeared, and the confessor's door was immediately knocked at, to communicate to him that the queen was dead.

The severe vengeance with which God visited the king of Morocco and his subjects was also noticed. The right hand with which this prince had struck the holy martyrs, and the whole of his right side, from the head to the feet, was paralyzed and became perfectly dry. During three years, no rain fell in the whole country, and an infinity of people died by pestilence and famine, which scourges lasted five years, God choosing to proportion the duration of the punishment to the number of the martyrs.

All these marvels which he wrought in their favor, and the title of martyrs, which the Church gives them, must convince every faithful Christian, enlightened by the wisdom which is from above, that it was by a particular impulse from the Holy Ghost that they exposed themselves to death with so much ardor, against the advice of the other Christians. Human prudence is very rash when it takes upon itself to blame what is approved by God and by His Church.

It would be difficult to express the joy which filled the heart of Francis, when he learned that his brethren had suffered martyrdom. He said to those who were with him:—"It is now that I can rest assured that I have had five true Friars Minor!" and he called down a thousand blessings on the convent of Alanquer, where they had prepared themselves for martyrdom, which had such effect, that there have been always since a great number of religious there, and at least one who has been distinguished for religious perfection.

Brother Vital, who had been the superior of these generous martyrs, was delighted on hearing of their triumph, and greatly regretted not having shared therein. It was not in good-will that he was deficient; he was only arrested by his illness, of which he died at Saragossa some time afterwards.

One of the authors of the life of St. Dominic, tells us that this great patriarch, who held his general chapter at the time, was in ecstasies of joy, when he heard that five Friars Minor had received the crown of martyrdom; that he looked upon it as the first fruits of the plans of his friend Francis, and, at the same time, as a powerful incentive for his brethren to aspire to what is most perfect, which is to suffer for the faith of Jesus Christ. The Friars Preachers have profited by the example, as is evinced by the great number of martyrs of their order, by whom the Church has been enriched.

It was not without a special dispensation of Providence that the relics of the five martyrs were deposited at Coimbra, in the Church of the Canons Regular of Santa Cruz, since our Lord made them subserve to the vocation of St. Anthony of Padua, who is one of the most striking ornaments of this renowned Order.

He was a native of Portugal, of a very noble family of Lisbon, born in the year 1195, and had received the name of Ferdinand in Baptism. The first years of his life had been passed in innocence and piety; the fear of being seduced by the world, and the wish to consecrate himself wholly to God, made him take the resolution, at the age of fifteen, to enter the Order of Regular Canons, in the Convent of St. Vincent, at Lisbon. Two years afterwards, in order to avoid the frequent visits of his friends, which interfere with habits of retirement, he asked permission of his superior to remove to the convent of Santa Cruz at Coimbra, which is of the same order. He had some difficulty in obtaining this leave, because they had great esteem for him personally. He made use of the quiet he now enjoyed to apply himself to the study of sacred literature, and, as if he had foreseen what he was to do at a future period of his life, he not only taught himself what was requisite for his own sanctification, but also what was useful for instructing others in the paths of virtue; he gathered also from the Holy Scriptures, and from the study of the Fathers, what could serve to confirm the truths of faith, and to impugn error. The assiduity with which he pursued his studies, together with the excellence of his memory, and his surpassing talents, with the light he received from Heaven, rendered him in a short time very learned.

The relics of the five Friars Minor who had been martyred at Morocco, and which were taken to Santa Cruz, at Coimbra, at that time, inspired in his heart an anxious desire to die for Jesus Christ as they had done, and made him entertain the thought of becoming a member of that Order, as the school of martyrdom. Some old authors add that St. Francis, who was then at Assisi, appeared to him, and induced him to embrace his Institute, foretelling him what would happen.

The Friars Minor of the convent of St. Anthony of Olivares, near Coimbra, having come to the Canons Regular of Santa Cruz to quest, Ferdinand could not control his zeal, but taking them aside, he opened to them the wish he had to enter their community. They were highly pleased on hearing this, and fixed the day with him for putting his design into execution. In the meantime, he asked leave of the Superior of Santa Cruz to effect the change, and with great difficulty obtained it. The Friars Minor returned on the appointed day, and gave him the habit of the Order, in the Convent of Santa Cruz itself, and took him back with them to that of St. Anthony. The loss of so estimable a member was very distressing to the canons; one of them who felt it more than the others, said to him with bitterness, as he left the house:—"Go, perhaps you shall become a saint." To which Ferdinand answered with humility:—"When you hear that it is so, you will doubtless give praise to God." He was not satisfied with having changed his order; he chose likewise to change his name, in order by that means to disappoint those who might endeavor to seek for him; and as St. Anthony was the titular saint of the convent, he begged the superior to call him Anthony, which is the name he was ever after known by, and to which was added of Padua, because his body reposes in that city, and is there honored by the faithful.

The wish to shed his blood for the faith of Jesus Christ, which was the source of his vocation, was constantly increasing in his mind and gave him no rest. He solicited leave from the superiors to go into Africa, which was granted to him, as had been promised him, when he entered the Order. Being come into the land of the Saracens, he was seized with a violent illness, which confined him the whole winter, and obliged him to return to Spain in the spring for his recovery. He embarked for this purpose, but the Almighty, who had destined him for the martyrdom of the apostolical life, and who intended by his means to convert an infinity of souls in Italy and France, gave him a passage in a contrary direction. The wind drove the vessel he was in to Sicily, where he landed, and from thence he went to Assisi, where we shall meet him in the general chapter at St. Mary of the Angels.

It was in the year 1220, that the Friars Minor, Angelus and Albert, both natives of Pisa, after having stayed some time at Paris in order to arrange the first establishment there, crossed the channel to England, whither Francis had sent them at the general chapter of 1219. The religious of St. Dominic had already a convent at Canterbury, where they received the two new comers with great charity. King Henry III, who reigned at that time, settled them with royal magnificence at Oxford. There he held his court, and he conceived so great a liking for them that he had a lodge built near their convent, to which he occasionally retired in order to converse with them.

The reason which primarily induced him to show them so much consideration, was his having learnt from authentic sources what had occurred to them on their journey from Canterbury to Oxford. The prior, the sacristan, and the cellarer of the abbey of Abingdon, who were at one of their farms, contrary to the usual practice of their order, where hospitality is always given, as recommended by St. Benedict, refused it to these poor religious, and turned them from their doors, although it was at nightfall. A young religious, who was in their company, seeing that they were about to pass the night in the wood, introduced them secretly into the barn, brought them some food, and recommended himself urgently to their prayers. In the night he had a dreadful vision of the justice with which God visited the prior and the two others, but which did not fall on him, because he had been charitable. In the morning he went to them with a view of telling them what he had seen in his sleep, and found them all three dead in their beds. Struck with astonishment he left the farm, from whence the two Friars Minor had departed before daybreak, and went to relate what had happened to the abbot of Abingdon; they both had serious reflections on this subject, which ended in their entering into the Order of Friars Minor. So extraordinary an occurrence could not be kept secret; many persons heard it; the king was made acquainted with it, and this caused the favorable reception he gave to Angelus and Albert.

His open protection, with the sanctity of their lives, caused the Institute to flourish throughout the kingdom. Several doctors of theology embraced it; and subsequently Robert Maideston, Bishop of Hereford, an enlightened prelate of great distinction at court, obtained leave from Gregory IX to give up his bishopric to take the poor habit of St. Francis, under which he became a model of humility and poverty.

Three hundred years after, King Henry VIII destroyed all these monuments of science and religion, which his predecessor Henry III had raised with so much zeal, and tyrannically treated the successors of those who had been received with so much benevolence. The strange revolution which the incontinence and heresy of this prince brought about in England, reduced the Friars Minor, and all other missionaries, to the necessity of running greater risks in endeavoring to maintain the remnant of faith, than what they had to incur amongst the infidels.

We suppress all comment on so deplorable a subject, and we are satisfied with offering up our prayers to the Almighty that He might deign to cast the eyes of His mercy upon those islands which formerly gave so many saints to the Church; that by His grace, the talent and learning which are found there, may be employed in searching for the truth and appreciating that truth which the illustrious Pope St. Gregory had taught there in the sixth century; that these talents may be no longer employed in the defence of a variety of sects, equally at variance with the doctrines of antiquity, condemned by the principles of the Christian religion, and by the rules of right reasoning; and that it shall no longer be said that men of learning make use of the light they have received and cultivated, to countenance every description of falsehood; so that, as St. Leo said of idolatrous Rome, dictating to almost all other nations, she herself was the slave of all their errors.

Francis, having received the resignation of his vicar general, on his return from his visitations, deferred the choice of his successor till the assembly of the chapter which was held on Whitsunday. He consulted God on the election, who made known to him by revelation that Brother Elias should be restored; he communicated this to his companions, and when the chapter met, he named Elias vicar-general.

We may feel assured that after having deposed him for laxness, he would not again have placed him at the head of his Order, had he not been certain that God himself had ordered it. As soon as the saints are made aware of the will of God, they have no thought but of obeying, whether it be that they know His reasons, or that they be hidden from them. Thus, three hundred years before St. Francis, St. Stephen, the third Abbot of Citeaux, did not fail sending Arnaud to Morimond to be its first abbot, although he knew by divine inspiration, that this post would be prejudicial to him, and that it would not turn out well: it was enough for him that it was God's will that he should be so sent. Thus we find in Holy Writ that Eliseus, by God's order to Elias, consecrated Hazael King of Syria, who, he foresaw would bring such great evils on the people of God, that the foresight moved him to tears. Human prudence must not censure in the saints what they have only done from supernatural views, against their own impressions, and their own inclinations. In these extraordinary cases we must only adore the counsels of Divine Wisdom, without endeavoring to penetrate them: we must acknowledge, as Tobias did, that all His ways are ways of mercy, truth, and justice; and say with one of the prophets: "Thy loss comes from thyself."

At the chapter Francis sat at the feet of Elias and, as his infirmities prevented him from making himself heard, it was through Elias that he proposed all that he wished to communicate to the assembly. Towards the close he pulled him by the tunic and told him in a low tone of voice his intention of sending some of the brethren into parts of Upper Germany, into which they had not yet penetrated. Elias laid the affair before the brethren in the following terms: "My brethren, this is what the Brother says" (for thus they designated Francis, as a mark of great respect). "There is a part of Germany, the inhabitants of which are Christians and devout; they go, as you know, through our country during the heats with long staves and great jack-boots, singing the praises of God and His saints, and thus visit the places of devotion. I sent some of our brethren into their land, who returned often having been sorely ill-treated. For this reason, I compel no one to go thither, but if there are any sufficiently zealous for the glory of God and the salvation of souls, to undertake this journey I promise him the same merit as is attached to obedience, and even more than if he made a voyage over the sea."

About ninety offered themselves for the mission which they considered as an opportunity for suffering martyrdom. The chief was named with the title of Provincial Minister of Germany, and Brother Caesar, a German, was selected for that office. He was an ecclesiastic of Spire, who had been drawn into the Order by the preaching of Brother Elias, sometime before, he himself having the character of a good preacher. He had permission to select those whom he desired to take with him from among those who had volunteered; however, he only chose twenty-seven, twelve of whom were priests, and fifteen lay-brethren, among whom there were some Germans, and some Hungarians, excellent preachers. He remained nearly three months in the Valley of Spoleto, with leave from Francis, and sent his companions into Lombardy to prepare themselves for the great work they were about to undertake; then they set forth dividing themselves into small groups of three and four. We shall further on give the details of their journey, and of their labors and success.

In the choice which Casar made of those whom he thought adapted to the German mission, something occurred which at first was amusing, but which turned out very serious and very useful. Someone having suggested to him to take one of the brethren named Jourdain, he went to him and said:—"And you Brother Jourdain, you will come with us?" "I?" replied he, "I am not one of yours; if I rose up, it was not with any intention of going with you, it was to embrace those who were about to go into Germany, and who, I am certain, will all be martyred." He was so apprehensive that the Germans by their cruelty, and the heretics of Lombardy by their artifices, would be the causes of his losing his faith, that he daily prayed to God for the favor of being kept away from the one and from the other.

Casar, continuing to urge him to go with him, and Jourdain continuing to refuse, they went to the vicar general, who, after having been informed how the matter stood, said to Jourdain:—"My brother, I command you, on your holy obedience, to decide absolutely upon going into Germany or not going." This order put his conscience in a dilemma: if he should not go, he feared its reproach for having followed his own will, and did not like to lose a glorious crown; and, on the other hand, he could not determine on going, thinking the Germans so cruel as he had been led to believe. In order to come to a conclusion, he consulted one of the religious who had greatly suffered in the first mission, and had been stripped in Hungary no less than fifteen times, who said to him:—"Go to Brother Elias, and tell him that you are neither willing to go into Germany nor to stay here, but that you will do whatsoever he shall desire you to do. You will hardly have addressed him, then your difficulties will be done away." He followed this advice, and Elias ordered him by the obligation of obedience to accompany Brother Casar into Germany. He went and labored assiduously, and more than any of the others, to extend the order throughout the country. His obedience quieted his mind for a man is never more satisfied with himself than when he obeys. "Experience shows," says St. Bernard, "that the yoke of obedience is light, and that self-will is oppressive."

Anthony had heard in Sicily that the chapter was to assemble at St. Mary of the Angels, and although he was still in a state of weakness, he had come to it with Philippinus, a young lay brother of Castile. When the chapter was over, the brethren were sent back to their convents by the vicar general, but no one asked to have Anthony, because no one knew him, and he appeared so feeble, that he did not seem fit for work. He offered himself therefore to Brother Gratian, who was Provincial of Bologna, or of Romagna, whom he begged as a master, to instruct him in the rules of regular discipline, making no mention of his studies, or of any talent he had, and showing no other desire than to know and love the crucified Jesus. Gratian delighted with these his sentiments, asked to have him, and took him with him into his province, with Philippinus, who was sent to Citta di Castello, and from thence to Columbario, in Tuscany, where he died a holy death. Anthony, who only wished for solitude, had leave from the provincial to live at the hermitage of Mount St. Paul, near Bologna, where he wished to have a cell cut in the rock, which was separated from all the others; this the brother who had cut it out for himself ceded to him. There he lived in as much solitude as obedience allowed him, devoting himself to contemplation, fasting on bread and water, and practising such other austerities, as to be thereby so weakened, that, according to the savings of his brethren, he could hardly stand when he came to them. Although he was full of zeal, he did not dare attempt to preach; the martyrdom which he had escaped in Africa had rendered him timid; he abandoned himself to Divine Providence, without any other anxiety than that of inciting himself to the more perfect love of God, and strengthening himself in the hope of enjoying the good things of Heaven, and resisting the attacks of the tempter, who strove to dissuade him from the holy exercise of prayer. Living thus in great simplicity among his unpretending brethren, he disguised under a plain exterior the vast light he received from Heaven; but by that humility he deserved to be brought forward for the accomplishment of the designs of Providence, who generally prepares those in secret, whom he destines to splendid ministrations.

Chapter 4

FROM HIS THIRD ORDER OF PENANCE TO THE TIME OF HIS LAST ILLNESS

After the chapter, Francis, notwithstanding the bad state of his health, actuated by his zeal, undertook to preach repentance in the towns adjacent to Assisi, where he dilated, in forcible language, on vice and virtue, and the sufferings and happiness of a future life. The inhabitants of Canaria were so moved by his preaching, that they followed him in crowds, forsaking their usual occupations. Many also, from the neighboring villages, joined them, and all together solicited him to teach them how to profit by his instructions.

Many married men were desirous of separating themselves from their wives, in order to embrace the religious state, and many married women were anxious to shut themselves up in cloisters; but the holy Patriarch, not wishing to break up well-assorted marriages, nor to depopulate the country, advised them to serve God in their own houses, and promised to give them a rule by which they might progress in virtue and live as religious, without practising the austerities of that state of life.

He was under the necessity of repeating the same injunctions in several towns in Tuscany, particularly in Florence, where similar views prevailed, and where they had already commenced building a monastery for females, who were desirous of renouncing the world. While he was yet ruminating on the mode of life he should prescribe for them, he assembled them all, and formed them into two congregations: the one of men, and the other of women; and having given each of them a president, they gave themselves separately up to exercises of piety and practices of mercy, with so much fervor, that a contemporary author compares them to the Christians whom Tertullian so eloquently eulogizes. With the alms which the two congregations collected, they built a hospital for the sick and aged, on the outskirts of the town where all the virtues of charity were assiduously exercised; an establishment which is extant to this day. St. Antoninus, when Archbishop of Florence, removed these pious assemblies to a locality near the Church of St. Martin, for the convenience of the poor. The vicinity of the church and their good works procured for them the name of the "Good Men of St. Martin;" and they were afterwards called the "Penitents of St. Francis," because they followed the rule of the Third Order of Penance, which the Saint instituted.

One day St. Francis having gone from Florence to Gagiano, near Poggibonzi, in Tuscany, met a shop-keeper of his acquaintance, whose name was Lucchesio, who had been very avaricious, and an enthusiastic partisan of the faction of the Guelphs, but who, having been converted a few months before, now lived a very Christian-like life, gave away great sums in alms, attended the sick in hospitals, received strangers hospitably into his house, and endeavored to instil similar sentiments into Bonadonna, his wife. They had already asked Francis to put them in a way of sanctifying their lives, which should be suitable to their position; and the holy man had given them this answer: "I have been thinking of late of instituting a Third Order, in which married persons might serve God perfectly; and I think you could not do better than to enter it." After having given the subject serious consideration, Lucchesio and his wife entreated him to admit them into this new Order. He made them assume a modest and simple dress, of a grey color, also a cord with several knots in it for a girdle, and he prescribed verbally certain pious exercises, which they were to follow until such time as he should have composed the rule.

This was the beginning of the Third Order of St. Francis, which many persons in the environs of Poggibonzi embraced, and which was soon established in Florence by the congregation of men and women of which we have just spoken. The following year, at latest, the Founder composed a rule for this Order, which he called the Order of the Brethren of Penance, in which the sisters were comprised, which was also called the Third Order, or the Order of Tertiaries, as relative to the two older Orders: the Order of Friars Minors, which is the first, and that of the Poor Clares, which is the second. This rule was subsequently confirmed by Pope Nicholas IV, and Leo XIII, with some changes, which they considered advisable as well in regard to the times as to the Order itself.

The holy Patriarch manifests therein not only the zeal which animated him in all that concerned the purity of the faith, but also the prudence which guided all his actions. He requires that all those who apply for admission into the

Order shall be carefully examined in the Catholic faith, and their submission to the authority of the Church, and he directs that they shall only be received after having made profession of all the orthodox truths; and that great care shall be taken not to admit any heretic, nor anyone suspected of heresy; and should any such be detected after having been admitted, he insists on their being immediately informed against. He, likewise, directs that their previous conduct may be inquired into, to ascertain whether any notorious crimes are imputed to them, or whether their morals are irreproachable, and he desires that they be warned to restore what they have which belongs to any other person; he also forbids receiving any married female into the Order without the consent of her husband.

The profession consists in a promise to keep all God's commandments, and to perform such penances as the visitor shall enjoin for faults committed in breach of the practices required by the rule. The habit is similar to what was given to Lucchesio and his wife; but so, that this may be dispensed with, according to the state of life of the persons, and the customs of the country in which they may be. The spiritual exercises laid down in the rule, have nothing in them which can interfere with the different stations of persons living in the world. Days of fasting and abstinence are prescribed, but modified prudently for the infirm, for pregnant women, for travellers, and for laboring people; and it is clearly explained that these observances are not obligatory under pain of sin, and that they only bind the transgressor to perform the penance imposed on him, unless the transgression has at the same time contravened any law of God, or commandment of the Church.

St. Francis, moreover, strenuously recommends to the brethren and sisters, to avoid all words tending to swearing or imprecation, the theatre, dancing, and all profane meetings; to undertake no law-suits, and to live in fraternal union; to take great care of the sick of the Order, to bury the dead, and to pray for them.

He adds to this, an article which is deserving of peculiar notice; it is, that all persons who enter the Order and have property over which they have the disposal, shall make their wills within a few months after their profession, lest they should die intestate. We see that his intention was to make them think on death, and to have their minds free for meditating on the important affair of their salvation, and to prevent those dissentions which frequently occur after the death of such as have not regulated their temporal affairs, before being called away. Wills which are made during a last illness are frequently exposed to deceit and fraud. They are never better made than when executed while the testator is in good health, in possession of all his faculties.

By the institution of the Third Order, Francis proposes to himself to reanimate the fervor of the faithful, to induce all the world, those in orders, laics, married persons of either sex, and such as were living in a state of celibacy, to a stricter observance of God's commandments, to live a more Christian and Catholic life, and to add the practice of virtues to the duties of civil life. His views met with astonishing success; the Order was established, and spread with the greatest rapidity through all conditions of life. Cardinals, bishops, emperors, empresses, kings, queens, considered themselves honored in being admitted into it, and it has given to the Church an infinite number of saints and blessed of either sex, who are publicly revered with her sanction. Wading says, that in his day, (that is in 1623,) there were at the court of Madrid more than sixty lords who belonged to the Third Order; and Cardinal Trejo, who had joined it, wrote to him in these terms on the subject of the works of St. Francis, which that author was about to give to the public with learned notes.

"You praise me with some surprise, that wearing the purple of a cardinal, I should have taken the habit and made solemn profession to adhere to the rules of the Third Order of St. Francis. Could I do less than devote myself wholly to his Order, I, who owe to him all that I have, and all that I am? Does not the cord of St. Francis deserve to gird even royal purple? St. Louis, King of France, St. Elizabeth, Queen of Hungary, wore it, as well as many other sovereigns and princesses. In our own day, Philip III, King of Spain, died in the habit of the blessed Father; Queen Elizabeth, wife of Philip IV, the reigning monarch of Spain, and the Princess Mary, his sister, have made their profession in the Third Order. Why, then, should it be a subject of astonishment to you, that a cardinal should cover his purple with a garment of ash color, and gird himself with a cord? If this dress seems vulgar and vile, I require it the more, because, finding myself raised to a high degree of honor, I must humble myself the more in order to avoid pride. But is not the garb of St. Francis, which is of ash color, a real purple, which may adorn the dignity of kings and cardinals? Yes, it is a true purple, dyed in the blood of Jesus Christ, and in the blood which issued from the stigmates of His servant. It gives, therefore, a royal dignity to those who wear it. What have I done, therefore, in clothing myself with this garment? I have added purple to purple, the purple of royalty, to the purple of the cardinalate; thus, far from being humiliated by it, I have reason to fear that I have done myself too much honor, and that I derive from it too much glory."

These sentiments of this learned and pious cardinal, are well calculated to silence the proud and irreligious spirits who turn into ridicule practices which the Church approves, and which her most illustrious children embrace with fervor. We have seen Queen Ann of Austria receive, at Paris, the holy habit of a penitent, and make profession of the rule of the Third Order of St. Francis; Queen Maria Theresa of Austria, wife of the renowned king, Louis XIV, follow this example, and even permit herself to be chosen superior of the sisters of the congregation, established in the church of the great convent of the Observance, under the protection of St. Elizabeth of Hungary, and assist at the various pious exercises with great edification.

The Holy See has loaded the brethren and sisters of the Third Order with many spiritual favors; and has granted them many privileges and indulgences. It has given to them a participation in all the merits which are gained in the other two Orders. What is singular is, that shortly after its institution, congregations of Tertiaries were formed, in which they lived in community of property, making the three vows of poverty, chastity, and obedience, and practising the works of mercy. God and the Sovereign Pontiff raised them to a religious body. Thus, besides the secular Third Order, there is now a religious one, of both sexes, which Pope Leo X confirmed and extended by his bull, dated 28th of January, 1521, in which he abridged the rule and adapted it to the observances of the religious state. St. Elizabeth of Hungary, being a widow, joined the three vows of religion to the profession of the Third Order of St. Francis, three years after the death of the blessed Patriarch, which makes her to be justly considered as the mother of the religious of both sexes of the Third Order, since she was the first Tertiary who took these solemn vows.

Lucchesio and his wife, who were the first Tertiaries whom St. Francis received, acquired by the exercise of prayer and good works, a holiness which God honored by many miracles during their life and after their death; but the wife was sanctified by the husband. Although she had embraced, after his example, the state of piety, she continued to disapprove the great donations of alms which he made, and to prevent them as much as was in her power, in consequence of that spirit of avarice and self-interest, which constantly induces such tempers to fear that they shall come to want.

One day, Lucchesio having given all the bread that was in his house to the poor, he begged his wife to give something to others who followed. She flew into a passion, like the wife of Tobias; and having reproached him with the care he took of strangers to the prejudice of those of his own household, she said that it was quite plain that his fasts and watchings had disordered his brain. The husband, as patient as he was charitable, was not irritated by these reproaches, but quietly requested his wife to look into the place where the bread was kept, thinking of Him, who by His power had satiated several thousand persons with a few loaves and fishes. She did so, and found a large quantity of fresh bread, sufficient to supply the wants of all the poor. This miracle had such an effect upon her, that from that time forward, he had no occasion to exhort her to the performance of works of mercy; both husband and wife gave themselves up to them with emulation, and devoted themselves to them until their deaths. The husband's charity shows us that almsgiving does not impoverish; but that, on the contrary, God increases, even sometimes by miracles, the property of such as give liberally; and the conversion of Lucchesio's wife shows that the spirit of interest and avarice, covered by pretence of economy, renders piety false and deceitful.

After having established his Third Order, Francis preached in several parts of Tuscany, and received an establishment at Columbario, in a very solitary situation, which was the more agreeable to him from the great attraction he had for contemplation. He had it erected under the title of the Annunciation of the Blessed Virgin, in honor of her Divine maternity; he then returned to St. Mary of the Angels.

An abbess was requested from the Monastery of St. Damian for that of Moncel, of the same institute, which was forming at Florence; he consulted thereon the cardinal protector, and by his advice he selected Agnes, the sister of Clare. Agnes, out of obedience, set out willingly; she found a very fervent, very united, and very submissive community, and the Sovereign Pontiff granted all that she required for their spiritual wants. But Agnes was seriously grieved to have to part from Clare, and to satisfy her heart, she wrote to her a most affectionate letter, full of the most tender sentiments, in which we see that the feelings of nature are elevated and sanctified by virtue, instead of being weakened.

At that time, about the month of October, Francis obtained the famous indulgence of St. Mary of the Angels, or of Portiuncula, of which we shall here relate the circumstances.

The great lights and inspirations which this holy man received in prayer, discovered to him the wretched state of sinners; he deplored their blindness, and was moved to compassion, and he often prayed for them. One night, when he was soliciting their conversion from God with great fervor, he was directed by an angel to go to the church, where he would find Jesus Christ and his Blessed Mother, accompanied by a host of celestial spirits. Greatly rejoiced, he went and prostrated himself to render due homage to the Majesty of the Son of God. Our Saviour said to him: "Francis, the zeal which thou and thy followers have for the salvation of souls is such, that it entitles thee to solicit something in their favor, for the glory of my name." In the midst of the marvels which enraptured him, he made the following prayer: "O Jesus, my Saviour, I entreat Thee, although I am but a miserable sinner, to have the goodness to grant to men, that all those who shall visit this church may receive a plenary indulgence of all their sins, after having confessed them to a priest; and I beg the Blessed Virgin, Thy Mother, the general advocate of humankind, to intercede that I may obtain this my request." The Blessed Virgin did intercede, and Jesus Christ spoke the following words: "Francis, what thou askest is great, but thou wilt receive still greater favors; I grant thee this one; I desire thee, nevertheless, to go to my vicar, to whom I have given power to bind and to loose, and to solicit him for the same indulgence." The companions of the Saint who were in their respective cells, heard all these things; they saw a great light which filled the church, and the multitude of angels; but a respectful fear prevented them from approaching nearer.

In the early morning, Francis assembled them, and forbade their speaking of this miraculous event, and then set out with Masse of Marignan for Perugia, where Pope Honorius then was.

When he came into his presence, he said to him: "Most Holy Father, some years ago I repaired a small church in your dominions; I beg you to grant to it a free indulgence, without any obligation of making an offering." The Pope replied, that the request could not reasonably be granted, because it was but just that he who wished to gain an indulgence should render himself deserving of it by some means, particularly by some work of charity. "But," added he, "for how many years do you ask me for this indulgence?" "Most Holy Father," replied Francis, "may it please your Holiness, not to give me so many years but so many souls." "And in what way do you desire to have souls?" rejoined the Pope. "I wish," added Francis, "that it may be the good pleasure of Your Holiness, that those persons who enter the Church of St. Mary of the Angels, are contrite, shall have confessed their sins, and have properly received absolution, may receive an entire remission of their sins, as well in this world as in the next, from their baptism, to the time of their so entering the church." The Pope then said to him, "Francis, what you solicit is a thing of great importance. The Roman court has not been accustomed to grant any similar indulgence." "Most Holy Father," returned Francis, "I ask not this for myself, it is Jesus Christ who sent me; I come from Him." Upon which, the Pope said publicly three times: "It is my desire that it be granted to you."

The cardinals who were present, represented to him, that in granting so important an indulgence, he was subverting the throne of the holy law, and that of the sepulchre of the holy Apostles. "The concession is made," replied the Pope, "nor is it right it should be revoked; but let us modify it." And recalling Francis, he said to him: "We grant you this indulgence which you have solicited. It is for all years in perpetuity; but only during one natural day; from one evening including the night, to the evening of the following day." At these words Francis humbly bowed down his head. As he went away, the Pope asked him: "Whither art thou going, simple man? What certitude hast thou of what thou hast just been granted?" "Holy Father," he replied, "your word is sufficient for me. If this indulgence is the work of God, He will make it manifest. Let Jesus Christ and His Blessed Mother, and the angels, be the notary, on this occasion, the paper, and the witnesses. I require no other authenticated document." This was the effect of the great confidence he had in God.

He left Perugia to return to St. Mary of the Angels, and midway he stopped at a village named Colle, at a leper hospital, where he rested awhile. On awaking, he had recourse to prayer; then he called Masse, and said to him with great exultation: "I can assure you that the indulgence which has been granted to me by the Sovereign Pontiff is confirmed in Heaven." The day had not been fixed, however, until the beginning of the year 1223.

Clare wished to see once more the Church of St. Mary of the Angels in which she had renounced the world, and to take another meal with Francis, her spiritual Father. He refused her his leave for some time; but his companions having represented to him that he treated a virgin whom he himself had consecrated to Jesus Christ, with too much harshness, he consented to what she wished. An appropriate day was fixed on, and she came to the convent of Portiuncula, accompanied by some of her nuns, and some Friars Minor who went on purpose to the convent of St. Damian.

After having prayed fervently in the church, and visited the convent, the Friars and the nuns seated themselves round the reflection which St. Francis had laid out on the ground, in pursuance of his usual practice of humility, which was his daily observance, whenever it was in his power. The first nourishment they took was for the soul. The holy Patriarch spoke of God, but in so moving a manner, and with so much unction and animation, that all who heard him were thrown into ecstasy, as he was himself. At the same time, the convent, the church, and the woods seemed to the inhabitants of Assisi and environs, to be on fire. Many ran thither to afford their aid; but finding everything in good order, they entered the convent, where they saw, with still greater surprise, the whole assembly in a state of ecstasy. By that they were made aware that what had seemed to them to be a fire, was the type of the fire which inflamed these holy bosoms, and they returned greatly edified.

By this marvel the Lord clearly showed that He approved the request, which Clare had made, to be allowed to come to the Portiuncula; as by another marvel He approved of the prayer which St. Scholastica made to detain her brother, St. Benedict, whom she wished to hear speak of the happiness of the future life, in the place in which they had just dined together. Such, was the condescension of His goodness for the consolation of these two saints, and it is thus that, according to the words of the Prophet, "He fulfils the wishes of those who fear Him."

The repast finished without any one having chosen to eat anything, so much were they filled with celestial aliment; and Clare returned to the Monastery of St. Damian, where her sisterhood received her with so much the more satisfaction, as they had been fearful that they would have given her the direction of some new establishment, as they had, a short time before, sent her sister Agnes to Florence as abbess. They knew that Francis had said to her on other occasions: "Be prepared to go wherever it may be necessary;" and that she had obediently answered, "My Father I am ready to go whithersoever you may send me." Her having gone out seemed to them a preparation for some longer journey and their grief for having lost Agnes, their dear companion increased the fears they had, lest they should lose Clare, also, who was in their regard a most excellent mistress of spiritual life. But they had not, thereafter, any similar alarms; this was the only time in forty-two years that their holy mother left the enclosure.

Elias, the vicar general, gave Francis great uneasiness, by his erroneous views. Many of the Friars Minor came to see their Patriarch, who received them with every mark of kindness. The vicar made great distinction between them. He was very particular in honoring those whom science and dignities rendered considerable in the Order; he never failed giving them the first places, and he took care to satisfy all they needed; while he left the others in the lowest places, and often without attending to their necessary wants. In his station he did what the Apostle St. James forbids all Christians to do.

Their common Father, who could not endure that so great a difference should be made, particularly amongst persons of the same Institute, affected, one day, at table, after grace had been said, to call two of the most simple of the brethren, and to place one on each side of him, without showing any attention to the merits of others.

He did this, not because he disapproved of peculiar consideration being shown to those to whom it is due, according to the maxim of St. Paul, in consequence of their character, their dignity, or their personal qualifications, but because he did not choose that these considerations should be to the disadvantage of those who had not similar circumstances to recommend them, and to whom, according to the same apostle, besides the feelings of charity to which they and all others are entitled, a certain degree of honor should be shown.

The vicar general, who was not impressed with a similar way of thinking, was highly indignant at this act of the Saint, and murmuring to himself, he said: "Ah! Brother Francis, it is quite certain that your extreme simplicity will be the ruin of the Order. You place alongside of you, men who have neither learning nor talents, and you affront those who are the support of the Order by their science." Francis, who by a supernatural revelation, was made aware of what his vicar had passing in his mind, replied immediately to his thought: "And you, Brother Elias, you do much greater injury to the Order by your vanity, and by the prudence of the flesh, with which you are filled. The judgments of God are impenetrable; He knows you as you are, and nevertheless, He chose that you should be Superior of the Order; and it is His desire that I leave it in your hands. Alas! I fear that the people, and he who governs them, resemble each other, and that God has only given a pastor, such as He foresees the flock will be." The holy Patriarch well knew that the whole of the flock would not be corrupted by Brother Elias, and that the majority of the members would resist him, as it came to pass. And thus the fear which he experienced in general terms, was a warning to keep them all to their duty. But what he added was a true prophecy: "Unhappy man, as you are, you will not die in this Order; God has so decreed. You have been weighed in the balances, and have been found wanting, because you are puffed up with the science of the world."

The following is the way in which this matter is related in the ancient legend which is followed by St. Antoninus. Francis, knowing by a revelation that Brother Elias would die out of the Order, and would be damned, avoided conversing with him, and even seeing him. Elias noticed this, and did not rest till he discovered the reason. Terrified and dismayed at such a prophecy, he threw himself at the feet of his kind master, and entreated him to intercede with God to prevent one of the flock committed to his care, from perishing eternally: "Let not the sentence which has been revealed to you, discourage you; for the Lord may change His decree, if the sinner corrects his sin. I have such confidence in your prayers, my very dear Father, that I should think they would mitigate my sufferings even if I were in hell, as you have been told I shall be. Pray for me, my Father; pray, and I have no doubt but that God will modify His decree, and that I shall be converted." Francis prayed, and obtained from God that Brother Elias should not be damned, but he could not obtain the reversal of the decree which said that he should not die in the Order. It was, in fact, out of the Order that he died; but, previous to his death, he gave great signs of contrition.

Wading makes on this a judicious remark, worthy of a sound theologian. He says that Brother Elias, who was universally admitted to be a learned man, was not ignorant that the decrees of God which are absolute, are immutable, because He Himself is incapable of change; but he also knew that the Lord sometimes expressed Himself in absolute words against sinners, which decrees are merely threats, which may be changed by their repentance, without His changing, according to what He has said by the Prophet Jeremy: "I will suddenly speak against a nation, and against a kingdom, to root out, and to pull down, and to destroy it. If that nation against which I have spoken shall repent of their evil, I also will repent of the evil that I thought to do them." Jonas sent from God, had positively announced that in forty days Nineveh should be destroyed, and nevertheless the penitence of the Ninevites hindered the destruction of their city. St. Gregory says, that in this sense God changed His decrees, but did not change His design; and St. Thomas says, that God proposes the change of certain things, but that in His will no change takes place. Sinners, however, must not abuse this doctrine, and imagine that God only threatens them, and that He will not damn them, for He has an absolute will to damn eternally those who die in mortal sin, as well as to crown with immortal glory such as die in a state of grace. In truth, it is His wish that sinners should be converted, and He places the means in their power by His mercy: "But," says St. Augustine, "He has not promised a to-morrow to your delay;" and as the Apostle has it: "According to thy hardness and impenitent heart thou treasurest up to thyself wrath against the day of wrath, and revelation of the just judgment of God, who will render to every man according to his works."

The example of the holy Patriarch, who had sought three times, the crown of martyrdom, and the triumph of the five brethren martyred at Morocco, had inspired many with an ardent desire to die for Jesus Christ. Shortly after Elias had been restored as vicar general, Daniel, Minister in the Province of Calabria, asked leave to go and preach the faith to the Moors, with six other brethren, whose names were Samuel, Donule or Daniel, Leo, Hugolin, Nicholas, and Angelus. Having received the permission of the vicar general, and the blessing of Francis, they embarked in a port of Tuscany, from whence they sailed to Tarragona. Their first intention was to have gone to Morocco, to mingle their blood with that of their martyred brethren, but some reasons, probably favorable to their intention, induced them to go to Ceuta.

Daniel arrived first with three of his companions, the master of the vessel not having thought proper to take on board more. They lived out of the town, in a village inhabited by traders from Pisa, Genoa, and Marseilles, because Christians might not enter the town without a particular permission. Their occupation here was to preach to these traders, until they should be joined by their companions, who arrived there on the 29th of September.

The following Friday, which was the first of October, they consulted together as to their future plans, and the aids they should require in the formidable combat they were about to sustain. On the Saturday, they confessed and received the Holy Communion, without which, when it is possible to receive it, St. Cyprian would not suffer confessors to be exposed to martyrdom for the faith, because it is the Body and the Blood of Jesus Christ which gives the strength to endure it. St. Chrysostom and St. Bernard, also, say that it is the firmest defence which can be opposed to the temptations of the devil, and to the allurements of sin, which are powerful motives for having recourse to frequent Communion.

The seven brothers went forth from the holy table, according to the expression of St. Chrysostom, "as roaring lions, breathing fire and flames," and they could not restrain the zeal which animated them. On the evening of the same day, they washed each other's feet, in order to follow the example of the Son of God, who washed His disciples' feet before His Passion; and very early on the Sunday morning, before there were any persons in the streets, they entered the town, having their heads strewed with ashes, and commenced crying out with a loud voice, "There is no salvation but through Jesus Christ."

The Moors soon collected, abused and beat them, and led them to the king. The missionaries then repeated, in presence of the learned in the law, what they had previously said to the people, "That it is requisite to believe in Jesus Christ; that there is no salvation in any other name than His," which they proved by the most forcible arguments. The king, who fully understood that in thus upholding the name of Jesus Christ they rejected that of Mahomet, looked upon them as idiots, and thought that their shaven heads, with a crown of hair round them, was a proof of their folly. However, to prove their constancy, he had them confined in a loathsome jail, where he kept them eight days in irons, and where they were cruelly treated.

Their confinement did not prevent their finding means to write to the Christians who were in the vicinity of Ceuta. Their letter was addressed to Hugh, Cure of the Genoese, and to two religious, one of their own Order, and the other of the Order of Friars Preachers, who had just returned from the farthest part of Mauritania. They blessed, in the first instance, the Father of

Mercies, who consoled them in their tribulation; and, after having quoted several passages from the Scriptures to justify their mission and to animate themselves to suffering, they assured their brethren that they had borne witness, and strongly argued in presence of the king, "that there is no salvation but in the name of Jesus Christ;" and they concluded by referring to God the glory of all that they had done.

The judge, whose name was Arbold, wishing to see what they did in prison, saw that they were no longer chained, that their faces shone with a splendid light, and that they sang the praises of God with extraordinary joy. The king, having been apprised of this, caused them to be brought before him on Sunday, the tenth of October, and offered them great wealth if they would become Mussulmen. They boldly replied, that they utterly despised all the things of this world and of the present life, in consequence of the happiness of the future life. They were then separated, and each was separately tempted, by promises and threats, but they were all found steadfast in their resolution. Daniel, speaking with great energy, one of the Moors cut him across the head with his scimitar, from which he did not even wince, and another exhorted him to embrace the law of Mahomet, to save his life with honor. "Wretch!" exclaimed Daniel, "your Mahomet and all his followers are but ministers of Satan, and your Koran is but a series of lies; be no longer misled, but embrace the Christian faith."

As soon as the seven brothers were collected together, six of them threw themselves at Daniel's feet, who had procured this mission for them, and who was their leader, and said to him with tears of joy: "We give thanks to God and to you, our father, for having procured for us the crown of martyrdom; our souls will follow yours; bless us and die; the struggle will be soon over, and we shall enjoy eternal peace."

Daniel tenderly embraced them, gave them his blessing, and encouraged them by these words: "Let us rejoice in the Lord; this is for us a festival day; angels surround us, the heavens are opened to receive us; this day we shall receive the crown of martyrdom, which will last forever."

In fact, the king, seeing that they were resolute, and not to be shaken, condemned them to be beheaded. They were stripped, had their hands tied behind them, and were taken to the place of execution, whither they went as to a banquet, preceded by a herald, who proclaimed the cause of their death, and where, after having recommended their souls to God, they were decapitated, on the tenth of October, in the year 1221.

Infidel children and adults broke their skulls to pieces, and mutilated the remains of the holy martyrs; but these precious relics were gathered up by the

Christians, and removed into the storehouse of the Marseillese, and were afterwards buried in their dwellings beyond the walls of Ceuta. It is asserted that some years afterwards they were transferred to the Church of St. Mary, near Morocco, and that God manifested them by miracles, and particularly by a splendid light, which even the Moors saw during the night; and that some time afterwards an Infant of Portugal, having obtained them from a King of Morocco, had them removed into Spain, where fresh miracles rendered them celebrated. Whatever truth there may be in the account of these translations, it is not known now where the relics of these seven martyrs are. This is certain— that the faithful had their memory in great veneration, and that in 1516, the Friars Minor solicited leave from Pope Leo X, to recite an office in their honor, which leave he most willingly granted to them, placing them in the number of martyrs recognized by the Church, as they are commemorated in the Roman Martyrology on the 13th of October.

We may imagine the satisfaction their triumph gave to Francis, from the ardent desire he always evinced for the crown of martyrdom, and the tender love he bore for his children. He had, moreover, in this year another great consolation on this subject. Pope Honorius sent to almost all the bishops of Europe, desiring them to send him four men from each province, or at least two, noted for their science and the integrity of their lives, whom it was his intention to commission to preach to the idolaters, and to the Saracens, for whose conversion he was most anxious, and amongst the number thus selected there were many Friars Minors, and Friars Preachers who generously exposed themselves to every sort of peril for the salvation of souls.

The intimate union which the love of God had formed between St. Dominic and St. Francis, induces us to note here, that the blessed Patriarch of the Dominicans died this year, on the sixth day of August at the age of fifty-one years. The eminent sanctity of his life, the great miracles he performed; the ardor and splendor of his zeal for the destruction of heresy; his inviolable attachment to the holy See; his tender piety to the Blessed Virgin, whom he causes to be generally and daily honored in the devotion of the Rosary; and the establishment of his Order, so useful by its science, by its piety, and by the great service it still renders to the Church, cause him to be illustrious through the entire Church. Among the Friars Minor, there is not one who, if animated by the spirit of St. Francis, must not have a special devotion for Him, and a respectful affection for those of his order.

Charity, which inflamed the breast of Francis, soon drew him from his retreat. He set out at the beginning of the year 1222, for the Terra di Lavoro,

Apulia and Calabria, and, in the course of this journey, God worked many splendid miracles by his hand.

Passing, first, through the Town of Toscanella, on the road to Rome, he received hospitality from a knight, whose only son was lame in both legs, and was in a state of suffering through his whole body. The afflicted father asked him to procure the cure of his son from God; he abstained from doing this for some time out of humility, esteeming himself unworthy of being loved by others, but being prevailed upon by reiterated entreaties, he placed his hands upon him, and made the sign of the cross upon the boy, who, at the same moment, stood upright and firm on his legs, and was entirely cured, to the great astonishment of his whole family.

At Rome, he made acquaintance, and became intimate with a nobleman, named Mathew de Rubeis, of the illustrious family of the Orsini. One day, on which he had been invited to dinner there, and having got there at the appointed hour, not finding his host yet returned from town, he joined, unperceived, the poor to whom they were giving a meal, and he received the alms with them. The nobleman arrived shortly after, and inquired where Brother Francis was, and as they did not find him, he declared he would not eat his dinner, if he did not come. While they were looking for him, he saw him seated in the yard with a group of poor. He went to him, and said: "Brother Francis, since you won't dine with me, I am come to dine with you;" which he did, placing himself on the ground near him, and in the group, where he found himself very comfortable in that company. When he heard that the holy man had established a Third Order for secular persons of all ranks, he prayed for admission into it, and had himself instructed in the practices to be observed. The consideration which his rank in life gave him in the world, threw great splendor on the new institution, and drew many persons to it.

There was a little child called John whom he requested Francis to bless; the servant of God gave him his blessing; he took him in his arms and foretold to all there that he would bring great glory to his house, and that he would be Sovereign Pontiff. Then, fixing his eyes upon the child, he spoke to him as if he had had the use of reason; he entreated him seriously, and in most affectionate terms, to be favorable to his Order; after which the prophet continued as follows: "He will not be a religious of our Order, but he will be its protector; he will not be reckoned among its children, but he will be acknowledged as its father; and our brethren will be delighted at seeing themselves under his shadow. I consider the immense benefits we shall receive from this child, I see them already in his little hands." Such a prediction caused as much pleasure as surprise to the lord of the family of the Orsini, but he never spoke of it till he saw its fulfilment, which happened fifty-five years afterwards. His son, cardinal, under the title of St. Nicholas, was chosen Pope in the year 1277, and took the name of Nicholas III. His singular benevolence for the Order of the Friars Minor showed that its holy Founder had not spoken in vain to him in his infancy.

From Rome Francis went to visit the Grotto of St. Benedict. He considered with great attention the bush covered with thorns, into which the great Patriarch of the monastic life had the courage to throw himself, in order to overcome a temptation of the flesh. In admiration of such extraordinary fervor, he touched this bush as a sacred relic; he kissed it, and made on it the sign of the cross. God, in order to honor his two servants, changed it immediately into a beautiful rose-tree, the flowers of which have served in many cases for the cure of the sick; the place has since been held in greater respect. In a chapel which is near it, and which was consecrated by Gregory IX, we see that Pope, with Francis on his left hand, who holds a scroll of paper, on which these words, taken from the Gospel of St. Luke, are written, "Peace be to this house," words which he constantly used as a salutation.

The remainder of his journey was remarkable for many other wonders which were worked through his means, in announcing the word of God. While preaching at Gaeta, on the border of the sea, seeing that a crowd of people were anxious, from a devotional feeling, to touch him, he threw himself into a boat to avoid these demonstrations of respect, which were disagreeable to him. The boat, which had no sailors in it, floated to a certain distance out to sea, and then became stationary; from thence he gave instruction to those who were on the shore, and the crowd dispersing after having received his blessing, the boat returned of itself to its former place. St. Bonaventure thereupon says:—"Who, after this, will have a heart so hardened and so irreligious as to despise the preaching of Francis, to which inanimate things lent their aid, as if they had reasoning faculties?"

The inhabitants of Gaeta, admiring the power which God gave to His servant, entreated him to stay some time in their town, and to permit them to build there a convent for his Order. He assented to this, and the work was commenced forthwith. While the church was in progress, a carpenter was crushed by the falling of a beam. As the other workmen were carrying him home, Francis, who was returning from the country, met them, and directed them to lay the dead man on the ground; he then made the sign of the cross on him, took him by the hand, called him by his name, and commanded him to arise. The dead man rose immediately and went back to his work. This is well-known in the country by successive tradition, and a small chapel has been erected, under due authority, on the spot where the miracle was performed, in order to perpetuate the memory thereof.

The earliest authors of the life of our Saint record a very singular miracle which he performed on his route, in the house of a gentleman. All the inhabitants of the place were gone to the great square to hear him preach. A female servant who had been left in a house to take care of a child, wishing to hear the sermon, left the child alone. On her return, she found the child dead, and half-boiled in a copper of hot water, into which it had fallen. She took it out, and in order to hide the disaster from the father and mother, she shut it up in a trunk; the parents, however, learnt their misfortune, which was the more afflicting as this was their only child. The husband entreated his wife not to let her distress appear, out of respect for the servant of God, who was to dine with them. During dinner, Francis endeavored to inspire them with a holy joy, knowing what the Almighty had in store for their consolation, and at the end of the dinner he feigned a wish to eat some apples. They expressed their regret that they had none to offer him; but pointing to the trunk in which the child was shut up, he said: "Let them look there, and some will be found." It was in vain that they assured him that there were none there; he insisted on having the trunk opened. The gentleman, to oblige him, and with a view of hiding the object of their grief, opened the trunk, when, judge of his astonishment on finding his child alive and well, and, with a smiling countenance, holding an apple in each hand. Transported with joy, he carried the child and placed it in the arms of the holy man.

The people of Capua were so moved by his preaching, and by the miracles he performed, particularly on his having saved from the waters a woman whom the river Volturnus had carried off, that the town made him the offer of a convent. St. Anastasius, Bishop of Civita di Penna, gave him another, with great marks of regard, after having gone out to meet him, on an inspiration he had in his sleep that Francis would come the next day to his town, a circumstance which is recorded by a painting in the church, and is explained in two Latin verses.

The servant of God having preached during the entire day at Montella, went to pass the night in a wood in the vicinity of that town, where he seated himself with his companion under an evergreen oak. Some persons who passed by, in the morning, perceived that there was no snow where the two religious sat, although there had been a heavy fall in the night, and they related the circumstance to the Lord of Montella, who sent for Francis, and entreated him to remain in that country, or to leave some of his companions amongst them, for the instruction of the people. He left two, for whom they built a house on the very spot where heaven had been so favorable to him.

The force which God gave to his discourses, and the miracles of which He made him the instrument, converted sinners, and animated the piety of the good. Both the one and the other were anxious to retain him amongst them, or, at least, to have some of his religious. In this journey alone, he founded more than twenty houses, among which was one at Amalfi, whither his devotion had led him to honor the relics of the Apostle St. Andrew. The inhabitants of Acropoli, who at first had been deaf to his instruction, were penetrated with contrition, and gave him a convent, after having been reproached with the hardness of their hearts by a multitude of fish, that God caused to collect round a rock from which Francis preached those truths which this people had refused to listen to.

The Emperor Frederic II was, at that time, with his court at Bari. The servant of God went there, no doubt, to venerate the relics of the great bishop St. Nicholas; he preached in the town, and as his discourses were always made suitable to the wants of his auditors, he spoke energetically on the dangers of the court, and particularly against impurity.

On leaving Bari, he found on the road a purse, which appeared to be full of money. His companion, who was aware of his great charity, said that he ought to take it for the poor. Francis refused to do so, saying that it was only a snare of the devil, and that, if it was really money which had been lost, it would not be right to take what belonged to others to give away in alms; so they continued their route. His companion was not satisfied; he thought that an opportunity was lost of doing a good action, and he tired Francis with his remonstrances. The holy man, who was very mild and very obliging, returned to the spot where the purse was, not intending to do what his companion wished, but to expose to him the artifice of the evil spirit. A young man was passing at the time, in whose presence he told his companion to take up the purse; he, trembling from a secret misgiving of what was about to happen, would have been glad not to have anything to do with it; but, obliged to obey, he put his hand to it, which he had no sooner done than he saw a large snake slide out, which disappeared with the purse. On which, Francis said to his companions: "Brother, money is, as regards the servants of God, but as a venomous serpent, and even the devil himself." We may here add, that it is the same thing for those who are too fond of it, and who avariciously keep it, or make it serve for the gratification of their passions. A chapel, which has been built in that place, is a memorial of the teaching of the Patriarch to the poor of Jesus Christ.

His devotion induced him also to visit the grotto consecrated by the apparition of the Archangel Michael, on Mount Gargano. They wished, out of respect, to take him to the very spot where the blessed spirit was manifested, and where mass is offered up, a privilege which is not allowed to all. But through humility he stopped at the door, and, as he was urged to enter, he said: "I dare not go farther; this place is awful; it is the dwelling of angels, whom men should respect in all ways." The place where he stopped to pray is shown to this day. These sentiments of humility should abash those Christians who crowd round our altars in unbecoming postures, and particularly those worldly women who, in immodest postures and in an air of vanity, approach contemptuously the sanctuary in which the Sacred Body of Jesus reposes.

Francis placed some of his religious near Mount Gargano and in some other parts, after which he came to Gubbio, where he cured a woman, the sinews of whose hands were contracted.

Near Gubbio, a soldier called Benvenuto, asked to be admitted into the Order; he was admitted as a lay-brother, with directions to wait upon the lepers. Profound humility, implicit obedience, an ardent charity, the love of poverty and of silence, assiduity in prayer, perfect patience in sickness, and a tender devotion to the Blessed Sacrament, rendered this soldier an excellent religious. God honored him with so many miracles during his lifetime and after his death, which happened in the year 1232, that Pope Gregory IX had information taken on the subject, in 1236, through the Bishops of Malfi, Molfetta, and Venosa, and permitted these three dioceses to allot to him an office, which is now said by the whole Order of Friars Minor.

There lived, between Gubbio and Massa, an old advocate of the Roman court, called Bartholomew Baro, who had retired thither to avoid the tumults and dangers of the world, and lived in great reputation of sanctity. Francis, delighted at what he had heard of him, wished to see him. They discoursed on spiritual things, and Bartholomew, hearing that there was a Third Order, willingly entered it. The holy Founder who saw that great prudence was associated with his consummate piety, placed confidence in him regarding the affairs of his Order, and left some of his religious with him.

St. Antoninus relates, that Bartholomew had in his hermitage a man possessed by the devil, who was incessantly talking, but who did not speak a word during the three days that Francis was there. After his departure he recommenced talking, and Bartholomew having asked him why, during the stay of Francis, he had kept silence: "It was," he said, "because God had so tied his tongue that it was out of his power to speak a single word." "How is it, then," replied Bartholomew: "is Francis so great a man, that his presence has such an effect?" "Truly," rejoined the demoniac, "his virtue is so great, that all the world will see in him most wonderful things. It is not long since our prince called us all together, and told us that God, who in all times had sent men for the conversion of sinners, has similar designs in regard to this man, and that Jesus Christ proposes to renew His passion in Francis, in order to imprint it in the hearts of men from whence it is obliterated."

As this was said two years before Francis received the stigmata, it would seem that the prince of darkness had some knowledge of the favors which Jesus Christ intended to confer on Francis. St. Augustine says, that the Son of God made Himself known to the demons on earth, making certain signs to them of His presence; but that it was only as far as He thought proper; that He made use of it, when necessary to inspire them with terror; and that, at other times, He left them in doubt as to His divinity. According to this doctrine, it might be said that God, to confound the demons, had made known to their chief His intention to renew the Passion of Jesus Christ in the person of Francis, without informing him in what manner this was to happen, for it is certain that this spirit of darkness, neither by his natural lights, nor by conjectures, had the means of discovering a favor which solely depended on the Divine will.

At length, having labored for the salvation of souls with great fatigue, nearly the whole year, the holy Patriarch returned to his dear home, St. Mary of the Angels, to attend more immediately to his own sanctification. He there received Brother Casar of Spire, who had returned from Germany, and the subject of whose mission we must now resume, having lost sight of it since the year 1221.

This zealous missionary left Italy with twenty-seven companions, divided into small parties, and before the Feast of St. Michael, they arrived successfully at Trent, where they remained fifteen days, during which the bishop provided liberally for all their wants. On the day of the festival, Casar preached to the clergy, and Barnabas to the people.

An inhabitant of the town, named Pellegrino, was so moved by Barnabas's discourse, that he had all the brethren newly clothed, and shortly afterwards he sold all his property, gave it to the poor, and took the same habit himself.

Casar left some of the brethren at Trent, exhorting them to the practice of patience and humility, and then set out with the remainder. On their way they attended with greater interest to spiritual than temporal wants, although they had commissioned some of their companions to provide what was necessary for them. The Bishop of Trent, whom they found at Posen, detained them for some days, and gave them leave to preach in the whole of his diocese. From thence they went to Brixen, where the bishop received them very charitably; but from thence they had much to suffer in the mountains, where they could procure nothing to eat, after long and fatiguing marches, and were reduced to feed upon wild fruits, and even then they had a scruple of tasting these on Friday morning, because it was, by their rule, a fast, although they had slept in the open air, and had had scarcely anything to eat the preceding day. But God supported them, and they reached Augsburg, where the bishop embraced them all, and gave them special marks of his benevolence.

In 1221, near the Feast of St. Gall, which is on the sixteenth of October, Casar assembled the first chapter of the Order which had been held in Germany; there were about thirty of his brethren, whom he distributed in several provinces of this vast country. Some were sent to Wurtzburg, Mentz, Worms, Spire, and Cologne, where they exerted themselves with much success for the salvation of souls, and built convents. Giordano was sent with two companions to Saltzburg, and the archbishop of that city received them with great benevolence. Three others went to Ratisboa, where they founded an excellent establishment. The provincial followed them, animating them by word and example. While at Wurtzburg, he gave the habit of the Friars Minor to a young man of good family, named Hartmod, who had enjoyed a good education. He called him Andrew, because the day of his reception was that of the holy Apostle. Andrew, having taken holy orders sometime after, became a celebrated preacher, and was the first warden in Saxony. Rodinger was also admitted into the Order, who was afterwards warden of the convent of Halberstad, and director of St. Elizabeth of Hungary, before Dr. Conrad of Marburg.

In 1222, Casar, having received a great number of novices, some of whom were made priests, assembled a chapter at Worms, and finding that the Order was taking firm root in Germany, he instituted as vice-provincial, Thomas de Celano, and returned into Italy with Simon de Collazon, who had preferred the humble state of Friar Minor to the nobility of his birth. The reason of Casar's return was the anxious desire he had to see once more his holy Patriarch, and his companions in the Valley of Spoleto, with whom he was intimately united through virtue. He was a man greatly attached to contemplation, very zealous for holy poverty, and highly esteemed by his brethren, who, after their holy Father, looked up to him above any other.

The religious whom he had left in Germany pursued their mission with great success. Even in this year, or shortly after, they penetrated, with the Friars Preachers, into the Kingdom of Sweden, and into some other countries of the North, according to the testimony of John the Great. Archbishop of

Upsal, and Legate of the Holy See, who notices this circumstance in the history of his church.

This prelate remarks that one of the first who entered the Institute of the Friars Minor, was Laurence Octavius, an illustrious man, whose conversion made such a sensation, that it drew into the Order many persons of high rank. The poor habit which he wore, and which he honored by his splendid virtues, and particularly by love of suffering, did not render it less venerable than his sciences.

Octavius could not avoid giving his consent, in the year 1244 or 1245, to the election which was unanimously made of his person, by the clergy and people, for the Archbishopric of Upsal, which was confirmed by Innocent IV. In this dignity, he continued to live the life of a true Friar Minor, and did so much for the salvation of his flock, as well as for the benefit of the whole kingdom, that, if heresy had not destroyed in Sweden all sentiments of piety with the light of faith, his memory would still be honored there as one of their greatest as well as holiest persons. He died a saintly death, in the year 1267, and chose to be buried among the Friars Minor, with whom he would have gladly spent his life.

While the Institute of St. Francis thus flourished in Germany and in the North, a treasure was discovered in Italy, which had been up to this time overlooked. It was the great St. Anthony of Padua, who was leading a hidden life in the Hermitage of St. Paul near Bologna.

His superior sent him, with some others, to Forli, in Romagna, to take orders. Some Friars Preachers were also present. Being assembled together at the hour of conference, the superior of the place requested the Friars Preachers to give them an exhortation. As they excused themselves because they were not prepared, he turned to Anthony, and without being aware of the depth of his learning, he ordered him to say whatever the Holy Spirit should suggest to him. Anthony replied with great humility that he was ill fitted for such a task, and that he was much more qualified for cleaning the plates than for preaching. However, yielding to the superior's reiterated order, he began to discourse with simplicity and timidity; but God, proposing to place conspicuously the lamp which was hidden under the bushel, he continued his discourse with so much eloquence, and showed himself to possess so profoundly learned a doctrine, that the audience was most agreeably surprised, and admitted that they had never heard anything to equal it; and they did not know which most to admire, his learning or his humility.

It was, indeed, requisite to be possessed of rare and extraordinary humility, to hide with so much care such sublime learning, and talents so varied; for Anthony had earnestly requested the guardian of the convent in which he was, to employ him in cleaning the plates and dishes, and in sweeping the house. This man, who, according to the saying of the Apostle, was "A vessel of honor, sanctified and profitable to the Lord, prepared unto every good work," treated himself, and wished to be considered by his companions, as one of the vilest amongst men. He was deserving of the highest place, and took the very lowest. He was so deeply versed in the Holy Scriptures, that his memory served him as a book; and he penetrated so well into the most obscure passages that he was the admiration of the most profound theologians; but he was more anxious to be confounded with the unlearned, and to be unknown, than to let his learning be discovered, and to appear capable of instructing others.

We may here notice a reflection of St. Bernard on a somewhat similar case: "Let this passage be remarked by those who undertake to teach what they have not learnt themselves; seeking for scholars, without having had masters, they are the blind leading the blind. But justice is done them; although it is admitted that they have some talent, it is soon found that they have nothing solid, and they are treated with contempt."

The fortunate discovery that was thus made of the talents of Anthony, soon reached the ears of Francis, who ordered him to apply himself to the pulpit. He desired, however, that the preacher, in order to exercise his ministry with the greatest effect, should study theology at Vercelli, under the Abbot of St. Andrew, who gave lessons with great reputation, and who is supposed to have been the celebrated Doctor Thomas, a canon regular of the Abbey of St. Victor of Paris. He was sent to be the first abbot at the Abbey of St. Andrew of Vercelli, which was founded about the year 1220. Anthony had as a fellow-student another Friar Minor, named Adam de Marisco, an Englishman, who was afterwards a doctor of the University of Oxford, the holiness of his life, his learning, and his writings rendered him famous throughout the whole realm of England. He was subsequently elected Bishop of Ely.

The application which Anthony gave to the study of theology did not prevent his preaching during all Lent at Milan, and at other times in some parts of the duchy. But his preaching was no hindrance to his studies, because the lights he had previously acquired, and those he received from above, together with his splendid talents, gave him an insight into the most sublime truths. His progress was so quick and so great, that his master often declared, that he learnt many things from his scholar. Speaking of the book of the celestial hierarchy which he was explaining, he said that his scholar ran over the several orders of blessed spirits with so much precision, and a penetration so surprising, that it might have been thought that the whole heavenly host passed before him. This exalted wisdom, joined to his eminent virtues, induced his illustrious preceptor to give him the name of Saint, and to apply our Blessed Lord's eulogy of St. John the Baptist to him: "He was a burning and a shining light." Anthony was requested by his fellow-students to communicate to them the learning in which he abounded, and to give lessons in the convent, but he would not take upon himself to exercise the functions of master, without having first consulted the holy Founder of the Order. He wrote to him on the subject, and received the following answer:

> "To my dear Brother Anthony, Brother Francis sends greeting in Jesus Christ.
> "I entirely approve of your teaching the brethren sacred theology; in such a manner, however, that the spirit of prayer be not extinguished in you or in them, according to the rule which we profess. Adieu."

This is a proof that Francis was not hostile to study, but that he only wished it to be conducted in a religious manner, without prejudice to piety. Anthony, having obtained leave, taught first at Montpellier, and then at Bologna, where studies were again set on foot, to which disobedience had put a stop, as has been said; then he taught at Padua, at Toulouse, and in other places where he was stationed: always joining to this holy exercise, that of preaching with wonderful success.

At the time when he began taking lessons from the Abbot of Vercelli, the most celebrated doctor of the University of Paris took the habit of the Friars Minor. This was Alexander d'Hales or d'Hels, or Hales, thus named from the place of his birth in the County of Gloucester, where, from the year 1246, Richard, Earl of Cornwall, had founded a convent of the Order of Citeaux. Having gone through his course of humanities in England, he came to Paris, where he studied philosophy and theology, took a doctor's degree, taught, and was universally admired.

St. Antoninus believes that what led to his vocation was this: having made a vow to grant, if he possibly could, whatever should be asked of him for the love of the Blessed Virgin, for whom he had a singular devotion, a person who was questing for the Friars Minor, came and said to him: "It is now long enough that you have been laboring for the world, and you have acquired celebrity in it. I entreat you, for the love of God, and of the Blessed Virgin, to enter into our Order, which you will honor, and you will sanctify yourself." The doctor was surprised at this request, but God touched his heart, and he replied to the brother: "I shall follow you very soon; and shall do as you wish," and shortly after, he took the habit of a Friar Minor. Others, however, are of opinion, that he was induced to quit the world by the example of his fellow-countryman, John of St. Gilles, an illustrious doctor, who, preaching one day to the clergy, with great energy, on voluntary poverty, in the convent of the Friars Preachers, descended from the pulpit in the middle of his sermon, and in order to give force to his words by his example, he took the habit of St. Dominic, and returned to the pulpit to finish his discourse.

However this may be, the holy life and happy death of Alexander Hales in the Order of St. Francis, bore testimony to his having been called by God. It is said that, at first, the practices were difficult to him, and that some interior suffering made him think of leaving the Order, but that, in this agitation, he saw in spirit Francis bearing a heavy wooden cross, and endeavoring to carry it up a very steep hill; that he offered to assist him, but that the holy Patriarch spurned his aid indignantly, saying: "Begone, you feeble man; you have not the courage to bear your own light cross, and you would attempt to bear this heavy one!" This vision having enlightened the doctor who was a novice, he was delivered entirely from the temptation under which he labored.

He continued to teach with the same repute; and the faculty of theology, to do honor to his merits, gave him the privilege of presenting one of his brethren and disciples for a doctor's degree; which he did the first time by an interior revelation, in favor of Brother John de la Rochelle, who afterwards became very celebrated. Alexander had many other disciples distinguished both for their learning and their piety, but there are none who have done more honor to his instructions than St. Bonaventure, and, according to the opinion of many authors, St. Thomas Aquinas. Among his writings, which are very numerous, and on all sorts of subjects, his Summa is much esteemed, in which, by order of Pope Innocent IV, he arranged methodically the theological subjects. This is the first Summa which was compiled, and it has served as a model for all others. Pope Alexander IV spoke in the highest terms, both of the author and of his work.

Gerson, Chancellor of the University of Paris, in speaking of Alexander's doctrine, expresses himself as follows: "It is not to be told how many excellent things it contains. I declare to have read in a treatise, that someone having asked St. Thomas what was the best mode of studying theology, he replied, 'To study the works of a single theologian;' and being asked what theologian it was desirable to fix on, he named Alexander Hales. Thus," continues Gerson, "the writings of St. Thomas, and principally the Seconda Seconda, show how familiar the works and doctrine of Alexander were to him."

So then learned men entered the Order of Friars Minor, as St. Francis had foretold; and this is the reason why he recommended that prayer should be joined to study, lest learning should obliterate piety.

The indulgence granted to St. Mary of the Angels, or the Portiuncula, two years previous to this time, had not yet had the day fixed on which the faithful could gain it. Francis waited till Jesus Christ, who first conceded so precious a boon, should Himself mark the day, nor was he disappointed. It occurred as follows:

> One night, when he was praying in his cell, at St. Mary of the Angels, in the beginning of the year 1223, the tempter suggested to him not to watch and pray so much, but rather to adopt other modes of penance, because, from his age, more sleep and rest was absolutely necessary for him, and these watchings would be his death. Being aware of the malice of his infernal enemy, he retired to the woods, and threw himself down into a bush of briars and thorns, till he was covered with blood. "For," said he to himself, "it is much better that I should suffer these pains with Jesus Christ, than that I should follow the advice of an enemy who flatters me."

A brilliant light which surrounded him, disclosed to him a great number of white and red roses, although it was the month of January, and the winter was very severe. This was an effect of the power of God, who had changed the briars into rose-trees, which have ever since been evergreen and without thorns.

Angels, who appeared in great numbers, said to him: "Francis, hasten to return to the Church, Jesus Christ is there, together with His Blessed Mother." At the same time, he perceived himself miraculously clothed with a new habit of pure white; he gathered twelve roses of each color, and went to the church. After a profound adoration he addressed the following prayer to Jesus Christ, under the protection of the most Blessed Virgin: "Most holy Father, Lord of heaven and earth, Saviour of man, deign, through Thy great mercy, to fix the day of the indulgence which Thou hast been pleased to grant to this sacred place."

Our Lord answered him, that it was His desire that it should be from the evening of the vigil of the day when St. Peter the Apostle was delivered from his chains, to the evening of the following day. Francis, again asking in what manner this should be publicly made known, and whether his own assertion would be given credit to, he was directed to present himself before the vicar of

Jesus Christ, to take with him some white and red roses as testimonials of the truth of the fact, also a number of his own brethren, who would testify to what they had heard; for, from the cells which were near the church, they had, indeed, heard all that had been said. Then the angels sang the hymn "Te Deum laudamus." Francis took three roses of each color in honor of the Most Blessed Trinity, and the vision disappeared.

Francis, accompanied by Brothers Bernard de Quintavalle, Peter of Catania, and Angelus of Rieti, set out for Rome, where he related to the Pope all that had happened at St. Mary of the Angels, in proof whereof, he presented to him the roses he had brought, and his companions testified to what they had heard. The Pope, astonished to see such beautiful and sweet-smelling roses in the depth of winter, said: "As to myself, I believe the truth of what you tell me, but it is a matter which must be submitted to the cardinals for their opinions." In the meantime, he directed his attendants to see that they should not want for anything.

The next day, they came before the consistory, where Francis, by the Pope's desire, said, in presence of the cardinals: "It is the will of God that whoever shall, with a contrite and humble heart, after having confessed his sins, and received absolution by a priest, enter the Church of St. Mary of the Angels, in the Diocese of Assisi, between the first vespers of the first day of August and the vespers of the second day, shall obtain an entire remission of all the sins he may have committed from his Baptism until that moment." The Sovereign Pontiff, seeing that the words of Francis were not thought to have any deceit in them, having conferred with the cardinals thereon for some time, confirmed the indulgence. And he subsequently ordered the Bishops of Assisi, Perugia, Todi, Spoleto, Foligno, Nocera, and Gubbio, to meet at the Church of St. Mary of the Angels, on the first of August of that year, and there solemnly to publish this indulgence.

All these prelates met on the day specified, and having mounted a large platform, which had been prepared outside of the church, they made Francis mount there also, to explain to the assembly, which was very numerous and gathered from all parts of the country, the cause of their meeting. He spoke with so much fervor that it seemed to be rather an angel who addressed the meeting than a man, and he ended his discourse by announcing the plenary and perpetual indulgence which God and the Sovereign Pontiff granted to this church every year on that day. The bishops were not satisfied with his publishing it to be in perpetuity. "Brother Francis," they said, "although the Pope desires us to do on this occasion whatever you wish, it is not, however, his intention that we should do things which are not suitable; therefore you must give notice that the indulgence is only to last for ten years." The Bishop of Assisi was the first to restrict it to this time, but he could not help saying, as St. Francis had, "in perpetuity." The other bishops endeavored successively to announce this restriction, but God permitted that, without intending it, they should all say, "in perpetuity." By this, they were made sensible of the will of God, and willingly proclaimed the indulgence to be perpetual.

Many of those who were at the sermon preached by Francis, have left testimony in writing to the effect, that he had in his hand a small scroll on which was written these words: "I wish you all to go to Paradise. I announce to you a plenary indulgence which I have obtained from the goodness of our Heavenly Father, and from the mouth of the Sovereign Pontiff. All you who are assembled here to-day, and with a contrite and humble heart have confessed with sincerity, and have received absolution from a priest, will have remission of all your sins; and in like manner, those who come every year with similar dispositions, will obtain the same."

Such is the way in which the famous indulgence of St. Mary of the Angels, or of Portiuncula, was published on the second day of August; an indulgence which the Sovereign Pontiffs have since extended to all the churches of the Order of St. Francis.

The seven prelates consecrated the Church of St. Mary of the Angels, and performed a similar ceremony for the Church of St. Damian, at the request of Francis and Clare. The remembrance of this is commemorated yearly at Assisi, on the ninth of August.

The benevolent feeling which Honorius III expressed to the holy Patriarch, when he was at Rome, for the indulgence of the Portiuncula, induced him to wish that this Pontiff would authorize solemnly the Rule of the Order, which Innocent III had only verbally approved. He had in the night the following revelation, which is thus recorded by St. Bonaventure:

It seemed to him that he had taken up from the ground some very small crumbs of bread, in order to distribute them to the half-starved brethren who surrounded him, and how, fearful lest such small crumbs should fall out of his hands, a heavenly voice said to him: "Francis, collect all these crumbs and make a host of them, and give of it to such as wish to eat of it." He did so, and all those who did not partake of it devoutly, or treated it contemptuously, after having received it, seemed to be infected with leprosy. In the morning, he related all this to his companions, and was distressed at not comprehending the mystery. The following day, while he was at prayer, a voice from heaven said to him: "Francis, the crumbs of last night are the words of the Gospel, the host is the Rule, and the leprosy is iniquity."

The term of Host, to designate the Rule, is worthy of particular consideration. Its import is that, as bread without leaven, which is called the Host, is made of the finest flour, so the Rule is composed of what is most perfect in the Gospel; and as this bread, by the words of consecration, is changed into the Body of Jesus Christ, the true Host immolated on the altar, so those who make profession of the Rule, must be transformed into hosts, or victims, and immolate themselves to God. It is thus that St. Paul warns Christians, "To become as a new paste without leaven," and to pass the whole time of their lives as a continual festival, "presenting their bodies a living sacrifice, holy and pleasing unto God." St. Peter also says to them, that they are a "Spiritual house, a holy priesthood, to offer up spiritual sacrifices acceptable to God by Jesus Christ."

The oracle of Heaven communicated to Francis that the Rule which he sought to have approved, and which was composed of sentences from the Gospel, required abridgment, and putting into order with greater precision. In order to effect this, he was inspired, after the publication of the indulgence, to go to Mount Columbo, near Rieti, where he retired into an opening in the rock, with Brothers Leo and Bonzio, fasting on bread and water; and this fast, according to the statement of Marianus, lasted forty days. There he wrote the Rule, according to the dictation of the Holy Spirit manifested to him, in prayer. On his return to St. Mary of the Angels, he put it into the hands of his vicar, Brother Elias, to read it, and keep it. Elias thought it too severe, and some days afterwards, in order to suppress it, he feigned to have lost it by negligence. The holy men returned to the same place, and wrote it out a second time, as if God had dictated it to him with His own mouth.

The vicar-general communicated to some of the provincial ministers what had happened, and told them that the Founder was desirous of imposing upon them a stricter mode of life than that to which they had hitherto adhered. They concerted together what they should do to avert this, and it was agreed that Elias, as vicar-general, should go and represent to him the inconvenience of such increased austerity, and the objections of his brethren. Elias, who was aware of the firmness of Francis in these matters, and had been severely rebuked by him on other occasions, acknowledged that he did not dare execute this commission alone, but he offered to accompany them for the common cause, and they consented to this arrangement.

While they were drawing near to the mountain, Francis had a revelation of what was passing. When they had reached the top, he left the opening of the rock quickly, and demanded of Elias what he and all these ministers who were with him wanted. Elias, with downcast eyes, and trembling, said, in a low tone of voice: "These ministers, having learnt that you were about to give them a new Rule above the strength of man to endure, have engaged me to come here, in my capacity of vicar-general, to entreat you to modify it, because they will not receive it, if it is too austere."

At these words, the Saint, in great emotion and shuddering, raised his eyes to heaven and exclaimed: "Lord, did I not say that these people would not believe me? As to myself, I will keep this Rule to the day of my death, with those of my companions who love poverty; but I shall not have it in my power to compel those who do not choose it, and who make so much resistance."

Jesus Christ appeared in a luminous cloud above Francis, and said, so that all heard him: "Little man, why are you discontented, as if this is your work?—It is I who have dictated the Rule; no part of it is yours. I insist on its being literally observed to the very letter—to the very letter, without gloss or comment. I know what frail man can endure, and what support I can and will give him. Let those who will not keep the Rule leave the Order; I will raise up others in their place; and if it be requisite, I will bring them forth from these stones."

Then Francis, from the top of the rock on which he had knelt down, addressed these words to the vicar-general and to the others, who were greatly alarmed: "You now know that your conspiracy has been solely an opposition to the will of God, and that instead of taking into consideration what He can do for us, you have only consulted the feeble light of your human prudence. Have you heard, have you, yourself, heard the voice which came forth from the cloud, and which spoke so audibly? If it did not resound in your ears, I will take steps to cause you to hear it once more." Upon this, Elias and his companions, astounded and beside themselves, retired without saying a single word.

The holy Patriarch having returned to join his faithful children in the small fissure of the rock, in which they lay prostrate at the voice of the Lord, said to them: "Rise up now, and fear nothing, but as true soldiers of Jesus Christ put on the armor of God, in order to be on your guard against the snares which the devil will not fail to throw in the way of your following Him." He left the mountain and went to the nearest convent to show the Rule to his brethren, intending to communicate it afterwards to the others, in order to know what each one thought of it. His countenance, animated and shining, was a manifestation that God himself had dictated to him the rule of life which he proposed to them. It was a striking representation of Moses coming down from Mount Sinai, his face shining brightly. The resemblance cannot be too much admired in its several relations. Moses, after a fast of forty days, received, on a mountain, the Law which God gave him. Jesus Christ having fasted forty days, was on a mountain when He taught that doctrine which embraces, as St. Augustine observes, all the perfection of the Christian life. And it was on a mountain that it was His pleasure to give His servant Francis, who fasted rigorously, a Rule in which the perfection of the evangelical life is contained.

Some having read the Rule, said to Francis, that it was necessary that his Order should have something in common, as the other religious orders had; seeing that the number of the brethren was already very great, and that, according to all appearance, the Order would be so extended; that it would not be possible to exist in so restricted a state of poverty. The Saint returned to the place he had left, and having had recourse to prayer, he consulted Jesus Christ, the true Legislator, who gave the following reply: "It is I who am their portion and their inheritance, I do not choose that they should be encumbered with the things of this world. Provided they adhere strictly to the Rule, and that they place their confidence in me, I will take care of them; I will not suffer them to stand in need of anything necessary to life; the more their numbers increase, the more will I manifest my providence to them."

We must here render to that adorable and loving Providence the justice due to it. It has never been wanting to the Order of St. Francis, and they have never had greater proofs of His care than when they have chosen to live most poorly. We see verified to the letter, in these poor evangelical brethren, the imitators of Jesus Christ crucified, what is said in the twenty-first psalm, in which the Son of God has clearly foretold His Passion: "The poor shall eat and shall be filled, and they shall praise the Lord that seek Him, their hearts shall live forever and ever." Were He now to ask the Religious of St. Francis, as He asked the Apostles: "When I sent you without purse, or scrip, and shoes, did you want for anything?" There is not one who would not answer as they did: "No, we have not wanted for anything." For a poor evangelical brother is bound to consider himself as not wanting anything while he lives, and to look upon having nothing but what is necessary as the treasure of his state of life.

A religious order which, without any revenue, maintains many thousand men, was a subject of admiration for an infidel prince, and the Founder was considered by him as a very great man. He was not aware of the cause of this wonderful effect, but religion teaches us that it is God himself who provides for the wants of His servants, by the charity with which He inspires the faithful.

Francis communicated to the ministers what our Lord had said to him. They submitted to everything, and returned with him to St. Mary of the Angels, where the Rule was approved by the brethren who were there, and was then sent into the provinces to be examined before it was submitted for confirmation.

Speaking of the Rule, he said to his children: "I have not put anything into it of my own; I caused it all to be written as God revealed it to me;" and he adduced this motive to incite them the better to keep it. He confirmed the revelation in his will, in the following terms: "When the Lord confided to me the guidance of the brethren, no one communicated to me how I was to behave towards them, but the Almighty Himself revealed to me that I ought to live according to the form prescribed by the Gospel; I caused it to be written out in few and simple words," etc.

This is the eulogium he passed on it: "My brethren and my dear children, a very great favor was done to us in giving us this Rule; for it is the book of life, the hope of salvation, the pledge of glory, the marrow of the Gospel, the way of the cross, a state of perfection, the key of Paradise, and the bond of our eternal alliance. None of you is ignorant how greatly advantageous to us holy religion is. As the enemy who fights against us is extremely clever in inventing and executing everything which is malicious, and strews in our way all sorts of snares to effect our perdition, there are many whose salvation he would have brought into great peril, if religion had not been their shield.

Study, therefore, your Rule, all of you, not only for alleviating your pains, but in order that it may remind you of the oath you have taken to keep it. It is necessary that you should employ yourselves in meditating on it, that it may sink into your hearts, and be always before your eyes, so that you may observe it with exactness, and hold it fast at your deaths."

St. Bridget being in prayer at Jerusalem; where she was interceding for a Friar Minor who had some conscientious scruples on the subject of the Rule, our Saviour caused her to hear the following words: "The Rule of St. Francis was not the composition of the human mind; it is I who made it; it does not contain a single word which was not inspired by my spirit; and thus Francis gave it to the others."

Pope Nicholas III says, that it bears on the face of it, the evidence of the Trinity; that it is descended from the Father of Light, that it was taught to the apostles by the example, and by the doctrine of His Son, and that the Holy Ghost inspired it to the blessed Francis and to those who had followed him. He also declares, as Gregory IX had done before, that it is established on the word of the Gospel, authorized by the life of Jesus Christ, and supported by the actions and words of the Apostles, who founded the Church Militant. It consists, according to the remark of St. Bonaventure, in observing the Holy Gospel of our Lord Jesus Christ, because all its substance is taken from the pure source of the Gospel. It is, therefore, no new rule; it is only a renewed rule; literally the same as what the Son of God laid down for the Apostles, when He sent them forth to preach; and that ought always give great spiritual consolation to those who keep it. This holy doctor considers the impressions of the wounds of Jesus Christ, which Francis received from the hand of the living God, sometime after the revelation of the Rule, as a bull of Jesus Christ, by which that High Pontiff confirmed it; and Pope Nicholas III was of the same opinion, in his decrial.

Finally, the Rule of the Friars Minor, given by St. Francis, is wholly Evangelical, and wholly Apostolical; there never was one which was so universally and so promptly followed. Men illustrious by their birth, by their knowledge, by their talents, by their virtue, embraced it and have followed it, during a number of centuries, in all parts of the Christian world; it has given to the Church a new family, in numbers most extensive, whose fecundity does not become exhausted, and it has produced a great galaxy of saints.

The children of the Patriarch, having most willingly received it, he left them in the month of October, in order to solicit the approval of the Sovereign Pontiff. When at Rome, he was invited to dine with Cardinal Ugolino, the Protector of the Order, who had a sincere affection for him; but he did not come to the invitation, until he had begged some pieces of bread, as he was accustomed to do, when he was to dine with persons of rank. Being at table, he drew this bread from his sleeve and began to eat of it, and he gave some to the other guests, who partook of it from devotion. After dinner, the cardinal embraced him, and said, smiling: "My good man, why, as you were to dine with me, did you put the affront on me, to go and beg bread first and bring it to my table?" "My Lord," replied Francis, "far from doing anything to affront you, I did you honor, in honoring, at your board, a much greater Lord than you are, to whom poverty is very agreeable, especially that which goes as far as voluntary mendicancy, for the love of Jesus Christ. I have resolved not to give up in favor of false and passing riches, this virtue which is of royal dignity, since our Lord Jesus Christ became poor for us, in order that, by His poverty, we might become rich and heirs to the kingdom of heaven."

An admirable reply, which is quite in unison with what was said by St. Gregory Nazianzen. "If I am reproached for my poverty, I am sure that it is my treasure;" and with these words of St. Ambrose, on the birth of Christ: "His poverty is my patrimony; He chose to want for everything, in order that all others might be in abundance."

The cardinal presented Francis to the Pope, that he might solicit the confirmation of his Rule. The Holy Father read it, and, finding it too severe, he desired some changes might be made in it; but, the man of God protesting by everything that was most sacred, that he had not put a single word into it, and that Jesus Christ had dictated it, as it there stood, the Pontiff, after discussing it with the cardinals, confirmed it. His bull commences thus:

> "Honorius, bishop, the servant of the servants of God. To our dearly beloved sons, Brother Francis, and other brethren of the Order of Friars Minor, health and apostolical benediction. The Apostolic See is accustomed to assent to pious intentions and to favor the laudable wishes of those who solicit her favors. For which reason, our dear children in Jesus Christ, we confirm by apostolical authority, and we strengthen by this present writing, the Rule of your Order, which was approved by Pope Innocent, of glorious memory, our predecessor, expressed in these terms, etc."

After having gone through it all, he concludes as follows: "Let no person, therefore, have the temerity to violate the contents of our present confirmation, or to contravene it. Should any one dare to do so, let him know that he will incur the indignation of Almighty God, and that of His blessed Apostles, St. Peter and St. Paul. Given in the Lateran palace, the twenty-ninth day of November, 1223, the eighth of our pontificate."

The original of this bull, with its leaden seal, is preserved as Assisi, in the Convent of St. Francis, where Wading saw it, in 1619, with a copy of the Rule written by St. Francis' own hand.

While Francis was still at Rome, he proposed to himself to celebrate the Festival of the Nativity of our Lord Jesus Christ at Grecio, with all the solemnity possible, in order to awaken the devotion of all in that vicinity. He wrote a letter on the subject to his friend, John Velita, begging him to prepare all things; and in order that there should be no room for censuring what he was about to do, he spoke to the Pope about it, who approved highly of this pious ceremony, and granted indulgences to those who should assist at it.

St. Bonaventure informs us that, before his departure from Rome, he went to pay his respects to Cardinal Leo Brancaleone, titular of Santa Croce, with whom his friendship began in 1210, when he first came to have his Rule approved. This cardinal invited him to stay some days in his palace, because the severity of the weather and the floods might impede his journey; it was the month of December. He retained, to remain with him, with Francis' leave, Brother Angelo Tancredi, whose miraculous conversion we have related; at that time, there were but few of the cardinals who did not wish to have some of the Friars Minor in their company; such was the veneration they had for their virtue at the Roman court. Francis, however, found excuses for not spending more than two or three days in the palace of Brancaleone, saying that it was not fitting for the poor to dwell in the palaces of princes. The cardinal told him that he would receive him as a pauper, and give him a bed, not in his palace, but in an adjacent tower near the city walls quite out of the way of any noise, where he might repose from his fatigue for some time. Tancredi entreated him not to refuse this satisfaction to a prince of the Church, who was a person of great piety, and a generous benefactor to the Order; therefore, out of respect, and from gratitude, he consented to stay, and with his companion took up his abode in the tower.

The following night, when he was about to take some repose, the devils came and beat him so long, and so violently, that they left him half-dead. He called his companion, and told him what had happened, and he added: "Brother, I believe that the devils, who can do nothing without the leave of the Almighty, have ill-used me to this degree, because of my having remained with great people, here; if so, it augurs no good. My brethren who dwell in very poor houses, knowing that I am the guest of cardinals, might suspect that I enter willingly into the concerns of the world, that I glory in honors, and that I am living daintily. I therefore think that a man who is to be an example to others, should leave the court, and dwell humbly with the humble, in places adapted to the profession of humility, in order that he may inspire those with fortitude, who suffer the inconveniences of a life of poverty, by suffering with them." In the morning, he took leave of the cardinal, and set out for Grecio.

It is necessary here to remark that St. Francis, who permitted some of his brethren to remain with the cardinals, did not think that he himself, who was the superior, ought to spend a single night in their palaces, lest others should be disedified thereby, and that it was his duty to give good example to all. This shows how much persons in power should strive not to do anything calculated to give bad examples, and to abstain from certain things which, though irreprehensible in themselves, and which would not be noticed in a lowly individual, might be a cause of scandal in one of high station, who ought to be a model of virtue. On this principle, St. Paul said to the Christians: "All things are lawful for me, but all things are not expedient. All things are lawful for me, but all things do not edify. I do all for your edification." He recommended his disciples, Timothy and Titus, whom he had ordained bishops, to be "an example to the faithful, in word, in conversation, in charity, in faith, in chastity, in the practice of good works." St. Gregory, St. Bernard, and all the Holy Fathers have always required of prelates, as a primary qualification, that they should greatly edify; which is the more necessary in the superiors of religious communities, as their example is under more immediate observation.

The bad health of Francis, the beating which he had received from the devils, and a constant fall of rain, compelled him to ride on an ass. During his journey he dismounted to say the Divine Office, standing; he remained on the same spot without paying attention to the rain, and did not mount till he had quite finished.

Having reached Grecio, he found all things prepared for the celebration of the festival by his friend Velita. They had prepared a crib in the wood, in which was represented the Nativity of our Saviour; they had placed straw there, and, during Christmas-night, also took there an ox and an ass. Many Friars Minor had arrived at the wood from the neighboring convents, and the people of the environs came in crowds to the ceremony. The wood was lit up by numerous torches, and resounded melodiously from the sound of a thousand voices which sang the praises of God with untiring zeal. Francis, full of devotion, and with his eyes bathed in tears of holy joy, knelt before the manger, above which an altar had been placed, where mass was celebrated at midnight; he acted as deacon, and after having sung the Gospel, he preached on the birth of the newborn King, became poor.

Velita, who had prepared the ceremonial, assured them that he had seen a most beautiful child in the manger, who was asleep, and whom Francis tenderly embraced in order to awaken it. There is so much the more reason for giving credit to this marvel, says St. Bonaventure, since he who relates it, having been an eye-witness thereof, was a very holy man, and since it was confirmed by many miracles; for the straw on which the child appeared to be sleeping, had the virtue of curing various maladies amongst cattle; and, what is still more wonderful, those who came to visit the spot, however tepid and indevout they may have been, were inflamed with the love of God. After the death of the Saint, a chapel was erected on the spot, and the altar was placed at the manger, in order that the flesh of the man-Cod immolated on the cross, might be eaten on the spot on which He had chosen to appear as a sleeping infant.

After the ceremony, Francis retired to the convent of Grecio, where some of the provincial ministers had collected, who had come thither to communicate to him the affairs of their respective provinces. The refectory had been set out in a better style than usual, with napkins and glasses, not only on account of the solemnity of the day, but to show respect to the guests. Francis was displeased at this, and, during dinner, he went to the door of the convent, and took the hat and staff of a pilgrim who was soliciting alms, and then, in this garb, came to the refectory to beg as a poor pilgrim. The superior, who knew him by his voice, said to him, smiling: "Brother pilgrim, there are here very many religious, who stand in great need of what has been bestowed upon them out of charity; however, come in, and they will give you what they can." Francis came in and sat himself on the ground, where he ate very contentedly some scraps of bread and other things which they gave him on a platter, without choosing to have anything else.

Francis remained some time at Grecio, where, one night, when he intended to lay himself down to sleep, he felt a severe headache, and a shivering over his whole body, which quite impeded his resting. Thinking that this might be caused by a feather pillow which his friend Velita had compelled him to accept, in consequence of his infirmities, he called his companion, who was near his cell, and said: "Take away this pillow: I believe the devil is in it." His companion, who took it away, found it extremely heavy, and he had hardly left the cell, when he found himself motionless and dumb. The Father, not doubting of the malignity of the devil, ordered the brother, under obedience, to come back directly; the wicked spirit having immediately left him, he came back and related the state in which he had found himself. The Saint, confirmed by this in the idea with which he had been impressed, that what he had suffered had been brought on by his enemy, said:—"It is true that yesterday, when reciting Compline, I perceived that the devil was approaching, and I prepared to resist him. He is full of malice and artfulness; as he could not sully a soul which God protects by His grace, he endeavored to injure the body, and to prevent the necessary aid being afforded to it; desiring to induce it to commit some fault, at least of impatience, and prevent its having recourse to prayer." The holy man was delivered from his sufferings, and got the rest he could not obtain, when his head was laid upon a feather pillow. To what a height of perfection did not God propose to raise this His faithful Servant? He did not even allow him to have a small relief from his sufferings. He is a holy God, jealous of the sanctity of souls, who desires to have them purified by all sorts of sacrifices; but, then, His rewards are great.

Whilst Francis was at Grecio and in its environs, Peter of Catania, his first vicar-general, died in the Convent of St. Mary of the Angels, on the 2d day of March, 1224. As soon as he was in the tomb, God bore witness to his merit by many miracles. The people crowded to his grave, and left valuable offerings, which greatly disturbed the quiet of the religious, and caused them much uneasiness on account of their strict poverty. Francis, having been informed of it, went to the tomb, and, moved by holy zeal, he addressed the dead man in a commanding tone, with which God alone could have inspired him: "Brother

Peter, whilst you were living, you always obeyed me punctually: I command you to obey me similarly now. Those who come to your grave are very troublesome to us. Our poverty is offended, and our quiet infringed on, so that our discipline becomes relaxed; thus, I command you, by your vow of obedience, to refrain from performing any more miracles." His order was obeyed. From that moment no more miracles were performed at the tomb of Brother Peter.

An ancient manuscript chronicle which is preserved in the Vatican, mentions that Francis, having directed the body of Brother Peter to be removed sometime afterwards, it was found that it was turned and kneeling, the head bowed down, and in the posture of one who obeys a command given him. To mark the value of obedience and the respect due to it, God was pleased to permit a dead person to obey the orders of a superior, as if he had been living.

A similar prohibition from performing miracles after death, is recorded in the life of St. Bernard. Gosvin, Abbot of Citeaux, who was at his funeral with many other abbots of his order, seeing the commotion caused by the numerous miracles which were worked there, and fearing this would become prejudicial to regular discipline, approached respectfully to the coffin, and forbade the saint from performing any more miracles, in virtue of his obedience. And, in fact, from that time, there were no more performed at that shrine publicly, although God performed others privately by his invocation. The author adds, that St. Benedict requires in his rule, an obedience without reserve, according to the example of Jesus Christ, who was obedient unto death, and that the soul of St. Bernard rendered itself obedient even after death to a mortal man.

Clare, and her daughters of the Monastery of St. Damian, now asked Francis to give them a written rule, and a form of life similar to that of the Friars Minor, in order that, in his absence and after his death, they and those who should succeed them, might live up to it. These Religious of St. Damian, did not wish to receive the rule of St. Benedict, nor the constitutions prepared by Cardinal Ugolino, which the other monasteries, established on the plan of St. Damian, had willingly accepted, and which were of great severity: these nuns desired to have a rule which should be of even greater rigor.

The holy Patriarch consulted the same cardinal on this subject, he being the protector of both Orders; and they jointly composed a rule in twelve chapters, which was similar in all respects to that of the Friars Minor, with modifications and usages proper for females. If anything made Francis hesitate, the cardinal gave his opinion either to modify certain parts, or to take precautions on others. He also used some articles from the constitutions which had before been drawn up. While he was writing, he could not help shedding tears, in reflecting that young females were willing to practise austerities of such a nature.

St. Clare says in her will, addressing herself to the sisters: "Our blessed Father, St. Francis, has written for us a form of life, principally that we may ever persevere in the practice of holy poverty, to which he has exhorted us, not only by his word and example, but by many writings which he has left us. Pope Innocent IV expressly declares in the bull which he issued at the earnest entreaty of St. Clare, three days before her death, that the rule which he confirms was given them by St. Francis. All is his, except some very trifling things, in no way essential, which seem to have been added to it by Cardinal Ugolino, by St. Clare, and by the Pope.

"It was in the year, 1224, that the marvellous apparition recorded by Wading was seen, which is noted as follows in the legend of St. Bonaventure:

"Although Francis could not attend the provincial chapters, the order which he had laid down for these assemblies, the fervent prayers which he put up for their success, and the influence of the blessing which he gave them, were as if he were present at them. Sometimes even, God, by His almighty power, caused him to appear among them in a sensible manner, as it happened at the chapter at Arles. While that excellent preacher Anthony was discoursing to the brethren on the Passion of the Son of God, and on the inscription on His cross, 'JESUS OF NAZARETH, KING OF THE JEWS,' one of the religious, named Monald, a man of exemplary virtue, moved by the Spirit of God to look towards the door of the chapterhouse, saw the blessed Francis, raised into the air with his arms extended as a cross, giving his blessing to the assembly. They then became filled with great spiritual consolation, which was an interior testimonial assuring them of the presence of their Father, and confirming what Monald had seen. This became more certain, afterwards, by the avowal which Francis made respecting it."

"We should have no difficulty in believing this," continues St. Bonaventure, "for God, by His almighty power, rendered the holy Bishop St. Ambrose, during a mysterious sleep, present at the funeral obsequies of St. Martin; in a similar manner it was His pleasure that the truths announced by His preacher Anthony, on the subject of the Cross of Jesus Christ, should receive greater weight by the presence of His Servant

Francis, who carried the cross with such exemplary courage, and preached it with such zeal."

Having given a rule to the sisters of St. Damian, and transacted all that related to the three orders, Francis recommended strongly to Brother Elias, to attend carefully, and to see that everything was carried into effect, and then thought it necessary to take some time to attend to his own interior. For it was his custom to go from one good work to another, in which he imitated, St. Bonaventure says, the angels whom Jacob saw in his dream, going up and down the mysterious ladder, the feet of which rested on the earth, but its summit reached the heavens. This angelic man so employed the time which was given him, in which to amass treasures of merit, that he was constantly occupied either in descending to his neighbor by the laborious ministries of charity, or in elevating himself to God in the quiet exercise of contemplation. When circumstances had compelled him to give more time to the service of souls, he afterwards retired to some lonely and noiseless place, to remove from himself, by giving his thoughts solely to God, all the filth which might have attached itself to him in his intercourse with men. Our Lord often gave His apostles examples of retreats, and they cannot be too often recommended to those who labor for the salvation of their neighbors.

Francis, therefore, went with some of his brethren to meditate in the convent of Celles, near Cortona. He met on the road a lady of good family, who was very pious and in great affliction, having a husband who used her cruelly, and prevented her from serving God. She told him that she was come to pray to God for the conversion of her husband, and he made her this answer: "Go in peace; and rest assured that your husband will soon afford you consolation; only tell him from God and from me, that now is the time of mercy, and that afterwards will be the time of justice." The lady received the Father's blessing, and said what she had just learned to her husband. The Holy Ghost descended at the same moment on this man, and he became so changed, that he said to his wife in a mild tone of voice, "Madam, let us serve God and work out our salvation." He passed thus many years with her in continence, with which she had inspired him, and they died most holily on the same day.

We saw in the first two Tertiaries, a wife sanctified by her husband. This is precisely what St. Paul says: The one may contribute to the sanctification of the other. In fact, St. Chrysostom thinks that a virtuous woman who is mild and prudent, is more likely to bring back a profligate husband to the service of God, than any other person; and that the solid piety of a husband, with good manners and discreet firmness, may soften the asperity of an ill-tempered woman, or at least render her less fractious.

All that Francis did at Celles, was to give himself up to contemplation; and, in order that the place itself should be favorable to meditation, he resolved, after having been there a short time, to retire to the desert of Mount Alvernia; it was the Holy Ghost who inspired him with the desire to go thither, where he was to receive the glorious privilege of the stigmata. As he passed through the country of Arezzo, his great infirmities compelled him to ask for an ass to continue his journey. There was not one in the village, but a person offered him a horse, which he was under the necessity of accepting: it was the only time that he had been on horseback since his conversion; for, whenever he had been forced to ride, he took the most despicable animal, in order to set an example to his brethren. In the village to which the horse was sent back, there was a woman who, for several days, was suffering cruelly from labor-pains, without being able to be delivered, so that no human hope remained of saving her life. The people of the place, seeing the horse brought back which had carried the Saint, took the bridle and placed it on the woman's bed, in full confidence that he who had had the use of it, would come to her aid; and, in fact, she was immediately, most fortunately, delivered. This fact is one of those related by St. Bonaventure.

On Mount Alvernia Francis reaped extraordinary consolations in meditation; he was filled with ardent desires of heaven, and, at the same time, he felt that the celestial gifts were communicated to him in greater abundance. These interior feelings which threw his soul into ecstasies, raised his body into the air to greater or less height, in proportion to their degree, as if an extreme disgust for everything that was connected with the earth, gave him a stimulus to raise himself to his celestial home.

Brother Leo, his secretary and his confessor, attests to have seen him raised sometimes to the height of a man, so that one could touch his feet, sometimes, above the tallest beech-trees, and sometimes so high, that he was elevated out of sight. When he was not raised higher than the height of a man, Leo kissed his feet and watered them with his tears, with tender devotion, saying the following prayer: "My God, be merciful to me, a sinner such as I am, by the merits of this holy man, and deign to communicate to me some small portion of Thy grace." When he lost sight of him, he prostrated himself and prayed, on the spot on which he had seen him elevate himself.

St. Thomas and many others believed that St. Paul in his rapture may have been elevated in body and soul into the third heaven, that is, into the Empyrean, into Paradise, into the place where the angels and the blessed are;

and we must not call this in question, since the apostle himself says, that he does not know whether he was raised up in the body or out of the body. St. Theresa, whose works are published by authority, says that she had sometimes raptures in which she was raised from the ground by a supernatural power, whatever resistance she might make; that others saw her in this state, and she saw herself in it. We may therefore believe that God raised the body of His Servant Francis, while his soul was in raptures by interior operations; more particularly, as the fact is attested by so trustworthy a witness as Leo, who certifies having seen it with his own eyes. "God," says St. Theresa, "grants extraordinary favors to a soul, to detach it entirely from everything that is earthly, by the body itself, so that life becomes burthensome to it, and that it suffers a sort of torment brought on by a violent desire of possessing God, which is a martyrdom both agreeable, and, at the same time, painful; but we must be under the conviction, that with ordinary grace, which God increases in proportion to faithfulness, we may attain to an entire disengagement from worldly affairs, and to that longing for heaven which, as Christians, we are obliged to feel."

One day, when Francis was restored from one of the ecstasies which had raised him from the ground, Jesus Christ appeared seated at a low stone table, where the Saint was in the habit of taking his meals, and speaking to him with the familiarity of a friend, as to the protection which He proposed to give to the Order, after his death, He made known to him the following points: first, that the Order would last to the end of the world; secondly, that those who should persecute the Order, would not be long-lived, unless they became converted; the third and fourth points, related to favors which our Saviour promised not only to the Friars Minor, but to those who were sincerely attached to them.

When our Lord had disappeared from the table, Brother Leo, not knowing what had happened, was about to prepare it, as usual, for their meal, but Francis stopped him, saying: "It must be washed with water, with wine, with milk, with oil, and with balm, for Jesus Christ has condescended to sit on it, and to make known to me from thence what will be communicated to you hereafter." As Brother Leo had not the articles he required, he only took oil, as Jacob had done, to consecrate this table to the Lord, and, having poured oil on it, he pronounced these words: "This is the altar of God." He then told his companion the four favors which had been promised and added that there was a fifth which he should not repeat: it was thought that it was out of humility; for, after his death, it was revealed to Brother Leo, that it consisted in that God, in consequence of the merits of the Saint, had deferred punishing the country by famine, to give sinners time to be converted; and, as they did not avail themselves of it, after his death, this scourge fell on the land, and was followed by a great mortality.

Towards the Feast of the Assumption of the Blessed Virgin, he retired into the most secret part of the mountains, where his companions built for him a small and unpretentious cell. He remained there with Leo, having forbidden the others to return to him till the Feast of St. Michael, and on no account to permit any persons whomsoever to have access to him. It was then the time of the fast which he prescribed for himself, in honor of the archangel; one of the nine periods of fasting he observed during the year, which will be noticed elsewhere. Proposing to fast this year more rigorously than in the preceding years, he directed Brother Leo to bring him nothing but bread and water once a day, and that, towards evening, and place it at the threshold of his cell. "And when you come to me for Matins," he added, "don't come into the cell, but only say in a loud voice, 'Domine, labia mea aperies;' and if I answer, 'Et os meum annuntiabit laudem tuam,' you will come in, otherwise you will go back." His pious companion, who had nothing more at heart than to obey him, and be useful to him, complied minutely with all he said; but he was often obliged to return in the night, because the holy man was in ecstasy, and did not hear him.

The reward of his solicitude was to be freed from a mental agitation, which he had found very troublesome; although it was not a temptation of the flesh, he nevertheless was ashamed of it, and did not dare make his Father acquainted with it; he only wished to have something written by him, which he thought would enable him to overcome the temptation, or at least enable him to bear it with less difficulty. The Father, knowing by revelation the state of his mind and his wish, desired him to bring him paper and ink, and he put on the top of the paper, in large characters, the letter "T," after which he wrote some praises of God, with his blessing: "May the Lord bless you and take you into His keeping, may He show you His countenance, and take pity on you, may He turn His eyes towards you, and give you His peace. May God bless Brother Leo." "Take this paper," he said, "and keep it carefully all your life." Leo had no sooner received it than his temptation left him; he preserved it carefully till his death, knowing the virtue that was attached to it. This writing is still extant at Assisi, in the sanctuary of the Church of St. Francis, and God has permitted it to be frequently used for the cure of diseases. St. Bonaventure says that, in his days, it had been the means by which several miracles were effected.

Francis experienced on Mount Alvernia, what had occurred to St. Anthony in the Desert of Thebais: after having been the means of freeing others from the attacks of the devil, he was exposed to them himself. The subtle spirit often suggested evil thoughts to him. He placed horrid spectres before him, and he even visibly struck him severe blows. Once in a very narrow path, and on the edge of a deep precipice, he appeared to him in a hideous figure, and threw himself upon him to cast him down; as there was nothing by which he could support himself, Francis placed his two hands on the rock, which was very hard and slippery, and they sank into it, as if it had been soft wax, and this preserved him from falling. An angel appeared to him to put away his fright, and to console him, causing him to hear celestial music, the sweetness of which in so far suspended the powers of his soul, that it seemed to him that his soul would have been separated from his body, had the music lasted much longer.

He resumed his prayer in which he returned thanks for having escaped the danger, and for the consolation he had received; then he set about considering what might be the will of God. He was not, as St. Bonaventure remarks, like to those inquisitive minds, who rashly endeavor to scrutinize the ways of God, and who are overwhelmed with His glory; but as a faithful and prudent servant, he endeavored to discover the intention of his Master, only from the anxiety he felt to conform himself to it in all things. A divine impression induced him to think that, if he opened the Book of the Gospel, he would learn from Jesus Christ what in him and for him would be most agreeable to God. Having, therefore, again prayed with great fervor, he told Brother Leo to take the New Testament from the altar, and open it; Leo opened it three times in honor of the most Holy Trinity, and, each time, he opened it at the Passion of our Blessed Lord. Francis, who was filled with the Spirit of God, understood from this, that, as he had imitated Jesus Christ in the actions of His life, he must now conform himself to His sufferings, and in the pains of His Passion.

Although his body was greatly weakened by the austerities he practised, by which he incessantly carried the cross of the Son of God, he was not alarmed at the idea of having new sufferings to endure; on the contrary, he put on fresh courage for martyrdom, in which, he thought, conformity to the Passion of Jesus Christ consists—hence the pious wish he had three times entertained of exposing himself to it. For the love he had for the good Jesus, remarks St. Bonaventure, was so lively, that the following words of the Canticles seemed to be applied to him: "His lamps are lamps of fire and flame." The charity which inflamed his heart was so ardent and forcible, that all the waters of tribulation, and all the fury of persecution would have been

From His Third Order of Penance to the Time of His Last Illness 203

unable to extinguish it. It is in this sense that St. Paul said: "Who shall separate us from the love of Christ? shall tribulation? or distress? or famine? or nakedness? or danger? or persecution? or the sword?" Such is the exalted love which Christians should have for God, if they desire to love Him eternally; their hearts must be ready and willing to make every sacrifice, and to suffer everything in order to preserve this divine love.

Some days after the opening of the book of the Gospel, Leo had come at midnight to say aloud, at the door of Francis' cell, "Domine labia mea aperies," according to the order he had received; and receiving no reply, he had the curiosity to advance a step further, and to look through the chinks of the door, to see what was going on. He saw the cell entirely illuminated, and a bright ray of light come from heaven, and rest upon the head of the Saint; he heard voices which made questions and answers; and he remarked that Francis, who was prostrate, often repeated these words: "Who art Thou, O my God, and my dear Lord? and whom and I? a worm, and Thy unworthy servant." He also saw him put his hand out three times into his bosom, and each time stretch it out to the flame.

The light disappeared, the conversation ceased, and Leo wished to retire quickly; but the Father heard him, and rebuked him severely for having watched him, and thus seen what ought to have been secret. Leo asked pardon, and having obtained it, humbly entreated his master to explain to him, for the greater glory of God, the things he had seen, which Francis did in these terms:—

> "God manifested Himself to me in the flame which you saw; He explained many mysteries to me, by His infinite goodness, and He communicated to me an immense knowledge of Himself, and I was so overpowered with admiration, that I exclaimed: 'Who art Thou, Lord, and who am I?' For nothing has tended more to my knowledge of what I am, than the contemplation of the infinite and incomprehensible abyss of the perfections of God, although from afar, and under obscure veils.
>
> "The Lord then having condescended to disclose to me, as much as I am capable of knowing of His infinite greatness, I could not avoid making this reflection; that it is certain that every creature is a mere nonentity before God. While I was thus meditating, it was His pleasure to direct that, for all the good He had done me, I should make Him some offering; I replied that my poverty was so great, that except the poor habit which I wore, I had nothing in the world but my body and my soul, which I had long since dedicated to Him. The Lord then urged me to offer Him what was in my bosom, and I was surprised to find there a beautiful piece

of gold, which I immediately offered to Him; I found three pieces successively, which I presented to Him in the same manner; it was when you saw me extend my hand in the flame. I gave thanks to God for His many benefits, and for the means He put in my power to make Him some acknowledgment. He gave me to understand that the three pieces of gold, which were highly agreeable to Him, represented the three modes of life which it had been His will that I should institute, and also the three vows of poverty, obedience, and chastity."

When he said that nothing had tended so much to the knowledge of what he was, as the contemplation of the infinite perfections of God, he well knew that the best mode to attain the knowledge of God is to know one's self, as St. Augustine and St. Bernard teach us; that is to say, that in order to our obtaining peculiar lights which open to us the grandeur of God, it is necessary to be thoroughly impressed with our own vileness, be sensible of our misery, and annihilate ourselves, because the Divine Majesty only communicates itself to the humble. But St. Francis proposed to himself to explain that, when it pleases God to manifest Himself in some manner to a soul which is duly sensible of its nothingness, it is better impressed with its own nothingness, by the disproportion it sees between the Sovereign Being and His creature, which discovers to it a thousand imperfections which it was not previously aware of, as a ray of the sun penetrating into a room, discovers a multitude of atoms of which we were previously unaware. We may also form to ourselves an idea of this by our knowledge of human ignorance; an ignorant man is less sensible of his ignorance and sometimes he is not at all aware of it; he thinks he knows everything; but a very learned man knows that he is ignorant of an infinity of things, and finds his mind very confined. So also souls which are interiorly enlightened as to the greatness of the Divinity, are more perfectly aware of their own nothingness, and are more humble than those who have not similar views. The mode adopted by the former is to dive into his own nothingness by the light of faith, to humble himself continually, in order to attain to a more exalted idea of the greatness of God and to repeat frequently this prayer of St. Augustine: "O God, who art always the same! may I know myself, may I know Thee."

The self-knowledge which St. Francis possessed in such perfection, prepared him sufficiently for the signal favor which God proposed to confer upon him, according to the principle of St. Augustine, that deep foundations are requisite for a building of great height.

About the Festival of the Exaltation of the Cross, which is on the fourteenth of September (it is believed that it was on the eve), an angel appeared to him and gave him notice as he afterwards communicated to some of his companions, to prepare himself for all that God would do for him. "I am prepared for everything," he replied, "and I shall not in any way oppose His holy will, provided he condescends to assist me with His grace. Although I am a useless man, and unworthy that God should cast a thought on me, nevertheless, as I am His servant, I beg He may act by me, according to His good pleasure."

This generous concurrence, which had martyrdom in its view, was the last disposition which the Almighty required previous to giving to Francis the peculiar and signal prerogative of the stigmata, that is to say, previous to imprinting on his body the five wounds of our Saviour Jesus Christ. We are about to put on record this marvellous event as nearly as possible in the very words of St. Bonaventure, which we have extracted from his two legends. He does not name the precise day, but Wading assigns good reasons for thinking it occurred on the Festival of the Exaltation of the Cross.

"Francis, the servant and truly faithful minister of Jesus Christ, being one morning in prayer on one side of the Mountain of Alvernia, elevating himself to God by the seraphic fervor of his desires and by the motives of tender and affectionate compassion, transforming himself into Him who, by the excess of His charity, chose to be crucified for us; he saw, as it were, a seraph, having six brilliant wings, and all on fire, descending towards him from the height of heaven. This seraph came with a most rapid flight to a spot in the air, near to where the Saint was, and then was seen between his wings the figure of a crucified man, who had his hands and feet extended and fastened to a cross. His wings were so arranged that he had two of them on his head, two were stretched out to fly with, and he covered his whole body with the two others.

"At the sight of such an object, Francis was extraordinarily surprised; joy, mingled with grief and sorrow, spread over his soul; the presence of Jesus Christ, who manifested himself to him under the figure of a seraph in so marvellous a mariner, and with such familiarity, and by whom he found himself considered so favorably, caused in him an excess of pleasure; but the sorrowful spectacle of His crucifixion filled him with compassion, and his soul felt as if it was pierced through with a sword. Above all, he admired with deep concern that the infirmity of His sufferings should appear under the figure of a seraph, well knowing that this does not agree with His state of immortality; and he could not comprehend the intention of the vision, when our Lord, who appeared outwardly, communicated to him interiorly, as to His friend, that He had been placed before him in order to let him know that it was not by the martyrdom of the flesh, but by the inflammation of the soul, that he was to be wholly transformed into a perfect resemblance to Jesus Christ crucified.

"The vision vanished, after having had a secret and familiar conference with him, leaving his soul filled with seraphic ardor, and imprinting on his body a figure similar to that of the crucifix, as if his flesh, like softened wax, had received the impression of the letters of a seal. For the marks of the nails immediately began to show themselves on his hands and feet, such as he had seen them on the figure of the crucified man. His feet and hands were seen to be perforated by nails in their middle; the heads of the nails, round and black, were on the inside of the hands, and on the upper parts of the feet; the points, which were rather long, and which came out on the opposite sides, were turned and raised above the flesh, from which they came out. There was, likewise, on his right side a red wound, as if it had been pierced with a lance, and from this wound there often oozed a sacred blood, which soaked his tunic, and anything he wore round his body."

This is the new prodigy which Jesus Christ chose to exhibit in favor of Francis, in order to render him more like to himself. He marked him and ornamented him with His own wounds, by a singular and glorious prerogative which had never, previously, been conceded to any one, and which justly excites the admiration of the Christian world. St. Bonaventure is of opinion that all human encomium falls short of what it deserves. In fact, in the midst of all the marvels which we find in the life of St. Francis, we are compelled to admit that this is the one which, without any exaggeration, may be termed incomparable. What can there be so beautiful as to be visibly clothed with Jesus Christ, to bear on the body the lively resemblance of those wounds which are the price of our redemption, the source of life, and the pledge of salvation? What interior conformity must the Servant have had with his Master, to have deserved to have so marked a one exteriorly, for, no doubt, the one was in proportion to the other! This faithful Servant having embraced the cross from the very commencement of his conversion, he carried it in his heart, in his mind, in his body, and in all his senses; all his love, all his desires, were centred in the cross, it was the standard of his militia. Therefore did Jesus Christ, whose goodness appears with magnificence towards those who love Him, after having honored the zeal of Francis by various apparitions in His crucified state, choose, as a crowning of all His favors, that he should be himself crucified, in order that, as the love of the cross constituted his merit before God, the glory of being so miraculously fastened to it, should render him admirable in the sight of mankind.

Such was the sort of torment which God reserved for him in order to satisfy the extreme desire he had to suffer martyrdom, on which St. Bonaventure exclaims: "O truly fortunate man, whose flesh not having been tortured by the racks of a tyrant, has nevertheless, borne the impress of the Lamb that was slain! O fortunate soul, thou hast not lost the palm of martyrdom, and yet thou art not separated from the body by the sword of the persecutor!" Must we not also admit that the impression of the five wounds of our Savior Jesus Christ on his body was a true martyrdom—a precious martyrdom; rigorous in one sense, and the more so, as it was not the consequence of the cruelty of executioners, but was owing to the darts of divine love, and to the very influence of the Son of God, the operation of which is most powerful; sweet and delicious in another sense, and the more so, as it was the effect of a most affectionate communication, and brought about more intimate relations? Out Savior, thus, in some degree, represented in His creature the situation in which He had been on the cross, enjoying sovereign beatitude, while He suffered all the pains and violence of the execution.

It was in all probability after this favor of the stigmata, that Francis composed the two Italian canticles which are found amongst his works. In the first, the burden of which is, "In foco l'amor mi mise, in foco l'amor mi mise," he describes very practically, with figurative and very lively expressions, the struggle he had with divine love, and the attacks he had himself made on that love, the wounds which he received, the flames by which his heart was kindled, and the state of languor and faintness to which he found himself reduced, and, finally, the strength, with a tranquillity of feeling exceedingly refreshing, which Jesus Christ had imparted to him. In the second, which is much longer than the first, he describes the strength, elevation, and tenderness, the vehemence of the divine love in his heart; he enters into conversation with Jesus Christ, who answers him; and this love constantly increasing, he declares that he can resist no longer, that he consents to everything, and that he wishes no other relief than to die of love.

St. Theresa, speaking of her situation at prayer, in which she often found herself, as it were, intoxicated with the love of God, and quite beside herself, said: "I know a person who, without being a poet, sometimes made very good extempore verses in spiritual canticles, which expressed beautifully her sufferings. It was not from her mind that they originated; but, by order of the glory so delicious a suffering caused her; she laid her complaint in this manner before God. She would have wished to tear herself to pieces to show the pleasure she experienced in this delightful pain." These spiritual and divine emotions are neither known nor relished by profane minds and hearts, who only learn from their own corruption, and from the pestiferous books which encourage it, the extravagances and transports of criminal love; but pure minds, who know what it is to love God, and to be loved by Him, are not astonished at the effects which this holy reciprocated love produced in a St. Francis, in a St. Theresa, and in many others. Neither is it surprising that the saints who are full of the thoughts of God, should have had recourse to poetry to express the feelings of their hearts, since the sacred writers, inspired by the Spirit of God, have composed many of the sacred books in poetry; this also is practised by the universal Church in her Divine Office.

The precious wounds which Francis had received, were a subject of great embarrassment to him; for, in the first place, he wished to conceal them wholly, well knowing that it is "proper to conceal the secrets of the king," as the angel said to Tobit; and, in the second place, he saw that the wounds were too conspicuous to remain long hidden from those of his companions who had familiar intercourse with him. His hesitation was, whether he should tell them what had occurred, in confidence, or whether he should be silent on the subject, for fear of making known the secrets of the Lord. He called some of them to him and laid before them his difficulty in general terms, and solicited their advice. Brother Illuminatus, he from whom he had received such excellent advice in the camp before Damietta, opining, from the look of astonishment which he remarked in him, that he had seen something wonderful, said: "Brother, you ought to know that it is not only for your own edification, but for that of others also, that God sometimes discovers his secrets to you, for which reason you should be fearful of being reprimanded for having hidden the talent, unless you make known what is to be of service to many."

Francis was struck with this advice, and although on other occasions he was in the habit of saying with Isaiah, "My secret is to myself," he communicated to them all what had passed in the apparition, but always with great fear; adding, that He who had appeared to him, had communicated things to him which, while he lived, he never would disclose to any one. We must believe, as St. Bonaventure remarks, that the seraph whom he saw attached to the cross in so wonderful a manner, or rather, Jesus Christ Himself in the appearance of a seraph, had said to him, as he had to St. Paul, "Secret words, which it is not granted to man to utter;" either because there are no words in which they can be expressed, or, as a respected author thinks, because there are no souls sufficiently disengaged from sensible objects, and sufficiently pure, to understand them.

The confidence which Francis had reposed in his companions, did not prevent his taking every precaution possible to hide, as much as it was in his power, the sacred marks with which the King of kings had secretly favored him. From that time forward, he kept his hands covered, so that the nails should not be seen, and he wore slippers, which covered those of his feet. Wading saw in the Monastery of the Poor Clares at Assisi, the sort of slippers which St. Clare made for her spiritual Father, so neatly contrived that the upper part covered the heads of the nails, and, the underneath being somewhat raised, the points did not prevent his walking; for these miraculous nails did not take from him the use of his hands and feet, although it was painful to him to use them.

But all the precautions which his humility had suggested, became useless; it is God's providence to reveal, for His greater glory, the wonderful things which He does. The Lord Himself, who had secretly marked on Francis the impressions of His Passion, by their means worked miracles, which manifestly disclosed their hidden and marvellous virtue. Moreover, the Saintly Man could not prevent his wounds from being seen and touched by persons whose veracity cannot be called in question, and who rendered public testimony thereto; besides which, after his death, all the inhabitants of Assisi saw, touched, and kissed them. The Sovereign Pontiffs of those days were so convinced of this admirable event, that they issued bulls to exalt it by their praise, and to repress by their authority those who refused credence to the fact, because they had not seen it with their own eyes. Pope Alexander IV certified it, as having been an eye-witness to it, in a sermon and in a bull; and St. Bonaventure says that the proofs then collected made it so certain, that they were sufficient to dispel every shade of doubt. This degree of certainty is still further enhanced and rendered more respectable, since Popes Benedict XI, Sixtus IV, and Sixtus V have consecrated and extolled the impression of the stigmata on the body of St. Francis, by having instituted a particular festival in their honor, which is found in the Roman Martyrology, on the 17th of September, and which is kept in the universal Church.

The forty days which Francis had resolved to pass in solitude and fasting having terminated on Michaelmas Day, this new man, whom perfect love had transformed by a lively resemblance into Him whom he loved, descended from the mountain, carrying with him the image of Jesus Christ crucified, not modelled by the hand of a workman on wood or stone, but stamped on his very flesh by the finger of the living God Himself, as St. Bonaventure expresses it. He became more partial than ever to Mount Alverno, where he had received this sacred image, and recommended to his brethren to cherish great respect for this holy place.

As he descended the mountain, he met a number of the country people who had already heard of the marvellous occurrence; it is probable that God had informed the people of it by some extraordinary manifestation. At the time when it occurred, they saw at break of day the mountain illuminated by a most brilliant light, and what they heard, informed them of the reason. They wished to kiss his hands; but they were tied round with bandages, and he only offered them the tips of his fingers.

In a village near Arezzo, they brought him a child of about eight years of age, who had been dropsical for four years, whom he cured instantaneously by touching him. He went afterwards to Montaigne, where Count Albert, the lord of that place, who was his good friend, and at whose house he often took his bed, received him with great pleasure. But the count was distressed to hear him say that his infirmities would not allow him to return there anymore, and that the time of his death was hastening on. To mitigate the grief of such melancholy tidings, he entreated the Saint to leave him some memorial of their friendship; to which Francis replied, that he had nothing to give but the miserable habit he had on, but that he would willingly leave it him, provided he could get another.

The change was soon effected; and it cannot be told how much Albert prized the habit in which Francis had received the impression of the precious pledges of our redemption. After the death of St. Francis he enfolded this poor habit in rich stuffs of silk and gold, and he placed it with great veneration on the altar of the church. The Lords of Montaigne, from father to son, had it long in their possession; and it, at length, came in the manner related by Wading, into the possession of the Grand Dukes of Tuscany, who preserve it as a precious relic.

The great infirmities which the man of God suffered, obliged him to take an ass to carry him from Montaigne to Mount Casal, through the borough of Saint Sepulchre. When he reached the latter place, which is very populous, the crowd surrounded him, touched him, and pressed upon him, but he was insensible of it; he was as a dead person, in no way aware what was doing, insomuch that, having proceeded a good way from thence, and coming to himself, as one returned from the other world, he inquired of some lepers at the door of the hospital, whether they would soon get to Saint Sepulchre. His mind, contemplating, says St. Bonaventure, with deep attention the brilliant lights of heaven, had not noticed the difference of time, place, or persons; so penetrated was he with divine communications, that he was not aware of what passed around him.

On reaching Mount Casal, he learned that one of his religious was suffering under an extraordinary disorder, which some considered to be epilepsy, and others thought it a true case of possession by the devil, for he had all the violent contortions of those possessed. The Father, who was full of tender compassion for the suffering, was greatly afflicted at seeing one of his children in this deplorable state, and he sent him a mouthful of the bread he was eating, the virtue of which was so great that, as soon as the sick man had swallowed it, he was cured, and thenceforward had no relapse into the disorder.

From Mount Casal Francis went to Castello, and at the house where he went to lodge, he was required to lend his aid to a female whom the devil possessed, and compelled to talk without ceasing. The servant of God with great prudence first sent one of his companions to see and hear her, to examine into the case, to see whether it was really one of possession, or whether the woman was not counterfeiting. She gnashed her teeth,—she imitated the cry of an elephant with a dreadful countenance; she affected to laugh when she saw the religious, and ordered him to go away, saying that she did not care about him, but she was afraid of him who hid himself. The Saint, who was in prayer, having heard this, came into the room, where this woman was speaking without any reserve, before many who were there. As soon as she saw him, she fell on the ground, trembling. He reproached the demon with his cruelty in thus torturing one of God's creatures, and ordered him to leave her, which he did instantly, but with so much noise as manifested his wrath. In the same town he cured a child who had an ulcer, by making the sign of the cross on the dressing which covered it. When the parents of the child took off the dressing, they saw with surprise, in lieu of the ulcer, a fleshy excrescence, like a red rose, which remained during the whole of the child's life, as a sensible proof and memorial of the miracle which had been performed.

After an abode of a month at Castello, the man of God set out on his return to Saint Mary of the Angels. Brother Leo, who accompanied him, assures us, that during the whole way, and until his arrival in the convent, he saw a beautiful golden cross, shining—with various colors, preceding him, which stopped where he stopped, and advanced as he went on. This pious companion understood from this, that God had chosen to give to His Servant the consolation of seeing with the eyes of his body that cross which he had always in his heart, and which he likewise bore in his flesh by the wounds of Jesus Christ.

Nothing is more affecting than what St. Bonaventure says of the feelings of St. Francis after having received the impression of these sacred wounds. These are the words of the holy doctor:—

> "Francis, being crucified with Jesus Christ in mind and body, not only burned with the ardent love of a seraph, but he likewise participated in the thirst for the salvation of souls which the Son of God felt on the Cross. As he could not go, as he usually had done, into the towns and villages, on account of the large nails he had on his feet, he had himself carried thither, to animate every one, although he was in a deplorable state of languor and half dead with his infirmities, to carry the cross of our Saviour. He used to say to his brethren: 'Let us now begin to serve the Lord our God, for up to this time we have made but little progress.'"
>
> "He was also ardently desirous of returning to his first practices of humility,—to attend the lepers, and to bring his body into subjection, as he had done in the first days of his conversion. Although his limbs were enfeebled by his exertions and sufferings, that did not prevent his hoping that, as his mind was yet vigorous and active, he should still combat and be victorious over his enemy. Under the guidance of Jesus Christ, he proposed to perform some extraordinary things; for when love is the spur, which admits of no neglect nor slackness, it urges to the undertaking of things of greater importance. His body was in such unison with his mind, so submissive, so wholly obedient, that, far from resisting, it was forward in some measure, and went as it were of itself towards the attainment of the great elevation of sanctity to which he aspired."

It being God's will that he should acquire the summit of merit, which is only attained by great patience, He tried him by many sorts of maladies, so grievous, that there was scarcely any part of his body in which he did not suffer excruciating pains. These reduced him to such a state, that he was scarcely more than skin and bone, almost all his flesh was wasted away; but these sufferings he did not consider as such, he denominated them his sisters, to show how much he cherished them.

These words of Saint Francis to his brethren, "Let us begin to serve the Lord our God, for until now we have made little progress," contain one of the most important lessons of all spiritual life. The Wise Man says of the knowledge of the works of God: "When a man hath done, then he shall begin," St. Augustine applies this sentence to the obscurity of the sacred writings, when he says that, the deeper they are searched, the more hidden mysteries are found in them; and it is equally applicable to Christian and religious perfection. It is an error condemned by the Church to believe that a man is capable of attaining in this life such a degree of perfection, as not to be able to increase it; but it would be a deplorable illusion to make use of the language condemned by Saint Bernard; "I have done enough, I will remain as I am: neither become worse, nor better." The just man never says, "It is enough;" he has always hunger and thirst after justice; as the apostles, "He forgets the things that are behind, and stretches himself to those that are before, to press towards the mark." To believe that we have made progress is not to do so; not to strive to advance is to go back, and to lose one's self. What instruction do we find here for the most perfect, in the example of a saint who deems himself to have made little progress in the service of God, and who wishes to begin all afresh, at a time when he is found deserving to bear on his body the wounds of Jesus Christ!

His disorders were only afflicting to Francis inasmuch as related to the vast projects he unceasingly formed for the good of souls. He was most grieved at the state of his eyes, which made his sight begin to fail. Notwithstanding his other infirmities, whenever he could, he mounted on an ass, and went about, preaching penance, announcing the kingdom of God, and addressing these words to all his hearers: "Jesus Christ, my Love, was crucified." He spoke with so much fervor, and with such assiduity, visiting sometimes five or six towns in the course of a single day, that it might be paid that God gave him, as to the prophet, the agility of a deer. However, although in the person of St. Francis the interior man was renewed from day to day, yet it necessarily followed that the exterior man, borne down by so much, austerity and fatigue, began rapidly to decay. The acute pains in his eyes, and the tears he constantly shed, brought on blindness, besides it was impossible for him to preach any longer, however desirous he was to do so. Moreover, he would not have recourse to remedies, although his brethren urged him to avail himself of them, because, being already in heaven in mind and heart, he wished, as the Apostle had done, "to have his conversation in heaven."

Brother Elias, vicar-general, who felt the loss which the death of his holy founder would be to the Order, was most anxious to procure him relief. His feelings also induced him to wish it; for, with all his faults, he was tenderly attached to his father, and was as a mother to him by the care he took of him: of this all the first writers of the life of Saint Francis bear testimony. He used entreaties and argument to induce him to have recourse to medicine for his disorders, and quoted the following Scriptural texts: "The Most High hath created medicines out of the earth, and a wise man will not abhor them." He also on this occasion made use of the power he had received from the Saint: he commanded him, on his obedience, not to resist his cure. Cardinal Ugolino, Protector of the Order, urged him also to the same effect, and warned him to be careful, lest there should be sin instead of merit in neglecting to take proper care of himself.

The sick man yielded to the advice of his friends. He was removed to a small and poor cell, very near the Convent of Saint Damian, that he might be nearer to Clare and her sisterhood, who loved him as their father, and who prepared the medicines for him. He remained there forty days with the Brothers Masse, Ruffin, Leo, and Angelo of Rieti; but the disorder of his eyes became so painful, that he could get no rest night or day; when he endeavored to procure a little sleep, he was prevented by a number of rats, which infested the hut, and ran over his table and bed so daringly, that it was thought to be a stratagem of the evil one.

Seeing himself overwhelmed by an accumulation of disorders, he made the following prayer humbly to God: "My Lord and God, cast Thine eyes upon me, and lend me Thine aid; grant me grace to bear with patience all these ills and infirmities." A voice forthwith made him this answer: "Francis, what price should be set upon that which shall obtain a kingdom which is above all price? Know that the pains you suffer are of greater value than all the riches of the world, and that you ought not to be rid of them for all that is in the world, even though all the mountains should be changed into pure gold, all its stones into jewels, and all the waters of the sea into balsam." "Yes, Lord," exclaimed Francis, "it is thus that I prize the sufferings Thou sendest me; for I know that it is Thy will that they should be in this world the chastisements of my sins, in order to show me mercy in eternity." "Rejoice, then," added the voice, "it is through the way in which you are, that heaven is reached." At these words he rose up full of fervor; and wishing that Clare, who was almost always ill, should benefit by what he had just heard, he sent to her, and informed her of the tender goodness of God to man, even in the dispositions of His Providence, which have the appearance of being the most severe.

Men who are enlightened by the light of faith,—must they not be convinced of these Christian truths: that the most perfect have some sins to expiate; that the saints can only attain to heaven by suffering; that the Kingdom of Heaven, which is invaluable, cannot be purchased at too great a price; and that God never manifests His paternal regard in our favor more evidently than when He afflicts us in this world in order to show us His mercy in the next? What fruit might not be gathered from sicknesses and other sufferings; what alleviations, what consolations, and even what joy, might not be found, if these holy truths were but reduced to practice, which unfortunately are only viewed theoretically, and with little or no application!

Francis being one day at dinner, and beginning to eat, stopped suddenly, and, with his eyes raised to heaven, exclaimed in a loud voice: "May God be blessed, glorified, and exalted above all!" Then leaving the room in an unusual manner, he threw himself on the ground, where he remained motionless in ecstasy during a whole hour.

When he came to himself, one of the brethren whose name was Leonard, who had witnessed what had passed, and had heard what he had exclaimed, spoke to him of it, as if what he had done had been very unbecoming. "My dear brother," said Francis, "I had great cause for what I did, which I will communicate to you confidentially, upon condition that you will tell no one of it during my lifetime. If a king promised to give a kingdom to one of his subjects, would not that person have great reason to rejoice? What, then, did I do that was unseemly,—I whom the Almighty assured of His kingdom? I was so overpowered with joy, that I could not control the emotions of my heart; you must excuse the excess in the expressions of my satisfaction, whatever it may have been, and however it may have seemed to transgress the rules of decorum. But what I did is not enough, I will praise God still more; I will unceasingly praise His holy name. I will sing hymns to His glory during the remainder of my days."

After which he sat down, and after having reflected a little, he got one of his companions to write an Italian canticle, which begins thus: "Altissimo, Omnipotente, bon Signore; tue son le laude, la gloria, l'onore, ed ogni benedizione," etc. "O God, most high, most powerful, most good! to Thee belong praise, honor, glory, and every blessing: these are solely to be referred to Thee; neither is any man worthy to pronounce Thy holy name. Praise be to Thee, O Lord, my God! by all thy creatures." He speaks of the sun as the most brilliant of all, of the moon, the stars, the air, the wind, the clouds, the seasons, the water, the fire, the earth and all that it contains; giving praise to God for each of His creatures, whose beauties and properties He recites.

This canticle resembles that which was sung at Babylon, in the fiery furnace, by the three young men who were thrown into it, for not having adored the statue of Nebuchodonosor. They called upon all creatures, inanimate and irrational, to praise God, as David had done before; and St. Francis calls upon all to praise Him, because of His creatures.

This has the same result; for inanimate creatures, as St. Jerome observes, only praise God by making Him known to men, and by placing before them His magnificence. "When they are considered as His work," says St.

Augustine, "we find in them numberless reasons for singing hymns to His glory; and if His greatness is manifested in His glorious works, He is not less great in those which are less so. Whatsoever God has made, praises God; there is only sin, of which He is not the author, which does not praise Him." It was Francis's desire that all his brethren should learn his canticle, and recite it daily, and that Brother Pacificus, the famous poet, of whom we have before spoken, and who was then in France or in the Low Countries, should put it into well-sounding verse. He called it the Canticle of the Sun, because of the preeminence of that beautiful planet, in which, David says, God seemed to have taken up His abode, in order to show Himself to us.

As his malady did not show symptoms of amelioration, Elias had him removed from the Convent of St. Mary of the Angels to Foligno, in hopes that change of air might be of service to him. And he was in fact somewhat relieved by it; but God made known, by an extraordinary revelation, that he would continue to suffer until death. Elias found himself overpowered with sleep, and in his slumber he saw a venerable old man, clothed in white, with pontifical ornaments, who told him that Francis must prepare himself to suffer patiently for two years more, after which, death would deliver him, and would cause him to pass into perfect repose, free from all pain. He communicated this to Francis, who said that the same thing had been communicated to him; and then, filled with joy, not only on account of the eternal felicity again promised him, but because the time was fixed when his soul was to be released from the prison of his body, he added this further couplet to his canticle: "Be Thou praised, my Lord, for death our sister, from which no living man can escape," etc. "Blessed are they who, at the hour of death, are found conformed to Thy holy will, for they will not be overtaken by the second death. Woe to those who die in mortal sin! May all creatures praise and bless God, obey Him and serve Him with great humility!" If we are surprised to find St. Francis call death our sister, we must bear in mind that the holy man, Job, said to rottenness: "Thou art my father; and to the worms, you are my mother and sister."

The whole of the year 1225, Francis passed in various illnesses and in great sufferings. Towards autumn, Cardinal Ugolino and Brother Elias induced him to be removed to Rieti, where there were able physicians and surgeons who could attend to the state of his eyes. As soon as it was known in the town, all the inhabitants met, and went to meet him; but, in order to avoid all the honors preparing for him, he had himself taken to St. Fabian, a village two miles from Rieti, where he lodged at the cure's.

The Pope was at Rieti, with all his court, at that time: many of the principal persons of the court, and even cardinals, came to St. Fabian to visit the holy man. While they were in conversation with him, the persons of their suite went into the cure's vineyard to eat grapes, and they gathered so many that the vineyard was nearly stripped. The cure was much displeased at this, and complained to St. Francis, who asked him, how much he thought he had lost? "I usually," replied the cure, "have made fourteen measures of wine, which were sufficient for the consumption of my house." "I am sorry," said Francis, "that they should have done you so much damage, but we must hope that God will find a remedy for it, and I firmly believe He will, and that, from the grapes which remain in your vineyard, He will give you fourteen measures of wine and more." The cure saw this prophecy fulfilled, for he made twenty measures from the few grapes which had been left. The magistrates of Rieti caused, at a subsequent period, a convent to be built for the Friars Minors on this spot; and the same Pope, Gregory IX, out of respect for the Saint, chose to consecrate the church himself, in which are still seen representations of the miracle.

After some days Francis could no longer avoid going to Rieti, where the persons of the court received him with honors, which he gladly would have dispensed with.—He lodged there with a pious citizen, named Theobald, a Saracen, who had settled in the town.

The dejection of spirits which his sufferings had brought upon him, made him desirous of having instrumental music to cheer him; "but," says St. Bonaventure, "decorum did not allow him to ask for it, and it was God's pleasure that he should receive this agreeable consolation by means of an angel. The mere sound, which was marvellously harmonious, raised his mind so entirely to God, and filled his soul with so much delight, that he thought himself in the enjoyment of the joys of the other world. His intimate companions perceived it, and they frequently observed that God gave him extraordinary consolations, for the effects they produced on him were so manifest, that it was impossible for him to disguise them, and then he admitted to them from whence they arose."

This shows that, if the saintly sufferer wished to hear some instrumental music, it was in order to listen to it for the glory of God, as St. Augustine observes was the case with David, and not for any purely human gratification, nor to take any ordinary pleasure therein, nor even for the assuagement of his violent sufferings.

It is true that harmonious sound will procure this relief; and without referring to what ancient writers say on this head, without noticing Saul, we know that there are feelings of the body and mind, in which we experience what the wise man supposes to be a common occurrence, "that music rejoices the heart." Man being born with a taste for proportion, and finding himself full of concert and harmony, it is no way surprising that the harmony and proportion of sounds should cause strong and vivid impressions on him.

St. Francis, who may have been naturally more affected by music than others, may also have reasonably wished for its solace, more from a desire to prevent the depression of his spirits, than from the violence of his sufferings, or from being deprived of its solace by a principle of mortification. For he was too spiritual a man not to have us convinced that his wish proceeded from a purer and more noble motive. He desired to prevent his mind from being too greatly depressed, in order to render himself more equal to interior operations, and to unite himself more easily and more intimately to God—as the Prophet Eliseus, who, having been greatly excited against the King of Israel, caused a canticle of the temple to be sung to him, with a harp accompaniment, in order to calm his irritated mind, and to prepare him for the lights of the Lord, as to the knowledge of future events. St. Augustine also observes, that, after his baptism, the chant of the hymns and psalms sung in the church excited in his heart tender sentiments of piety, and drew from his eyes floods of tears.

We may say: Music is a science given to men by the liberality of the Creator, to represent to them the admirable harmony by which He governs the world, in order to guide them by the channel of the senses, and melody of sounds, to the knowledge and love of immutable truth. This is also the true use of music, and it is only with this view that the Church permits it in the Divine Service. That which is soft and effeminate, which is calculated to excite the passions, by multitudes of ambiguous expressions, (not the less dangerous for being so cloaked) should be considered by Christians as an abuse the more deplorable, as it has even been censured and condemned by the pagans.

All the skill of the physicians and surgeons of Rieti not having had any effect towards the cure of their patient, he had himself taken to his Convent of Fonte Colombo, where they were to continue their remedies; and it was their opinion that a hot iron should be applied above his ear, from which it was expected he would obtain relief. For this reason his brethren urged him to give his consent, which he willingly did, in hopes to recover his sight thereby, and then to continue his exertions for the salvation of souls; and also because, the operation being very painful, he would have an opportunity of voluntary suffering.

When they were about to apply the red-hot iron, he could not avoid feeling a natural sense of fear; in order to overcome it, he addressed the fire as we should speak to a friend: "My brother," said he, "the Most High has given you great beauty, and has made you most useful; be favorable to me on this occasion. I entreat the great God who created you, to temper your heat, so that I may be able to bear it." He then made the sign of the cross on the instrument, and without any fear presented himself to receive the impression. His companions, not having courage to witness the operation, left the room. The physician and surgeon remained alone with him, and the hot iron was pressed from over his ear to his eyebrow, into his flesh.

After the operation, the brothers having returned, he said to them: "Praise the Lord, for I assure you I neither felt the heat of the fire, nor any pain." Then he reproached them mildly in these words: "Why did you fly, you pusillanimous men, and of little faith? He who preserved the three young men in the furnace of Babylon, could He not temper in my favor the heat of my brother, the fire?" We shall see further what an exalted principle it was which induced him to qualify all creatures by the names of his brothers and sisters. He said to the physician: "If the flesh is not sufficiently burnt, replace the hot iron." The physician, struck with so much fortitude in so feeble a body, saw that it was miraculous, and said to the religious: "I see truly to-day a most wonderful occurrence."

St. Bonaventure, who relates this, makes the following observation: That Francis having attained so high a degree of perfection, his body was subject to his mind, and his mind to God; with admirable harmony it followed from thence, by a peculiar disposition of Divine Providence, that inanimate creatures which obey God, obeyed His servant also, and forebore from hurting him, according to the words: "O Lord! the creature being subject to Thee, as to its Creator, renovates its strength to torment the wicked, and softens it to contribute to the good of those who trust in Thee."

It is, moreover, remarkable that St. Francis feared when he saw the red-hot iron,—he who had consented to have the remedy applied, because it was severe, and who had offered, when in Egypt, to cast himself into the fire to prove the truth of the Christian religion. It is thus that God permits His saints to become sensible of their natural weakness in trifling things, in order that they may be sensible that in greater things all their strength depends upon His grace.

The disorder in the eyes of St. Francis was caused by the tears he continually shed. His physician told him he ought to restrain them, unless he wished to lose his entire sight; and this is the reply he gave him: "My dear Brother Doctor, for the love of corporal sight, which we enjoy in common with flies, we must not set aside for a single instant the Divine illustrations; for the mind has not received the favor on account of the body, it has been granted to the body on account of the mind." He liked better, says St. Bonaventure, to lose corporal sight than to check for a single moment that tender and affectionate devotion which calls forth tears, by which the interior sight is purified and rendered competent to see an infinitely pure God.

In order to show some gratitude to the physician for the trouble he took in his regard, Francis one day desired the brethren, in his presence, to take him to dine with them. They represented to him that their poverty was such that they had nothing which was fit to place before a person of his consideration, for this physician was in great estimation, and very rich. "Men of little faith," replied the Saint, "why have you these doubts? Why have you not considered more favorably the merit of obedience? Go and take to the refectory our honorable brother, the doctor." They took him, seeing that he would consent to partake of their poor fare out of devotion, but, just as they were sitting down to table, there was a ring at the bell; it was a woman, who brought, in a basket, several dishes exceedingly well dressed, which a lady, who lived at a country house, six miles off, sent to the servant of God. He desired that these might be offered to the physician, and that he might be told that the Lord took care of His own. The doctor admired the hand of Providence, and said to the religious: "My brethren, we do not sufficiently understand the holiness of this man; and even you who live with him, have no conception of the secret virtue with which his mind is replenished."

This physician was not less charitable than learned; he had great pleasure in prescribing for this sick man, he frequently visited him, and paid the expense of the medicines he required. God, who considered as done to Himself what was done to His servant who could not repay him, rewarded him in this world by a miracle worked in his favor.

He had laid out all his ready money in building a house which was only just finished, when one of the principal walls was found to have a large crack in it from the top to the bottom, which no human art could make good. Full of faith and confidence in the merits of Francis, he begged his companions to give him something which the holy man had touched. After many entreaties they gave him some of his hair, which he placed at night in the fissure in the wall. He came back in the morning, and found the whole so completely closed, that it was not only impossible to get back the hair, but it was no longer perceivable that there had been any rent in the wall. The good offices which he had manifested to a worn-out body prevented, says St. Bonaventure, the ruin of the house he had just built.

Some days after, Francis was taken to Rieti, where the bishop lodged him in his palace; they brought to the foot of his bed, upon a tressel, one of the canons, who was dangerously ill; he had been a very worldly man, who had lived a dissipated life, but who, struck with the fear of approaching death, entreated the Saint to make the sign of the cross upon him. "How," said Francis, "shall I make the sign of the cross on you, who, without any fear of the judgments of God, have given yourself up to the lusts of the flesh? I will do it, however, because of the pious persons who have interceded in your favor. But, bear in mind that you will suffer much greater ills, if, after your cure, you should return to your vomit, for the sin of ingratitude and relapse makes the last state of man worse than the first." He then made the sign of the cross upon the sick man, who immediately arose, praised God, and exclaimed, "I am healed." All the bystanders heard his bones crack, as when dry sticks are broken. That unhappy man, however, did not remain long without plunging again into vice; and one night, as he was in bed at the house of a canon where he had supped, the roof of the house fell in and crushed him, without hurting anyone else.

"It was," says the same holy doctor, "by a just judgment of God; for the sin of ingratitude is a contempt of the graces of God, for which we ought to be most thankful; and the sins into which we again fall after repentance, displease Him more than any others. Will it never be understood that, in the diseases of the soul, as in those of the body, there is nothing so dangerous as a relapse?"

The pains felt by Francis were in some degree assuaged, his sight was restored, and he made use of this interval to have himself taken into several parts of Umbria, of the Kingdom of Naples, and of the adjacent provinces, in order to work for the salvation of souls. At Penna, a young religious who was naturally good, and of great promise, came to ask his pardon for having left the Order, which he had only done at the instigation of the evil spirit, who persuaded him that by living privately, he could better sanctify himself. As soon as the Saint saw him, he fled to his cell, and shut the door; when he came out again, his companions expressed their surprise at what he had done: "Do not be astonished," he said, "at my having fled; I saw on this young man a frightful demon, who was endeavoring to throw him down a precipice, and I acknowledge to you that I could not bear his presence. I have prayed as earnestly as I could for the deliverance of this poor brother from such a seducer, and God has heard my prayer." Then, having sent for him, and telling him what he had seen, he exhorted him to be on his guard against the snares of the devil, and not to separate himself again from his brethren: "For, if you do otherwise," he added, "you will not fail to fall into the precipice from which the mercy of God has preserved you." The docile and faithful religious passed the remainder of his days in great piety, and in the exercises of a regular life.

At Calano, a town of the Duchy of Marsi, in the farther Abruzzo, where Francis was come to preach, a common soldier pressed him so earnestly to come and dine with him, that he could make no excuse. He therefore went, with one companion, who was a priest,—a circumstance which was very serviceable. The poor family of the soldier having received them with great joy, the Saint began to pray, as was his custom, and he had his eyes constantly raised to heaven. He then said to the soldier, privately, "My brother and my host, you see I have acceded to your request in coming to dine with you. Now, follow my advice, and make haste; for it is not here, but elsewhere, that you will dine. Confess your sins with as much exactness and sorrow as you can; the Lord will reward you for having received His poor ones with such good religious intentions." The soldier, placing confidence in what the servant of God said to him, made his confession to Francis' companion, regulated his temporal affairs, and prepared himself, as well as he could, for death. When that was done, he sat down with the others at table, and a minute afterwards he expired suddenly. Then were the words of the Gospel fulfilled, that he who should receive a prophet as a prophet, that is to say, not seeing in him any other qualification, receives also the reward of the prophet, inasmuch as the prediction of Francis enabled him to fortify himself by penance against death, which he did not think to be so near at hand.

It was probably in this apostolic tour that the Servant of God performed a miracle on the person of St. Bonaventure, who, under the dispositions of Divine Providence; was to become one of the most illustrious of his children. He was born at Bagnarea in Tuscany, a town belonging to the Ecclesiastical States, in the year 1221, and he was baptized by the name of John. His father, John Fidenza, and Ritella, his mother, joined to the nobility of their birth a large fund of piety. In his infancy he was seized with a mortal illness, of which he was cured by St. Francis, which was one of the reasons why he determined to write his Life. "I should fear," he says in his preface to his Legend, "that I should be accused of criminal ingratitude if I neglected to publish the praises of him, to whom I acknowledge that I owe the life of my body and my soul."

It is reported, with the circumstances which he himself may have told, and the memory of which may have been preserved by tradition, that his mother, having no further hopes of saving him by means of medicaments, came and presented him to St. Francis, who was renowned in Italy, at that time, for the splendor of his sanctity and his miracles; she implored the aid of his prayers, and made a vow that, if the child was saved, she would give him to his Order.

The holy man consoled the afflicted mother, and obtained from God the cure of her son, to the astonishment of the physicians, who had deemed his disorder incurable. At the sight of this miraculous cure, he said, in the Italian language: "O buona ventura!" "How fortunate!" from whence came the name of Bonaventure; and finally, he foretold that the child would become a great light in the Church of God, and that through him his Order would receive great increase of sanctity.

In the year 1243, being then twenty-two years old, he proposed to fulfil his mother's vow, and take the habit of a Friar Minor. This is not the place to narrate his illustrious actions, but we must notice two remarkable circumstances which are connected with St. Francis.

The first is, that, as this blessed Patriarch bears the name of Seraphic, because of the Divine love with which he was inflamed, when Jesus Christ, under the figure of a seraph, imprinted on him the sacred stigmata, so St. Bonaventure has been called the Seraphic Doctor, "because his whole doctrine, as well as his whole life, breathes the fire of charity." It is a torch which burns and illuminates; it influences while instructing; whatever truths he expounds, he brings back all to God by love, and, to define him properly, he should be styled the Seraphic and Cherubic Doctor. Tis thus that Gerson, the Chancellor of the University of Paris, expresses himself.

"If I am asked," he continues, "who amongst the doctors seems to me the best calculated to instruct, I answer, without detracting from any other, it is Bonaventure, because he is sure, solid, exact, and devout, at one and the same time; and separating from his theology all questions foreign from the purpose, all superfluous dialectic, and that obscurity of terms with which so many others load their works, he turns into piety all the beautiful lights he gives to the mind. In a word, there is not a doctrine more mild, more salutary, more sublime, than his; and in devotion alone can neglect it. As to me," he adds, "having recommenced studying it since I am grown old, the more I advance the more I am confounded, and I say to myself:

> "What is the use of so much talking, and so much writing? Here is a doctrine which is quite sufficient of itself, and it is only necessary to transcribe and to spread it into facts.'"—Such is the opinion of the celebrated Gerson as to St. Bonaventure, before he was canonized, declared a Doctor of the Church, and honored by the title of Seraphic, which he shares with his blessed Father. The Abbot Trithemius, of the Order of St. Benedict, passes a similar eulogium on him, to which the Sovereign Pontiffs, Sixtus IV. and Sixtus V., have added the crowning

point in their bulls, the one for his canonization, the other for his doctorship.

The second particularity of his life, which had relation to St. Francis, is, that he gloriously verified his prediction as to the fruits of sanctity which he was to bring to the Order. Having been elected general when he was five and thirty years of age, in consequence of his great talents and eminent virtues, he governed his brethren for eighteen years with so much zeal, light, mildness, and wisdom, that he perfectly made amends for the evil which the relaxation of some and the perplexity of others had occasioned. He prepared such judicious regulations for the form of government, for the recital of the Divine Office, for the regularity of discipline, that they have served as a basis and foundation for all the statutes which have since been introduced into the Order.

He decided on the difficulties which occurred as to the observation of the rules, and this with so much precision, that, in order to follow them exactly and conscientiously, without scruple, it is only necessary to practise what he has clearly laid down. He composed spiritual treatises, so elevated, so instructive, and so affecting, that they are alone sufficient to guide the Friars Minors, or all other persons of piety, to the sublimest perfection. He answered, with so much strength and judgment, the philosophers of his day, who attacked the Mendicant Orders, despite of the Sovereign Pontiffs, by whom they were approved, that his works, with those of the Angelic Doctor, St. Thomas Aquinas, will ever cover with confusion whosoever may attempt to renew the former disputes on this head.

The exertions which St. Francis made, during a short interval from pain, for the salvation of souls, in an unfavorable season of the year, increased all his maladies. His legs became inflamed, and he was obliged to lie by in a small hamlet near Nocera. When this was known at Assisi, the fear they had lest he should die on the way, and lest his country should be deprived of his precious remains, induced the authorities to send means to bring him into town.

This deputation, returning with the patient, arrived at the dinner hour in the Village of Sarthiano, where they found nothing to be purchased for their meal, although they offered a double price for everything they wanted. Upon their complaining of this, Francis said: "You have not found anything, because you have had greater confidence in your flies than in your Lord" (he called their money flies); "but return to the houses where you have been, and ask them humbly for alms, offering to pray to God for them in payment. Don't think, under false impressions, that there is anything mean or shameful in this, for, since sin came into the world, all the good which God so liberally bestows on man, on the just, and on sinners, on the worthy and unworthy, is done by means of alms, and He is the chief almsgiver." These men overcame their bashfulness, and went cheerfully to beg for the love of God, and got whatever they wanted, although they had not been able to obtain it for money; God having so touched the hearts of the inhabitants, that, in giving what they had, they even offered spontaneously every service.

The Bishop of Assisi had the man of God brought to his palace, and kept him there till the spring of the year 1226, providing him with everything he required, with great affection. One day, when his stomach loathed everything, he expressed a wish for a particular sort of fish, which the severity of the winter made it difficult to procure, but, at the very moment, a messenger sent by Brother Gerald, the guardian of the convent of Rieti, brought three large fishes of this species, with certain sauces which were calculated to sharpen the appetite and strengthen the patient. Thus it is that it sometimes pleases the Lord to give sensible relief to His friends who have neglected their health and crucified their flesh for His sake.

The children of the holy patriarch, and particularly Elias, his vicar-general, who saw that there was no amelioration in the state of his health, but that, on the contrary, his disorders increased with the renewal of the year, entreated him to allow himself to be removed to Sienna, where the mild climate and the excellence of the physicians might afford him some relief, if there were no hopes of a cure. And they urged this so energetically, that, as he was mild and obliging, he consented to be taken thither at the beginning of April. But all his ills continued, and the disorder of his eyes was greatly increased. A red-hot iron was again applied to both sides of his head, from the ears to the eyebrows, but this had no good effect, though he suffered no pain from it, God having renewed the miracle He had before performed in his favor.

So the mild air of Sienna, and the kind care of the physicians, did not prevent the sufferings of Francis from continuing and increasing. During one night he vomited so much blood, and he was to such a degree weakened from it, that it was thought he was about to expire. His children, cast down and in tears, came to him, like the disciples of St. Martin, when he was on the point of death, and said to him, sobbing:—

> "Dear Father and Master, we are greatly distressed to see you suffer so intensely, but we are likewise afflicted for ourselves. After all your labors you are about to go to the enjoyment of eternal repose, but we shall remain without our Father and Pastor, you have begotten us in Jesus

Christ by the doctrine of the Gospel, and we are scarcely born before we lose you. Who will instruct us? Who will console us? You have been everything to us, your presence has been our happiness. To whom do you consign us, in the desolate state in which we are? Alas! we foresee that after your departure ravenous wolves will invade your flock. Leave us, at least, something of yours to remind us of your instructions, in order that we may follow them when you are no more; and give us your blessing, which may be our shield against our enemies."

The holy patriarch, casting his eyes affectionately on his children, called out to Brother Benedict of Piratro, who was his infirmarian, and who, during his illness, said Mass in his room: "Priest of God," said he, "commit to writing the blessing I give to all my brethren, as well to those who are now in the Order, as to those who shall embrace it to the end of the world. As my great sufferings and extreme weakness prevent me from speaking, here are in a few words my intentions and last wishes: 'May all the brethren love each other as I have loved them, and as I now love them. May they always cherish and adhere to poverty, which is my lady and my mistress; and never let them cease from being submissive and faithfully attached to the prelates and all the clergy. May the Father, Son, and Holy Ghost bless and protect them! Amen.'"

His sufferings being in some degree modified, and his weakness no longer so intense, his zeal induced him to think of instructing and exhorting the absent, for, by the example of the Son of God, he loved his own even to the last.

As soon as Brother Elias, the vicar-general, learnt the extreme danger in which the Father was, he came in great haste to Sienna, and proposed to him to be removed to the convent of Celles, near Cortona. Francis was very glad to see him, and was quite willing to be removed to Celles, where he was attended with great care by the relations and friends of Elias, who were of that country. But, as he became swollen, and the sufferings of his stomach and liver were greatly increased, he requested to be taken to Assisi; which the vicar-general had done with all the care and precaution possible. His return was a source of extraordinary gratification to the inhabitants, who had been fearful of being deprived of so great a treasure had he died elsewhere. They went in crowds to meet him, with great expressions of pleasure, and the bishop received him again into his palace.

Before we put on record the last acts and precious death of St. Francis, it will be proper to notice the state in which his Order was at that time. There were some of his brethren in all parts of the known world. In Europe, they filled all Italy. Greece furnished them a province. The esteem of the great, and the love of the people, procured for them, daily, new houses in Spain, Portugal, France, the Low Countries, and England. They had spread into Scotland, and began to be received in Ireland. Brother Albert, of Pisa, had sent missioners into Upper and Lower Germany, with great success. They had penetrated into Poland, and into the countries of the North. In Asia, those whom the holy Patriarch had left, with others who followed, multiplied the missions among the Saracens. In Africa they continued to preach Jesus Christ to the Mohammedans, and we see by letters dated from Rieti, the 7th October, 1225, which Pope Honorius addressed to the Friars Preachers and Minors, destined by the Apostolic See for the mission into the kingdom of the Miramolin, "that they renounced themselves, and desired to sacrifice their lives for Jesus Christ, in order to gain souls for Him."

> The Second Order instituted by Francis, and called that of the Poor Dames,
> spread itself also throughout Europe, and the Third Order of
> Penance made stupendous progress.

The children of this holy Patriarch, being thus spread in all parts, preached the Gospel to the infidels, repressed heresies, attacked vice, inspired virtue, and gave admirable examples of poverty, humility, penance, and all perfection.

Anthony, of Padua, preached in Italy and France with so much lustre, that he has ever been considered as one of the most marvellous preachers whom Italy ever saw. The strength and the unction of his discourses, the eminent sanctity of his life, the evidence of his miracles, changed the face of the towns in which he announced the word of God. His auditors, penetrated with conjunction, and bursting into tears, excited each other to works of penance; the revengeful, the lascivious, the avaricious, the usurers became converted, and resorted so to the tribunals of penance that the number of priests were insufficient to hear the confessions.

In the year 1225 he came to Toulouse, and visited other towns of France, where his principal object was to confront the heretics. Animated with the same spirit which inspired his Father, Francis, with so perfect an attachment to the Roman Church, and the Holy See, he was the declared enemy of all errors, and he labored with all his strength to root them out. By quotations from the Holy Scriptures, with which he was intimately conversant, and the sense of which he perfectly understood, and by the solidity of his reasoning, he confounded the sectarians, and created a great horror of the false doctrines they taught. With admirable tact he discovered their artifices and frauds, which he laid before the people, to preserve them from their seduction; and, in fine, he pursued them with so much vigor and perseverance, that the faithful gave him the name of the indefatigable mallet of the heretics; none of them ventured to enter the lists with him, not even to say a word in his presence.

God favored him by converting a very great number of their supporters, and, what is very singular, many of the heads of their party. At Bourges a man whose name was Guiald, and whom the historian calls an heresiarch, was so convinced by the power of his words, and by a marked miracle of the real presence of Jesus Christ in the Eucharist, that he persevered till death in the Catholic faith, and in submission to the Church. Another named Bonneville, or Banal, who is also stated to have been an heresiarch, who had been thirty years buried in the darkness of errors, was converted in a similar manner at Rimini by the sermons of St. Anthony, and had a like perseverance.

The state in which, as we have just shown, St. Francis left his Order when on the point of death, must be looked upon as one of the principal marvels of his life. God had predestined him for this great work; he labored at it for eighteen years without ceasing, with all possible assiduity, and, on the eve of quitting this world, he might say, in conforming himself to Jesus Christ, after having profited by His grace: "I have glorified Thee on earth; I have finished the work Thou gavest me to do, I now go to Thee." Happy the Christian whose conscience bears him thus out on the bed of death, who can say that he has endeavored to do what God required of him, and fulfilled the duties of his profession.

Chapter 5

FROM THE TIME OF HIS LAST ILLNESS TO THE HONORS PAID TO HIM AFTER HIS DEATH

The cruel and continued pain under which the holy Patriarch suffered, did not prevent his giving instruction to his children, his providing for their spiritual wants, and his answering, with admirable presence of mind, to various questions which were put to him relative to the observance of the Rule, and the government of the Order.

He spoke as freely, and with as much composure, as if he felt no inconvenience. As his body became weaker, his mind seemed to acquire fresh vigor.

One day, when his sufferings were greatly aggravated, he saw that the brothers took great pains in endeavoring to afford him relief, and fearing that fatigue would cause some of those who were about him to become impatient, or that they might complain that their attendance on him prevented them from observing their spiritual exercises, he addressed them affectionately, saying: "My dear children, do not tire of the trouble you take for me, for our Lord will reward you, both in this life and in the next, for all you do for His little servant; and if my illness takes up your time, be assured that you will gain more from it, than if you were to labor for yourselves, because the aid you give me is given to the entire Order and to the lives of the brethren. I also assure you that God will be your debtor for all that you will do for me."

It is very true that those who assisted the Saint in his illness labored for the entire Order, and for the spiritual life of his brethren, because they aided in the preservation of him who was so necessary to his Order; and they put it in his power to give further instructions to his brethren who were now in it, and to those who were to enter it in future.

On another occasion, when his sufferings were apparently bringing him to extremity, one of his infirmarians said to him: "Brother, pray that God may treat you with less severity, for it seems that His hand presses too severely upon you." At these words Francis exclaimed in a loud voice: "If," said he, "I was not aware of the simplicity and uprightness of your heart, I should not dare to remain in the same house with you from this instant. You have had the rashness to criticise the judgments of God in my regard;" and immediately, notwithstanding the weak state in which he was, he threw himself on the ground with such violence that his worn-out bones were all bruised; he kissed the ground and exclaimed: "My God, I return Thee thanks for the pains I endure, and I pray Thee to add to them an hundred-fold, if such should be Thy good pleasure. It will be pleasing to me to know that, in afflicting me, Thou dost not spare me, for the greatest consolation I can enjoy is, that Thy holy will shall be fulfilled." He had in his sufferings similar feelings to those of holy Job, and he expressed himself in a similar manner. Ought not all Christians to have such feelings in their illnesses and other afflictions? Are the saints not to be imitated in this? May we not, by the grace of God, which assuredly will not be wanting, practice those virtues by which they became saints?

Clare and her daughters, hearing that their father was so dangerously ill, sent to express to him the grief which it caused them, and they entreated him to mitigate their sorrow by sending them at least his blessing. The holy Patriarch, full of tenderness for these pious virgins, and sympathizing in their grief, and in that which they would feel on his death, sent them some verses he had composed in the praise of the Lord, and added to them a letter of exhortation, in which doubtless he gave them his blessing most amply; but this is not found in his works. We find only the following fragment, which may belong to the letter he had written to them at that time:—

> "I, Brother Francis, little man, I choose to follow the example of the life and poverty of Jesus Christ, our most high Lord, and that of His holy Mother, and to persevere in it to the end. I beg you also, all you whom I consider as my Ladies, and I recommend you to conform yourselves at all times to this life and to this poverty, the sanctity of which is so great. Be careful not to swerve from it in the least, nor to listen to any advice, nor to anything which may be said to contravene it."

The oldest historians of the Order say that, in the letter he sent them shortly before his death, he entreated them, that, as the Lord had brought them together from many places, in order that they might apply themselves to the practice of the sacred virtues of charity, humility, poverty, and obedience, they should use every effort to pass their lives accordingly, and to die in holy perserverance. He exhorts those of his sisters who were suffering from sickness, to have patience under their ills. And because he knew how austere they were, he recommended them to use with discretion, and with joy and thankfulness, the alms which Divine Providence sent them. He promised Clare that she should see him, and, in fact, after his death she and her daughters did see him, as shall hereafter be related.

The same writers add, that he had always entertained peculiar affection and regard for these holy religious females, thinking that the holiness of their life, which had been from the beginning one of great poverty and mortification, reflected glory on the religious state, and was a source of great edification to the whole Church. He wrote to them several other times, to encourage them in virtue, and particularly in the love of poverty, as we find in the will of St. Clare, but the letters are not extant.

Even to this day we are sensible of the truth of what he said; nothing is more glorious for the regular state, and nothing more edifying for the whole Church, than to see the nuns of St. Clare, who keep the rule of their Order without the slightest mitigation, who renounce the possession of any property whatsoever, whether private or in common, who live wholly on alms, and in such a state of rigorous austerity, that the stronger sex would find to be quite appalling.

As soon as it was known in Assisi that the holy man was at the point of death, the magistrates placed guards round the episcopal palace, with orders to keep strict watch, lest his body should be taken away the moment he should have expired, and thus the city would be deprived of so precious a treasure.

The physician, whose name was John Lebon, a native of Arezzo, communicated to him that death was approaching; his brethren told him the same thing. Full of joy, he began to praise God, and having caused some of the choir-singers to be called in, he sang with them in a loud voice the last verses which he had added to the Canticle of the Sun: "Be praised, O Lord! for death, our sister—which no man living on earth can escape."

Elias, whose thoughts were always governed by human prudence, was fearful lest his singing should be considered a weakness of mind arising from the fear of death, and entreated him to stop. "Brother," replied Francis, with extraordinary fervor, "permit me to rejoice in the Lord, and to thank Him for the great tranquillity of my conscience. I am, through His mercy and His grace, so united to my God, that I have just reason to manifest the joy that He gives me, who is the high and most liberal Giver of all good gifts; and do not imagine that I am so wanting in courage as to tremble at the approach of death."

>He had his children brought to him, and he blessed each one of them as the Patriarch Jacob had done, giving to each an appropriate blessing.
>Then, after the example of Moses, who blessed all the faithful Israelites, he gave a general and ample blessing to the whole Order.

As he had stretched his arms one over the other in the form of a cross, as Jacob had done in blessing the children of Joseph, his right hand came upon the head of Elias, who was kneeling on his left. He asked who it was, for his sight was quite gone, and being answered that it was Brother Elias, he said: "'Tis well, my right hand is properly placed on him. My son, I bless you in all and above all. Inasmuch as under your hand the Most High has increased the number of my brethren and children, thus I bless them all in you. May God, the Sovereign Lord of all things, bless you in Heaven and on earth! As for me, I bless you as far as is in my power, and even more than that—may God who can do all, do in you what I cannot! I pray that God may bear in mind your labors and your works, and that He may give you a share in the rewards of the just, that you may obtain the blessings you wish for; and may what you solicit worthily be fulfilled!"

The reader may perhaps be surprised that Francis, who knew Brother Elias, and who had learnt by revelation that he was to die out of the Order, should have given him a share in his blessing; but we must recollect that He who enlightens the saints, inspires them with views similar to His own. He loves and favors those who are in a state of grace, although He foresees the great sins they will commit hereafter. What affection had He not for David, and what favors did He not heap upon him before he became guilty of the adultery and homicide which rendered him so criminal! Thus, in a manner, the holy Patriarch, in blessing Elias, only had in consideration the good dispositions in which he believed him to be at that time, independent of the future, which God had revealed to him, and which was not to guide him in this instance. Moreover, Elias was his vicar-general, and was so by an order from on high; he had labored usefully in the works of the Lord; the talents he possessed put it in his power to do still more good service; we cannot deny that he was sincerely and tenderly attached to his Father, and that he had an ardent zeal:—all these circumstances united might have induced the Saint to give him an ample blessing, nor was it without good effect, since he died in sentiments of true repentance.

The man of God finding the day of his death, which Jesus Christ had revealed to him, draw near, said to his brethren in the words of the Prince of the Apostles: "The laying away of this my tabernacle is at hand;" and he begged them to have himself taken to the Convent of St. Mary of the Angels, wishing, as St. Bonaventure remarks, to render up the spirit which had given life to him, in the place where he had received the Spirit of grace. He was, therefore, removed, according to his desire; and when he had come to the place between the town and the convent, he asked if they had reached the hospital of the lepers, and, as those who were carrying him replied in the affirmative, he said: "Turn me now towards the town, and set me down on the ground." Then raising himself upon the litter, he prayed for Assisi, and for all its inhabitants. He likewise shed tears, in considering the ills which would come upon the city, during the wars which he foresaw, and he then gave it this blessing: "Be blest by the Lord, O city, faithful to God! because many souls will be saved in thee and by thee. A great number of the servants of the Most High will dwell within thy walls, and among the number of thy artisans not a few will be chosen for eternal life."

Sometime after his arrival at St. Mary of the Angels, he called for paper and ink, that he might acquaint Dame Jacqueline de Septisal of the proximity of his death: she was the illustrious Roman widow who was so much attached to him. "It is right," he said, "that, dying, I should give that consolation to a person who afforded me so many consolations during my life." This is what he dictated for her:

> "To the lady Jacqueline, the servant of the Most High, Brother Francis, the poor little servant of Jesus Christ, sends greetings, and communication with the Holy Ghost, in Jesus Christ."
>
> "Know, my very dear lady, that Jesus Christ, blessed for ever, has done me the favor to reveal to me the end of my life: it is very near. For which reason, if you wish to see me alive, set out as soon as you shall have received this letter, and hasten to St. Mary of the Angels, for, if you arrive later than Saturday, you will find me dead. Bring with you some stuff, or rather, a sackcloth, to cover my body, and some wax-lights for my funeral. Pray bring also some of those comfits which you gave me when I was sick at Rome."

At these words he stopped, having his eyes raised to Heaven. He said it was not necessary to go on with the letter, nor to send a messenger, because the lady had set out, and was bringing with her all that was required; and, in fact, she arrived shortly after with her two sons and a considerable suite, bringing with her the stuff, a quantity of wax-lights, and certain electuaries which were comforting for the stomach.

The religious asked her how she could have come so opportunely, without having had notice given her, and how she came to bring all that was requisite for the time. She told them that during the night she had received an order from Heaven, and that an angel had requested her not to leave out any of the things which had been desired.

On Friday, October the 4th, Francis again collected all his brethren together, blessed them a second time, and having blessed a loaf of bread with the sign of the cross, he gave to each a piece as a symbol of union and fraternal charity. They all partook of it with great devotion, representing to themselves, in this repast of love, the last supper which Jesus Christ ate with His disciples. Brother Elias, who wept bitterly, was the only one who did not eat his portion, which was perhaps a mournful foreboding of the division he was to introduce into the Order. In truth, he kept the piece he had received from their Father respectfully in his hand; but, as if he had cast aside the charity which was offered him, instead of, at least, keeping the morsel of bread, he gave it to Brother Leo, who asked him for it. Great care was taken for its preservation, and God permitted that it should be subsequently used for the cure of many maladies.

All the brothers had melted into tears, and the holy Patriarch inquired where Bernard, his eldest son, was. And Bernard having drawn near, he said: "Come, my son, that I may bless you before I die." Feeling that he was kneeling on his left, while Brother Giles was on his right, he put his hands again crosswise, so that his right hand came on the head of Bernard, to whom he gave this blessing:—

> "May the Father of our Lord Jesus Christ bless you with all the spiritual blessings which He has shed from on high on His Son. As you were chosen the first to give good example of the Evangelical law in this Order, and to imitate the poverty of Jesus Christ, to whom you generously offered your goods and your person in the odor of sweetness, so may you be blessed by our Lord Jesus Christ, and by His poor servant; and may you be so blessed in your going out and coming in, waking or sleeping, living and dying. May he who blesses you, be filled with

blessings; and may he who curses you, not remain unpunished. Be the lord of your brethren, and let them be all subject to you. Let all those whom you shall approve, be admitted into the Order, and all whom you shall reject, be rejected. Let no one have authority over you, so that you may be at liberty to go and dwell where you think proper."

Bernard having retired, with his eyes bathed in tears, Francis said to the others: "My intention is, and I direct that whoever may be appointed minister general, may so love and honor Brother Bernard as myself, and that all the provincial ministers, as well as all the brethren of this Order, may look upon him as they have done on me; in fact, I leave him to you as the half of my soul. There are few who are able to appreciate his virtue: it is so great, that Satan never ceases from tempting him, molesting him, and laying snares for him. But, by God's help, he will get the better of all, to the great profit of his soul, and he will find himself in an extraordinary manner in perfect tranquillity." Those who were present, and who afterwards lived with Bernard, witnessed the fulfilment of these predictions. His eminent sanctity, well known to Francis, and of which he foresaw the perseverance, was the reason why he ordered the others to respect him as their master, and why he rendered him independent, in order that he might have full leisure to give himself up to contemplation, which had such charms for him. For a similar reason, he gave him power to admit or reject novices, as his prudence should dictate: a privilege which was the more appropriate, as Bernard had been the first to enter into the Order.

St. Bonaventure is silent as to the manner and fervor with which the Servant of God received the last sacraments, following in that the method of many old authors who, in the lives of saints, only notice those things which are peculiar and marvellous, without speaking of the common and ordinary actions of all Christians. But we have only to bear in mind the great respect St. Francis had for all the practices of the Church; the spirit of penance by which he was animated; the vivid and tender affections of his heart towards the Passion of the Son of God, and the mystery of the Holy Eucharist; the ardor of his zeal to cause Jesus Christ to be adored in the august sacrament, and revered in all that related to it; his eagerness in recommending the frequent approach to the Holy Communion, and the constant recourse he himself had to this balm for the soul, so that for fear of being deprived of it, he chose to have Mass said in his own room during his illnesses:—all these recollections, being united, are demonstrations of what must have been the dispositions of the Saint when the last sacraments were administered to him.

He particularly desired all his brethren to have a peculiar veneration for the Church of St. Mary of the Angels, because it had been revealed that the Blessed Virgin had a singular affection for this church among all those which were dedicated to her name, and upon this subject he spoke as follows, with great animation:—

"It is my desire that this place shall be always under the direction of the person who shall be minister-general and servitor of the Order; and that the minister shall be careful to select for its service only good and holy brethren; and that the clerics who shall be appointed to it shall be taken from those of the Order who are the best and the holiest, and are the best instructed for the celebration of the Divine Offices, so that their brethren and the seculars may be edified in seeing and hearing them. Let them also be particular in choosing the lay brethren to be placed there; let them be discreet, mild, and humble men, whose lives are holy, who shall serve the others without entering into idle discourse, not talk of the news, or what is passing in the world, nor of anything which does not relate to the salvation of souls. It is also my desire that none of the brethren shall come here except the minister-general and his companions, and that no secular shall be admitted, in order that those belonging to the place may the better preserve themselves in purity and holiness, and that the place itself may remain pure and holy, being solely devoted to singing the praises of the Lord. When God shall be pleased to call any one of them to Himself, I desire that the minister-general may send another whose life shall be equally holy. My intention is, that, if the brethren shall swerve from the path of perfection, this place shall be ever blest, and shall remain as the example and model for the whole Order; as a beautiful torch before the throne of God, and before the altar of the Blessed Virgin, where lamps shall be ever burning, to obtain from the goodness of God that He may grant His pardon to the brethren for all their faults, and preserve and protect this Order which He has planted with His own hand."

"My children," he continued, "be careful never to abandon this spot, and if you are driven out on one side, return by the opposite one; for it is holy, it is the dwelling-place of Jesus Christ, and of the Blessed Virgin, His Mother. It is here that the Lord, the Most High, has multiplied our numbers, from being very few; here, by the light of His wisdom, He enlightened the minds of His poor ones; here, by the ardor of His love, he inflamed our hearts; here, whoever shall pray devoutly, will obtain whatever he may ask; and whoever shall sin here, will be punished with greater rigor. Wherefore, my children, have a great veneration for this place, which is truly the dwelling of the Almighty, peculiarly beloved by

Jesus Christ and His blessed Mother. Employ yourselves here joyfully, and with your whole hearts, in praising and blessing God and His Son, our Lord Jesus Christ, in unity with the Holy Ghost. Amen."

The day at length arrived which had been fixed by Divine Providence for terminating and rewarding the labors of this faithful Servant of God: it was a Saturday, the fourth of October. St. Bonaventure who considers him on his death-bed as a work well finished by the chisel of suffering, as a precious jewel cut and polished, to be placed in the sacred edifice of the celestial Jerusalem, remarks, that, finding himself near his end, and animating himself with fresh fervor, he stretched himself on the ground.

All the brethren were penetrated with grief and shed tears. One of them, whom the holy man called his guardian, knowing by inspiration what he wished for, went quickly to fetch a tunic, a cord, and the other parts of the dress of a Friar Minor, and brought them to him, saying: "Here is what we lend you, as to a poor man; take them out of obedience." He accepted this alms, and was rejoiced that he was faithful to the last to poverty, which he called his dame and his mistress; then raising his hands to heaven, he gave glory to our Lord Jesus Christ, that, being disengaged and free from everything, he was about to go to Him.

At the beginning of his conversion he stripped himself before the Bishop of Assisi, in imitation of the poor life of our Saviour; and to resemble Him more completely in His state of poverty, of nudity, and of suffering on the cross, he stripped himself before his brethren at his death, and chose to leave this world poor as he came into it, or, at least, only in a habit which he had received as an alms: such was his love of poverty.

"Oh!" exclaims St. Bonaventure, "with what truth may it be said that this was verily a Christian man, who has rendered himself perfectly conformable to Jesus Christ while living, or dying, or dead, and who has merited the honor of such a conformity, by the impression of the five wounds!"

What is further remarkable is, that they asked him where he desired to be buried, to which he answered: "In the vilest of places, on the Infernal Hill, on that side where criminals are executed."

This place was out of the Town of Assisi, near the walls, vulgarly called the Infernal Hill, perhaps on account of its being the place of execution. The Servant of God wished to be buried there, in order to be in strict conformity with his Divine Master, "who chose," says St. Jerome, "to be crucified in the usual place of execution, as a criminal among criminals, for the salvation of men, and to be placed in a tomb which was close by." His wish became a prophecy, for, two years after his death, as will be explained hereafter, a church was built in his honor on the Infernal Hill, when the name was changed into that of the Hill of Paradise, and the site of the church was so contrived that his body was placed precisely on the spot where the gallows had been formerly erected.

Seeing his last hour drawing nigh, he summoned all his brethren who were in the convent, and after having addressed some words of consolation to them, to mitigate the grief they felt for his death, he exhorted them to love God as a tender Father. Then he spoke to them for a long time on the care they should take to persevere in the faith of the Church of Rome, in poverty and in patience, under the tribulations which awaited them, as well as in successes of their holy undertaking. He made use of the most moving expressions in recommending to them to make progress towards eternal goods, to be armed with vigilance against the dangers of the world, and to walk exactly in the paths of Jesus Christ; remarking to them that the observance of His Gospel was the basis and essence of their Institution, and that all their practices had this in view.

After the holy man had made known his last wishes, he sent for Brother Leo, his confessor, and for Brother Angelo, whom he directed to sing in his presence the Canticle of the Sun, because death was very near: this is the canticle of which we have spoken, in which he gives glory to God for all His creatures, and also for death. As he was assured by revelation that death would remove him to eternal life, its proximity filled him with joy, which he evidenced by causing the praises of God to be sung.

When the canticle was finished, he placed his arms one over the other in the form of a cross,—a saving sign, to which he had been always devoted, as St. Bonaventure remarks—and stretching them over his brethren who stood around him, he gave his blessing for the last time, as well to those who were present, as to those who were absent, in the name and by virtue of Jesus crucified. He then pronounced the following words with great mildness and suavity: "Adieu, my children, I bid you all adieu; I leave you in the fear of the Lord, abide ever in that. The time of trial and tribulation approaches; happy those who persevere in the good they have begun. As to me, I go to God with great eagerness, and I recommend you all to His favor"

He then called for the book of the Gospels, and requested them to read to him the Gospel of St. John, at that part where the history of the Passion of our Blessed Saviour begins by these words: "Ante diem festum Pascha," before the Feast of the Passover. After this had been read, he began himself to recite, as well as he could, the hundred and forty-first psalm, "Voce mea ad Dominum clamavi:" "I have cried to Thee, O Lord, with my voice;" and he continued it to the last verse, "Me expectant justi, donec retribuas mihi:" "The just wait for me, until Thou reward me." In fine, all the mysteries of grace having been fulfilled in this man, so beloved by God, his very soul, absorbed in Divine love, was released from the shackles of his body, and went to repose in the Lord.

Such a death makes good what the Holy Fathers of the Church say, that the perfect Christian dies with joy, and with pleasure. There is no one who would not wish for such a death. The most worldly would desire with Balaam, that their life should end as that of the just; but the perfection of the just must be imitated to afford any hope of the end being similar: death is only mild and consoling in proportion to the fervor of a Christian life.

St. Bonaventure places on record many proofs which they had of the glory of St. Francis at the moment of his death. One of his disciples saw his blessed soul, under the figure of a brilliant star, rise upon a white cloud, above all the others, and go straight to heaven. This marked, says the holy doctor, the splendor of his sublime sanctity, with the plenitude of grace and wisdom, which had rendered him worthy of entering into the regions of light and peace, where, with Jesus Christ, he enjoys a repose which will be eternal.

Brother Austin, of Assisi, Provincial of the Terra di Lavoro, a just and saintly man, who was in the last stage of a severe illness, and had ceased to speak, suddenly exclaimed: "Wait for me, my Father, wait for me; I will go with you" The brethren, quite astonished, asked him who he was speaking to. "What," said he, "don't you see our Father, Francis, going up to Heaven?" At that very moment his soul separated itself from his body, and followed that of his Father. Thomas of Celano, and Bernard of Bessa, companions of St. Bonaventure, also mentioned that a holy man of their day had a revelation to the effect, that the souls of several Friars Minors were delivered from the sufferings of purgatory, and were joined with that of the holy Patriarch, to enter Heaven with him.

The Bishop of Assisi being then on a devotional tour to Mount Gargano, to visit the Church of the Archangel Michael, Francis appeared to him on the night of his death, and said: "I leave the world, and am going up to heaven." The prelate, in the morning, mentioned to those who accompanied him what he had seen; and on his return, having made exact inquiry, he found that the apparition had appeared to him at the very time of the Saint's death.

The body of St. Francis, after his death, was an object worthy of admiration, according to this description of it, given by St. Bonaventure on the testimony of those who had seen it, and reported verbally to him all the circumstances, conformably to what had been taken down in writing: On his hands and on his feet black nails were seen as of iron, wonderfully formed of his flesh by Divine power, and so attached to his flesh, that, when they were pressed on one side, they protruded farther on the other, as hard excrescences, and all of one piece. Nothing now prevented the wound on his side from being seen, which he hid with so much care during his lifetime,—this wound, which had not been made by the hand of man, and which resembled the opening in the side of our Blessed Saviour, from which the sacrament of our redemption issued, and that of our regeneration. Its color was red, and the edges, rounded off, gave it the appearance of a beautiful rose. The flesh of the Saint, which was naturally of a brownish color, and which his diseases had rendered tawny, became extraordinarily white. It called to mind the robes whitened in the blood of the Lamb, with which the saints are clothed. His limbs were flexible and pliable as those of an infant; evident signs of the innocence and candor of his soul. The whiteness of his skin contrasted with the black nails of his hands and feet, and with the wound in his side, which resembled a fresh-blossomed rose, exhibited a variety of tints which was beautiful and pleasing, and was the admiration of those who saw it. His body, in fine, was the representation of the Passion of Jesus Christ by the wounds imprinted on it, and of the glorious resurrection by the qualifications it had received after death.

This marvellous and novel sight mitigated the affliction of his children; it strengthened their faith, inflamed their love, and quite enraptured them; and, although the death of so amiable a father caused them to shed torrents of tears, they, nevertheless, had their hearts filled with joy when they kissed the impressions of the wounds of the great King imprinted on his flesh.

As soon as the news of his death was spread, and the circumstances of the stigmata came to be spoken of, the people came in crowds to see them: each person wished to see them with his own eyes, and assure himself of the truth of an event which was the cause of so much joy to the public. A great number of the citizens of Assisi were permitted to approach, to see and to kiss the sacred stigmata. One of them named Jerome, belonging to the army, a learned and prudent man, whose reputation was very extensive, finding it difficult to give credit to so wonderful a circumstance, examined the wounds more particularly and more minutely than the rest, in presence of the brethren, and of many persons of the town. He felt the feet, the hands, and the wound in the side of the Saint's body; he moved the nails, and convinced himself so perfectly of the truth of the fact, that he was afterwards a most zealous advocate and witness to it, and made oath to its truth on the holy Evangelists. "It was," St. Bonaventure remarks, "a case similar to that of the Apostle St.

Thomas, who, from being incredulous, became a faithful witness after having put his hands into the wounds of the Saviour, in order that his faith, preceded by incredulity, should strengthen our faith, and prevent us from becoming incredulous."

The brethren, who had been present at the death of the blessed Patriarch, passed the remainder of the night in singing the praises of God around the body, with a number of other persons, who had collected there for the purpose, insomuch that it more resembled a feast of celestial spirits than the funeral service of a mortal.

The next morning, which was Sunday, the holy corpse was carried to Assisi on the shoulders of the principal persons of that city, and those of the highest rank among the Friars Minors; hymns and canticles being sung the whole way, while the concourse followed, carrying in their hands lighted torches, or branches of laurel. The procession passed on to the Church of St. Damian, where Clare and her nuns awaited it, and where it halted for a short time, to afford them the consolation of seeing and kissing the stigmata. In admiring this extraordinary prodigy, and lamenting the death of such a father, they called to mind the promise he had made them during his last illness, that they should again see him before their death. Clare endeavored to draw the nail from one of his hands, which, as the head of it was raised above the palm of the hand, she thought she would be able to effect, but she found it impossible. She, therefore, only dipped a piece of linen in the blood which exuded; and she took the measure of the body, by which she had a niche made of similar size, on that side of the choir which the religious occupied, in which the image of the saint was afterwards placed. These pious virgins would have been glad to have detained the body longer, but it was necessary to resume the route to Assisi, where he was buried in the Church of St. George, with every possible veneration and respect. It was there he had received the first rudiments of education, it was there he had preached for the first time, and there was his first place of repose.

Brother Elias, in his quality of vicar-general, wrote a circular letter on his death, which he sent into all the provinces of the Order. The copy which the Provincial of France received, was thus directed: "To my well-beloved brother in Jesus Christ, Brother Gregory, minister of the brethren who are in France, and to all his brethren, and to ours, Brother Elias sends greeting."

He first expresses his grief in very affecting terms, and in alluding to the loss the Order had sustained, he passes a high eulogium on the sanctity of their common Father, with many citations from the Sacred Scriptures, very aptly applied. Then, he says, that what must console the children of the blessed patriarch is, that his death opened to him eternal life, and that previously he had pardoned all the offences which he might have sustained from any of them. This article only regarded Brother Elias and his adherents, for they were the only ones who had caused him any displeasure, and, according to all probability, Elias only adverted to it to soften the feelings of many who were irritated with him in consequence of his relaxation. After this preliminary he communicates to them a great cause for rejoicing in the miracle of the stigmata, which he treats as follows: "We had seen our Brother and our Father, Francis, sometime before his death as one crucified, having on his body five wounds similar to those of Jesus Christ, nails of the color of nails of iron, which perforated his hands and feet, his side being laid open as by the wound of a lance, from whence blood often percolated. Immediately after his death his face, which was not handsome during his life, became extraordinarily beautiful, white and brilliant, and pleasing to behold; his limbs, which the contraction of the muscles, caused by his great sufferings, had stiffened like to those of a corpse, became pliant and flexible as those of a child: they could be handled and placed in any position which might be wished."

He then exhorts them to give glory to God for so great a miracle, and adds: "He who used to console us in our afflictions is no more, he has been taken from us; we are now orphans, and have no longer a father. But, since it is written, that 'to the Lord is the poor man left: He will be a helper to the orphan, let us address our prayers to Him, my dear brethren, and let us entreat Him to give us another chief, who, as a true Machabee, shall guide us and lead us to battle." At the close of the letter he ordered prayers for the deceased, saying: "It is not useless to pray for the dead; pray for him, as he requested we should: but at the same time pray that we may obtain from God a participation in His grace. Amen." It was signed, "Brother Elias, a sinner."

Although Elias doubted not that the holy man was in glory, he, nevertheless, prescribed praying for him, not only to comply with the wish of the deceased, and not to forestall the decision of the Holy See, but, also, because he bore in mind what St. Augustine had said, that the sacrifices and prayers offered for the dead whose life has been irreproachable, are acts of thanksgiving.

Conclusion

We have yet to mention what the Holy See did to glorify St. Francis and to make his name memorable for all times. Pope Honorius III died on the 18th of March, 1227, to the great grief of the entire Church.

He dearly loved St. Francis and had approved the Rule of the Friars Minor. The morning after his death the cardinals assembled and elected Cardinal Ugolini as his successor, who took unto himself the name of Gregory IX. Cardinal Ugolini was the intimate friend of Francis, the Protector of his Order and the founder of several Franciscan Convents; as was recorded above, St. Francis predicted his Pontificate.

A riot at Rome shortly after caused the Holy Father to flee to Rieti, he then went to Spoleto, and from thence to Assisi. At Assisi he was greeted with the greatest enthusiasm by the people. His deep piety prompted him to visit the grave of our Saint, where he spent a long time in prayer. At the general chapter held at Rome, June 7, 1227, in which Brother Elias was re-elected, His Holiness was petitioned by all present to canonize Francis whom God already made illustrious by many miracles. Now a favorable opportunity presented itself to pay special heed to this petition. He caused a rigorous examination to be made of all the miracles attributed to the intercession of the Saint after his death. This was not a difficult matter for there were a great number of witnesses in the city and neighboring places. In the meanwhile the Holy Father went to Perugia to attend to some affairs of state. When the validity of the proofs regarding the miracles and virtues of St. Francis could in no way be questioned, Gregory returned to Assisi.

The canonization took place with the greatest solemnity on Sunday July 16th, in the Church of St. George, where the body of the Saint reposed. Amidst an immense assembly of cardinals, bishops, priests, clerics, members of the

Franciscan Orders, knights, lords, and dignitaries of the, provinces and a vast multitude of people the Sovereign Pontiff pronounced from his throne, the following solemn words:

> "To the glory of the Most High God, Father, Son, and Holy Ghost, the glorious Virgin Mary, the blessed Apostles Peter and Paul, and to the honor of the whole Roman Church, we have resolved, in concert with our brethren and other prelates, to inscribe in the catalogue of the saints, the blessed Father Francis, whom God has glorified in Heaven, and whom we venerate on earth. His feast shall be celebrated on the day of his death."

At once the cardinals intoned the Te Deum, the people responded by their cries and shouts of joy. Thereupon prayers of thanksgiving were recited and then the august Pontiff celebrated Holy Mass. It was a day of grace, of exultation and triumph for Assisi, for the Franciscan Family and for the whole Church. Thus was St. Francis canonized but a few years after his death.

The humble Saint had asked to be interred on the "Infernal Hill," the hill on which criminals were buried. Up to the present his desire could not be fulfilled. The City of Assisi waited to make that place of ignominy a worthy abode for the remains of its most saintly and illustrious citizen. A magnificent double-church was erected on the spot. The Sovereign Pontiff declared that henceforth the place shall be called "Hill of Paradise" and later on laid the corner-stone for the new edifice. The lower church was completed in 1230. The elaborate portal is a plan of Baccio Pontelli. The stained glass windows by Bonino, a native of Assisi, render a soft and mellow harmony of light no less charming than that of the mosaic interior of San Marco, Venice. Famous frescoes which influenced all the great movements of art that followed, cover the walls of the church. Those in the sanctuary by Giotto are particularly fine. They represent St. Francis espousing Humility, Charity, and Poverty. The gold and blue of the backgrounds upon which the numerous scenes are painted, harmonize beautifully in the general color scheme of the sacred edifice. In the fourteenth century nine chapels were added along the walls of the lower church, mostly memorial chapels of cardinals and bishops.

Two years after the construction of the lower church with its vaulted top, the building of the upper church began. The Gothic form of architecture was chosen for the building, so that the high and pointed arches be emblematic of the lofty spirit of St. Francis, and of the towering strength of his followers, whose object it is to raise the spirit of men to a higher standard of religion and devotion. After its completion in the year 1253 Pope Innocent IV came in person to Assisi and consecrated the upper and lower church. At the same time the Holy Father, who resided in the monastery at Assisi with the Franciscan Fathers for five months, solemnly canonized the Bishop and Martyr Stanislaus of Cracow. The upper church again afforded the genius of artists ample opportunity to blossom forth. Zimabue enriched the sanctuary with brilliant frescoes from the life of the Blessed Virgin Mary whom St. Francis had chosen to be the Patroness and Protectress of his three orders for all future times. The choir-picture, the Assumption of the Virgin, is the finest of the series. In the apse are frescoes of St. Peter and St. Paul to whose tomb (at Rome) St. Francis made a pilgrimage to ask for grace and light at the beginning of his conversion. Other frescoes of Zimabue, also in the apse of the church, represent various passages of the Apocalypse, relative to the rejuvenation of the Church; St. Francis was called and appointed by God to restore the church which was falling into ruins. Along the lower wall-spaces of the nave are twenty-eight large frescoes from the life of St. Francis by Giotto, Taddio, Gaddi and Giunto Pisano; the upper spaces have representations of the Old and New Testament by Pietro Cavallini and his school. These upper paintings are now in ruins, but even in their ruins they are precious pearls of mediaeval art. The stained glass windows are of such exceptional beauty and artistic correctness that their equal cannot be found in all Italy. Speaking of the Church of St. Francis at Assisi, a traveller says in substance as follows: In its tremendous proportions the gigantic Church of St. Francis can only be compared to the pyramids of Egypt; and both are symbolic of their times. The pyramids were erected by the iron will and the cruel might of the Pharaohs, the blood of nations stain every stone and they are bedewed with many tears. The Church of St. Francis was built by the self-sacrificing love and heartfelt gratitude of nations. Its stones are worn by the footsteps and the tears of millions and millions of people, who came there, perhaps sad and weary, but returned with the love and the peace of the Saint in their heart.

When the lower church was completed (1230), the venerable remains of St. Francis were translated to their new resting-place. Such numbers were present at this translation, that many had to sleep out under tents during the night, the walls of Assisi not being able to contain so vast a multitude. The people of Assisi, having observed a commotion in the crowd, began to fear that an attempt was being made to deprive them of their sacred treasure: accordingly they rushed to the bier, took possession of the Saint's body, entered the church, locked the doors, and interred the body, without allowing any of the clergy, religious, or people to enter. In consequence of this event, an impenetrable veil of secrecy long hung over the place where the body had been laid. In 1818, Pope Pius VII gave permission to the General of the Conventual Minors to make researches under the high altar. Many previous researches had been made; they grew to such gigantic proportions that the foundations of the massive structure were partly undermined. To prevent the ruin of the basilica at Assisi, the Holy See finally forbade all further researches without the special consent of the Sovereign Pontiff. When Pope Pius VII gave the necessary permission, the researches were again taken up, but very carefully and in great secrecy. The workmen were employed for fifty-two nights in hard labor. At length, after having broken through rocks and massive walls, an iron grating was discovered, beneath which was a skeleton in a stone coffin, which when opened, exhaled the most fragrant odor. The Holy Father deputed the Bishops of Assisi, Nocera, Spoleto, Perugia, and Foligno, to make a juridical examination, to certify the authenticity of the body. Then, in accordance with a decree of the Council of Trent, he named a commission of cardinals and theologians, and, all being settled, on the 5th of December, 1820, he declared in a Brief that "this body is verily the body of Saint Francis of Assisi, Founder of the Order of Friars Minor." The sacred body of St. Francis now lies beneath the main altar of the lower church, mentioned before, in an exquisitely beautiful little chapel hewn out of the solid rock. The remains repose in their original sarcophagus, which is bound by broad girders of steel.

Seven hundred years have elapsed since the death of this humble servant of God. His memory has outlived all the storms that have agitated the world. The good seed that he sowed is still bringing forth fruit a hundredfold. Like the Apostles of old, he labored in the vineyard of the Lord, and opened up to others, Heavenly treasures of untold value. Yet more, in the person of St. Francis, Jesus of Nazareth lived again for the instruction and edification of the whole world, as He had never done in any individual, since the great Apostle of the Gentiles. At he word of St. Francis a revival of primitive Christianity sprang into existence at a time when all civilization seemed unhinged on account of the almost universal decay in morals. He taught men afresh that the commands of Jesus Christ could be literally obeyed and that the Sermon on the Mount was as applicable to the men of the middle and all succeeding ages as to the first age of Christian history. This New Abraham begot through the Gospel the largest family of Christ's followers and of missionaries the Catholic Church has ever produced. It is well known that the history of the Church from the thirteenth to the sixteenth century was largely the history of the rise and growth of Franciscanism in every part of Europe. To-day, after seven centuries have elapsed, we find no symptoms of decay in the great Franciscan Family. The priests and laybrothers of the First Order are to be found laboring assiduously in every country. In efficiency and number their active missionaries are second to none. They are storming the strongholds of Satan from one end of the world to the other. The Second Order stands before us as of old, a beautiful lily in the Sanctuary of God. The Holy Virgins, of the Second Order, called "Poor Clares," seek voluntary oblivion and by their pure and pious life of the greatest austerity, of seclusion, silence, penance and prayer, daily open the floodgates of God's graces to mankind. The wonderful and healthy growth of the Third Order, especially since the great Encyclical on St. Francis and on the Third Order by Pope Leo XIII (1882), need not be mentioned; it is a fact known to all. Since the work of the Seraphic Saint is so prosperous at present, we need not doubt about the future. As we have previously seen God Himself revealed to St. Francis that his institution shall remain till the end of times. Thus the Most High glorified and rewarded the poor, humble man of Assisi, "the greatest of sinners," as he loved to call himself. St. Francis now reigns in Heaven, brilliant as the Morning Star, and showers his blessings upon his many children. Let us praise God for the grace and glory He gave his humble Servant and let us deeply impress upon our mind the words of the Holy Ghost: "God resists the proud, but gives his graces to the humble." "He that humbleth himself shall be exalted."

"St. Francis Sealed with the Character of Jesus"

The eminent perfection of St. Francis was grounded on a tender and fervent devotion to Jesus Christ crucified. This adorable object had a powerful attraction for his heart, was the source of all the graces he received, and the model of all the virtues he practised. From the sufferings of our Saviour he made for himself, as St. Bernard had done, a nosegay of myrrh, which he always carried in his bosom; he considered attentively the sufferings of his Beloved, he suffered them himself, and they called forth his sighs and his tears; it was his wish that the fire of this love might transform him entirely into Him who had borne them.

The poverty of the Son of God, in His birth, during His life, and at His death, made such impression on the heart of Francis, that he embraced this virtue with inexpressible ardor.

Seeing that it was rejected by the world, and looking upon it as the pearl of the Gospel, to acquire it, he abandoned father, mother, and all that he had. No person ever sought after riches with so much avidity, and no one ever guarded his treasure with so much care. He never wore, until his death, anything but a worthless tunic, and he refused himself everything but what was absolutely necessary. He would yield to no one in poverty, although he considered himself the most abject of all. If he saw any one worse dressed than he was, he considered it as a reproach to himself. One day, meeting a poor man who was almost naked, he said to his companion with a sigh: "There is a poor man who shames us. We have chosen poverty for our greatest riches, and in him you see it shine far more than in us."

For his nourishment, he greatly preferred what he solicited for the love of God from door to door, to what was offered to him. He frequently considered within himself, and it brought tears into his eyes, how poor our Saviour and His Blessed Mother had been in this world, and the reflection induced him to live in greater poverty.

As to the cells, he always chose the smallest. One of his secular friends having had one built, which was only made of wood, though pretty neat, in the hermitage of Sarthiano, he found it too fine, and said he would not enter it a second time unless it was put into a state of poverty; so that, in order to induce him to return, it was necessary to cover it roughly with branches of trees, both without and within. He left it afterwards because one of his companions had said to him, "Father, I am come to look for you in your cell." "I will not occupy it any longer," he replied, "because you consider it mine in calling it my cell: another may live in it, to whom it will not be appropriated."

This is what his companions tell us on the subject:—"We have often heard him say, we, who have lived with him: 'I will not have as mine either dwelling-place, or any other thing, for our Master has said: "The foxes have lairs, and the birds of the air, nests; but the Son of Man hath not where to lay His head."'"

He was also accustomed to say: "When our Lord went to fast in the desert, where He remained forty days and forty nights, He had no cell prepared for Him, nor any other covering; it was only in some crevice of the mountain that He took repose." The same authors add, that, in order to imitate Jesus Christ perfectly, Francis desired to have neither convent nor cell which could be called his. And, moreover, if sometimes, on arriving, he pointed out to his brethren the cell which he proposed to occupy, he checked himself immediately, as having shown too much solicitude, and went into another, which had not been prepared for him. Shall, then, the children of the Patriarch of the poor be censured when they imitate this tenderness of conscience; and when, to show their aversion to the possession of property, they call even the things which are most essential for them to have the use of, by terms which show that they do not even hold them in common, and that they have nothing which is their own?

Although the servant of God possessed every virtue in a very high degree, yet it was remarked that the virtue of poverty was the one which was above all the others; and this it pleased the Almighty to make known by an admirable vision. When the saint was going to Sienna, three very poor women, who resembled each other both in size and countenance, and appeared to be of the same age, presented themselves before him, and greeted him in these words: "May the Lady Poverty be welcome!" This salutation filled him with joy, because nothing was more grateful to him in greeting him than to speak of poverty, which was so dear to him. The vision immediately vanished, and his companions, who had seen it, had no doubt that there was something mysterious in it; that God meant thereby to discover to them something which related to their father.—"In fact," says St. Bonaventure, "these three women, who were so like to each other, were not bad representations of chastity, obedience, and poverty, which constitute the beauty of Evangelical perfection, and were the very eminent characteristics of the saintly man; yet the expressions which these women made use of in greeting him, showed that he had chosen poverty as his special prerogative, and the principal object of his glory; and, indeed, he was in the habit of calling it sometimes his lady, sometimes his mother, and sometimes his spouse or his queen."

It is not possible to record in this place all the praise which the holy Founder gave to this Evangelical virtue. He called it the Queen, not only because it shone with splendor in JESUS CHRIST, the King of kings, and in His Blessed Mother, but because it is elevated above all earthly things, which it tramples under foot. "Know," he used to say to his brethren, "that poverty is the hidden treasure of the Gospel, the basis on which an order rests the special path to salvation, the support of humility, the mother of self-renunciation, the principle of obedience, the death of self-love, the destruction of vanity and cupidity, the rod of perfection, the fruits of which are abundant, though hidden. It is a virtue descended from Heaven which acts within us, and enables us to despise everything which is despicable; it subverts all the obstacles which prevent the soul from perfectly uniting itself to God by humility and charity; it causes those by whom it is beloved to become active as pure spirits, and enables them to take their flight towards Heaven, to converse with angels, though still living on earth. It is so excellent and so divine a virtue, that vile and abject vases such as we are, are not worthy of containing it."

In order to obtain the grace of poverty, he often recited the following prayer to Jesus Christ: "O Lord Jesus! point out to me the ways of poverty, which are so dear to Thee. Have pity on me, for I love it with such intensity that I can find no repose without it, and Thou knowest that it is Thou who gavest me this ardent love. It is rejected, despised, and hated by the world, although it is a dame and a queen, and Thou hast had the goodness to come down from Heaven to make poverty Thy spouse, and to have from her, by her, and in her, perfect children. My Jesus, who chosest to be extremely poor! the favor which I ask of Thee is, to give me the privilege of poverty; I ardently desire to be enriched by this treasure; I entreat of Thee that it may be mine, and of those who belong to me, and that we may never possess anything of our own under heaven for the glory of Thy name, and that we may exist, during this miserable life, on those things only which are given to us, and that we be very sparing in the use we shall make even of these. Amen."

This friend of poverty did not confine it to the repudiation of all external things: he carried its perfection to the most elevated spiritual point. "He who aspires to its attainment," he said, "must renounce not only all worldly prudence, but in some degree all learning and science, so that, being stripped of all sorts of goods, he may place himself under cover of the protection of the Most High, think only of His justice, and cast himself into the arms of the Crucified. For it is not to renounce the world entirely, if any attachment to its lights, and to one's own feelings, remains in the secret recesses of the heart." He did not assert that, in order to arrive at the perfection of poverty, it was necessary to be without learning, but he required that learning should not be considered by the possessor as an interior property, from which self-love should be fed; that there should not be that secret attachment to mental illumination, which is the primary source of error, and the basis of the obstinacy of heretics; that all of knowledge should "be referred to God, and that we should in some sense strip ourselves of it to acquire the perception of God alone, and of His holy law. St. Hilary said, speaking in the same sense, that we must always bear in mind that we are men, that we have nothing of our own, not even the use of our senses and faculties; that these come from God, and that we must only use them as things which are in a continual dependence on His will. This is an important instruction for the consideration of the learned."

The lively affection which St. Francis bore for the crucified Jesus, from the moment of his conversion, rendered him very austere towards himself. Not only could he not suffer that the tunic which he wore should have anything soft in it, but he chose that it should be rough and harsh; when he found that it had become too soft, he put knotted cords on the inside to counteract the softness.

It was usually on the bare ground that he laid his body down,—that body which was worn out by fatigue; sometimes he slept, sitting with his head resting on a stone or piece of wood. As to food, he scarcely took what was absolutely necessary for his nourishment. When in health, he seldom permitted anything to be put before him which was cooked, and then he either strewed ashes upon it, or added water to it, to take away the taste. Pure water was his only beverage, and then he drank so little that it was insufficient for quenching his thirst. Besides the Lent kept by all Christians, he kept eight others in the course of the year. The first, of forty days, from the day after the Epiphany, in memory of our Lord's fast in the desert, after He had been baptized by John, which took place on the sixth day of January, according to the old tradition of the Church. The second was from the Wednesday in Easter week, to Whit-Sunday, to prepare himself for receiving the Holy Ghost. The third, from the day after the Festival of Pentecost to the Feast of SS. Peter and Paul, in honor of these blessed Apostles. The fourth, from the day after their festival to the Assumption, in honor of the Blessed Virgin. The fifth in honor of St. Michael, from the Assumption to the feast of that angel. The sixth, from that feast is the first of November, in honor of all the saints. The seventh, from All-Souls to Christmas, to prepare himself to celebrate the birth of Christ. The eighth, from the Feast of St. Stephen to the Epiphany, in honor of the three kings. Thus was his life a perpetual fast.

When he went abroad he ate whatsoever was put before him, not only to observe the direction of the Gospel, but in order to gain worldlings to Jesus Christ, by conforming to their ways; but when in the convent, he resumed his habits of abstinence, and this mode of life was very edifying to laymen. The more he advanced towards perfection, the more he mortified himself. We cannot form a more correct opinion of the Evangelical hatred he bore his body, than by noticing the terms he made use of to express it. After having finished Complin, and spent a considerable time in prayer, in a deserted church, in which he passed the night, he wished to take some rest. As the evil spirits prevented him from so doing, by suggestions which frightened him, and made him tremble, he mustered courage, rose, made the sign of the cross, and said in a loud voice: "Devils, I declare to you from Almighty God, that you may use against me all the power given to you by my Lord Jesus Christ, and do all the harm you can to my body. I am ready to suffer everything, and assuredly you will oblige me greatly, for this body is a great burden to me; it is the greatest enemy I have, the most wicked, and the most crafty; and you will revenge me by so doing."

He exhorted his religious to austerity in their food, in their clothing, and in everything else. For he was convinced, as was St. Augustine, that it is difficult to satisfy the demands of the body, without in some degree sacrificing to sensuality; and he used to say, "Our Saviour praised St. John the Baptist for his having clothed himself coarsely. According to the words 'Behold they that are clothed in soft garments, are in the houses of kings,' soft garments must not be found in the huts of the poor. I know by experience that the devils fly from those who lead an austere life; and St. Paul teaches us, that they who are Christ's have crucified their flesh with its vices and concupiscences." We remember that he knew how to temper what seemed to be excessive in the mortifications of his brethren.

Francis taught persons to flee from idleness. "I desire," he said, "that my brethren may work and be occupied. He who desires to live by the labor of others, without doing anything, deserves to be nicknamed Brother Fly; because, doing nothing that is worth anything, and spoiling what is good, he becomes odious and despicable to all the world." If he came upon any one wandering about, and without occupation, he applied to him these words of the Apocalypse: "Because thou art lukewarm, I will begin to vomit thee out of my mouth." His example was an excellent lesson for not losing time, and fostering the idleness of the flesh; he employed himself always holily, and he called his body brother ass, which required to be well worked, to be severely beaten, and to be badly fed.

Silence was not considered by him to be a small virtue; he considered it as a guard to the purity of the heart, according to the maxim of wisdom: "Life and death are in the power of the tongue;" by which he understood the intemperance of speech, as well as that of taste. But he principally wished his brethren to become exact in keeping Evangelical silence, which consists in abstaining from all idle conversation, of which an account must be rendered at the day of judgment, and he severely reprimanded those who were in the habit of saying useless things. In fine, his instruction was, that they should endeavor to destroy all vice, and to mortify the passions; and that, in order to succeed in this endeavor, everything should be cut off which could serve as an attraction, and, therefore, that the exterior senses by which death enters into the soul, should be continually mortified.

As soon as he felt the smallest temptation, or if he only foresaw it, he took every precaution for resisting it. At the beginning of his conversion he frequently threw himself in the depth of winter, into freezing water, in order to subdue his domestic enemy, and to preserve his robe of innocence without stain, asserting that it is far less painful to a spiritual man to suffer the rigor of the severest cold, than to feel interiorly the slightest attack upon his purity.

We have seen, in his life, that he threw himself into the midst of thorns, to drive away the tempter who wanted to induce him to moderate his watchings and his prayers. One of his actions, the circumstances of which are thus related by St. Bonaventure, shows how great the purity of his heart was, and with what force he resisted the impure spirit.

One night, while he was at prayer in his cell, at the hermitage of Sarthiano, he heard himself called three times by his name. After he had answered, a voice said to him: "There is no sinner in the world whom God does not pardon if he be converted; but whoever kills himself by too rigorous a penance, will never find mercy." Francis was made aware by a revelation that these deceitful words emanated from the old enemy, who wished to induce him to relax in his austerities, and he soon had sensible proof of it, for, "he who by his breath sets fire to coals," as holy Job says, "tempted him strongly to sin against purity." As soon as he became aware of it, he inflicted a severe discipline on himself, saying to his body: "O brother ass! this is what suits you, this is the way in which you should be chastised. The tunic you wear is that of religion, and is a mark of its holiness. It is not permitted to one who is impure to wear it: that would be a theft." As the devil represented to him probably that he might marry and have children, and have servants to wait upon him, he responded to that by turning his own body into derision, and treating it cruelly. With admirable fervor he burst from his cell, and threw himself upon a large mound of snow; he made seven balls of it with his hands, and then said to himself: "The largest of these snowballs is thy wife, four others are thy two sons and two daughters, and the two last are thy man and thy maid-servants. I must think of clothing them, for they are perishing with cold." Then he added: "If this solicitude is overpowering, think hereafter of nothing else than of serving God fervently." At this the tempter fled, and the Saint returned victoriously to his cell. He never after had a similar temptation. One of his brethren, who was at prayer in the garden, saw by the light of the moon what was going on, and Francis, being aware of it, could not avoid explaining to him the whole temptation: "But," said he, "I forbid you strictly from saying a word on the subject during my lifetime." It was only known after his death.

Those who know how far the scrupulousness of chaste souls will carry them, will not feel surprised that, after the example of many other saints, he had put in practice such severe mortification, to shield himself from the slightest taint on his purity. His lively and agreeable turn of mind are apparent in the way in which he taunted his body when suffering from extreme cold; this also shows how much self-possession he had under the severest trials, and by what sentiment he was actuated in his penances.

St. Bonaventure says that, as a skilful architect, he laid down humility for the foundation-stone of his spiritual edifice, and that it was from Jesus Christ that he had acquired this wisdom. The foundation was so solid that humility became natural to him, as well as poverty, and thus it is justly that he is called the humble St. Francis. He was in the eyes of all a mirror of holiness, but in his own eyes he was but a sinner; on all occasions he sought to vilify himself, not only in his own mind, but in that of others.

Upon one occasion Brother Pacificus, while praying with him in a church, was raised in an ecstasy, and saw several thrones in the heavens, among which there was one more splendid than the rest, ornamented with precious stones. As he was pondering for whom this magnificent seat could be destined, a voice said to him: "This was the seat of an angel, and now it is reserved for the humble Francis." Some short time after, when conversing with the Saint, he led to the topic of the knowledge of one's self, and he asked him what idea he had of himself, upon which St. Francis answered quickly: "I consider myself the greatest of sinners." Pacificus maintained that he could not conscientiously either say so or think so. "I am convinced," replied Francis, "that, if the most criminal of men had experienced the great mercies I have received from Jesus Christ, he would be much more grateful for them than I am." This beautiful effusion confirmed Pacificus in the opinion he had entertained, that the vision he had seen was a true vision; and it is quite in accordance with the maxim of the Gospel that, "whosoever shall exalt himself, shall be humbled; and that he that shall humble himself, shall be exalted." It is humility that raises men to those places from whence pride cast down the fallen angels.

We have seen the extraordinary things which Francis did in order to humble himself; from the same motive he felt no difficulty in making public the defects he thought he discovered in himself. If he found himself attacked by any temptation to pride, vain-glory, or any other sin, he never failed communicating it to those who were present, whether they were religious or seculars. One day when he was followed by a great concourse of people, he gave his cloak to a poor woman who had asked him for an alms, and some minutes after he turned round to the crowd and told them in a loud voice that he had sinned from vainglory in so doing. We may imagine that his humility was at that moment very great, which prevented him from distinguishing between voluntary consent and the feeling over which we have no control.

He took great care not to do anything in private which he should have had any hesitation in doing in public, and which was not in conformity with the opinion people had of his sanctity. His illness rendered it necessary that he should eat meat in the Lent he kept before Christmas, but this relaxation consisted only in the use of lard; yet he, nevertheless, accused himself of it in public, as an act of gluttony. His companions have recorded what he said: "I wish to live in hermitages and in other solitary places, as if I was seen by all the world; for, if people have a great opinion of me, and I were not to live as they think I do, I should be guilty of scandalous hypocrisy." The vicar of his convent suggested that he should permit his tunic to be lined with fox-skins, to keep his chest warm, which his disorder had greatly weakened. "I consent to this," he replied, "provided you put a similar set of skins outside, that the world may know the relief which is inside also." This condition put a stop to the proposition.

Praise mortified him, and he liked that people should blame him, and he rejoiced in being despised. When he heard people express by acclamation the merits of his sanctity, he made some of the brethren say to him, "You are a vulgar man, ignorant and useless in the world, a nobody;" and when he answered, with pleasure depicted on his countenance, "May the Lord bless you, my dear child, what you say is quite true, and is exactly what the son of Peter Bernardo deserves to hear." To those who called him a saint he used to say: "Do not praise me; I have no assurance that I shall not sin; a person must never be praised whose end cannot be known." And he addressed the following words to himself: "Francis, if the Most High had bestowed so many favors on a thief as He has on you, he would be much more grateful than you are."

One day when great honors were paid him, his companion remarking that he received them without showing any reluctance, said: "Father, do you not see what they are doing in your honor? and far from refusing to receive the applause manifested in your regard, as Christian humility requires, you seem to receive them with complacency. Is there anything which a servant of the Lord should more sedulously avoid?" This is the reply which the holy man made him: "Brother, although it may appear to you that they are paying me great honors, nevertheless, know that I consider them as little or nothing in comparison to those which ought to be paid me." His companion was not only surprised, but almost scandalized, on hearing him utter such sentiments; but, not to expose his follower, Francis added: "Now be attentive to this, and understand it properly. I refer to God all the honor which is paid me, I attribute nothing to myself; on the contrary, I look upon myself as dirt by my baseness.

I am as those figures of wood or stone for which respect is had. All goes back to what they represent. Now, when men know and honor God in His creatures, as they do in me, who am the vilest of all, it is no small profit to their souls."

This is the magnanimous humility of which St. Thomas speaks, by which a man honors in himself the great gifts of God, permits them to be there honored, and practises great virtues to render himself more worthy to receive new ones, while he shrinks from the contemplation of his own merits. Such was the humble Francis, in permitting, for the glory of God, and the salvation of his neighbor, that the supernatural gifts which had been imparted to him, should be honored in his person, while he himself only considered his own nothingness; and afterwards he retired into solitary places, where he passed whole nights in meditating upon this nothingness, and on the infinite mercy of God, which had loaded him with graces.

Being one day with Brother Leo in one of these solitudes, and being without the books necessary for saying the Divine Office, he invented a sort of humiliating psalmody for glorifying God during the night. "My dear brother," he said to Leo, "we must not let this time, which is consecrated to God, pass without praising His holy name, and confessing our own misery. This is the verse which I will say: 'O Brother Francis! you have committed so many sins in this world, that you have deserved to be plunged into hell.' And you, Brother Leo, your response will be, 'It is true; you deserve to be in the bottom of hell.'" Leo promised, however repugnant he felt, to answer as his father desired; but, instead of that, he said: "Brother Francis, God will do so much good through your means, that you will be called into Paradise." The Father said to him, with warmth: "You don't answer as you ought. Here is another verse: 'Brother Francis, you have offended God by so many bad deeds, that you deserve all his maledictions.' Answer to that: 'You deserve to be among the number of the cursed.'" Leo promised again; but when the Saint had said his verse, striking his breast, and shedding abundance of tears, Leo pronounced these words: "Brother Francis, God will render you such, that, among those who are blessed, you will receive a peculiar blessing." "Why don't you answer as I desire you?" said Francis, surprised. "I command you, under obedience, to repeat the words which I am going to give you. I shall say: 'O Brother Francis, miserable man, after so many crimes committed against the Father of mercies, and the God of all consolation, do you think he will have any pity on me? In truth you are undeserving of pardon.' Brother Leo, answer immediately: 'You deserve no mercy.'" Leo, however, said: "God, our Father, whose mercy infinitely surpasses our sins, will pardon you all your sins, and will load you with His favors."

Then Francis said somewhat angrily: "Why have you dared to transgress the rule of obedience, and to answer so often differently to what I desired?" Leo excused himself most respectfully, saying: "My very dear Father, God is my witness that I had each time intended to repeat the words which you had directed me, but He put into my mouth the words I uttered, and caused me to speak, notwithstanding my resolution, according to His good pleasure." The humble Servant of Jesus Christ admired this disposition of the Lord; but persisting, nevertheless, in his intention of humbling himself, he entreated Brother Leo to repeat, at least once, the following words, which he pronounced with many sighs: "Oh Brother Francis, miserable little man! do you think that God will have mercy on you, after so many crimes which you have committed?" "Yes, my Father," replied Leo, "God, your Saviour, will have mercy on you, and will grant you great favors. He will exalt you, and glorify you eternally, because he who shall humble himself shall be exalted. Nevertheless, pardon me for not having said what you desired. It is not I who speak, it is God who speaks in me." Finally Francis bowed to what Leo communicated to him, who only disobeyed him by an impulse of the Holy Ghost; and they conversed during the remainder of the night on the great mercy of God to sinners.

It has been already remarked, with St. Bonaventure, that St. Francis had given to his brethren the name of Minors, and to their superiors that of Ministers, in order that their very name should cause them to be humble. These are the maxims by which he used to impress this upon them:—"The Son of God debased Himself in coming from the bosom of His Father to us, to teach us humility by His example and by His word, as our Lord and Master." "What is exalted in the eyes of man is an abomination before God." "Man is nothing but what he is before God, and is nothing more. It is folly to feel glorified by the applause of man; it is better to be blamed than praised, for blame induces the person to correct himself, while praise leads to his fall. No man should pride himself for doing those things which a sinner may do as well as he. A sinner may fast, pray, weep, macerate his body, but what he cannot do, as long as he is a sinner, is to be faithful to his God. Now, this is what we may glory in, to render to God the glory which is due to Him, to serve Him faithfully, and to return with like fidelity all that He has given. Happy the servant who finds himself as humble amidst his brethren, inferiors like himself, as in presence of his superiors! Happy the servant who does not believe himself better when men load him with praises, than when he appears in their eyes simple, vile, abject and despicable! Happy the servant who bears reprimanding with meekness, who acknowledges his fault with humility, and voluntarily punishes it; who is sufficiently humble to receive a reprimand without offering an excuse. Happy the religious who has not been desirous of the elevation he has attained, and who always wishes to be at the feet of the others! Woe to the religious who has been raised by the rest to an honorable position, and who has not the inclination to descend from it."

The example of Jesus Christ, who "was obedient unto death, even to the death of the cross," inspired St. Francis with great love for obedience. Although he was appointed superior by order of God and of the Pope, he was always desirous of obeying rather than commanding. In his travels, he promised obedience to him who accompanied him, and he rigidly kept that promise. One day he communicated the following in confidence to his companions: "Among all the graces which I have received from the bounty of God, this is one, that, if they were to appoint a novice of an hour's standing to be my guardian, I would obey him as implicitly as if he was the oldest and the most serious of our brethren." He was not satisfied with having renounced being General of the Order, to obey the Vicar-General; he asked Brother Elias, who filled that position to give him a guardian, on whose will he should depend in all things. Brother Angelo of Rieti was given to him, and he obeyed him with entire submission.

The instructions he gave his brethren on the subject of obedience contained all the perfection which could be given them: 1st. To renounce their own will, and to look upon it as the forbidden fruit, which our first parents could not eat of without being guilty. 2d. To abandon themselves wholly to their superior, so that they should neither do nor say anything which they know he would not approve of; and that they should do what he wishes the moment he has spoken, without waiting for his speaking a second time. 3d. Not to examine whether what is ordered is difficult or impossible, for, said St. Francis: "When I order anything which is above your strength, holy obedience will enable you to effect it." 4th. To submit their lights to those of the superior, not with a view of obeying him in anything manifestly contrary to salvation, but to act upon his views, although they may think their own better and more useful. 5th. Not to consider the man, nor his qualifications, in the obedience they bow to, but the authority he has, the place he fills, and the greatness of Him for whose love they are subject to man.

This last point is the greatest sacrifice of a religious life; but a necessary sacrifice, one which is just, and worthy of God, and the most certain proof that our obedience is grounded on our love for God. It is not difficult to follow the dictates of a superior of acknowledged talent and merit; the hardship is to submit with humility, without remonstrance or murmur, to one who has not these qualifications. This also it is which enhances in the eyes of God the value of religious obedience; it may then be considered as a sort of martyrdom of the mind, as well as that of the body, which will receive its crown in heaven. Nevertheless, it is requisite to be cautious, lest antipathy or some other motive, and the natural revolt of the human heart against authority, should cause a superior to appear contemptible, who really is not so. Finally, the religious are highly interested in practicing holy obedience, whoever may be the superior; it is, as St. Francis remarks, so abundant in fruits, that such as bend to the yoke pass not a moment of their lives without some spiritual profit: it increases virtue, and procures peace to the soul.

He was asked one day, who was to be considered to be truly obedient, and he instanced a dead body. "Take," said he, "a dead body, and place it where you please; you will see that it shows no repugnance at its removal, it utters no complaint at its situation, nor of dissatisfaction at being left where it is. If you put it in an honorable place, its eyes will remain closed, it will not raise them. If you clothe it in purple, it will only be paler than before. That is true obedience; it asks no reason as to why it is put in motion, it is indifferent as to where it is placed, and does not require to be removed.—If a Minor is raised to the dignity of superior, he remains equally humble; the more he is honored, the more does he think himself unworthy of it. I have often," he said, "seen a blind man led by a little dog, the man went wherever his guide took him, in good roads and in bad. This is another resemblance of one who is perfectly obedient; he should shut his eyes, and be blind to the commands of his superior, think of nothing but submitting immediately to him, without stopping to examine whether the thing be difficult or not, only keeping in view the authority of him who gives the order, and the merit of obedience."

Disobedience is insupportable; he considered it as the unfortunate offspring of pride, which is the source of all evils, and of which he had great horror. One day while praying in his cell, and meditating between God and his brethren, he saw in spirit one of them who refused to perform the penance imposed on him in chapter by the vicar-general, and excusing himself as to the fault of which he had been accused. He called his companion, and said: "I saw on the shoulders of this insubordinate brother the devil, who was wringing his neck, and leading him as by a bridle. I prayed for him, and the devil, abashed, loosed his hold immediately. Go to him, and tell him to bend immediately to the yoke of obedience," In fact, the brother did submit as soon as he was told this, and threw himself humbly at the feet of his superior.

Another, who had erred in some way against obedience, was brought to Francis, that he might correct him; but he appeared so penitent, that the Saint, who liked the humility of repentance, felt himself inclined to pardon the fault. Nevertheless, lest the facility of pardon should be abused, and to show what chastisement disobedience deserves, he ordered his cowl to be taken from him, and thrown into the fire. Some minutes after, he desired it to be taken out of the fire, and to be returned to him, when it was found that the fire had not injured it in the least; "God having shown by his miracle," St. Bonaventure observes, "the power He gave to His Servant, and how agreeable to Him humble repentance is."

The conduct of the holy Founder was more severe to one of his brethren, who was obstinately disobedient. He desired the others to put him into a pit, and to fill it up with earth, in order to bury him alive; when they had filled it up to his chin he said:—"Brother, are you dead?" The religious, absorbed in grief, replied: "Yes, Father, and I ought to die in reality for my sin." Francis, moved by compassion, had him dug out, saying: "Come forth from thence, if you are truly dead, as a good religious ought to be, to the world and its concupiscences. Obey the smallest sign of the will of your superiors, and make no more resistance to their orders than a dead body could do. I wish for followers, not living, but those who are dead."

He once called Brother Juniper to employ him a little while, and this brother not having immediately obeyed, because he was busy in planting a juniper tree, he cursed the tree that it should never grow, and it remained always in a dwarf state. The Fathers of the Desert were similarly exact in their attention to obedience, insomuch as to leave a letter unfinished when they had to attend to the orders of a superior.

The virtues of St. Francis, which we have recorded, and those which we have yet to narrate, were cultivated by the exercise of prayer. He had the gift as soon as he was called to the service of God; and he followed it up so faithfully, that he consecrated to it his heart, his body, all his actions, and all his time. In-doors, or out of doors, walking or seated, working or resting, his mind was always raised to heaven; he seemed to live with the angels. As he was always diffident of himself, he had recourse to prayer, and consulted the Almighty, with perfect confidence in His goodness, in all that He had to do. Although he could pray in any place he might happen to be in, nevertheless, he found solitary spots best adapted for recollection; he sought them out, and often retired to them. This shows us why he made so many houses of his Order, where there had previously been hermitages only.

Careful in attending to the interior calls of the Holy Spirit, if he perceived one coming on, he let his companions go forward, and stopped, not to receive it in vain, and to enjoy it to its full extent. When he prayed in community, he avoided all exterior signs, which might discover the secret dispositions of his mind, because he loved secrecy. He did not find the precaution difficult, because he was wholly absorbed in his interior, and united himself so intimately to God, that he was almost without exterior motion. If it happened that he was surprised by a visit from heaven in the presence of his brethren, he had always something ready to propose to them, to take off their attention. When he returned from prayer, in which he had been marvellously transformed, he strove to conform himself to his brethren, lest what they might perceive might draw from them applause, which would deprive him of his reward by inspiring him with vanity.

But in the solitudes he was under no restraint, and gave his heart entire liberty. The woods resounded with his sacred sighs and laments, the earth was moistened with his tears, and he struck his breast with violence. Sometimes he addressed himself to God as to his Sovereign Lord; sometimes he spoke to Him as to his Judge; sometimes he prayed to Him as to his Father; and at other times, he conversed with Him as a friend converses with his Friend. He solicited the pardon of sinners with loud and energetic exclamations; and he expressed his horror at the Passion of Jesus Christ in loud laments, as if he had been present at it. All this was seen and heard by someone or other of his companions, who had the pardonable curiosity to watch his proceedings. The devils tormented him severely during his prayers, and that in a very sensible manner, as St. Bonaventure informs us; but, protected by celestial aid, he continued his prayers with additional fervor, in proportion to the efforts they made to distract him.

God favored him with the gift of contemplation in a sublime degree. His companions bear witness that they have often seen him in a state of ecstasy, in which he had lost all the use of his senses, and in which all the powers of his soul were suspended. Once they saw him, during the night, raised from the ground, and his arms extended in the shape of a cross, surrounded by a luminous cloud, as if to betoken the Divine light which filled his mind. St. Bonaventure says that they had efficient proof that God at such times revealed to him some of the great secrets of His wisdom; but His faithful Servant only made such parts of them known as were for the glory of his Master, or the utility of his neighbor.

One of his brethren, not finding him one evening in his cell, went to look for him in the wood. Having penetrated a short distance into it, he heard him praying, with loud cries, for the salvation of men, and addressing the Blessed Virgin with moving sighs, humbly imploring her to show him her Son. He then saw the Blessed Mother of God descend from Heaven, with great splendor, and place her Son into the arms of Francis, who received Him as Simeon had received Him in the temple of Jerusalem, with the profoundest respect; he caressed the Infant most tenderly, entreating Him for the conversion of sinners, and the salvation of the world. At this sight the religious fell on the ground, half dead, and remained on the spot where he fell. Here the Saint found him, as he was returning to the convent for Matins; he brought him to himself from this fainting, but strictly forbade him from telling anyone what had occurred; but he, thinking it for the glory of God not to be obliged to obey in this instance, communicated the marvel to all the others.

A novice whom the holy Patriarch had received, and whom he was taking to the convent of the novitiate, wished to know what he did during the night. In order to succeed, he tied his cord to that of the Father, whom he saw asleep in the fields, in which they had been obliged to remain, and laid himself down near him, in order that he might be roused as soon as he should stir. A few hours afterwards, Francis wished to get up, but finding himself fastened by the cord, he untied the knot, and went to pray under some neighboring trees. The novice, not finding him when he awoke, went to seek him under the trees. A celestial light caused him to draw near a spot, where he stopped, and from whence he saw Jesus Christ, surrounded by angels, His Blessed Mother, and John the Baptist, who were in conversation with him. His astonishment made him fall on the ground, where he remained till Francis, to whom God had imparted the circumstances, came and raised him up, and restored him to his senses, forbidding him to speak of the vision. The young man, who continued to live very holily, kept the secret; but, after Francis's death, he published what he had seen.

God chose that his Servant should be respected in the secret retirements to which he went to pray, and that he should not be disturbed at those times. The Bishop of Assisi knew this by his own experience. One day, when he had come to the Convent of Portiuncula, as he frequently did, he wished to go at once into the cell where the Saint was at prayer; but scarcely had he seen him in that attitude, when he was pushed back by an invisible hand, his body became stiff, and he was unable to speak. Much astonished at this accident, he made his way back, as well as he could, to the other brethren; God restored his voice, and he made use of it, to acknowledge that he had committed a fault. The Celestial Spouse, in the Canticles, conjures the daughters of Jerusalem, "not to awaken her whom he loves, and not to disturb her repose until she awakes of her own accord." St. Bernard, on this, says that such as are given to prayer should not be troubled about useless affairs, and that those who disturb them when they are conversing with God, become enemies of heaven.

In consequence of the knowledge which Francis had of the sweets and fruits of mental prayer, he constantly urged his brethren to practice it, and they profited so fully by his instructions, that most of them became spiritual and contemplative men. "A religious," he said, "must principally desire to acquire the spirit of prayer. I believe that, without this, peculiar favors cannot be obtained from God, nor any great progress made in His service. When one is sorrowful and uneasy, he should have immediate recourse to prayer, and remain before his Heavenly Father, until such time as the joy of salvation is restored to him. If one remains in this state of depression and disturbance, this disposition, which comes from Babylon, will increase, and produce rust, unless it be purified by tears."

He taught them to shun the tumult of the world, and to seek for solitary places in which to pray, because he knew that the Holy Ghost communicates Himself more intimately to souls in such places; but he recommended them to be perfectly secret as to the favors they might receive; his maxim being, that a slender human communication often causes the loss of that which is of inestimable value, and has the effect of preventing the Lord from again communicating what He had previously given; that when one is visited by God, he should say: "It is Thou, O Lord! who hast sent me this consolation from Heaven,—to me who am a sinner, wholly unworthy of thy bounty. I commit it back to Thy keeping; for I feel myself capable of stealing Thy treasure from Thee;" and when he returns from prayer, he should show as much humility and self-contempt as if he had received no peculiar favor.

All the masters of spiritual life have had similar opinions of the value of mental prayer as this contemplative Saint, and they have pointed out the necessity of it for advancing in the ways of virtue. St. Teresa wrote so sublimely on this practice, that the Church prays to God that "her Heavenly doctrine may be our nourishment." She declares that she was near being lost, from having given it up, but that our Lord had done her the signal favor to urge her to resume it; she exhorts all to apply themselves to it, even should they make but small progress in it, because it is always useful, and, if persevered in, will be attended with great benefit. This is what directors might represent to those who seriously wish to attend to their salvation, and to say to them, with the same saint, that "mental prayer is nothing else but holding friendly intercourse with God, often remaining alone in conversation with Him, who, we know, loves us."

The practice of mental prayer no way diminished the zeal of St. Francis for vocal prayer, which every Christian ought to resort to as he did. Vocal prayer was practised and taught by Jesus Christ; the Church employs it in her public worship. "We require it," says St. Austin, "to assist our memory and understanding, and to animate our fervor; finally, God desires that we should offer to Him "a sacrifice of praise," and that it shall be "the fruits of our lips and hearts, giving glory to His name," because our body and soul belong to Him. Piety had inspired the holy man to compose vocal prayers on various subjects, which he often repeated, and some of which he recited daily. He said the Lord's Prayer, with particular devotion, weighing all the words, and meditating on the sense they contain, as is seen by the paraphrase of it he composed, and which we think it useful to insert at length:

"'Our Father,' most happy and most holy, our Creator, our Redeemer, and our Consoler. 'Who art in Heaven;' in the angels, in the saints, in the illuminated, in order that they may know Thee, who inflamest them by Thy love; for, O Lord! Thou are the Light and the Love who dwellest in them, and Thou art their Beatitude by satiating them: Thou art the Sovereign and Eternal Good, from whom all good proceeds, and without Thee there is no other good. 'Hallowed be Thy name:' in order thus to make Thyself known to us by vivid lights, so that we may see the full extent of Thy bounty, the duration of Thy promises, the sublimity of Thy majesty, and the depth of Thy judgment. 'Thy Kingdom come:' in order that Thou mayest reign in us by grace, and that Thou mayest bring us to Thy Kingdom, where Thou art clearly and perfectly loved, where we become happy in Thy society, and where Thou art eternally enjoyed. 'Thy will be done on earth as it is in Heaven:' in order that we may love Thee 'with our whole hearts,' thinking always of Thee 'with our whole soul,' ever longing for Thee, 'with all our mind,' referring to Thee all our views, seeking Thy glory in all things; 'with all our strength,' employing in Thy service, for Thy love, all the strength,' of our bodies and souls, without making any other use of them; that we may love our neighbor as ourselves, using all our efforts to draw them to Thy love; rejoicing in all the good that happens to them, as if it was our own; being grieved at any ills which may befall them, and giving offence to none. 'Give us this day our daily bread:' it is Thy beloved Son, Jesus Christ; we ask Thee for Him, in order to remind us of the love He has shown us, and of what He has said, done and endured for us; we ask Thee to make us fully comprehend these things, and cause us to revere them. 'Forgive us our trespasses,' by Thy infinite mercy, by the passion of Thy beloved Son, our Lord Jesus Christ, by the merits and intercession of the Blessed Virgin Mary, and of all the elect. 'As we forgive them that trespass against us:' what may be not altogether remitted on our part, grant us the favor, O Lord! to remit entirely, in order that, for love of Thee, we may sincerely love our enemies, and may intercede for them fervently at Thy throne; that we may not render to any one evil for evil, and that in Thee we may endeavor to do good to all. 'And lead us not into temptation,' hidden, manifest, sudden, grievous. 'But deliver us from evil:', past, present, and to come. Amen: willingly and gratuitously" These two words show that he ardently desired what he prayed for; and that it was purely for the glory of God, without any temporal interest.

He recited the Divine Offices with a devotion full of respect, and with great fervor. St. Bonaventure says that, although he suffered greatly from pains in his head, from his stomach, and from his liver, he never leant while reciting it; that he stood during the whole time, with his head uncovered, his eyes looking down. In travelling, he always stopped to say it; however much it might rain, he never omitted this pious practice, and he gave this reason for it: "If the body rests, in order to take its food, which will, as well as himself, soon become the food of worms, with how much tranquillity ought the soul to take its spiritual nourishment, which is to cause it to live eternally!"

The verse, Gloria Patri, etc., made a lively impression on his heart; once he repeated it in thankfulness to God for His bounty after each verse of the Magnificat, which Brother Leo was reciting, and he exhorts all to say it frequently. A lay brother, who was strongly tempted to apply himself to study, having come to ask his permission, was told: "My dear Brother, learn the Gloria Patri, and you will know the whole of the Holy Scriptures."—The brother obeyed, and had no further temptation on that head.

The distractions which his lively imagination caused him during the holy exercises, appeared to him to be great faults, and he never failed to confess them, and to expiate them by penance, asserting that we ought to be ashamed of being distracted by trifles when speaking to the great King. Once during Tierce, the thought of a little vase which he had made came into his head, and called off his attention; he immediately went and took it, and threw it into the fire, saying: "I will sacrifice it to the Lord, whose sacrifice it has hindered." But he acquired the habit of reciting the Office so attentively, that this sort of distractions seldom importuned him.

His application was equally strong and respectful in reciting the psalms, as if God had been present in a sensible manner; and he found so much sweetness in the name of God, that he seemed to have the taste of sweetness on his lips, after having pronounced it. Thus the Prophet said to the Lord: "How sweet are thy words to my palate! more than honey to my mouth." Francis had also an interior joy in pronouncing the holy name of Jesus, which communicated itself to his exterior, and produced on his senses a similar effect as if he had tasted something agreeable to his palate, or heard some harmonious sounds.

He desired that all the holy names should be peculiarly reverenced, not only when people thought of them, or pronounced them, but whenever they saw them written. This is the reason why, in his last will, he recommends his brethren to pick them up should they find them scattered about in unseemly places, and put them in a better locality, lest they should be disrespectfully trampled upon. This must be considered not as a mere nicety of feeling, but as a sentiment inspired by faith, which teaches us to venerate the word of God. If a great bishop has thought it proper to compare the abuse of the sacred word, when it is announced, to the profanation of the Body itself of Jesus Christ, may we not, in the same spirit, say that he who permits that word to be trampled upon when it is written, becomes in some measure as guilty as if he had allowed the Sacred Body of our Saviour to be treated with similar indignity?

It was the love of God which gave St. Francis so much zeal for mental prayer, as well as for that which is vocal. He sought his Beloved, from whom he was only separated by the wall of his flesh. To be present to Him in spirit, and to contemplate Him, were his sole consolations, and his anxiety to gain these was intense. But then the frequent exercise of prayer increased his love, and inflamed it to that degree, that St. Bonaventure does not think it possible to find words to express it. This Divine charity penetrated his whole interior, as fire penetrates a burning coal. Only by hearing the term of the love of God pronounced, he was moved and inflamed, and this movement made the affections of his soul thrill, as the strings of a musical instrument sound on being touched.

To incite himself more and more to the love of God, he made use of all creatures, as of so many mirrors, in which he viewed the Supreme Reason, the Sovereign Beauty, and the Principle of being and of life. They were for him as so many steps by which he raised and united himself to the object of his love, as so many streamlets in which he tasted, with inconceivable unction, the Infinite Purity of the source from whence all that is good is derived; so many delightful strains whose harmony resounded on his ears, and which, as David in his psalms, he invited to praise and glorify Him who had given them their being. Wholly inflamed with love, he prayed to be enabled to love still more, and he addressed the following prayer to God, which is found among his works: "Grant, O Lord! that the mild vehemence of Thy ardent love may separate me from everything which is under Heaven, and may consume me entirely, in order that I may die for the love of Thy love, since it was for the love of my love that Thou didst deign to die. I solicit this through Thyself, O Son of God! who livest and reignest with the Father and the Holy Ghost for ever and ever. Amen."

And here is another, which he used to say every day: "My God and my All, who art Thou, O sweet Lord! and who am I, Thy servant, a miserable worm? I wish to love Thee, most holy Lord, I wish to love Thee. O God! I have consecrated to Thee my heart and my body. If I had the means of doing more for Thee, I would do it, and I ardently wish I had the means."

This poor Evangelical could not give more to God than his body and soul. He continually offered the sacrifice of his body, by the rigor of his fasts, and that of his soul, by the vehemence of his desires; "by which," says St. Bonaventure, "he conformed in a spiritual manner to the practice of the Old Law, which was to offer holocausts out of the tabernacle, and to burn incense within it."

The sacrifice of his desires went to a great extent. For the love of God he had renounced all the things of this earth; he had stripped himself of everything; he had embraced the severest poverty, and practised the most austere penitential life; he had devoted himself to the ministry of preaching, and to the establishment of his Order; his life was but a course of labors and fatigue, but he reckoned all that as nothing; he wished to do much more, to mortify himself more rigorously, to forward thereby the glory of God, because, according to the words of our Saviour, this is the greatest mark of love which a friend can give to his friend. This was the motive of the ardent desire he had to endure martyrdom, and of the three voyages he undertook in search of it; seeing that he could not succeed, he lowered his views to wishing for and soliciting grace to know what he could do, to testify his love for God. The Lord granted his desire, favoring him with the impression of His five wounds, which rendered him a living and, at the same time, an expiring martyr; but it inflamed his heart to such a degree, that then he wished to die for love, and to be absorbed in the love of Him whom he loved.

Inflamed with divine love, he endeavored to spread the fire on all sides. He often made it the subject of his discourses, and it was usually the motive he employed to animate his brethren to the practice of virtue. When he proposed anything that was difficult to them, such as to go about soliciting alms, "Go," he would say, "and ask it for the love of God." He found a noble prodigality in asking it for that motive, and he thought those demented who preferred money to the love of God, the price of which is incalculable, and sufficient to purchase the Kingdom of Heaven, and which the love of Him who has so loved us must make infinitely dear to us. They were surprised one day to find that he could bear the severity of winter in so miserable a habit as that which he wore, and, full of fervor, he gave this reason, which contains a very useful lesson; "If we were inwardly inflamed with a longing for our celestial country, we should easily bear exterior cold." It was his wish that a Friar Minor should love God with an effective, liberal, and generous love, which should enable him to suffer calmly and joyfully pain and opprobrium for the object of his love. This is what he said one day to Brother Leo, on the subject, in a conversation which Leo himself has recorded at full length: "If a Friar Minor had a clear and distinct knowledge of the course of the stars, and of all other things in the universe; if he possessed all the sciences, all the languages, and a perfect knowledge of the Holy Scriptures; and if he spoke with the tongues of angels, cast out devils, performed all sorts of miracles, even that of raising one from the dead who had been four days in the tomb; if he had the gift of prophecy, and that of discerning the affections of the heart; if he preached to the infidels with such success as to convert them all, and if he should edify the world by his sanctity, all that would not be to him the subject of perfect and true joy."

Afterwards, to show in what this true joy consisted, he proposed a supposition, similar to one he had made on another subject, and very like to the hypothesis of St. Paul: "Who shall separate us from the love of Jesus Christ? Shall tribulation, or distress, or famine, or nakedness, or persecution, or the sword?" From which he concluded, that all that there is in Heaven or on earth could not separate him from the love of God, which is grounded on Jesus Christ, our Lord.

"Suppose," said St. Francis, "that we were to arrive at the Convent of St. Mary of the Angels very wet, covered with mud, perishing with cold, dying of hunger, and that the porter, instead of letting us in, were to leave us at the gate in this pitiable state, saying angrily, 'You are a couple of idle vagabonds, who stroll about the world, and receive the alms which the real poor ought to get.' If we bear this treatment with patience, without being discomposed, and without murmuring; if even we think humbly and charitably that the porter knows us well for what we are, and that it is by God's leave that he behaves thus to us, mark this down as perfect joy."

"Suppose, moreover, that we continue to knock at the door, and that the porter, considering us importunate, should come out and give us some severe boxes on the ears, and say, 'Get along, scoundrels, go to the hospital, there is nothing for you to eat here.' If we bear all these things patiently, and we pardon him from our hearts, and with charity, note, this would be a subject for perfect joy."

"Let us, in fine, suppose, that in this extremity the cold, hunger, and the night, compel us to entreat, with tears and cries to be allowed to enter the convent, and that the porter, in great irritation, darts out with a stick full of knobs, takes us by the cowl, throws us down in the snow, and beats us till we are quite covered with bruises:—if we bear all this ill usage with joy, with the thought that we ought to participate in the sufferings of our Blessed Saviour Jesus Christ, note this, and note it carefully, that this is, for a Friar Minor, the subject of a true and perfect joy."

"Now hear the conclusion of all this. Amongst all the gifts of the Holy Ghost, which Jesus Christ has granted and will grant to His servants, the most considerable is, that of conquering one's self, and of suffering pain and opprobrium for the love of God, in order to respond to the love He has for us. In all the miraculous gifts which I have noticed, there is not one from which we may derive so much glory; we have no share in it, it is all from God; we only receive what He gives us, and, as St. Paul says, 'If thou hast received, why dost thou glory, as if thou hadst not received it?' But we have our share in the tribulations which we suffer for the love of God, and we may make it a subject of glory, as the same Apostle has said: 'God forbid that I should glory save in the Cross of our Lord Jesus Christ.'"

St. Francis was far from thinking that we may glory in our sufferings, as of a favor which we have not received, since he acknowledges that it is the greatest gift of the Holy Ghost, conformably to what St. Paul said to the Philippians: "To you is given not only to believe in Jesus Christ, but also to suffer for His sake;" and to what is written of the Apostles: "And they, indeed, went from the presence of the council, rejoicing that they were accounted to suffer reproach for the name of Jesus." He only proposed to say that our sole cause of glory is, that God permits us to be associated to the Cross of Jesus Christ, in which alone we are glorified. Thus it is to God that he refers all the glory of our sufferings, which indeed is His, since, without the aid of His grace, we should not suffer as we ought, and without the Cross of Jesus Christ we should have no merit. But he correctly says, and he speaks the true orthodox faith, when he adds, that we have a share in the merit of what we suffer, and when he draws the distinction between that and miraculous gifts. St. Chrysostom has spoken in the same manner, and says that our virtues are in so far the gifts of God, that they are also merits of our will, for which God has been pleased to render Himself indebted to us, by the promise He has made to reward them.

The mystery of the Incarnate Word, "that great mystery of piety, which has been manifested in the flesh," produced in the heart of St. Francis sentiments so pious and so tender, that they were observable exteriorly, by actions of extraordinary fervor, as we saw in the grand solemnity which he celebrated at Grecio on Christmas night. "Consider," he says, in his letters, "that the most high Father has sent from Heaven His archangel, St. Gabriel, to announce that His most worthy, holy, and glorious Word should descend into the womb of the most Blessed Virgin Mary. And, in truth, He did so descend, and took from her true human flesh, passible and mortal, such as ours is: 'Being rich, He became of His own accord poor.' He chose, by preference, poverty in this world for Himself and for His Blessed Mother. He gave Himself thus to us, in conformity to the will of His Father, to wipe away our sins on the cross, by the sacrifice of His Blood, and to leave an example for us to follow in His traces, for it is His wish that we should all be saved through Him; but there are few who desire the salvation He proffers them, although His yoke is sweet, and His burden light."

When he spoke of the incarnation and birth of the Son of God, it was with affectionate devotion; he could not hear the words, "the Word made flesh," without manifesting great joy. The religious of a monastery where he was one day, remarked this emotion, and took occasion to ask him if it was right to eat meat on Christmas-day, when it fell on a Friday, or if it was not better to abstain from it. "Not only do I think," he replied, "that men may eat meat on this day, on which the Word was made flesh, but I wish that princes and rich persons would throw meat and corn in the highways, in order that the birds and beasts of the field should rejoice, in their way, in the joys of so great a festival; I wish, even, that some was placed on the walls, if they could derive sweetness from it."

We see plainly that these are hyperbolical expressions, flowing from his heart, by the emotions of his spiritual joy, by which he was actuated; but, in saying that men might eat meat on Christmas-day, although it fall on a Friday, he speaks in conformity with the usage of the Church, which, however, is a permission, and not a law. Pope Honorius III. pointed it out clearly to the Bishop of Prague, in Bohemia, in the following rescript of the year 1222: "We answer that, when the Feast of the Nativity of our Blessed Lord falls on a Friday, those who are not under the obligation of abstinence by a vow, or by a regular observance, may eat meat on that day, because of the excellence of the festival, according to the custom of the universal Church. Those, however, who abstain on that day, from devotion, are not to be censured."

St. Francis was, moreover, much affected by the goodness of our Saviour, who, after His baptism, went into the desert, and there fasted forty days and forty nights, without eating anything during that time, for the expiation of our sensuality, and to set us an example of fasting. He honored this holy retreat by a fast of forty days, which he commenced on the seventh day of January, and which he passed in some solitary place, confined to his cell, keeping strict abstinence in fasting and drinking, and employing himself solely in praising God and in prayer. It was also during this Lent that he received the most signal favors from Jesus Christ.

His soul was penetrated with ardor for the mystery of the Sacred Body and Blood of our Lord. The work of so tender a love, and of such condescending goodness, threw him into an excess of admiration, and put him quite beside himself. He communicated frequently, and with so much devotion, that it inspired others with similar feelings; they saw him almost always, after having communicated, as if in a spiritual intoxication, and raised into ecstasy by the sweetness he tasted in partaking of the Body and Blood of the Lamb without spot. At Mass, when at the Elevation, he said this prayer: "Celestial Father, my Lord and my God, cast Thine eyes on the glorious countenance of Thy Christ, and have pity on me and on other sinners, for whom Thy beloved Son, our Lord, has condescended to die, and who has chosen to remain with us in the Sacrament of the Altar, for our salvation and consolation: who with Thee, eternal Father, and the Holy Ghost, sole God, liveth and reigneth to everlasting ages. Amen."

The profound veneration which is due to the august mystery of the Eucharist, the solicitude which we ought to have to hear Mass, to approach to the sacred altar, and to prepare ourselves, in order worthily to communicate, were points on which he used to dilate in his conversations, in his instructions, and in his letters.

The life of the holy man has furnished many examples of the ardent and respectful zeal which animated him in all that regarded churches or altars, or all the things which were used for the Sacrifice of the Mass, and for the divine service. As he could not bear anything dirty or slovenly, in the country churches, he took the trouble of cleaning everything himself; and lest they should want altar breads for Masses, he made them himself in iron forms, which were made in a very workmanlike manner; he took them into the poor parishes: some of these moulds are carefully preserved in the convent of Grecio.

The great love which he had for Jesus Christ, and for the sacrament which contains His Body, His Blood, His Soul, and His Divinity, inspired him with a zeal and a tenderness of devotion to His Blessed Mother, which cannot be expressed, as St. Bonaventure remarks. He placed himself and his Order under the protection of this Blessed Mother of God, whom he chose for his advocate; and in her, after Jesus Christ, his chief confidence rested: "for," said he, "it is she who made this God of Majesty our brother; through her we have obtained mercy." He used, as we have noticed, to keep a Lent of six weeks, in honor of her glorious Assumption; and he observed it with great sentiments of piety. These are the prayers and eulogiums he was in the habit of addressing to her:—

> "Hail, Mary! Mother of God, ever a Virgin, most holy Lady and Queen, in whom is all the plenitude of grace and every sort of good. Amongst women there are none born like unto thee; thou art the daughter and the handmaid of our celestial Father, the great King; and he has chosen thee for the Mother of His beloved Son. Thou art the Spouse of the Holy Ghost, the Comforter. Hail to thee, who art the palace, the temple, and the Mother of our Lord Jesus Christ! I honor all the virtues with which thou art filled. Thou who art as mild as thou art beautiful, implore thy very dear Son, conjure Him by His great clemency, by the virtue of His most sacred incarnation and that of His most painful death, to pardon our faults. Amen."

The indissoluble ties of spiritual love, says the holy doctor whom we have quoted, united Francis to the hierarchy of the angels, caused in him marvellous fire which absorbs man in God, and influences the elect with noble aims. The ardent zeal he had for the salvation of souls, attached him intimately to the Archangel St. Michael, because his employment is to present man to the throne of the Divine Majesty. It was to honor these blessed spirits, that he kept every year a Lent of forty days, before the Feast of St. Michael, adding to it a continual exercise of prayer. He had prescribed to himself another Lent, to prepare for the Festival of All Saints, who seemed to him to be, according to the expression of Ezekiel, precious stones, glittering as fire, the memory alone of which excited him to a more fervent love of God. The great love which all the Apostles had for Jesus Christ, led him to revere them with peculiar devotion, particularly Saints Peter and Paul, in honor of whom he fasted from Whit-Sunday to their feast.

It is useful to remark here that this great Saint, who was raised to a sublime degree of prayer, did not neglect, nevertheless, the usual practices of piety with the rest of the faithful. This may serve as a preservative against an illusion which might lead to the belief that they are useless to the spiritual, and that those who are mystical, may dispense with them, to devote themselves to contemplation. His heart was so full and so penetrated with that true and sincere piety, of which charity is the soul, that it seemed to have entire possession of him. It united him incessantly to God, to the friends of God, and to everything which was holy; but, as the Apostle says, "prayer is profitable to all things"; it gave him a fund of all that was good, a spirit of meekness, of condescension, and of zeal, to communicate with his neighbor.

All men were dear to him, because he saw in them the same nature, the same grace, the image of the Creator, and the Blood of the Redeemer. If he had not taken care of the salvation of souls, which Jesus Christ had redeemed, he would not have considered himself among the number of His friends. "Nothing," he said, "is preferable to the salvation of souls;" and he gave several reasons for this, and principally this one: that, for them, the Only Son of God had condescended to be nailed to the cross. It was also for them that he labored and lived; for them, in some measure, he called in question the justice of God in prayer, and powerfully solicited His mercy; for them he frequently forewent he sweets of a contemplative life; he undertook journeys, he preached everywhere, he exposed Himself to martyrdom, and their edification was one of his motives in the practice of virtue. Although his innocent flesh, already perfectly under the control of the spirit, did not require to be chastised for any faults, he, nevertheless, mortified it in various ways for the edification of his neighbor. When he was censured for his too great austerities, he replied:—"I am sent to give this example; if I had not the charity to give it, I should be of little use to others, and of none to myself, although I spoke all the languages known to men and angels."

Seeing that a multitude of persons, stimulated by his example, fervently embraced the Cross of Christ, he became animated with fresh courage to put himself at the head of these pious troops, as a valiant captain, in order to gain with them a victory over the devil, by the practice of perfect and invincible virtue.

The sanctity of his life gave him great freedom in his manner of preaching. He spoke fearlessly, without any apprehension of what critics might say, because he had acted before teaching, and he felt and had experienced all he said. The zealous preacher knew not how to flatter. Far from sparing sinners by complacence, he reproached their vices in forcible language, and attacked their disorderly conduct with great vehemence. The presence of the great of the world did not intimidate him; he spoke to them as plainly and forcibly as he had done to the common people; and, as all souls were equally dear to him, he preached as willingly, and with as much zest, to a few people, as to a crowded auditory.

The tender love which St. Francis bore for souls redeemed by the Blood of Jesus Christ, rendered him very sensible to their misfortunes. When he knew of any one stained by the filth of sin, he lamented over it with deep grief. His charity, fertile in expedients, inspired him sometimes to give to wicked persons temporal assistance, with a view of getting them to return to the ways of salvation. One day, when he was at the Convent of Mount Casal, Brother Angelo, who was the guardian of it, told him that there were in the neighborhood three notorious robbers, who injured considerably the farmers of the vicinity, and daily came and extorted from them the bread which was destined for the convent, without their being able to prevent it. "Brother," he replied, "if you will do what I will point out to you, my confidence in God tells me that you will reform these men, and gain their souls. Go and seek them out: although they are robbers, they are still our brothers. Take them the best bread you have, and some wine, spread a cloth on the ground, and invite them to eat with you; while they are eating, speak to them of holy things, in an insinuating manner, both yourself and your companion; humbly entreat them to injure no one any more. If they promise you this, return to them the next day, and take them something to eat, with bread and wine as before, and tell them that you bring that, as to brethren and friends, who have granted you what you asked of them. If you do this a third time, do not doubt but God will enlighten them, and touch their hearts, and bring them into the right way."

Brother Angelo followed this advice, and gained over the robbers so completely, that they gave up their lives of plunderers, and began to render service to the convent, supplying them with fire-wood, which they carried to them on their shoulders. Their conversion was complete: one of them entered the Order, and the other two went elsewhere to embrace a penitential life. The guardian used similar means for converting three other robbers, who retired into the recesses of the mountain, after having induced the Saint to pray for them. All three afterwards entered the Order of Friars Minor and lived holy lives.

The affection which our Saint had always shown for the poor from his infancy, during the first years of his youth, and at the beginning of his conversion, became stronger and stronger, and was manifested on all occasions. St. Bonaventure says that he spared nothing to come to their assistance. Cloaks, tunics, books, the ornaments of the Church, all that he had he gave to them. Many times he has been seen taking the burdens from the poor he met on the road, and bear them on his own weak shoulders. When he returned from begging, he shared what he had received with any that solicited alms at his hands; and as long as anything remained, he never refused any one.

At Sienna, a small cloak had been given to him, which was very necessary for his infirmities; but, in leaving the town, he met a poor person, whose wretched state excited his pity, and he said to his companion: "Let us restore this cloak to him, for it belongs to him; we have only borrowed it, until such time as we should see someone poorer than ourselves." The companion, knowing that Francis really required it, endeavored to prevent his parting with it, but the father made him this answer: "If I did not give this cloak to a poor man, who had more need of it than I have, I should think I had committed a theft, which I should be convicted of by our Sovereign Lord, who is the universal almoner." It was for this reason that, when anything was given him, he asked leave to give it away, if he should meet with any one poorer than himself.

On the same principle, notwithstanding his infirmities, when he was at the convent at Celles, he gave another cloak, which he had received in charity, to a poor woman. One of the brothers having taken it back, promising to give the woman something else instead, the Saint said immediately:—"My brother, kneel down and acknowledge your fault; give the cloak back to the woman: she is poorer than I am." His companions got him another, and he gave it again to a man of Cortona, who came to solicit alms for the love of God, at the same convent at Celles. He told Francis that his wife was dead, that he had several little children, and that he had no food for them: "I give you this cloak," said the Saint, "on this condition, that, if you are asked to give it back, you do no such thing, unless you receive its full value." The brethren, indeed, did all they could to induce him to give it back: they told him there was no one poorer than the person who had given it to him, or who wanted it more on account of his bad health and the rigor of the season. But the man, referring to what his benefactor had said, answered that the cloak was his, and that he would not part with it, unless he received its full value. In order, therefore, to have it returned, they were under the necessity of taking him to a friend who gave him in money what the cloak was considered to be worth.

A very old woman, the mother of two of the Friars Minor, having come to the Convent of St. Mary of the Angels to ask for charity, Francis old the guardian to give her something; and he having said that there was not anything then in the convent which could be given, unless it was a book of the Gospel which the brethren read out of, when they were in the choir the Father said:— "Give it that the poor woman may sell it to provide for her necessities. I believe that this will be more agreeable to God, than reading out of it. What is it that a mother has not a right to require from us, who has given two of her sons to the religious?"

Another time, a poor man came to ask for an old habit. Francis desired them to look about well for one that was not used. As such an one was not to be found, he stole aside and began to unpick some breadths of his own, in order to give them to the man; the guardian, being informed of this, came down hastily and forbade his taking them out: "I will obey you, because you are my superior, but give this poor man something to cover himself with; otherwise I shall have a scruple, and shall be grieved to be obliged to wear an entire habit which is lined, to keep me warm, while this poor man is shivering with cold at the gate." He went to the poor man to console him, and did not leave him until the guardian had given him something wherewith to clothe himself; and this alms was no less comforting to his charitable feelings, than the clothing was to the misery of the poor man. By a similar impulse of charity, and in order to prevent curses against God, he gave his cloak to a servant who complained of the great injury his master had done him, cursing him and blaspheming Providence for allowing the poor to be so ill used. He gave him his cloak on the condition that he would leave off cursing and blaspheming.

The physician who saw the saint in his illness, near Rieti, having one day mentioned the extreme poverty of an old woman who was begging, he sent for the guardian and said: "Here is a cloak which I have worn until such time as someone should be found who has a greater right to it than I have; I beg you to send it, with some of the bread which has been received on the quest, by one of the brethren, to our sister, who is very poor, and let him say that we only give her what belongs to her. I conceive that what is given to us can only be ours until such time as someone shall come forward, who is more in want of it than we are." Not to vex the holy man, the commission was faithfully executed.

The blessed Patriarch wished that such of his children who had not studied, and had no talent for preaching, should be employed in serving their brethren, and should frequent the hospitals, there to render the meanest offices to the lepers, with humility and charity.

Brother James the Simple, who came from Perugia, was greatly distinguished by his zeal in this charitable exercise, insomuch that they gave him the name of the steward and physician of the lepers. Francis recommended one to him, whose body was a mass of sores, from his head to his feet. James took such care of him, that, by degrees, he regained his strength; and, thinking fresh air would contribute to his restoration, he took him with him, although still full of ulcers, to the Convent of Saint Mary of the Angels. This appeared to the Saint, who met him, to have been very indiscreet, and he said to Brother James: "You should not lead about, in this manner, the Christian Brothers; it is neither proper in you, nor good for them. I wish you to serve them in their hospital, but I do not wish you to take them out of it, for there are many persons who cannot bear the sight of them." The leper was distressed at hearing his benefactor thus reprimanded, and he blushed for shame. Francis, perceiving him to have been mortified, threw himself immediately at his feet, and begged his pardon, and, in order to console him, he ate at the door of the convent, out of the same plate with the leper, after which he embraced and kissed him, and dismissed him satisfied.

There was in the hospital a leper who was so impatient and so violent, that he abused and struck the Friars Minor who served him, and even went so far as to blaspheme God. They reported this to their Father, who offered himself to the sick man, to wait upon him: "What can you do for me more than your companions have done?" replied the invalid. "Ever since I have had this insupportable disorder, God has forgotten me. I am in despair, I can live no longer; no one can mitigate my sufferings; neither you nor anyone else." Francis, seeing that he was agitated by the evil spirit, left him for a while, prayed for him, and returned to exhort him by the most urgent motives, to be patient. As he saw that the man became calmer, he asked him what might seem most agreeable to him; what he should do for him. He said that he should now wash his whole body, that he could no longer endure the stench of the infection. The saint quickly got some water warmed, into which he put aromatic herbs, and began to wash him himself, while his companion poured out the water. As he washed, his cure advanced, and, at the same time, the grace of God made such impression on the mind of the patient, that, as the water flowed from his body, the tears flowed from his eyes. The washing having terminated, the leper being perfectly cleansed and converted, publicly confessed his sins, asked for mercy, and went through a rigorous course of penance. He died a few months afterwards, and appeared to the Saint, thanking him that, by his means, after a light punishment in purgatory, he was about to enjoy eternal glory.

God performed a different miracle on another occasion, to justify the charity of His Servant to the poor. At Alexandria de la Paille, a town of the Milanese, where he was received as a Saint, he was invited to dinner by a wealthy and pious man. While he was at table, a man of bad character, who was, however, jealous of Francis's reputation, watched all his actions, in order to decry and criticise them: this man counterfeited a beggar at the door, and solicited an alms for the love of God. As soon as Francis heard the appeal for the love of God, he sent him the wing of a fowl, to which he had been just helped. The sham beggar, to whom it was taken, kept it. The next day he produced it, in a large concourse of people, where the Saint was preaching, and, interrupting the discourse, he said in a loud voice: "This is the food on which the preacher feeds: should such a man be honored as a saint?" His malice received a signal check; the wing of the fowl which he exhibited, appeared to the bystanders to be fish, and he was thought to have lost his wits. He himself perceiving that what he held up was nothing but fish, was ashamed of what he had said, was touched with remorse, and published himself what had happened. After which, one miracle succeeded another; it was found that what had appeared to be fish, was in reality flesh. Thus did the Lord vindicate the virtue of His Servant, punish envy, and convert the envious. The malignity of envy often finds its punishment in the artifices it employs to injure persons of virtue, but it is very unusual for the envious to be so converted.

St. Bonaventure says that St. Francis felt a most tender compassion for all who suffered from temporal ills; that, indeed, he had naturally a feeling heart, but that the goodness of the heart of Jesus Christ, communicating itself to his, rendered it still more compassionate. He was the more sensible of the afflictions of others, as in all the poor, and in all those who suffered, he represented to himself his Divine Master, poor and suffering; in which, continues the holy doctor, he who was himself poor, showed that he was so as a perfect Christian.

When he had it not in his power to alleviate the sufferings of those in indigence or sickness, he endeavored, at least by soothing words, to assuage their feelings. One day, when he was about to preach, he was entreated by a poor and infirm man to recommend him to the auditors. His compassion was excited, and, with tears in his eyes, he said to his companion that he felt the man's ills as if they were his own. His companion answered the man rather drily, who was importunate in asking for alms, and in order to moderate the feelings of the Saint, he said: "If we judged by exteriors, this man is apparently in great misery; but, if we could penetrate his interior, we should, perhaps, find that in the whole province there is not an individual richer in wishes, or more eaten up with pride: such characters are frequently found among beggars." Francis censured him severely for having repulsed the poor man, and for judging him with so much asperity, and pointed out to him that in this he offended God. The religious acknowledged his error, and asked pardon on his knees. "I shall not pardon you," said Francis, "unless you take off your habit, prostrate yourself before the poor man, acknowledge your fault, entreat him to pardon you, and to pray for you." The humble penitent did immediately all that he had been desired to do, after which Francis embraced him, and said, with great mildness: "My son, it is not so much against the poor man that you have sinned, as against Jesus Christ, for He is in all the poor: they are so many mirrors, in which He represents to us His own poverty, and that of His Blessed Mother. Therefore, as often as you see the poor and the sick, respect them, and humble yourself in their presence; consider, with sentiments of piety, that the Son of God made Himself poor for our sakes, and condescended to take upon Himself our infirmities."

If we cherish these Christianlike views, we should not judge so harshly of the poor, of whom it is no less faulty to judge, than of the rich; and in their poverty we should find as powerful motives for loving Jesus Christ, as for affording the succor they require.

The heart of St. Francis was naturally so kind and so tender, that he felt an affection for creatures, but it was from a profound sentiment of piety that he called them his brothers and his sisters. Going back to the origin of things, St. Bonaventure says that he considered all that had being as having emanated from the bosom of the Divinity, and he acknowledged that they had the same principle as himself. In fact, the creation established amongst them a sort of fraternity: God being the parent of all nature, it is not to be denied that, in this sense, everything which composes it is brotherly. And who can censure a man who is wholly religious, for expressing himself in a manner which is grounded on the first principles of religion? This trait shows both the elevation of his mind, and the piety of his heart; heretics alone can blame it.

Among animals, those he preferred were such as reminded him of the mildness of Jesus Christ, or were the symbol of some particular virtue, or which gave rise to some edifying reflections; and God has sometimes shown by miracles, how much the motive of these feelings was pleasing to Him. Lambs were peculiarly agreeable to the holy man, in memory of the meek Lamb who permitted Himself to be led to the slaughter, for the redemption of sinners; he frequently had them purchased, to prevent their being killed.

While he was staying at the Monastery of St. Vereconda, which is in the Diocese of Gubbio, he found that on the previous night a sow had killed with its teeth a lamb, which had just been born. The Lamb without spot, whom sinners put to death, flashed immediately upon his recollection, and the pity this excited in him, caused him to lament sorely the death of the little animal, which was a symbol of meekness; to curse the cruel beast which had killed it, and to wish that neither man nor beast might eat of its flesh. The sow was at that moment struck with a disease, of which it died in three days. It was thrown into a ravine, not far distant from the monastery, and no animal ventured to touch it: it became dry and hard as a piece of wood. St. Bonaventure remarks, on this occasion, that if God was pleased to punish with death the cruelty of a beast, how infinitely more severe must not the punishment of cruel and pitiless men be in the other world.

A lad went to Sienna to sell some turtle-doves, which he had taken alive. Francis met him on his way, and said: "These are innocent birds, which are compared in Scripture to chaste and faithful souls I beg you earnestly not to put them into the hands of persons who would kill them, but to confide them to me." They were given to him, and he put them immediately into his bosom; he spoke to them as if they were capable of reasoning, not only by that natural impulse which induces us constantly to speak to animals, when we caress them, but also by an impression of the spirit of God. He told them of a great miracle, promising to prepare a nest for them, where they might increase and multiply, according to the intention of their Creator. Having taken them to his Convent of Ravacciano, near the walls of Sienna, he forced his stick into the ground before the gate, and the stick became, by the following day, a large evergreen oak. He let the turtle-doves fly into it, desiring them to make their nests there, which they did for many succeeding years; and they were so familiar with the religious, that they came to feed from their hands. Wading says that the tree was still there at his time and that many saw it.

Nor did the young man go unrewarded. Francis told him that he would become a religious of his Order, and that he would acquire eternal glory: he did, in fact, enter the Order, and lived so holily as to earn Heaven. The miracle was the cause of his vocation, and at the same time sanctioned the affection the Saint showed these birds: he only loved God through the affection he showed to His creatures. So also, St. Gregory Thaumaturgus, according to the testimony of St. Gregory of Nyssa, having planted his stick in a spot where a river was breaking down the dyke and doing damage through the country, the Lord changed it suddenly into a large tree, which checked the flood entirely, and served to honor the faith of his Servant, and incite the infidels to believe in Jesus Christ.

The Divine love which inflamed the heart of St. Francis, made everything appear amiable to him which could tend to the love and service of God. For this reason he was fond of birds, whose carol seemed to invite mankind to publish the glory of their Creator, for, according to the words of Jesus Christ, "neither do they sow nor reap, nor gather into barns: yet their Heavenly Father feeds them." It was gratifying to him to remark the gray and ash color of larks, the color he had chosen for his Order, so that the minors might often think on death. He also loved to admire the disposition of the plumage of such as were crested, which seemed to him to have some relation to the simplicity of his habit. On the lark rising into the air, and singing as soon as it has taken some grains of corn for its nourishment, he remarked with sensible pleasure that this example ought to teach us to give thanks to our common Father, who gives us wherewithal for our sustenance, only to eat for His glory, to despise the earth, and to raise ourselves up to Heaven, where our conversation ought to be. He was more fond of these small birds than of any others, because they induced holy thoughts, and he took as much care of them as he could.

As he had noble and spiritual motives for his simplest and most common actions, God made use of this for the instruction of men by the example of a bird. Near the Convent of Mount Ranier, or Mount Colombo, there was a nest of crested larks, the mother of which came every day to feed out of the hand of the Servant of God and took sufficient for herself and her brood: when they began to be strong, she brought the little ones to him. He perceived that the strongest of the brood pecked the others, and prevented them from taking up the grain. This displeased him, and addressing himself to the little bird as if it could understand him, "Cruel and insatiable little animal," he said, "you will die miserably, and the greediest animals will not be willing to eat your flesh," In fact, some days afterwards, it was drowned in a basin, which was placed for them to drink out of. It was given to the cats and dogs, to see if they would eat it; but neither would touch it. It may be thought that so trifling an anecdote was not worth recording, but there is nothing trifling in the moral it contains. It is a natural representation of those greedy and insatiable men who devour the substance of their brethren, and envy them all that they cannot despoil them of; enemies of mankind, unworthy of the name of men, thieves, ruffians, ravaging wolves, as they are designated in Scripture, whose voracity, say the Holy Fathers, surpasses that of wild beasts; whose life is a public calamity; hated and detested by all, during their lives, they die as they have lived, and their memory is held in execration.

The tender-heartedness which Francis evinced for animals has been ridiculed by heretics. Nevertheless, the Holy Ghost tells us, by the mouth of Wisdom, that "the just man regardeth the lives of his beasts." The Patriarch Jacob excused himself from following his brother Esau, because his ewes and cows were heavy, and he was fearful he should kill them if he hurried them. When St. Paul said, "Doth God take care of oxen?" he only wished to insinuate that God is far more interested in what regards men.

In this view St. Chrysostom, commenting on the words of Wisdom, which we have just quoted, says that the saints are tender-hearted; that they love all men, strangers as well as their own countrymen and their own families, and that their good feelings are extended to senseless animals.

Sulpicius Severus relates of St. Martin, that, seeing some hounds pursuing a hare, which they were on the point of catching, he ordered them to stop; he had no sooner spoken, than the hounds became immovable on the spot where they were, and they did not stir till the hare was placed in safety.

An author of the life of St. Bernard, who had been his secretary, says that not only men, but irrational animals, even birds, and other beasts, felt the effects of his tenderness. He adds that the Saint, in one of his journeys, coming close to a hare, which the dogs were about to catch, and where a bird was nearly seized in the talons of a hawk, delivered them both miraculously by the sign of the cross, and then told the sportsmen that all their efforts would be useless for taking this prey.

If it had been thought proper not to omit in his life, and in that of St. Martin also, these anecdotes of the goodness of their hearts, which were enhanced by supernatural evidence, and of which God approved by His wisdom and His power, what right can critics have to censure precisely similar circumstances in the life of St. Francis?

The glorious Patriarch, who praised God in the minutest things, procured his glory in the greatest. His principal care was to lead his brethren to perfection; to render them worthy imitators of Jesus crucified, capable of exciting His love in all hearts. It would be difficult to point out the founder of an order who had spoken more, taught more, or exhorted more, than St. Francis; and it may have been noticed that he instructed his disciples in the most solid and eminent virtues. He recommended them to put the Gospel in practice, as they had promised to do in making profession of the rule; to adore profoundly and with great devotion the Body of Jesus Christ; to hear Mass most devoutly; to celebrate the Divine Office with attention; carefully to keep all the ordinances of the Church; to have the greatest veneration for all priests, humbly to bow in their presence, and to kiss their hands. He even said that, if it could be done, they ought to kiss the feet of the horses on which they rode, to honor the power which they have of consecrating and administering the Divine mysteries.

When abroad, it was his desire that his religious should appear with so much modesty, reserve, and circumspection, that every one might be edified thereby, and glorify God therein. "Do not despise the men of the world," he said, "and judge not ill of them. You are not to judge other persons' servants, who are not yours; whether they stand or fall, it is not your affair, but that of their masters. Have peace in your own mind, make it known to others, inspire it to all; labor for the conversion of sinners, for that is your vocation."

Attentive to the regulation of the interior, he incessantly exhorted them to correct the smallest defects; to exercise themselves in the practice of holy prayer, to meditate on the Passion of our Blessed Saviour, and to use all their efforts to preserve union and fraternal love. "Happy," said he, "is the man who loves his brother when absent, as well as when they are together, and who would not say in his absence what charity would prevent his saying in his presence."

In the view of rendering his brethren more perfect, he frequently counteracted the bent of their devotion. Brother Masse was a very spiritual man, who was much attached to prayer. Francis, in order to try him, said to him one day, in presence of the others: "Brother, these have received from God a greater gift of contemplation than you have. For which reason, in order to give them more time to give themselves very freely to it, it seems proper that you, who seem more calculated for exterior duties, should have the care of the door and of the kitchen, and, if there is any time over, you will employ it in questing. Take great care that the strangers who may call, do not interrupt your brethren in their meditations. As soon as they may knock at the door, be there ready to receive them, satisfy them with fair words, and do everything which the others would have done, so that it shall not be necessary for any of them to make their appearance. Go in peace, and fail not in doing all these things, in order to have the merit of obedience."

Masse, bowing his head, submitted to the order of his superior, without hesitation or murmur, and, during several days, he acquitted himself faithfully of what had been directed. His companions, who knew his virtue, and the love he had for prayer, had scruples at seeing him in these employments, and begged their father to permit them to share these duties with him. He assented, and, sending for Masse, said to him: "Brother, your companions wish to relieve and assist you, and I also wish that they may have a share in the labors." To which Mass replied, "Father, I consider as coming from God whatever duties you direct, whether it be my work or prayer." St. Francis, seeing the charity on the one part, and the humility on the other, gave them an exhortation on these two virtues, and distributed the duties among them, with his blessing.

What he had ardently desired for himself, and what he was rejoiced to see some of his brethren look forward to most anxiously, was the perfection which consists in suffering martyrdom: in shedding one's blood for the faith. As he could not obtain this favor, and as it was only granted to a few of his brethren during his lifetime, he endeavored to make up for it by another species of martyrdom, which, as St. Bernard says, is indeed less cruel than the first, but is rendered more bitter by its duration. It is the martyrdom of mortification, and principally that of voluntary poverty. In fact, this poverty, as he compelled its observance, not only placed him and his brethren in the most humiliating situation in the eyes of the world, but deprived them, moreover, of all the comforts and conveniences of life; exposed them to hunger, thirst, want of clothing, and various other annoying discomforts. All this, however, was not, in his view, the consummation of this description of martyrdom. It was still further requisite to suffer patiently, in time of pain and sickness, the want of assistance, which poverty cannot command, to see the disease increase, and death about to follow, from want of necessary succor.

His charity had taken all possible precaution for procuring assistance to the sick of his Order. He had directed that, if any of the brethren fell sick, the others should attend upon them, as they would wish to be themselves waited upon in like circumstances, and with more affection than a mother has for a beloved son. Notwithstanding the great aversion he had to money, he required that the superiors should make application to their spiritual friends, to induce them to give coins, in order to assist the brethren in their sickness. But, as he foresaw that this measure might not always be successful, and that poverty in such a case would put it out of the power of the superiors to procure what was absolutely necessary for the sick, he pointed out to the brethren what perfection called upon them to do:

> "If one of the brethren, in health or in sickness, finds himself unable, through poverty, to procure what his absolute necessities require, provided he has humbly applied to his superior for them for the love of God, let him bear with the privation, for the love of Jesus Christ, who sought for consolation, but found none. It is a suffering which, will be in His sight a substitute for martyrdom; if this should even increase his disease, he must not fear being guilty of suicide, for he has done all he ought to have done, by applying humbly to his superiors." The maxim is well grounded. St. Chrysostom maintains, that to suffer generously the loss of all goods, as did holy Job, is a species of martyrdom. St. Bernard says the same thing of voluntary poverty, and remarks that, in the Beatitudes, a similar reward is promised to the poor and to martyrs. On those principles, is not a Friar Minor to be looked upon as a martyr, who, having embraced the strictest poverty, for the love of Jesus Christ, would, rather than contravene it, endure with patience every evil, and even death, and would generously make to God the sacrifice of his health and of his life, in order to practise this virtue to his last breath? St. Augustine affirms that a Christian suffers martyrdom in his bed, when he declines procuring his cure by forbidden means: thus, a sick Friar Minor, who has not the necessary assistance, brought about by his having embraced poverty, according to the Evangelical counsel, is a martyr to poverty.

Even supposing that it was less owing to poverty, than to the neglect or harshness of his superior, that he was without assistance, he would equally have gained the crown promised to this description of martyrdom, since it would be as an Evangelical pauper that he would suffer and die. But woe to that superior who should procure him such a crown! He would be like to those who have made so many martyrs in the persecution of the Church.

When St. Francis learnt that his brethren, by the sanctity of their lives, and by the efficacy of their preaching, brought back numbers of sinners into the paths of truth, and enkindled in their breasts the love of God, he said that such intelligence was to him as most pleasing odors and precious perfumes, by which he was wholly embalmed; and, in his spiritual joy, he loaded these holy and edifying religious with the most ample benedictions. On the other hand, he fulminated dreadful maledictions against such as dishonored religion by their conduct. "Most holy Lord," he would say, "may those who overthrow and destroy by their bad example what Thou incessantly raisest up by the saintly brethren of the Order, be accursed by Thee and by the whole celestial choir, and also by me, Thy little servant."

Any scandal given to little ones gave him so much affliction and heartsore, that he often might have died of it, if God had not supported him by interior consolations. One day, when he was suffering extreme grief on a subject of this nature, and was praying the Father of Mercies for his children, St. Bonaventure informs us that he received the following answer: "Poor little man, why do you disquiet yourself? Because I have appointed you the pastor of this religion which I have established, are you unmindful that I am its principal protector? I gave you the direction of it, to you who are a simple man, in order that what I should do through you might be attributed, not to human industry, but to my favor. It is I who called those who have entered it; I will preserve them, and provide for their wants; I will substitute others for those who will die off; I will cause some to be born, in order to come into it; and whatever may occur to shake this religion, which is founded on strict poverty. I will assist by My grace, that it shall be always upheld." Up to this day, the world has seen the verification of this prophecy. The Order of Friars Minor has been powerfully attacked, and has still many enemies; nevertheless, it still subsists.

To animate his brethren to perfection, he employed example, rather than precept. When he imposed punishments, if they appeared to him to be very severe, he took them also on himself. Having sent Brother Ruffinus to preach at Assisi without his hood, because he had sought to be excused from preaching, he reflected on the severity of this order, and went himself to the church where Ruffinus was preaching. The latter having left the pulpit to give it up to Francis, he began his discourse, and instilled into his audience so much compunction, that it was evident that God had blessed the obedience of the disciple and the example of the master.

This admirable preceptor taught no virtues which he did not himself practise in an eminent degree; and as those which are exterior make the greatest impression, he practised extreme austerity, in order that the others should imitate him. Having noticed, on a certain occasion, that some of his brethren had relaxed from the extreme poverty of their nourishment, he thus slyly reprimanded them: "My brethren may well believe that, with so infirm a body as mine is, I require better nourishment than what I get, but I am obliged to be their model in everything; for which reason I propose to give up every alleviation, and to cast aside, with disgust, everything resembling delicacy; to be satisfied with little in everything; to make use of those things only which are the commonest, vilest, and most conformable to strict poverty."

Being in a hermitage in some mountains, in mid-winter, when the weather was rigorously cold and severe, his companions prepared a habit for him, in which they lined the breast, to make it somewhat warmer for him, but he made them take this out, saying: "I am placed here to give example to others; my life must be their rule. I know that there is no harm in wearing a warmer habit in the state I am in, but I see many of our brethren who require it as much as I do, and who could not get it. I must therefore bear this poverty with them, and not differ from them in anything, lest it should be thought that I take greater care of myself than of the others. They will more willingly bear the privation of these wants, when they shall see that I voluntarily go without aid." His three companions, the writers of his life, observed that he refused his body the most lawful indulgence, in order that his children should be ashamed of taking those which were less so; and that his maxim was, always to give instruction more by example than by discourse.

He recommended his brethren, also, to preach by example, and, farther on, we shall see some beautiful sentiments in his maxims, relative to preaching. Rodriguez, of the Society of Jesus, an excellent master of spiritual life, mentions, on this subject, a lesson which our saint gave to one of his religious, which we give here, in the very words of the talented academician, who translated the Practice of Christian Perfection, of the pious author. St. Francis, taking one day one of his religious with him, said:—"Let us go and preach"; and thereupon he went out, and after having made a tour round the town, he returned to the convent. "But, Father," said his companion, "are we not going to preach?" "We have done so already," replied the Saint. It was the religious reserve which they had used in walking through the streets, which he considered to be an excellent sermon for the whole town. And, in fact, a mortified and humble exterior leads the people to piety and contempt of the world, it excites to compunction for sin, and raises the heart and desires to heavenly objects. It is a mute exhortation, which has often more effect than the most eloquent and sublime sermons.

To example and precept, the holy Patriarch added frequent and fervent prayers for the spiritual advancement of his children; well knowing that neither he who plants, nor he who waters, contributes to the fruit which the tree bears, but that the interior virtue which fructifies, comes from God. In fine, in order not to be wanting in anything which might be in his power, when his infirmities absolutely prevented his watching over the conduct of his children, he unceasingly exhorted the superiors to fulfil this duty with exactness, and he enforced it by the following powerful motive: that, if one of the brethren should be lost by their fault, they would be accountable for him to Jesus Christ on the day of judgment.

St. Francis, being ill at Assisi, cured a spiritual wound of a more serious nature than that of a scruple. One of his children, named Ricer, of Bologna, Provincial in the Marches of Ancona, a man of a very saintly life, had taken it into his head, at the suggestion of the devil, that the patriarch hated him, because he knew that he was to be damned, and he came to Assisi, in the hopes that this thought would be dissipated, if the saint should receive him kindly. The Saint, who had a revelation as to the state of his mind, and of his arrival at Assisi, said to Brothers Masse and Leo: "Go and meet Brother Ricer, embrace him, and kiss him from me, and tell him that, among all my brethren in the world, I love him the most tenderly." They executed the commission given them, and Ricer found himself strengthened in his faith, and filled with joy, and thanked God for the happy success of his journey. As soon as he appeared, Francis, weak as he was, ran to him, and, embracing him, said, with paternal affection: "Ricer, my dear son, you are, among all our brethren, he whom I love from the bottom of my heart;" and, after having made the sign of the cross upon his forehead, he gave him several kisses, and then added: "Ricer, my dear child, this temptation was visited upon you for your greater good. But if you do not choose to be a gainer at this price, you will henceforward suffer no more from this temptation, nor from any other;" and from that time, he never had another.

The holy Patriarch had so tender a love for his brethren, that he could not bear that a shade of sorrowfulness should pass over their minds, lest they should lose their spiritual joy. "My dear brethren," he said to them, "entertain interiorly and exteriorly the holy joy which God gives. When His servants seek to obtain and preserve His spiritual joy, which has its source in purity of heart, in the fervor of prayer, and in other virtuous practices, the devils can do them no injury; and they say: 'We can do no injury to these servants of God; we have no entry to them; they are always joyful, whether in tribulation or prosperity.' But they are highly gratified when they can deprive them of this happy temper of mind, or, at least, lessen its intensity; because, if they can succeed in instilling any of their own venom into them, they will soon turn what has only the breadth of a hair into a beam, by adding something by little and little, unless we endeavor to destroy their work by the virtue of prayer, of contrition, of confession, and satisfaction. For this reason, my brethren, since spiritual joy comes from purity of conscience and the frequent exercise of fervent prayer, labor principally to acquire these two blessings, in order that you always possess it; I am very anxious to see it in you, and to feel it in myself. It is for the devil and his satellites to be sorrowful; but as to us, we can always rejoice in the Lord."

Although the holy man had occasionally reason to be sorrowful, in consequence of the temptations to which he was exposed, or from the fear of the pains of hell, arising from the remembrance of his sins, yet he was ever gay. He was one day asked the reason of this, and he gave this answer: "My sins sometimes, indeed, make me very sorrowful, and Satan would wish to imprint this sadness on me, in order to make me fall into slothfulness and weariness; but when that occurs, I look on my companion: the spiritual joy I see in him, renews mine, and the temptation passes off. My joy is a torment to the devils, for they envy me the favors I receive from God. I know and see that, when they cannot injure me by making me sorrowful, they endeavor to strip this spiritual joy from my companions, and, if they cannot succeed either with them or with me, they retire in confusion."

We must notice, in this answer of the holy Father, two sorts of sorrow: the one arising from the anguish caused by sin, of which St. Paul says, that "it is according to God, and works penance unto salvation." This does not do away with spiritual joy; on the contrary, it produces it: nothing is sweeter, or more consoling, than the tears shed from the impulse of sincere contrition. The other sorrow is a depression of spirits, brought about by the devil, who endeavors to render us tepid and sluggish, to give us a disgust for pious exercises, and to induce us to give them up. A good conscience causes spiritual joy. No one has truly cause to rejoice, but he who is well with God, faithful to His law, and submissive to His will. A tranquil mind, free and disengaged from the tyranny of the passions, is, in the opinion of Wisdom, a continual feast. It is true happiness: "For a happy life is nothing more," says St. Augustine, "than the joy which is found in truth; that is, in God, who is truth, the sweet light of our souls, our salvation and our repose." Therefore David excites the just of Israel to manifest their joy, and St. Paul said to the Christians: "Rejoice always in the Lord; I say again, rejoice." What constitutes the Kingdom of God is the justice, peace, and joy, which come from the Holy Spirit. This disposition of the heart enables it to resist the evil spirit, according to the words of Esdras to the Jewish people: "The joy of the Lord is our strength." What can the evil spirit do against a soul whose sole pleasure is to serve God, who has no other solace than to love and praise Him? There is, moreover, nothing which makes so great an impression on the people of the world, as witnessing the interior contentment of a truly good man, which is seen in the serenity of his countenance. This is, according to St. Augustine, what compels them to admit that they themselves have not true joy, for that is reserved to God's servants.

It was not alone by the ardor of his zeal, and the tenderness of his affection, that the holy Founder led on his brethren, but by a wonderful discretion and prudence in the government of his Order. Although he used every endeavor to induce his religious to live austerely, he, nevertheless, recommended them to be guided by moderation; he did not countenance indiscreet penances.

Brother Sylvester, the first priest in his Order, having fallen into an illness of languor, brought on by excess in his mortifications, had a wish to eat some grapes: Francis, having been informed of it, hastened to procure him this relief. He took him, as well as he could, into the vineyard of one of his friends, which was near the convent, and, having made him sit down near a plant of vine, he blessed it, and ordered him to eat the grapes, and ate some with him. As soon as the sick man had eaten of them, he found himself perfectly cured, and he frequently afterwards related the circumstance to his brethren, with tears in his eyes, as a proof of the love the holy father bore to his children; it was, also, an effect of his discretion, for, disapproving of Sylvester's excessive austerities, he chose that he should take this sort of remedy, which nature seemed to call for, and it pleased God to render this the subject of a miracle.

This prudent and charitable Father came to know, one night, that one of his children who had fasted too rigidly, could not take repose, in consequence of the hunger which oppressed him. Not to leave him in so deplorable a state, he sent for him, offered him some bread, and pressed him to eat of it, eating some himself first, to give him confidence. The religious got over the shyness he at first felt, and took the nourishment he so greatly required, being well pleased to have been relieved from the peril his life was in, by the prudence and kindness of the Saint, and to see so edifying an example. In the morning, Francis assembled his brethren, and having told them what had occurred in the night, said:—"Brethren, take a precedent from this, not as to what I ate, but that I had recourse to, what was charitable." Then he pointed out to them that virtue should always have discretion for its rule and for its guide; not that discretion which the flesh inspires, but that which has been taught by Jesus Christ, whose most holy life is the finished model of all perfection.

"Let each man," he continued, "have regard to his constitution. If some of you are strong enough to support life well, while eating very little, I do not wish, on that account, that one who requires more nourishment, shall imitate them in this respect: such a one might give his body what is necessary for it; for, as in eating, we are obliged to avoid whatever is superfluous, which is hurtful to the body and soul, so also we must guard against excessive abstinence, and the more so because the Lord requires mercy rather than sacrifice. This is what God says by the Prophet Osee, which means that He prefers the practice of works of mercy to our neighbor, to the exterior exercise of religion; and that this worship which must be rendered Him, is not pleading to Him without mercy. Now, as we are commanded to love our neighbor with a love of charity, St. Thomas teaches us, as does St. Augustine, that the same love obliges us to have a similar regard for our own body; from whence it follows that, this charity not being found in immoderate abstinence, God does not approve of the sacrifice. To this we may add, that it is sometimes the devil who instigates a person to undertake immoderate fasting, in order to render that person incapable of spiritual exercises, and for other evil intentions."

The holy Founder cautioned his brethren to avoid excess in fasting, even more than excess in eating, because he knew that they were all animated by the spirit of mortification. Their fervor was so great that, in fasting very rigorously, they at the same time wore iron girdles, coats of mail, coarse hair-shirts, and took severe disciplines, which brought on frequent illnesses. For this reason he often recommended discretion to them. "My brethren," he said, "if a servant of God gives his body what is reasonable for its nourishment and for its repose, and if the body is nevertheless sluggish, lazy, sleepy at prayer, in watchings, and other good works, it must, then, be chastised, and treated as a horse that refuses to work, or an ass that won't go on, although they are well fed. But, if the body is deprived of its real wants, it is disabled from bearing the yoke of penance, and performing the functions required by the soul; it has, then, every right to complain."

We shall, perhaps, be surprised that St. Francis, who preaches discretion so admirably to his brethren, should have carried his own austerities to excess; but we must bear in mind that he was a man, guided in all things by the Holy Spirit, in whom God was pleased to show the abundant riches of His grace, and whose prodigious penitential exercises were to draw down an abundance of mercy on sinners. Thus, what appeared excesses in his mortifications, arose from his perfect fidelity to the extraordinary impulse he received from above; and this is true prudence.

Fervent persons are occasionally found who would wish to imitate the fastings and other austerities of the saints, but this is presumption, unless they are called thereto by God, and unless the vocation has been well sounded and approved by legitimate authority. The general and safe maxim, in cases of austerities, is not to undertake anything extraordinary, without the consent of superiors and confessors. Before granting any permission of this nature, the constitution and character of the person must be carefully examined, and inquiry minutely made whether the applicant practises regularly the ordinary mortifications, and if he is as zealous in controlling his passions and acquiring the virtues requisite in his station, as for the maceration of his body; for it is often found that those who solicit extraordinary penances, neglect those which are ordinary and common, and who, in mortifying their bodies, do not take sufficient pains to purify their hearts, to become humble, obedient, mild, and charitable.

It may not, perhaps, be believed that the holy Patriarch carried his discretion and condescension even to the buildings and the habits,—he who advocated extreme poverty on these two articles. He had carefully recommended to his brethren to build only small, low houses, surrounded only by hedges, in remote and solitary situations; but, as his own companions tell us, he admitted that in towns, and near towns, it was proper to act otherwise; that, in consequence of the number of religious who were there for the service of the faithful, it was necessary to have the convent surrounded by walls.

His companions also say that he allowed those who required it, to wear a softer and warmer tunic; on this sole condition, however, that the outward garment should be very poor, to keep up the spirit of humility by the contempt the world entertains for such as are poorly clothed. Finally, the same authors testify that, although he was very austere from the moment of his conversion, to his death, with a constitution very delicate and weak, yet he prudently moderated the austerities of his brethren; and that many things which he rigidly refused himself, he allowed to the others, from discretion and from charity. This, indeed, is characteristic in the saints; severe and inflexible to themselves, they spared their neighbors, and were indulgent in their regard; while hypocrites, such as the Pharisees, and certain heretics who resemble them, put heavy burdens on the shoulders of others, which they are unable to carry; overwhelm with austerities those whom they direct, often for the most trifling faults, while they themselves live in comfort and at their ease.

The discretion of St. Francis was apparent in every part of his conduct. Bernard de Besse, one of the writers of his life, and secretary to St. Bonaventure, says that he never spoke to his brethren but in terms of moderation and mildness; that he compassionated the weak, and encouraged the young in the practice of virtue; that he had great respect for old age; that whatever faults a priest might commit, he never reprimanded him but in private; in fine, that he had proper consideration for all those whose birth, merit, or dignity required it.

Brother Guy, who was beatified by the Holy See, and of whom we have before spoken, begged the saint to allow him to build a cell in the fissure of a rock which was opposite to the convent of Celles, near Cortona, in order that he might live there in great solitude, and give himself up to contemplation. Francis, who knew that Guy, although he was only in the novitiate, had the virtue of the ancients, and would raise himself up to an eminent degree of sanctity, permitted him this peculiar retreat, but upon this condition, that it was not to prevent him from attending all the offices said by the community, in order to preserve the uniformity of the observance, and to obviate the illusion which might mix itself up with unusual practices. This was also what the Saint himself practised; he quitted regularly his contemplation, to join in singing the praise of God in community.

St. Bonaventure says that some of his religious asked him one day if he thought it proper that persons who were already learned, when they were admitted into the Order, should continue to study the Holy Scriptures? To which he replied: "This is very pleasing to me, provided they follow the example of Jesus Christ, whom we find to have prayed more than He seems to have read."

A novice, to whom the vicar-general had allowed the particular use of a psalter, came to solicit Francis' confirmation of this permission, and this is the reply he got: "Charlemagne, Orlando, and other great captains, rendered themselves illustrious by their exploits; the martyrs are celebrated in the Church by their sufferings and death; but there are others who aspire to glory by the sole reading of the feats of these persons." The Saint intended to give him to understand that no one is estimable unless by his actions and conduct, and that there is nothing more vain than a reputation grounded on fruitless science.

Doubtless the holy Patriarch wished his brethren to have psalters and breviaries, since they were obliged to say the Divine Office. He knew, also, that books were necessary for them, to enable them, by study, to be capable to instruct their neighbors, according as their vocation required, for he himself read the Scriptures. But he did not approve that any one should have a book for his own peculiar use.

All study which is entered upon more through vanity than piety, and less to gain souls to God than to gain for oneself the praise of man, was his abhorrence.—He said of those whose desire for learning was out of curiosity: "In the day of tribulation, they will find nothing in their hands. It would be better that they should labor now to improve themselves in virtue, in order to have the Lord on their side at that time; for the time will come, when books will be thrown aside as useless. I do not choose that my brethren shall be curious in learning and books; what I wish is, that they be well grounded in humility, simplicity, prayer, and poverty, our mistress. It is the only sure way for their salvation, and for the edification of their neighbor, because they are called to imitate Jesus Christ, who followed and pointed out this path. Many will forsake this path, on pretence of edifying other men by their knowledge; and it will turn out that understanding the Scriptures, by which alone they fancied themselves filled with light, devotion, and the love of God, will be the cause of their remaining cold and empty. Thus, in consequence of having, in pursuit of vain and useless literature, lost the time which ought to have been given to living according to the spirit of the state they had embraced, they will not have it in their power to return to their primitive vocation."

St. Francis looked upon the ministry of preaching as the most agreeable sacrifice which could be offered to the Father of Mercies; this is also the grand idea which St. Paul entertains of it, when he says: "God has given me the grace that I should be the minister of Jesus Christ among the Gentiles, sanctifying the Gospel of God, that the oblation of the Gentiles may be made acceptable, and sanctified by the Holy Ghost." St. Chrysostom concludes from this, that preaching is a sacrifice; that the preacher is the priest; that an attentive and devout audience is the victim; that the Word of God is the sword which immolates, spiritually, and the grace of the Holy Ghost the fire which consumes. What exalted sentiments must not a preacher entertain, in exercising this sort of priesthood; and with what spirit of devotion should not those attend who are thus holily immolated!

The ardor of his love for Jesus Christ, and his great zeal for the salvation of souls, made him esteem all preachers very venerable. His intention was, that some of his Order should be brought up to that duty, and that they should be respected by the others, because it is they who instil life, who combat the infernal enemy, and who enlighten the world. But he desired that they should exercise their ministry in a spirit of charity, even more by example, by prayers, and tears, than by eloquent discourses.

"I desire," he said, "that these ministers of the Word of God should apply themselves solely to spiritual exercises, and let nothing turn them from this; for, as they are chosen by the great King to declare His will to the people, it is requisite that they should learn, in the privacy of prayer, what they are to make known in their sermons; and that they should be interiorly warmed, in order to make use of language which shall kindle fire in the hearts they address. Those who make use of their own lights, and who savor the truths they preach, are very praiseworthy; but it is a bad division when all is given to preaching, and little or nothing to devotion. As to those who sell their labors for the oil of approbation, such persons excite my pity."

"They are true brethren, whom I call Knights of the Round Table, who hide themselves in solitary places, to have better opportunities of devoting themselves to prayer, and whose sanctity, well known to God, is sometimes unknown to men, or even to their brethren. One day they will be presented by angels to the Lord, who will say to them: 'My beloved children, here are the souls that have been saved by your prayers, by your tears, by your good example. Receive now the fruit of the labors of those who only make use of their learning for this object. Because you have been faithful over a few things, I will set you over many.' They will thus enter into the joy of the Lord, loaded with the fruit of their virtues; while the others, who have employed themselves in studying the way of salvation, in order to teach it, without following it themselves, will appear naked and empty-handed at the tribunal of Jesus Christ, having on them marks of grief and confusion."

All that St. Francis says against vain learning,—a learning which is ostentatious and void of devotion,—is founded on the beautiful words of our Saviour: "Many will say to me on that day, Lord, Lord, have we not prophesied in Thy name? And then I will profess unto them, I never knew you, depart from me you that work iniquity;" and on these of St. Paul: "If I speak with the tongues of men and of angels, and have not charity, I am become as sounding brass, or a tinkling cymbal." "I chastise my body, and bring it into subjection, lest, perhaps, when I have preached to others, I myself should become a castaway."

But it may not be concluded from this that the holy patriarch had any wish to prevent his brethren from studying and becoming learned; for, 1st, he was not unaware of what St. Augustine teaches on that head. That learning is good in itself; that it is a gift of God; that it is most useful, when charity employs it; that it serves as a guide to piety; and that, when it has the Holy Scripture for its object, it powerfully excites to the love of God. How many learned men there are in whom humility, simplicity, and all the other virtues, are combined with deep reading! 2d. He positively declared, as has been reported upon the evidence of St. Bonaventure that he was well pleased that his brethren should study; it was his wish that schools should be opened in his Order, and he himself, as has been already noticed, instituted St. Anthony of Padua lecturer in theology. 3d. He wished to have his brethren Apostolical men, employed in the holy ministry for the salvation of souls, and he had inserted in his Rule a chapter which solely relates to the instruction of preachers. He desired, in consequence, that the Friars Minor should acquire the learning requisite for fulfilling their functions, which, in the ordinary course of things, is impossible without study. "It was, certainly, his intention," adds St. Bonaventure, "that his brethren should apply themselves to the study of the Holy Scriptures, for, one day, having but one copy of the New Testament, he divided it into leaves, which he distributed among them, that all might read and instruct themselves at the same time." The holy doctor maintains, in another place, that there are no religious who, by their position, are more employed in preaching than the Friars Minor; and he adds, that, as St. Francis required them to be correct and accurate in their discourses, it is clear that he himself obliges them to study, since, without such application, it is impossible to be accurate.

If the blessed founder has spoken more of humility and piety than of learning and study, it is, in the first place, because he well knew that, naturally, persons are more prone to learn than to practise; and, secondly, because the virtues which purify the heart, are gifts more precious and necessary than learning, which only enlightens the mind; and, in the third place, because he knew what St. Paul says, that "knowledge puffeth up," that a learned person easily becomes proud and presumptuous, if charity does not keep him in humility, and in mistrust of himself. Finally, let not his words be misconstrued to give color, under pretence of piety, to laziness and ignorance. He preferred, to vain and sterile learning, the humility and simplicity of the poor brethren, who spent their time in prayer: this was no more than right. "A rustical holiness," St. Jerome remarks, "is more valuable than vicious learning and criminal eloquence." But the blessed patriarch only spoke of the lay-brethren, who were not intended for the sacred ministries, or of those clerics whose talents were not equal to being employed in them, and whose occupations were limited to prayer and labor. In respect to the others, who, by study, might render themselves capable of serving their neighbor spiritually, he certainly would have censured them, had they continued in ignorance, even under the pretext of prayer and manual labor,—he, who had adopted, as we have seen, the maxim, that "nothing is preferable to the salvation of souls." He well knew that all the brethren did not resemble some among them whom God had supernaturally enlightened, and who, without any other aid than that of prayer, had sufficient light to be able to announce the Word of God. St. Jerome says, that as a man of talent must not persuade himself that holiness consists in the beauty of his composition, and in the ornament of eloquence, so also a simple and unpolished man must not imagine that his ignorance constitutes him a saint. This is even still clearer, when this man may not be ignorant. Now, it is self-evident that a Friar Minor, cleric, or priest, is obliged, in conscience, according to the talent he has received from Heaven, to study carefully, in order to be competent to fulfil properly the ministries of preaching and of the confessional; since the spirit of his vocation, and of his Order, is to labor for the salvation of souls. But he must always have before his eyes what his blessed Father wrote to St. Anthony of Padua: "I agree that you should teach the brethren sacred theology, in such manner, however, that the spirit of holy prayer be not extinguished, either in yourself or in others, according to the rule of which we have made profession."

While the holy Patriarch was ill at Sienna, a religious of the Order of the Friars Preachers, who was a doctor of theology, and a truly learned man, put several very difficult questions to him: he answered them so learnedly, and so clearly, that the doctor was quite surprised, and spoke of the circumstance with admiration. Truly, said he, the theology of this holy Father is an eagle, which soars to a great height; it is raised up, as if with wings, by the purity of the heart, and by contemplation, while our knowledge is as that of animals which crawl on the ground.

Thus, according to St. Athanasius, the great Anthony, who was illiterate, showed admirable knowledge in his controversy with the heretical Arians, and in his replies to pagan philosophers who strove to puzzle him. So also, according to the testimony of Sulpicius Severus, no one explained the Holy Scriptures more clearly than the celebrated Bishop of Tours, St. Martin, who had never studied.

Another Friar Preacher asked St. Francis how he was to understand these words of the Saviour to the Prophet Ezekiel: "If thou speakest not to the impious that he may be converted from his wicked way and live, the same wicked man shall die in his iniquity; but I will require his blood at thy hand." The humble Father having at first excused himself! saying that he should apply to learned theologians to learn the sense of the Holy Scriptures; but, as the religious urged him, nevertheless, to give his opinion, and expressed a great wish to have it preferably to that of others whom he had consulted, he gave him this answer: "I believe these words, if taken in the full extent, to mean, that the servant of God must be by holiness, and the good odor of his life, a torch which burns and enlightens, in order that the splendor of his example may be as a voice which censures the impious; for this is the way to warn and reprehend them all: if he act otherwise, and scandalize his neighbor, he will not escape the punishment of heaven."

St. Francis was not ignorant that the literal and immediate sense of this passage is, that pastors, and all those who are in authority, are obliged to instruct, warn, censure, and correct those who are committed to their charge; that they become guilty of the loss of souls, if they are silent when they ought to speak. He himself, faithful in the mission he had received from God and the Holy See, never ceased from exhorting his brethren to sanctify themselves, and from urging sinners to be converted; but he found in the above passage a more extended sense, and one of greater moral influence, which was, to preach by example; and he adhered to this for many reasons:—1. Because words produce small effect when they are not backed by example. 2. Because there are a greater number of superiors who instruct and censure, than of those who edify by example. 3. Because the number of persons who have no right to instruct and reprove, is the greater, and it is good that they should know that God will call them to account for the good example which it was their duty to have given, which might have contributed to the conversion of sinners. All this shows how solid and proper the Saint's reply was.

His style is plain, because he formed it on the Gospel, from which he would not in any degree deviate—besides that, his was not the age of elegant Latinity; but in all that he has written we do not find anything that is not clear and intelligible—there are even passages insinuating and persuasive: we have also reason to admire some parts which are beautiful from their simplicity. Let the cleverest men read his description of the rich sinner on his death-bed, and he will be obliged to admit that it would be impossible to draw a more natural or more striking portrait.

He had so completely the talent of persuasion, that neither popes, cardinals, nobles, nor any other persons could resist his appeals; whatsoever he wished, they complied with. It is not easy, for the sake of piety, to persuade to that which is contrary to the interests of a family: nevertheless, St. Francis succeeded in this. The following is an example, which, relating only to a very common subject, we, notwithstanding, select, because it contains wholesome instruction:—

> The Saint was one day sweeping in a country church, according to his usual practice, when a man, whose name was John, and who was ploughing in an adjoining field, came and took the broom from his hands, and after having swept the whole church, he said to him: "Brother, what I have heard of you and of your brethren, has inspired me with an idea of serving God as you do. I did not know how to come to you, but, since it has pleased God that I should find you here as I had wished, I offer myself to you: do with me as you please." Francis, knowing by an interior light, that this man had been sent him by the Lord, resolved to receive him into his Order, and after having instructed him in the Rule, he said to him: "If you resolve upon joining this Institute, you must renounce all you have, and give it to the poor." John went immediately to his plough, unyoked the oxen, and brought one to Francis, saying: "I have been long in the service of my father, and I maintain the family by my labor; I think I may take this ox for my reward, and do with it as you shall direct me." He immediately went home to take leave of his parents, and desired them to take care of the plough.

The parents, alarmed when they learnt his intention, ran in despair to the church, where Francis still was, and conjured him not to take a man from them who was so useful in work, who earned their means of living. He replied with mildness, and then said that he would come to dine with them, and sleep at their house, and would endeavor to console them. He went, and after dinner, addressing himself to John's father, he said: "My dear host, your son wishes to serve God, and it is God who has inspired him with this thought. This ought not to give you any displeasure; on the contrary, it ought to be gratifying to you, and you should give God thanks that He has been pleased to select one of your family for His service. This will be no small gain to you; for, in place of this son whom you give up, you will gain as many children and brethren as there are religious in the Order he is about to join. Moreover, your son is one of God's creatures; and if God has destined him for Himself, who shall dare to resist His will? Who shall say to Him, 'Why dost Thou do thus?' He is all-powerful, and He is also just. He only asks for what belongs to Him. May His will therefore be done, and may His mercy be extended to your son, whom I cannot and ought not to refuse to receive into the house of God, which he so anxiously wishes me to do. All that I can, and will do for you, is, to inform him to leave you the ox he had destined for the poor, according to the Gospel, and that, abandoning to the world what belongs to the world, he come stripped of everything, to throw himself into the arms of Jesus Christ."

This reasoning was so convincing to the parents, that they assented willingly and cheerfully to their son's leaving them, whom before they thought they could not part with. Human prudence will not fail to say that he ought to have remained with his parents, to provide for their subsistence by his labor; but will it say that James and John, being called by Jesus Christ, ought not to have left Zebedee, their father, who was poor, and whom they maintained by their fishing? Our Lord, in calling them, desired that they should obey His voice, and leave to Providence to provide for the subsistence of their father. St. Francis well knew that, under any other circumstances, this laborer would have been bound to work to provide for his parents; but, as he knew that his call was from God to a religious state of life, he wisely judged that the Lord would assist the family by some other means, and that the vocation ought to be followed.

The supernatural and miraculous gifts which St. Francis had received from God, gave great weight to his discourses. A man, who casts out devils, who raises the dead to life, who cures the sick, whose prophecies are verified, who discovers spirits, who commands animals, and makes them obey him,—a man who performs these prodigies, and many others, is listened to as if he were an angel, when he speaks.

The polish of language which St. Francis neglected, was wonderfully compensated by Divine Power. St. Bonaventura says that the Holy Ghost, from whom he had received his unction and his mission, inspired him with abundance of words to preach His holy doctrine, and continually assisted him; and that Jesus Christ, who is the strength of the Father, came invariably to his aid; that, indeed, he had recourse to the ornaments of human eloquence, in his discourses, but that inspiration was very perceptible; that his preaching was a great fire, which penetrated quite to the bottom of hearts, with so much efficacy, that the most obdurate were softened, and had recourse to penance. Men and women, young and old, nobles and plebeians, flocked in crowds to see and hear this extraordinary man, whom God had sent them. He seemed to them, in fact, to be a man from the other world, when they saw him, with his eyes elevated to heaven, with the view of drawing them thither; and, as soon as he spoke, they felt their hearts moved to compunction. All that he said against the public scandals, was received with respect; those whose crimes he censured, whatever confusion they might feel from it, did not dare complain— not even those in the highest station. Some of the learned were likewise noticed amongst his auditory, and they, more than any others, admired the powerful influence of his discourses, knowing him to be a man who had not gone through any course of study. In short, the public was so charmed by hearing him, that, after preaching one day at Cortona, and wishing to return to the convent of Celles, the guards at the gates of the town would not let him pass. After having preached for three successive days there he only got leave to go, after the strongest entreaties, and after having promised to leave Brother Guy there, whose sanctity he assured them would free Cortona from many evils. God punished, in a most frightful manner, an insolent young girl, who was making a noise with a sort of drum during the Saint's sermon; he called upon her three times to be quiet, but she laughed at him, and he was then inspired to say, in a loud voice, "Devil, take what is thy own." At the same moment the girl was raised up into the air, and she was seen no more. By this dreadful example, God proposed to teach them the respect they were bound to have for the instructions which His servants teach them, as once He taught the faithful not to lie to the Holy Ghost, by the deaths of Ananias and Sapphira, which followed the reproach which St. Peter had made them.

St. Bonaventure assures us that the gift of prophecy appeared in our Saint with great splendor; that not only did he foretell things to come, but also spoke of those things which were happening in his absence, as if they were present before his eyes; that he penetrated to the bottom of hearts, and saw the most secret recesses of consciences, so that it might have been said that he inspected the mirror of eternal light, and that its admirable splendor uncovered to him what was most hidden.

God revealed to him, in prayer, the loss of one of the religious, who had the reputation of being a saint, but who was so peculiar in everything, that, in order the more rigidly to keep silence, he usually confessed by signs. The blessed Father having come to the convent in which this religious was, he saw him, and spoke of him to the others, who were loud in their praises of him. "Brethren," said he, "cease all these praises, and give them not to inventions of the devil; know that all this is but a temptation, and an extraordinary illusion." The brethren could not persuade themselves that so many marks of perfection were but covers to imposture; but, a few days after, this pretended saint left the Order, which proved that St. Francis had probed to the bottom of his soul.

He knew, in the same manner, why another, who seemed to be adorned with every virtue, had thrown off the habit of the Order; and he replied to his brethren who expressed their surprise at it: "Do not be astonished, my brethren; this wretch is lost, because he was not grounded in humility, and in the fear of God. Believe me that, without this foundation, it is fruitless to endeavor to become virtuous."

Of two religious who were returning from the Terra di Lavoro, he saw in spirit that the senior did not by any means edify his companion. On their arrival, he asked the younger what had occurred on the road, who then replied, that all had gone on well. "Take care," answered Francis, "take care, and don't say what is false, on pretence of humility. I know, I know; but wait a little, and you will see." In fact, the giver of scandal abandoned his vocation shortly after.

The charitable father received, with great kindness, one of the brethren who had apostatized from the Order, and now returned, he even gave him the kiss of peace. But, pointing out to him the gallows erected upon a height, at some distance, he said: "If the devil induce you to leave the Order a second time, he will lead you to be hanged on the gallows which you see from hence." This weak penitent did not profit from this warning, but left the Order again, and led a libertine life, was taken up for a robbery, and hanged on the spot pointed out. St. Francis might have said of those, as St. John did of the apostates who left the Church, "They went out from us, but they were not of us; for, if they had been of us, they would no doubt have remained with us:" that is to say, that they were not firm in the Christian religion.

The knowledge of the human heart belongs to God alone; even the angels have it not unless imparted to them by His light, and He was pleased to communicate that light to Francis. We have had several instances of this, but we must add the following: The blessed Father, being at the hermitage of Grecio, two of his brethren came, from a great distance off, urged by a strong desire to see him, and to receive his blessing, which they had long been desirous of. Unfortunately, they reached the hermitage when he was retired to his cell, from which he did not come out to receive visits, and they could not see him. As they were going away, greatly disappointed, he came out, contrary to his usual custom, called them, and blessed them in the name of Jesus Christ, and made the sign of the cross upon their foreheads, as they had wished. Humanly speaking, he could not have known that they were come, but he knew it in spirit, as well as if he had seen them.

Having restored peace, and performed some splendid miracles in a town, he left the place early in the morning, without having taken leave of the bishop, who had given him a most honorable reception. At a spot where three roads diverged, he did not know which one he ought to take, and desired Brother Masse, who was his companion, to turn round and round, no doubt to put his obedience to the test. When he began to be giddy, he ordered him to stop, and to follow the road which was before him. Masse went first, and said to himself, "How uncivil! how simple! He not only has not taken leave of the bishop who received him with so much kindness, but he makes me turn round and round as a child." This interior murmuring did not last; these reflections followed: "How could I have so much pride as to despise a man who is so evidently beloved by God? Fool that I am, I deserve to go to hell for daring to censure the actions of Francis, through whom the Lord works such wonders, and whom I ought to look upon as an angel. And, after all, what reason has he given me for censuring him? He left the town without having taken leave of the bishop, but it was to avoid fresh honors being shown him; he made me turn round and round, but he made me take the right road." Then Francis exclaimed: "Ah, Brother Masse, how different are these feelings from those first entertained! From whence do these come, and from whence did those others arise?" Masse, seeing that his thoughts were discovered, threw himself at the Saint's feet, and solicited his pardon.

A particular gift which Francis received from God, was the control of animals. He gave them his commands, and they obeyed him, they did whatever he pleased; it was, moreover, noticed that they showed a sort of affection for him, and applauded what he did in their way. Upon which two observations occur. The first is taken from St. Bonaventure, who says that the state of innocence was represented in the power which God gave to His Servant over animals. Adam, just and innocent, had absolute control over them, and he exercised it in giving to each of them its proper name, when God made them pass before him, as we read in Genesis. His sin caused him to lose his privilege, with all the others which had been attached to this happy state; and we experience, as he did, the revolt of the animals, in punishment of his having disobeyed God. But when an eminent sanctity has brought men more to original justice, and has, in some measure, reestablished them in a state of innocence, it has sometimes pleased the Almighty to restore them to some of the privileges which man enjoyed in those times, and, in particular, this control over animals. This is what is seen in well-authenticated acts of many saints, and, in what St Bonaventure relates of St. Francis, on the testimony of ocular witnesses, as well as on the evidence of facts which were of public notoriety.

The second thing which deserves notice is, that, when this holy man compelled animals to obey him, and when they appeared to be attached to him, it never occurred but when it was to give authority to the Word of God, to do some good to a neighbor, to give a salutary lesson, or to excite to the practice of some virtue, as we shall now see. It is another proof that these marvels had their source in God, who proposes, in all He does, some end worthy of His wisdom.

Francis left Assisi one day, to go to preach, not having any longer a doubt but that he and his brethren were called for the service of souls, after the mission they had received from God, and from the Supreme Pontiff; this was confirmed by supernatural lights, as we have seen above. Being near to the Town of Bevagna, he saw on a particular spot a number of birds collected, of various species, and he went up to them, and said: "My sisters, listen to the word of God; you have great reason to praise your Creator; He has covered you with feathers; He has given you wings wherewith to fly; He has placed you in the air, where the breathing is so pure; and He provider you with everything which is necessary, without giving you any trouble." While he was thus speaking and saying other similar things, the birds remained where they were, turning towards him, and those which were perched on the branches of trees, bending their heads, as if to listen to what he said. It was a curious thing to observe the joy they appeared to feel and make known by their motions; they stretched their necks, they spread their wings, opened their beaks, and looked anxiously at the zealous preacher, who walked about in the midst of them, and sometimes touched them with his habit, without any of them stirring. They only took to flight after he had given them leave, and made on them the sign of the cross, to bless them.

It was God's intention to honor the ministry of the Saint, in the eyes of his companions, by this miracle, which they witnessed, and the circumstances of which they communicated to St. Bonaventure. It was also to show the attention which ought to be given to the truths of salvation; and this is the reason why Francis, in turning to them, said, with admirable candor: "I am very neglectful in not having as yet preached to the birds." He observed, by this apparent simplicity, which was full of good sense, that men often fail to listen to the preachers, as the birds had seemingly listened to him; in the same sense in which St. Martin had said, when complaining of the insensibility of the men of his times: "They do not attend to me, though the serpents obey me." This means that, with the aid of reason and grace, they will not do what unreasonable animals necessarily do, by the impulse of divine power.

But why preach to birds? will the sages of this age ask; but why did David say what the Church repeats daily in her Divine Office? "Whales, and all that move in the waters, bless the Lord. All ye beasts and cattle, fowls of the air, bless the Lord." The three young men who were in the furnace at Babylon, said the same thing. A heart full of love and gratitude would wish that all creatures should have hearts and tongues, to glorify the Author of their being;

he knows that even the beasts praise Him by the marks they bear of His power, wisdom, and goodness; in seeing them, in speaking to them, he commemorates His sovereign greatness.

On leaving Bevagna, Francis went to preach in the Borough of Alviano, and not being able to make himself heard, in consequence of the noise the swallows made, who had their nests there, he spoke these words to them: "Swallows, my sisters, you have made yourselves heard long enough; it is now my turn to speak. Listen, then, to the Word of God, and keep silence while I preach." Immediately, as if they had understood what he said, they ceased their noise, and remained where they were, to the end of his sermon. The fruit of this miracle was to revive the fervor and piety of the assembly, who glorified God, and listened to the preacher with wonderful deference. The circumstance was soon spread, and produced everywhere a similar effect.

St. Bonaventure, who gives us this anecdote, adds, that, sometime afterwards, a scholar at Paris, who was of good conduct, having been interrupted in his studies by the chirping of a swallow, said to his companions: "This is one of those who interrupted the blessed Francis in his sermon, and which he silenced;" having then addressed the swallow, he said, with great faith: "In the name of Francis, the servant of God, I order you to be silent and to come to me." It was instantly silent, and came to him; in his surprise he let it go, and was not again troubled by it. It was thus it pleased God to honor the name of His servant.

Other examples are found in the Saint's life, of the power he exercised over animals, when, by their noise, or by any other means, they interrupted his sermons or prayers, as on his return from Syria, near the lagunes of Venice, where he saw a great number of birds who were singing. He went into the midst of them to say his office, with his companions, but the noise the birds made prevented their hearing each other; Francis, upon that, ordered them to cease singing, till he had finished his office, and, in fact, says the holy doctor, the author of his life, from that moment they ceased their chirping until the ffice, being finished, he gave them leave to resume their song, which they did, as before. He took this opportunity to settle some of his religious there, to celebrate the praises of the Lord, as has been before noticed, St. Ambrose speaks of a circumstance as well known to all the world, that some of the faithful, having been assembled in a spot where the croaking of the frogs greatly disturbed them, a priest commanded them to be quiet, and to show respect for holy things, and that they immediately ceased from making any noise, and that these irrational animals respected what they were incapable of understanding.

We have already seen that when Francis was at Grecio, he freed the country from the wolves which had ravaged it. At Gubio, he tamed one in an extraordinary manner. He took it into the public square where he preached, and having pointed out to his auditors that God sends sometimes these carnivorous animals to warn sinners to return to their duties, he addressed the wolf, and made an agreement with it, the clauses of which were, that the inhabitants should feed it, and that the wolf should do no injury to any of them. This was faithfully attended to on both sides. During two years the animal came to the town to feed, and did no injury to anyone. The holy man had tamed, in a similar manner, at Carinola, a fox that stole all the poultry of a poor old woman, and from which she received no injury afterwards. Similar traits are found in the lives of many saints, whose acts are admitted to be authentic and certain, by the most talented critics.

St. Athanasius remarks, in the life of St. Anthony, that wild animals causing great damage in a field which he cultivated, he took one gently, and said to all the others, while speaking to the one he had caught: "Why do you injure me, who never did you any harm? go, and in the name of the Lord, never come here anymore." The holy doctor adds, that from that time they were never again seen in that place, as if they had been afraid of disobeying him. Sulpicius Severus relates of St. Martin, that he had an extraordinary control over all animals. Resting himself one day with his disciples, on the bank of a river, he saw a snake swimming over, and he ordered it in the name of the Lord to swim back again, upon which it was seen to return with as much speed as it had come. James, who wrote the life of St. Columban, given by the learned Father Mabillon, after Surius, states that the crows and the bears obeyed him, and that all the beasts of the field came at his call, in the same manner as those which are domesticated. It was in order to teach men to esteem and imitate a virtue which the Lord caused to be respected, even by dumb animals.

St. Francis, when at Rome, in 1222, had always with him a little lamb, to remind him of the Lamb of God, who chose to be sacrificed for us. When he was about to leave the eternal city, he confided the little animal to the care of the Lady of Septisal, the illustrious widow of whom we have often had occasion to speak. The little lamb, as if it had been trained to spiritual exercises by the holy man, followed this lady to church, stayed there, and returned with her, never leaving her. If she was behind her usual time of rising in a morning, it would go to her bed, where, by bleating or striking the bed with its head, or other motions, it seemed to call upon her to rise, and offer her grateful prayer to God. The lady was much attached to this lamb, and took care of it, says St. Bonaventure, as a disciple of Francis, which had become her instructor in devotion. A present was made to the holy Father, at St. Mary of the Angels, of a sheep; he received it thankfully, because of the innocence and simplicity of which it was a symbol, and he said to it, as if it could understand him, that it was necessary it should assist at the praises of the Lord, without incommoding the brethren; the sheep obeyed with great punctuality. When the religious went to the choir, to sing the office, the sheep went of itself to the church, placed itself at the foot of the altar of the Blessed Virgin, bent in its fore-legs, and bleated in a low tone, as if to pay its homage. It did the same at Mass, when the Host was elevated. St. Bonaventure remarks, that this animal, by the respect it manifested during the celebration of the Sacred Mysteries, taught the Christians the deep reverence with which they ought to assist at Mass, and at the same time passed a deserved censure on those who are irreverent or indevout during its celebration.

The smallest things raised the heart of St. Francis to God, and he made use of them to create similar feelings in the hearts of his disciples. The chirping of a grasshopper, which was on a fig tree, near his cell, inspired him with fresh fervor; he called it, and it came to him directly, and he made it sing on his hand, which it began anew, whenever he required it. At the end of eight days he said to his companions: "Let it now go; it has incited us long enough to praise God;" at the very moment the grasshopper flew away, and was seen no more. One day, as he was about to take his collation with Brother Leo, he felt himself interiorly consoled, on hearing a nightingale sing. He begged Leo to sing the praises of God alternately with the bird; the latter having excused himself, alleging the badness of his voice, he himself responded to the bird, and continued to do so till night, when he was obliged to give over, acknowledging that the little bird had beaten him. He made it come upon his hand, and praised it for having sung so well, fed it, and it was only after he had desired it to leave him, and given it his blessing, that the nightingale flew away.

In the impression which the power of God affected upon animals, in favor of St. Francis, there was this further circumstance, which was marvellous: that they seemed to have an affection for him, and appeared pleased when they saw him. It is St. Bonaventure who gives several examples of this.

The Servant of God, going to Sienna, passed near a flock of sheep which were feeding in a meadow. He greeted them, as was his custom, with an air of kindness, and immediately the sheep, the rams, and the lambs, left their pasture, came to him, lifted up their heads to greet him in their manner, which was greatly wondered at by the shepherds and by his companions. Hares and rabbits were presented to him, which had been caught alive; they were put before him on the ground, and they immediately sprang into his arms. Although he gave them their liberty, they remained with him, and he was obliged to have them removed far off into the country, by some of his religious, and put in a place of safety.

On the banks of the Lake of Rieti, a fisherman gave him a live water-fowl. After having kept it a little while, he tried to make it fly away, but in vain. He then raised his eyes to Heaven, and remained for more than an hour in a state of ecstasy, after which he mildly ordered the bird to go away and praise the Lord, and he gave it his blessing. The bird showed signs of pleasure by its motions, and flew away. On the same lake, a large fish which had been just caught, was presented to him; he held it for some time in his hand, and then put it back in the water. The fish remained in the same place, playing in the water before him, as if out of regard for him; it could not leave him, and did not disappear till it had received the Saint's leave, together with his blessing.

The first time that St. Francis went to Mount Alverno, he was surrounded by a multitude of birds, which lit upon his head, on his shoulders, on his breast, and on his hands, evincing by their beaks and wings the pleasure his arrival caused them, which he noticed to his companions, as a mark of the will of God that he should remain in this mountain. When he came thither, and received the stigmata there, the birds greeted him in a similar manner; and a hawk, which could only have come thither by a supernatural impulse, attached itself peculiarly to his person. When the hour of the night drew near, at which Francis rose to pray, the bird did not fail to come and make a noise at the door of his cell. This punctuality was very pleasing to the Saint, because it caused him to be watchful; but when his infirmities were more severe than usual, the bird, well taught by Him who controlled its movements, did not come to wake him till sunrise, and even then did not make so much noise as usual.

The numerous miracles of St. Francis attached men to him in a scarcely less degree than his extraordinary sanctity; and the gift he possessed of unbounded love—called for their admiration. This is the portrait we find of him in the legend we have before alluded to: "Our blessed ather was agreeable to all. Joy, serenity, kindness, and modesty, were perceptible in his countenance. He was naturally mild and affable, compassionate, liberal, prudent, discreet, gave sound advice, was faithful to his word, and full of courage; he was easy in his manners, accommodating himself to all sorts of tempers; he was all to all, he was a saint among the saintly, and among sinners, as if he was one of them; his conversation was graceful, and his manner insinuating; clear in his reasoning, energetic and compliant in matters of business; and, finally, simple in his actions and words."

These are qualifications well calculated to make their possessor beloved, particularly when joined, as in the case of St. Francis, with the purest morals, with the most ardent charity, the most profound humility, and a countenance which seemed angelical. After the portrait of his mind, we find in the same narrative the following description of his person: "He was of middle size, neither short nor tall, but well shaped. His face was oval, his forehead smooth, his eyes black and modest, his mouth pretty; his hair was of chestnut color, his beard black, but scanty, his body very thin, his skin delicate, his speech pleasing and animated, his voice strong and piercing, but altogether mild and sonorous."

We must receive in their true sense what was understood in saying that "he was simple in his actions and words." The term simplicity has two significations in English.—Firstly it is used to describe a person of little mind, narrow-minded, dull, not well informed, weak and credulous; it is also used to express candor, ingenuousness, and uprightness; to describe a person who is natural, without artfulness. It is in this sense that it is said that the greatest geniuses are the most simple; enemies of subtlety and trick, which are only appropriate to narrow minds. The simplicity of the just, in Scriptural language, is true virtue, solid without drawback, purity of heart, uprightness of intention; in opposition to every sort of duplicity or disguise—everything that St. Paul calls "the prudence of the flesh; the wisdom of this world." St. Gregory so explains it. This does not exclude prudence, but only malice and double dealing. Our Blessed Lord warns us "to be prudent as serpents, and simple as doves." St. Paul says: "I would have you to be wise in good, and simple in evil." Every Christian must be simple in faith, submitting himself purely and simply to the decisions of the Church, without any endeavor to elude them by crafty evasions, as some do in so scandalous a manner; simple in the intercourse of society, being frank and sincere, doing injury to no one; simple in devotion, going straight to God; following the way pointed out by the Gospel; not resembling those of whom the wise man says: "They go two ways, and have two hearts," the one for God, and the other for the world.

Such was the simplicity of St. Francis. He was simple because he had no other intention in his mind, no other movement in his heart, than to be conformed to Jesus Christ. In order to imitate His poverty, His humility, His sufferings, all His virtues, he did many things far above the ordinary rules of human wisdom; and, as to his language, it was formed on that of the Gospel.

St. Francis was simple, but he had great qualities of mind and heart; and his simplicity was a perfection in him—not a defect. If it induced him to do things of which human prudence disapproves, it was because he was guided by Divine light; it was because he sought to be despised by the world, to render himself more conformable to Jesus Christ. Men of his age were not deceived by it; they discovered the principle which made him act and speak with such simplicity. His constant endeavor to humble himself, and draw on himself contempt, only gave them a greater esteem for his person, and they loaded him with honors. If our age deems itself wiser, what reason has it for not doing similar justice?

May the tender holiness of St. Francis, which we have endeavored to portray, excite all those who read his life to love God, and to manifest their love, not only by their actions, but by their patience in adversities! May they love Him so, that the sweet violence of their ardent love separate them from all that is beneath the Heavens, and wholly absorb them, may they be enabled to kneel in spirit at the side of St. Francis and pray with him from the bottom of their heart:

My God and My All!

INDEX

A

abuse, 133, 169, 218, 266
Acts of the Martyrs, xiv
admiration, xii, 8, 22, 55, 174, 181, 189, 203, 206, 239, 271, 296, 307
agility, 213
Ambrose, xvi, xxi, 16, 56, 84, 122, 191, 197, 304
angels, vii, xiv, 1, 17, 18, 20, 24, 41, 42, 43, 44, 47, 53, 55, 56, 59, 63, 65, 66, 72, 75, 78, 87, 88, 98, 100, 104, 105, 107, 110, 131, 137, 140, 142, 145, 153, 156, 164, 165, 166, 171, 177, 178, 184, 185, 186, 187, 189, 195, 198, 199, 211, 216, 233, 236, 249, 254, 260, 262, 264, 268, 272, 273, 275, 276, 294, 301, 306
anger, 15, 51, 58, 83, 89
anxiety, 90, 107, 120, 131, 157, 202, 266
apparitions, xi, xiii, xiv, 18, 206
astonishment, xii, 2, 6, 40, 53, 90, 108, 126, 153, 162, 173, 175, 208, 223, 262
attachment, 5, 42, 95, 97, 140, 172, 227, 250
authority, xiii, xviii, xx, xxiii, 12, 33, 94, 95, 96, 103, 104, 111, 113, 114, 122, 132, 142, 161, 175, 192, 200, 209, 235, 258, 259, 291, 297, 302
aversion, 67, 105, 248, 284
Avitus, xvi

B

benefits, 20, 28, 42, 79, 81, 98, 173, 204
birds, 38, 81, 248, 270, 280, 282, 303, 304, 307
blame, 151, 255, 257, 279
blindness, 164, 213
blood, 10, 59, 62, 118, 131, 137, 152, 162, 169, 184, 206, 225, 240, 241, 242, 245, 283, 297
brothers, 98, 115, 117, 170, 171, 219, 229, 234, 274, 275, 279

C

Catholic Church, xxv, 120, 246
Catholics, xxii, 77, 95
children, xiv, 11, 24, 26, 27, 30, 34, 35, 36, 40, 44, 46, 47, 48, 52, 58, 63, 78, 81, 87, 89, 90, 91, 92, 94, 95, 111, 114, 117, 119, 123, 125, 139, 141, 163, 171, 172, 173, 188, 190, 191, 192, 211, 222, 225, 226, 227, 229, 232, 236, 238, 240, 241, 247, 248, 250,253, 275, 276, 285, 286, 287, 289, 294, 298
Christianity, 67, 111, 133, 246
Christians, xiii, xiv, xv, xxi, 1, 16, 83, 117, 118, 126, 127, 128, 130, 131, 132, 133, 134, 147, 148, 149, 150, 155, 159, 167,

170, 172, 177, 187, 193, 200, 203, 218, 230, 235, 251, 289, 306
clothing, 13, 22, 35, 86, 146, 162, 252, 253, 276, 284
community, 27, 41, 48, 58, 77, 117, 152, 163, 164, 260, 292
compassion, 3, 14, 15, 67, 82, 85, 100, 134, 139, 164, 205, 211, 260, 278
conformity, xix, 2, 9, 24, 34, 40, 57, 59, 89, 94, 117, 202, 206, 237, 255, 270
corruption, 25, 27, 104, 208
crimes, 83, 129, 161, 256, 257, 299
crowds, 38, 74, 138, 141, 159, 194, 226, 240, 299
crown, 68, 118, 124, 125, 128, 131, 151, 156, 169, 170, 171, 172, 259, 285
cure, xv, xxi, 14, 80, 121, 122, 173, 174, 201, 214, 216, 217, 218, 221, 223, 225, 234, 277, 284

D

danger, xviii, 54, 72, 94, 105, 129, 137, 202, 203, 226
deaths, 164, 190, 300
decay, 62, 143, 213, 246
defects, 4, 10, 48, 254, 282
defence, 103, 149, 154, 170
demonstrations, 174, 235
depression, 100, 218, 263, 288
destruction, 169, 172, 249
dignity, xvii, 36, 97, 162, 167, 180, 191, 259, 292
disorder, 211, 214, 219, 223, 225, 255, 277

E

ecstasies, xi, xiii, 151, 199, 200
ecstasy, 26, 86, 90, 101, 166, 201, 215, 254, 261, 271, 307
education, 49, 179, 241
effusion, 61, 254
Egypt, 127, 129, 131, 132, 134, 219, 245

enemies, 43, 60, 93, 94, 95, 96, 103, 116, 124, 132, 226, 262, 264, 281, 285, 308
Eon of Arle, xvi
Europe, 118, 126, 128, 150, 172, 226, 227, 246
evidence, xi, xvii, xxii, 58, 132, 190, 227, 282, 295, 302
evil, xix, xxi, xxiii, 2, 34, 46, 48, 50, 51, 67, 70, 92, 121, 129, 136, 169, 176, 202, 214, 221, 224, 251, 265, 277, 284, 289, 290, 308
execution, 11, 21, 30, 46, 55, 56, 66, 74, 93, 108, 124, 126, 152, 171, 207, 237
extreme poverty, 276, 286, 291

F

faith, xii, xiii, xiv, xv, xvi, xviii, xxi, xxiii, xxv, 9, 17, 22, 31, 36, 39, 46, 61, 72, 73, 93, 97, 100, 103, 104, 114, 115, 118, 123, 127, 129, 130, 148, 149, 151, 152, 154, 156, 160, 169, 170, 171, 180, 193, 204, 214, 219, 220, 228, 238, 240, 241, 266, 269, 280, 283, 287, 304, 308
families, 20, 25, 46, 47, 58, 66, 281
fasting, xv, 15, 45, 106, 135, 157, 161, 187, 201, 209, 270, 290
Father Candide Chalippe, ix, x
Father Paschal Robinson, ix
fear, xv, xix, 24, 27, 29, 35, 43, 45, 46, 50, 54, 58, 78, 82, 83, 96, 105, 111, 112, 119, 121, 127, 129, 140, 142, 147, 151, 162, 163, 165, 167, 168, 188, 208, 218, 221, 222, 224, 231, 235, 238, 245, 284, 288, 301
Feast, 90, 105, 116, 118, 178, 179, 201, 238, 251, 270, 272
feelings, xxiii, 3, 7, 15, 21, 30, 42, 45, 82, 86, 97, 104, 123, 139, 140, 144, 164, 168, 199, 208, 212, 213, 218, 230, 242, 250, 271, 276, 278, 279, 281, 302, 306
fever, 67, 69
food, 8, 15, 35, 39, 63, 74, 78, 79, 107, 147, 153, 251, 252, 265, 275, 277

force, xi, 12, 17, 56, 67, 87, 137, 176, 183, 253
France, xxv, 1, 2, 31, 73, 88, 89, 90, 93, 120, 128, 153, 162, 216, 227, 241
friendship, 4, 33, 36, 87, 92, 104, 107, 192, 210

G

Germany, 88, 117, 129, 155, 156, 178, 179, 180, 227
grants, 30, 81, 200
Greece, 117, 227
Greeks, xv
guardian, 78, 181, 225, 237, 258, 274, 275, 276
guidance, 30, 46, 55, 74, 87, 122, 144, 190, 212
guilty, 16, 137, 232, 255, 258, 266, 284, 297

H

happiness, 18, 55, 106, 122, 159, 167, 171, 226, 289
harmony, 218, 219, 244, 266
health, xv, 5, 24, 51, 68, 78, 112, 138, 148, 159, 161, 192, 194, 225, 251, 275, 284
history, xvi, xvii, xix, xx, xxii, xxiv, 49, 84, 99, 117, 137, 180, 238, 246
holy scriptures, xiii, 53, 96, 99, 128, 152, 181, 227, 265, 268, 292, 295, 296, 297
host, 41, 68, 70, 74, 75, 80, 164, 173, 182, 186, 222, 298
Hungary, 117, 156, 162, 163, 179

I

illumination, 26, 250
illusion, 213, 272, 292, 300
image, 7, 19, 35, 209, 241, 273
infancy, 3, 93, 174, 222, 274
innocence, 151, 240, 252, 302, 306
Ireland, 227
Israel, 30, 107, 114, 129, 218, 289

Italy, xxv, 1, 17, 47, 52, 65, 71, 72, 74, 85, 87, 94, 99, 113, 117, 118, 132, 136, 143, 146, 153, 178, 179, 180, 222, 227, 245

J

Jews, 47, 83
Jordan, 87

L

languages, xxiv, 268, 273
laws of nature, xi
learning, xvii, xxii, 2, 46, 105, 109, 110, 154, 168, 180, 181, 182, 183, 184, 250, 293, 294, 295
legend, xx, xxiii, 132, 168, 197, 307
liberty, xix, 6, 12, 20, 94, 235, 261, 307
lifetime, 121, 144, 145, 177, 215, 240, 253, 283
light, xii, xx, 1, 9, 20, 35, 40, 41, 54, 60, 61, 65, 72, 82, 86, 88, 95, 107, 113, 127, 149, 152, 154, 156, 157, 165, 171, 172, 180, 182, 183, 184, 188, 203, 204, 210, 214, 223, 224, 236, 239, 244, 245, 253, 261, 262, 270, 277, 289, 293, 296, 298, 300, 301, 309
lives of the Saints, xi, xii, xiii, xiv, xvi, xvii, xix, xx, xxi, xxv
Lucius Verus, xiv

M

Marcus Aurelius, xiv, xv
memory, xvii, 36, 91, 96, 97, 116, 136, 152, 172, 175, 180, 181, 192, 222, 246, 251, 264, 272, 279, 281
Metropolitan of Vienne, xvi
military, 5, 57, 73, 127
miracles, xi, xii, xiii, xiv, xv, xvi, xvii, xviii, xx, xxi, xxii, xxiv, xxv, 49, 50, 58, 60, 62, 68, 70, 73, 75, 77, 78, 79, 84, 85, 86, 88, 100, 117, 119, 120, 128, 138, 150, 163, 164, 172, 173, 175, 176, 177, 194,

195, 196, 201, 209, 222, 227, 243, 268, 279, 301, 307
mission(s), xxv, 19, 20, 27, 29, 31, 32, 45, 47, 66, 76, 89, 93, 94, 100, 117, 119, 120, 121, 122, 146, 155, 156, 171, 178, 179, 227, 297, 299, 303
Morocco, 68, 73, 74, 123, 124, 146, 147, 148, 149, 150, 152, 169, 172
Moses, 30, 129, 188, 232

N

neglect, 52, 77, 84, 212, 223, 272, 285, 291
New Testament, xiii, 202, 245, 295
Nile, 132
nobility, 64, 71, 85, 129, 179, 222
nuns, 59, 166, 196, 231, 241

O

obedience, xvii, 26, 28, 35, 36, 37, 46, 50, 59, 84, 88, 89, 96, 103, 107, 109, 123, 155, 156, 157, 163, 164, 177, 195, 196, 204, 214, 220, 231, 237, 249, 256, 257, 258, 259, 260, 283, 286, 301

P

pain, 16, 58, 108, 119, 161, 207, 216, 219, 224, 225, 229, 268, 269, 284
peace, 20, 23, 28, 29, 41, 50, 51, 57, 64, 89, 95, 114, 123, 126, 132, 137, 171, 198, 201, 239, 245, 259, 282, 283, 289, 301
physicians, 216, 218, 223, 225
pleasure, 3, 5, 6, 8, 15, 28, 29, 31, 34, 41, 47, 60, 72, 79, 86, 97, 113, 122, 149, 165, 173, 189, 197, 203, 205, 207, 210, 217, 220, 226, 230, 239, 255, 257, 280, 289, 307
Pontius Pilate, xiv
Pope St. Gregory, xvi, 154
Portugal, 74, 118, 146, 147, 149, 150, 151, 172, 227

prejudice, xi, xvii, xix, 30, 114, 129, 163, 182
principles, xviii, xix, xx, 11, 60, 61, 67, 154, 279, 284
prisoners, xvi, 4, 128, 132, 147
profit, 3, 23, 27, 77, 159, 235, 256, 259, 301
propagation, 104, 115, 133
proposition, xvii, 104, 116, 145, 149, 255
protection, 3, 10, 25, 37, 41, 56, 92, 94, 95, 97, 121, 124, 134, 135, 153, 163, 184, 200, 250, 271
punishment, 26, 98, 109, 129, 150, 277, 278, 279, 297, 302
purity, 3, 17, 49, 55, 68, 95, 107, 143, 160, 236, 252, 253, 288, 296, 308

R

reading, x, xxi, 68, 106, 120, 275, 292, 295
reality, 105, 260, 278
reasoning, 34, 94, 96, 129, 154, 174, 227, 280, 299, 308
reception, 66, 110, 142, 153, 179, 301
regulations, 32, 91, 135, 139, 224
relaxation, 143, 224, 242, 255
relief, 7, 145, 195, 207, 213, 217, 218, 225, 229, 255, 289
religion, xii, xiv, xviii, xix, xxi, 1, 28, 29, 45, 50, 56, 57, 77, 110, 130, 131, 132, 143, 146, 149, 154, 163, 189, 190, 219, 244, 253, 279, 285, 290, 301
remission, 26, 28, 165, 185, 186
reputation, 17, 55, 58, 64, 73, 78, 136, 177, 181, 240, 277, 293, 300
resistance, 65, 79, 91, 127, 188, 200, 260
resolution, 3, 6, 8, 12, 20, 21, 37, 74, 94, 129, 145, 151, 171, 257
revelations, xi, xiii, 26, 39, 60
Roman Senate, xiv
rules, xix, xx, 73, 85, 101, 112, 141, 154, 156, 162, 215, 224, 308

S

Saint Justin Martyr, xiv
saints, xi, xii, xiii, xiv, xvii, xix, xx, xxi, xxv, 272
school, 43, 139, 152, 245, 295
science, 69, 91, 139, 140, 145, 154, 167, 168, 172, 218, 250, 293
senses, 6, 9, 18, 27, 38, 206, 218, 250, 252, 261, 262, 265
sex, 62, 111, 119, 162, 231
shame, 16, 93, 141, 277
slavery, 12, 126
slaves, xvi, 133
society, xii, 3, 22, 29, 31, 41, 55, 109, 124, 264, 308
solitude, 6, 56, 140, 157, 209, 292
Spain, 68, 72, 73, 74, 75, 76, 88, 118, 120, 131, 143, 149, 152, 162, 172, 227
species, xiii, 42, 225, 283, 284, 303
St. Anthony, xvi, 19, 34, 73, 79, 118, 151, 152, 180, 202, 228, 295, 296, 305
St. Athanasius, xvi, xxi, 19, 79, 296, 305
St. Augustine, xii, xvi, xviii, xxi, xxii, 58, 62, 77, 91, 95, 106, 112, 140, 169, 178, 189, 204, 212, 216, 217, 218, 242, 252, 284, 289, 290, 295
St. Basil, xvi, xxi, 65, 112
St. Chrysostom, xvi, xviii, 45, 170, 198, 269, 281, 284, 293
St. Gregory of Nyssa, xvi, xxi, 280
St. Gregory Thaumaturgus, xvi, 280
St. Jerome, xvi, xix, xxi, 58, 83, 95, 119, 215, 237, 295
St. Martin, xvi, 75, 76, 160, 197, 225, 281, 282, 296, 303, 305
stained glass, 244, 245
statutes, 140, 224
subsistence, 24, 82, 107, 120, 147, 299
Sulpicius Severus, xvi, 281, 296, 305
supernatural, xv, xvii, 47, 56, 129, 155, 168, 200, 256, 282, 299, 303, 307
Sweden, 179, 180
Syria, 63, 124, 126, 131, 132, 135, 155, 304

T

talent, 31, 43, 54, 137, 154, 156, 181, 208, 258, 276, 296, 297
Theodoret, xvi
Third Order, v, vii, x, 159, 160, 162, 163, 164, 173, 177, 227, 247
Third Order of St. Francis, x, 160, 162, 163
thoughts, 19, 46, 73, 85, 113, 141, 198, 202, 208, 231, 281, 302
threats, 9, 48, 169, 171
treatment, 16, 29, 113, 268

V

Vatican, 196
veneration, 1, 19, 29, 42, 75, 90, 92, 95, 97, 130, 137, 146, 148, 172, 193, 210, 236, 241, 271, 282
victims, xvii, 110, 187
violence, 56, 57, 61, 67, 79, 109, 207, 218, 230, 261, 309
vision(s), xi, xiii, xv, xxi, 30, 33, 35, 46, 64, 92, 94, 97, 143, 150, 153, 183, 185, 205, 206, 249, 254, 262
visions, xi, xiii, xv, xxi

W

waking, 234
walking, 9, 33, 48, 51, 209, 260, 287
war, 2, 4, 5, 127, 129
water, 51, 70, 80, 81, 85, 128, 136, 148, 157, 175, 187, 200, 201, 215, 251, 252, 277, 307
weakness, xviii, xxi, 1, 4, 15, 20, 27, 44, 50, 70, 79, 109, 147, 156, 219, 226, 231
wealth, 86, 171
weeping, 20, 100, 124
witnesses, xxiii, 17, 40, 166, 243, 302
works of God, xii, 212